PERSUASION

PERSUASION

Robert N. Bostrom

University of Kentucky

Prentice-Hall, Inc., Englewood Cliffs, New Jersey 07632

Library of Congress Cataloging in Publication Data

BOSTROM, ROBERT N.
  Persuasion.

  Bibliography: p.
  Includes index.
  1. Persuasion (Rhetoric)   2. Persuasion
(Psychology)   I. Title.
PN207.B6 1983   302.2'4   82-12190
ISBN 0-13-661157-5

Editorial/production supervision: Dee Amir Josephson
Cover design: Wanda Lubelska
Manufacturing buyer: Ron Chapman

Printed in the United States of America

10 9 8 7 6 5 4 3 2 1

ISBN 0-13-661157-5

Prentice-Hall International, Inc., *London*
Prentice-Hall of Australia Pty. Limited, *Sydney*
Editora Prentice-Hall do Brasil, Ltda., *Rio de Janeiro*
Prentice-Hall Canada Inc., *Toronto*
Prentice-Hall of India Private Limited, *New Delhi*
Prentice-Hall of Japan, Inc., *Tokyo*
Prentice-Hall of Southeast Asia Pte. Ltd., *Singapore*
Whitehall Books Limited, *Wellington, New Zealand*

To my father,
CALVIN G. BOSTROM
(1908–1979)

CONTENTS

PREFACE

Writing a book of this type is much more rewarding than anyone might realize. Not only is the subject matter itself fascinating, but the strategies and approaches of individual communication researchers are also fascinating. Browsing through various research studies is much like traveling across the country, visiting many different universities, and talking with a number of different scholars. The fact that many of these scholars are my friends and coworkers enhances the sheer pleasure one gets in seeing a difficult question in persuasion answered.

Many persons might feel that the construction of a bibliography is dull going. True, there are a number of really dull aspects to assembling references, but one can learn a great deal from scanning such a bibliography once it is completed. The first thing I have learned is that persuasion, in spite of reports of its demise, is an extremely popular research topic in the 1980s. There are as many significant research endeavors underway as there ever were. Indeed, the significance of the research now is much greater, because the researchers themselves are much more sophisticated in method and knowledgable in content.

The second interesting fact about a bibliography is the general source of the studies. Fifteen years ago when I first started teaching a course in persuasion, the bulk of the research was found in psychology and sociology journals. Today, the bibliography of this book is drawn primarily from the pages of *Human Communication Research, Communication Monographs, Quarterly Journal of Speech, Journal of Communication, Central States Speech Journal, and Western Speech.* This means, of course, that communication, as a discipline, has truly come of age and has created a significant body of knowledge of its own.

The third interesting thing to be learned from a bibliography of this type is the extraordinary contribution of Gerald Miller and his students. These pages are sprinkled with references to Burgoon, Roloff, Berger, Hunt, Steinfatt, and many others who have truly enriched the field. I do not mean to minimize the extraordinary contributions of James McCroskey and Kenneth Sereno who have also made signal contributions to the field of persuasion, but Miller's truly unique contribution may well be in the distinguished body of students that have continued to study persuasion long after their dissertations were done.

It is my fondest hope that those who read this book can enjoy it as much as I have enjoyed writing it. I also hope that students will visit the library and follow through some of the research problems with those who have conducted it. You might imagine what it was like to construct the attitude tests, prepare the messages, score the responses, and you might puzzle over what it might mean. You might also suffer with the researcher when a critic or an editor discovers a hidden flaw that was missed at the outset of the study. The goal of all of these studies is, of course, not simply to be mentioned in a textbook like this, but to hope that the discovery will make a real difference in the way that we interact with one another. I also hope that some of you will be bitten by the same bug that plagues the rest of us. Pursuing the study of persuasion may motivate you to attend graduate school and to add your name to this discipline.

I have these hopes because we do not yet fully understand this subject. We know that individuals who are highly regarded and who generate messages often influence others with their messages. Exactly *why* this happens is still a mystery, as is why we wish to influence others. Perhaps it is enough to observe these events. But how much more rewarding is *understanding*! So let's keep at it.

Thanks are due to my dear wife Ann, who has encouraged and assisted and has spent countless hours typing and mailing permission slips, checking references, and generally making life livable while the work went forward. And I owe a great debt to my students, who, over the years, have made it all worthwhile.

PERSUASION

CHAPTER ONE
PERSUASION: COMMUNICATION AND HUMAN RESPONSE

Anyone who likes Western movies is familiar with the following scene: An angry mob mills outside the jail, where the sheriff and his loyal deputy have locked up the rustlers. The mob has learned that the rustlers are there and have decided that tonight's the night to hang them. Muttering ominously, the crowd carries rope and torches to the jail. "Give them to us, sheriff!" they cry, "We're gonna string them up!" As the noise mounts, the steely-eyed sheriff goes out on the porch of the jail. Facing the mob, he speaks. "Boys, I know they're skunks," he says, "but we gotta let the law take its course. I want to hang these rats as much as you do. But we need law and order in this here territory, and dadgum it, I aim to enforce it right here and now." After some more shouts and mutters, the mob finally drifts away—the sheriff has faced them down. A lesser person would have used a Gatling gun, but since the sheriff is the hero, he chose to use *persuasion*. Those who use force are ordinary people, but those who use persuasion are something special.

What is this distinctive act we call "persuasion"? How does it work? When can we use it? How do we manage to be effective in changing the course of human action? What can persuaders (like our sheriff) do to improve their persuasive abilities? Can we learn to do the same?

Persuasion is a complex topic involving many different approaches to communication and human behavior. Persuasion, of course, is the subject of this book. In it, we will analyze this fascinating social phenomenon to see how it works, when it works, and for whom it works. We will look at persuasion from a number of points of view: we will study sources, messages, channels, and receivers; we will look at theories and practical concerns; and we will try to study persuasion from the point of view of our society as a whole.

PERSUASION AND OUR SOCIETY

There are a number of ways to study persuasion, and no one way is the "correct" one. Persuasive activity takes place in a variety of settings and has a variety of uses. This activity is much more common than most of us would suppose. Let us look at some of the representative settings in which persuasion plays an important part.

Persuasion and Interpersonal Relationships

Most of us use persuasion in our interpersonal relationships in one form or another. We persuade one another in many different ways. Sometimes these are subtle, but at other times the attempts are very straightforward. Anyone who has ever asked a stranger for a date knows that information alone does not always achieve the desired response. Sometimes we need to put something in the message that tells more than where and when!

In our daily lives, we try to persuade our supervisors and our teachers that we are honest and hardworking, and that we deserve raises and good grades. Traditionally we have thought of persuasion as a one-to-many activity. Usually we think of propaganda campaigns, speeches, television commercials, and the like. All of these are important, of course. But the *interpersonal* dimension of persuasion is still probably the most important. Miller and Burgoon (1978) have described some of the interpersonal aspects present in persuasion, and Kathleen Kelley Reardon (1981) has developed an interesting new approach to persuasion based principally on interpersonal processes.

Sometimes this activity is desirable; sometimes not. Many of us need to improve our interpersonal "style" when we set out to influence other persons. Some of us seek to persuade more often than others, and we often term these persons as "argumentative," because they seem to be arguing so much. Often we feel that we need to "point things out," and miss the effect that this activity has on other persons. We all feel a need for agreement, and tend to want to persuade others in interpersonal situations. And when we take a point of view that we think is reasonable and just, we often are surprised when others do not agree and are offended. Clearly, what many of us need to do is to become more persuasive and less argumentative. Later in this book we will explore some of the implications of interpersonal relationships in persuasion.

Persuasion and Commerce: Advertising

Try as we may, none of us are able to escape advertising. In our culture, advertising is everywhere—on billboards, in newspapers and magazines, on radio and television. The ostensible purpose of advertising is to inform consumers regarding a product. But if this is really true, it is hard to understand how many present practices of advertisers fit the definition. Most of us would agree that advertisers use highly nonrational methods in selling their products. Occasionally, ads include "data" that at least sound factual, but most of the time, advertisers appeal simply to the senses without invoking any reasoning facilities that we may have. This may lead us to believe that persuasion is a truly "mindless" activity.

Advertising is often used for other kinds of persuasion. Many industries have begun to include more subtle messages in their advertising. In recent years, during Middle East tensions over oil prices and supplies, oil companies have been promoting political and economic views that favor unrestricted trade, and they call this advertising discussion of economic "philosophy." In other words, Mobil no longer tells us only that their gasoline is better than Shell, they tell us that we ought to believe in laissez-faire economics. Whether this is really advertising or not is problematical. Certainly it is persuasive.

Should advertisers be permitted to take political stands? How our society deals with this problem is an important modern issue. No sensible solutions can be found unless we know something about the nature and limits of persuasion. In a later chapter in this book, we will look at the use of persuasive activities of corporate America in some detail.

Persuasion and Politics

Political life abounds with persuasive activity. Indeed, some political scientists define politics as the art of persuasion. Even though this definition may be a little overstated, it is certainly true that much political activity is persuasive in its nature. When a candidate decides to run for office, he or she is faced with a great many persuasive tasks: assembling an organization, securing campaign funds, and gaining television time. The actual campaigning is only a small part of the persuasive activity involved in political life, but that small part seems very prominent to most of us. Most of the time, candidates seem to be making speeches in which they promise us everything under the sun. It is not unusual to hear a candidate tell us how taxes should be lowered, services should be raised, inflation should be fought, respect should be established abroad, and that motherhood should be reestablished as the foundation of the republic. In Kentucky, candidates for the legislature were fond of promising that they would "put God back in the classroom" after the United States Supreme Court had ruled that the practice of hanging the Ten Commandments on schoolroom walls was unconstitutional. It did not seem to bother these candidates that the state legislature had no power at all to reverse U.S. Supreme Court rulings. In other words, these promises were not real commitments to action but a persuasive device. Such promises often prove embarrassing, so many political figures have avoided them. Instead, they prefer to present a persuasive image of strength, good sense, and power, rather than promising specific action when elected.

Once in office, the politician finds that persuasion is an important daily activity. Legislators need to convince other legislators to support legislation, and mayors need to persuade the city councils to vote for new programs. Even the president needs to convince, not only the Congress, but the people that the policies are correct. President Johnson, for example, was quite effective in persuading the Congress that he was right, but he was ineffective in carrying the great mass of public opinion on the war in Southeast Asia. President Reagan, on the other hand, was quite effective in convincing the electorate that the budget should be cut, and was additionally effective in convincing the Congress.

Persuasion and Bureaucracy

Most of our large institutions are constantly persuading. In theory, these large organizations—government, churches, and corporations—have very specific functions, such as caring for the elderly or servicing computers. However, bureaucracies (private and public) have adopted another main purpose: preserving their existence and perpetuating themselves. In this activity, they constantly use persuasion. In an interesting book, Altheide and Johnson (1980) have shown how large bureaucracies continuously distort factual data to suit their own purposes. For example, in the U. S. Navy, junior officers soon learn "gundecking," the practice of turning in reports that show things to be in better shape than they really are because the higher echelons want it that way. It would never do for the Navy to be less fit than the Air Force!

The Pentagon tends to overestimate the size of the Russian missile forces, and the Department of Education tends to overestimate the number of illiterate young persons in the country. Whenever the police conduct a raid and seize narcotics, we are told that some small paper bag was worth hundreds of thousands of dollars in "street value." It seems that the very nature of large organizations leads to intensive efforts to persuade others that the organization is justified.

Persuasion and Religious Life

Various religions have been spreading the gospel for centuries. The word propaganda originally meant the dissemination of churchly information.[1] Evangelical movements have always had an important place in most churches.

Most Christian churches have been in the missionary business for centuries. One wonders what the American response would be if the Ayatollahs in Iran would send missions to America to start evangelistic activities! Yet this is exactly what many well-meaning American churches do when they send their missionaries to less well-developed countries. We tend to think it is fine for our own churches to have missionaries, but we are less tolerant of those who disagree with us. The success of the Reverend Sun Young Moon and the Hare Krishna groups have profoundly disturbed many Americans.

An unpleasant juxtaposition of religious activity and persuasion has been the formation of groups that aim at specific political activity based on a narrow ethical

---

[1]The *Congregatio de propaganda fide* was an organization in the Roman Curia instituted by Pope Gregory XV to oversee missionary activities. From this organization the word *propaganda* has evolved to its present unpleasant connotation.

point of view. One such group has called itself the "moral majority." Although many persons have protested that this group is neither moral nor a majority, its influence was felt during the 1980 presidential campaign and may have been instrumental in the election of President Reagan.

Persuasion and the Arts

In the late 1960s, Tom and Dick Smothers were featured in a very popular television show. Much of the show's content was highly relevant to young people: the draft, the war in Vietnam, and the Presidential election. The show's style was usually irreverent and occasionally highly satirical. But the show was popular, and CBS was happy with the good audiences the show produced.

Then the Smothers brothers did the unforgivable. They invited Pete Seeger, a folk singer and anti-war activist to appear on the show. This was Seeger's first appearance ever on national television. He had been blacklisted in the 1950s because of his early association with a group that some had labeled communist. Rather than downplay his sentiments, Seeger sang a song called "Knee Deep in the Big Muddy," a direct criticism of President Johnson's leadership.

The Smothers brothers were warned, but rather than backing down, they then invited another folksinger, Joan Baez, to perform. She not only performed, but spoke out against the war in an interview. This time, CBS censored the show, cutting out her remarks. When the Smothers brothers protested, CBS fired them and canceled the show (Wetmore, 1979, p. 157).

What is it that the network thought was so dangerous about a song sung by an aging liberal about political leadership? What was so offensive about a popular singer discussing her ideas about a government policy? The answer is that the arts have always played an important part in the attitudes and ideas in any culture. Songs, plays, records, and novels are intensely persuasive. The greatest of our novelists and playwrights have always taken political positions in their works. Persuasion is certainly not confined to messages delivered in straightforward ways. John Lennon may have been a more effective persuader (in the long run) than John Kennedy.

In Nazi Germany in the 1930s, the propaganda minister, Dr. Joseph Goebbels had complete control of the artistic life of the state. He commissioned the talented filmmaker Leni Riefenstahl to use her artistic powers to produce a number of films supporting the government, many of which are classics today. Goebbels encouraged Wagner and discouraged American jazz, especially the work of George Gershwin (who was considered, not only decadent, but an "animal" because he was Jewish.) At the same time the Soviet Union was producing films like *Alexander Nevsky*, in which the considerable talents of Eisenstein and Prokofiev were combined into a Pro-Russian, anti-German message. And we should remind ourselves that the use of the arts in persuasive activity is not necessarily a bad thing. Some of George Bernard Shaw's best plays (*Major Barbara*, for example) were frankly propagandistic. And who can forget John Wayne in *Green Berets*?

Persuasion and International Relations

Whether we admit it or not, one of the principal goals of our nation's foreign policy is to win other countries over to our side. We are extremely anxious, especially in the case of the developing nations, that America be seen as benign and benevolent and that the USSR be seen as the "bad guys." There is an official agency of the U.S. government, called the International Communication Agency, that coordinates all of the propaganda activity of the United States, including the Voice of America radio stations, cultural exchanges, films, speakers, and other activities. Even though it may seem that we put a great deal of time and energy into international relationships, the Soviet Union puts in more. In 1981, *Time* magazine estimated that the Russians spent $3.3 billion annually in propaganda activities of one kind or another, while the United States only spent $448 million.[2] The implications of this expenditure differential are profound.

> In radio broadcasting, this disparity means that American stations broadcast for 1,818 hours per week in 45 languages, mostly to Eastern Europe and the Soviet Union, while the Soviet Union broadcasts for a total of 2,022 hours a week in 82 languages to virtually every one of the world's 165 countries. (Isaacson, 1981)

According to *Time*, the Soviets were winning this propaganda war. But regardless of who we think is winning, it is clear that we tend to believe that persuasion is an important aspect of international diplomacy. Most Americans are especially concerned with the influx of Marxist governments in South America, and they feel that the United States needs to be a better persuader south of the border.

There is one troublesome factor that seems to characterize all persuasion. Specific instances of communicative influence all possess some questionable ethical problems. When persuasion works in interpersonal relationships it is for personal gain, in advertising it works for financial gain, in politics it works for the acquisition of power, in bureaucracies it is used to cover up the truth, and in the arts it is used to manipulate the masses. At this point, many students might conclude that the study of persuasion involves the study of lying for profit and the distortion of facts. Some of the ethical issues seem important. Cushman and Craig (1976) concluded that persuasion is an outdated phenomenon and that a more defensible approach to modern communication would be multivalued. In other words, we should be more tolerant of those whose values are different from ours, and not try to persuade so much.

CONFLICT AND CONFLICT RESOLUTION

However, there is another side to persuasive activity that is extremely important. Persuasion serves our society by serving as a nonviolent means to bring about social change. Many societies have evolved into repressive, monolithic systems in

[2] *Time* (1981), 117, pp. 15–16.

which the only change and adaptation comes from the top. In any society, we need to have some procedure for bringing about change. No society can remain static and survive. Cushman and Craig's appeal for tolerance should be considered in many persuasive interactions, but in others, agreement must be reached and a decision arrived at. In a democratic government, persuasion is the one device that enables citizens to retain their freedoms while government continues to function. This use of persuasion is a socially acceptable alternative to force and violence.

Differences of opinion are a phenomenon common to all of us; it is rare to experience a personal relationship that is free from disagreement. Some conflict is inevitable in anyone's life. Parents disagree with children, students with teachers. Factions form within clubs, within work groups, and even in churches. Disagreements between labor and management occasionally escalate beyond repair. The president disagrees with Congress, and consumers contend with power companies. Too often, the result of international conflict is armed confrontation. In the modern age of missile weaponry, the risks attendant on international conflict are enormous.

Most of us believe that we should resolve our disagreements, and that communication is one of the best tools available for doing this. Resolution is desirable for many reasons. When another individual disagrees with us, it is often unpleasant and sometimes intolerable. Privately, most of us feel that we are right and someone that disagrees with us is obviously wrong. Part of this chauvinism occurs simply because altering our views is uncomfortable. Sometimes resistance to change leads to an "agreement" to disagree. Other times we simply withdraw from the situation. Aside from the obvious unfairness of these reactions, they have another important fault—they do not always work. Many times we are bound together in groups that require mutual efforts. When we disagree about these efforts, we must agree somehow before we can proceed with day-to-day operations or activity.

Unfortunately, differences frequently intensify and take on a personal dimension. Then some conflicts lead to emotional involvement. Indeed, it has been customary to call this kind of communicative behavior *attack* or *defense*. As long ago as the Golden Age of the Greeks, argumentation was viewed as attack and defense. Aristotle, for example, wrote that "If it is a disgrace to a man when he cannot defend himself in a bodily way, it would be odd not to think him disgraced when he cannot defend himself with reason." (Rhetoric, i. 1335b) This emphasis is still with us. Jack Gibb (1961), for example, wrote extensively of "defensive communication." Most of us know that conflicting situations can be quite unpleasant; almost all of us have been in a shouting match generated by an interpersonal conflict. Therefore, most of us feel that anything that can help us avoid such unpleasantness is valuable. We might avoid conflicting situations entirely, and many of us do just that. However, another way of handling the problem is to emulate our steely-eyed sheriff—meet it head-on and try to change the situation.

If we are powerful, it is tempting to use our power to force the disagreer to change his or her attitudes or behavior. This approach is a traditional one that is strongly rooted in Western civilization. As late as the fourteenth century, trial by combat was an accepted method of settling a dispute. The disputants went outside and hacked away until the quarrel was settled. Under this system, peasants had definite disadvantages in disputes with knights, and weak knights were reluctant to argue with strong ones. We now view this custom as barbaric and unfair, but unfortunately many of us still practice it. In a large organization, it is often easier to threaten an employee rather than persuade. The military relies on coercion almost exclusively. Modern-day persuasion is certainly not free from coercion. Herbert W. Simons (1972) has illustrated how coercion has been necessary in bringing about the real dialogue between social groups.

Many of us do not realize how pervasive coercion and violence have been in our lives. Many of our present customs owe their existence to some of our violent traditions. For example, in the British House of Commons, members of opposing parties are confined to a space behind certain lines on the floor, and cannot cross over. The lines were drawn so that disputants could not reach one another with a sword during a debate. In some states, duelling is still prohibited by statute, which reminds us of how common it once was to settle an argument with formalized violence.

Most of us, however, would agree that some other form of conflict resolution is a desirable thing to have, not only for our personal relationships, but for managing group dissent, the existence of which is a wholesome thing in any society. The central activity in the settling of any dispute is *change*. For example, when planning to attend a movie, couples often disagree about which movie to see. Person A may wish to see movie A and person B may wish to see Movie B. They may end up seeing movie A, movie B, or even a third choice, movie C. Choosing either option implies change in one or both persons. It is not enough that one of the participants gives in reluctantly, grumbling all the way; this spoils the evening and is an external change only. What is necessary for the system to work is *real* change, not external change. The ideal solution for the couple is for both of them to *want* the same movie, and to accomplish that what is needed is an alteration of attitude, belief, perception, or whatever internal process would lead to a truly amicable solution.

WHAT IS PERSUASION?

Persuasion is the name we give to the type of communication that brings about change in people.

Traditional Definitions

One way to define any word is by consulting a dictionary. *Webster's Seventh New Collegiate Dictionary* defines the verb *persuade* as "to move by argument, or expostulation to a belief, position, or course of attitude." Two key elements appear in this definition that deserve more careful attention. The first, "to move by argument or expostulation," obviously applies to communicative activity of some kind. The second element is the result of persuasion—"belief, position, or course of attitude." To this, most modern thinkers would add *behavior*. In other words, persuasion is communicative activity that produces attitudes and behavior.

Everyone knows what a belief is. If you believe that Muhammad Ali was the greatest heavyweight fighter in history, and someone else convinces you that Joe Louis was even better, you have been persuaded because you changed your belief. However, you also believe that your car will start tonight and that the sun will rise tomorrow. Are these beliefs also involved in persuasion? It may be easy to convince you that your car might not start tonight, but to convince you that the sun will not rise tomorrow will be a little harder. Obviously we need a more precise definition of *belief*, as well as *attitude* and *move*.

Persuading and Informing

Some of the beliefs mentioned above are things that you know. When we *know* something, we typically do not think of it as being subject to persuasive activity. We know that salt is white and the ocean in Maine is cold. Information is something that is vital to communicative activity, but typically, information does not call for any overt response. Most writers would probably agree with Barker (1978, pp. 223–229) that persuasion is distinguished from other kinds of communication in that persuasion calls for a response on the part of the receiver. If that is so, then the next question is, What kind of response?

Definitions in Terms of Responses

It is not easy to define persuasion in terms of *responses*. Another approach is to say that persuasion differs from informing in that persuasion changes attitudes. This may be too simple, however. Many attitudes have cognitive elements and are only partially connected with overt behavior.[3] But most persons would accept a definition that says that persuasion changes responses or behavior. The nature of the changed behavior is not as easy to define.

Recent researchers have suggested that there are strong indications that individuals differ in their choice of desired outcomes in persuasive interactions. Applegate (1980a) suggests that more complex persons will probably exhibit greater concern for creating and establishing and/or maintaining a positive interpersonal relationship with the other person rather than achieving the desired response. Similar suggestions were made by Clark and Delia (1977) as well as Delia, Kline, and Burelson (1979). So although many typical definitions of persuasion tacitly assume nonrelational kinds of responses, it is probably more accurate to assume that the term *response* should be broadened to include responses to the other person in the interaction.

Another crucial element in a definition is the term *change*. If we think about it for a little, we can see that we might include almost any alteration as a change. What

---

[3] We will discuss specific relationships between attitudes and behavior in the next two chapters.

do we mean by behavioral change? Gerald Miller (1980) proposed that we look at the three kinds of end products of persuasion: changing responses, reinforcing responses, and shaping responses. Let us look at each of these in turn.

Changing responses.   As Miller put it, "smokers are persuaded to become nonsmokers, automobile drivers are persuaded to walk or to use public transportation, Christians are persuaded to become Moslems and so on (1980, p. 21)." You will recognize that these kinds of changes are perhaps the most difficult of all the persuasive interactions. To persuade a dyed-in-the-wool men's basketball fan that women's basketball is as exciting and as deserving of support as men's basketball is indeed a difficult task. It requires a good deal in the way of altering perceptions, life styles, and so on. To convince a farmer to use a technological innovation in producing or marketing crops is an extremely difficult job. Yet we know that all of these changes *can* be made, and they usually utilize communication as the principal means.

Reinforcing responses.   This is the kind of process that takes place when we only modify an existing attitude or behavior. At a political rally, for example, speeches are usually not aimed at converting persons from Democratic to Republican (or vice versa) beliefs. That is, no one goes to party rallies unless he or she is already convinced about the rightness of their party membership. What does happen at a party rally is that the attitude is *strengthened.* Individuals are urged to work harder, to get out the vote, and to make more phone calls. Sales meetings are typical examples of this aim of persuasion. Sermons, too, are usually addressed to those who are present in church and already have a basic set of attitudes, rather than the absent!

Miller's term, *reinforcing*, only tells part of the story, however. Often persuasion consists of *weakening* a response. If, for example, we recognize that excess drinking is an undergraduate health problem, we would use persuasive messages as part of our campaign to *reduce* undergraduate drinking. It would not be sensible to insist that everyone stop drinking entirely. The reduction would be an example of successful persuasion, but we could not say that it was an example of reinforcement. It is, of course, similar to reinforcement in that it implies a modification of an existing response (or attitude, or behavior).

Shaping responses.   This is the third end product of persuasion that Miller mentioned. Shaping is the process that occurs when persons are receiving a message about which they have no prior knowledge. For example, a message imploring us to give some consideration to the plight of the refugees from Baluchistan would involve neither change nor reinforcement, since there would be no preexisting attitude to change. Very few of us know where Baluchistan is, let alone whether they have refugees. Any response to this message would be entirely new, and is called response shaping.

Miller's three end products form the basis for a more comprehensive definition of persuasion: *Persuasion is communicative behavior that has as its purpose the changing, modification, or shaping of the responses (attitudes or behavior) of the receivers.* In our next chapter we will go into greater detail about the nature of the attitude-behavior-response relationship.

PERSUASION AND COERCION

Many persons do not distinguish between persuasion and coercion. Messages aimed at a specific response sometimes include a threat as part of the incentive for compliance. For example, a persuader addressing a city council might recommend that a given social program be undertaken in the city because the program would be helpful in forestalling street riots or other kinds of violence. This clearly is a type of "coercion." Burgess (1973) calls this kind of persuasion "crisis rhetoric" and equates it with the kind of threat given by a bank robber with a gun.

Clearly, many persuasive arguments have implied threats in them. To contend that Americans ought to conserve energy to avoid the threat of inflation and disproportionate influence of oil companies on our economy implies a threat. Similarly, to persuade cigarette smokers that lung cancer and emphysema are likely to result from continued smoking also implies a threat. However, these implications are quite different from the coercion that Burgess discusses. Where does persuasion fit into the continuum between free choice and coercion?

Easterbrook (1978, p. 15) contends that freedom of action and individual control are one and the same. The distinction between determinism on one hand and free will on the other is an interesting subject in the history of ideas. Physiological factors often determine our behavior, much as the dependence on a given drug determines the behavior of an addict. Nonetheless, the addict is still free (in a sense) to take corrective action, to try to reduce his or her dependence on drugs, and to engage in treatment programs. But it is probably not as easy for the heroin addict as it is for the cigarette addict to kick the habit. The principal point that Easterbrook makes is that free and determined behavior are not clearly bipolar categories: they are only positions on a continuum that goes from totally determined to totally free.

In communication study we have almost always been concerned with interactions in which the receiver is totally aware of the communicative purpose. Receiver awareness is as important as the presence or absence of coercion. Many times, we can figure out the implied purpose of a message. Even in conditioning experiments, most persons are aware of the conditioning process (Brewer, 1975). But what about the kind of communication in which the true purpose is masked? This, of course, is one of the most common persuasive devices in our society.

When a salesperson tells us, for example, that he or she is not going to get a commission as a result of the sale, we ought to get suspicious. Almost *all* salespersons do get commissions, and a common persuasive device is to claim that you don't. This kind of masked purpose is more common in everyday persuasion than

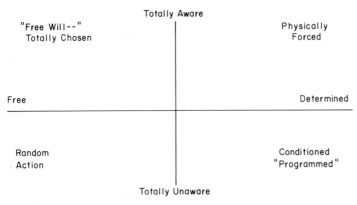

FIGURE 1-1

most of us would like to admit. Many persuaders like to hide their persuasive intent so that they will be more effective. Allyn and Festinger (1961), for example, arranged a situation where persons could overhear a communication that was designed to change attitudes. These overheard communications were more effective than ones presented in a more straightforward way. Many other kinds of persuasion take place when the receivers' awareness is attenuated. Should persons be totally aware before we can call the process persuasive?

A number of writers in communication theory have explored the question of whether individual choices should be studied from the point of view of actions or of behaviors. Actions, to these writers (Pearce, 1976, Cushman and Whiting, 1972) means behavior *plus* conscious intent. In other words, masked purpose is not one of the legitimate forms that communication may take. Although not everyone agrees with this point of view, we do need to look at how persuasion relates to coercion.

Let us imagine that we have two different dimensions, one an awareness dimension, and the other a determined dimension. We can draw lines to represent each of these dimensions, with one end of the line called totally aware and the other end called totally unaware. A line like this is called a *continuum*, meaning that no precise intervals are possible along the line. However, the awareness continuum is not the same as the determined continuum. Figure 1-1 illustrates how the two might look if they were placed at right angles to one another. This creates four quadrants that illustrate four different kinds of human action, ranging from totally determined to totally free, totally aware and completely hidden. On one side is behavior that is totally forced, such as that of a prisoner or an helplessly ill person. On the other side is behavior totally free from influence. Where does persuasion fit into these dimensions?

Most persons like to distinguish between what persuasion *is* and what persuasion *ought to be*. When asked what persuasion is, most persons construct a diagram like Fig. 1-2. Apparently many of us recognize that much persuasion is actually coercive in nature. When asked what persuasion ought to be, we usually

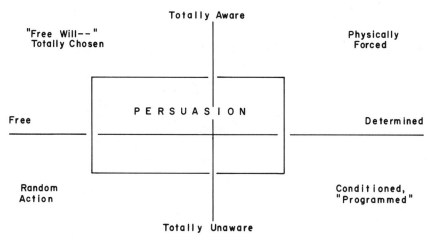

FIGURE 1-2

get a diagram with proportions like Fig. 1–3. In other words, most of us believe that a persuader ought not to deceive the listener, and that the receiver of the message ought to be as free as possible in choosing alternatives as a result of the interaction. Unfortunately, in the real world, persuaders often do not conform to our ideal of what we wish they would do. This adds a further dimension, the "ethicality" of persuasive activity. Is it ethical to influence another even if the strictures of freedom of choice and total awareness are observed? How do we decide if persuasion is ethical? At what point on the intersections of the other two dimensions does an influence become unethical?

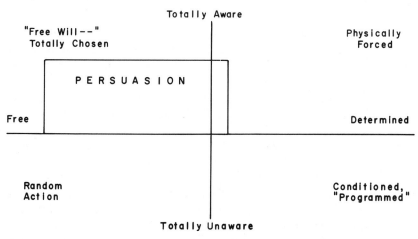

FIGURE 1-3

PERSUASION AND ETHICS

Earlier in this chapter we saw some examples of unethical persuasive activity. We also saw many ways in which persuasive communication can be used for socially accepted purposes. Is there any systematic way to deal with the question of ethicality?

The final chapter of this book will deal with the problem of persuasion and ethics in some detail. The problem is not a simple one and cannot be solved easily. But before we proceed in our study of persuasion, we ought to look at one or two principles concerning the ethical aspects of persuasion:

1. Persuasion can be viewed as an ethically neutral act; one that can be employed for ethical or nonethical ends.
2. Persuasion will be employed by many varieties of persons. Knowledge of the persuasive processes will often be useful as a defense against unscrupulous practitioners.
3. Ethical questions are often relative and can allow several acceptable answers.

What, then, is the place of persuasion in our society? We all feel the need to influence the values (or attitudes) of other persons, and through this, their behavior. This can be done by understanding the nature of the persuasive process; by understanding the values, attitudes, and behaviors of human beings and how the process affects them. In this book, we will relate the study of human behavior to the study of persuasion. Then we will examine some of the important elements that make up this body of knowledge: persuasive subject matter, the study of sources, messages, receivers, and social concerns.

PLAN OF THE BOOK

The principal plan of the book is from the simple to the complex. In Chapter 2, we discuss basic concepts concerning the nature of communication and how responses are defined. Because persuasion has been studied primarily from a behavioristic point of view, some of the principles of behaviorism are then discussed. Chapter 3 then examines the nature of attitudes and the ways in which they are measured, defined, and related to other responses. Following that, source credibility is explored.

Chapter 4 concerns balance, dissonance, and congruity theories and how they relate to persuasion. The elements of the persuasive process are then put together into a comprehensive model of persuasion and integrated into a system. In Chapter 5, more practical concerns are taken up: what topics or subjects are suitable for persuasive interactions. Chapter 6 integrates the separate elements of persuasion into a model, and Chapter 7 discusses selection of persuasive strategies. Then in Chapters 8–10, message elements such as evidence, language, and organization are discussed. Chapter 11 studies the specific nature of the receivers, that is, audience variables.

Persuasion in specific settings is discussed in the next three chapters. Small groups are examined in Chapter 12. Chapter 13 treats the nature of bargaining and negotiation. Persuasion in organizations is the subject of Chapter 14. The last chapter concerns the role of individuals in the resistance to persuasion and the nature of ethical choices that persuasion imposes upon us.

This persuasion process is one of the most fundamental of human interactions. The persuader and the persuadee are both enriched by the process, and usually the result is improvement of the individual or society. Although the general principles of persuasion remain fairly constant, the specific applications of them to particular subjects, audiences, and situations provide a fascinating insight into human affairs.

QUESTIONS FOR FURTHER STUDY

1. What does the word persuasion mean to you? Do you consciously try to persuade in everyday life or do you feel that you can get through life by informing other persons? Explain your answer.
2. What television commercials, if any, affect you? Did they persuade you to buy the product? What exactly persuaded you?
3. What do you look for in successful politicians? Do you want them to be persuasive or merely to reflect the wishes of the electorate?
4. Look at the quadrants in Fig. 1-2. Describe a persuasive attempt belonging in each of the four areas.
5. Can a university professor persuade in class? Why or why not?
6. How would you solve an argument with your parents over a person you were dating?

SUGGESTIONS FOR FURTHER READING

ALLYN, J. & FESTINGER, L.   The effectiveness of unanticipated persuasive communications. *Journal of Abnormal and Social Psychology*, 1961, *62*.

ALTHEIDE, D. & JOHNSON, J.   *Bureaucratic propaganda*. Boston: Allyn and Bacon, 1980.

BARKER, L.   *Communication*. Englewood Cliffs, New Jersey: Prentice-Hall, Inc., 1978.

EASTERBROOK, J.   *The determinants of free will*. New York: Academic Press, 1978.

GIBB, J.   Defensive communication. *Journal of Communication*, 1961, *11*, 141-148.

HOVLAND, C. & JANIS, I.   *Personality and persuasability*. New Haven: Yale University Press, 1959.

HOVLAND, C., JANIS, I., & KELLEY, H.   *Communication and persuasion*. New Haven: Yale University Press, 1959.

MILLER, G.   On being persuaded: some basic distinctions. In M. Roloff and G. Miller (Eds.), *Persuasion: New Directions in theory and research*. Beverly Hills: Sage, 1980.

MILLER, G. & BURGOON, M.   *New techniques of persuasion*. New York: Harper and
Row, 1973.
MILLER, G. & BURGOON, M.   Persuasion research: a review and commentary. In B.
Ruben (Ed.), *Communication yearbook II*. New Brunswick, New Jersey: Transaction
Books, 1978.
REARDON, K.   *Persuasion: Theory and context*. Beverly Hills: Sage Publications, 1981.

CHAPTER TWO
COMMUNICATION AND BEHAVIOR

Recently at a major midwestern university, the governor of the state was invited to present the commencement address. He released a statement to the press that he had something to say to the student body. Interest ran high in this prospective message. When the time came for the speech, the governor launched into a vigorous attack on recent activities of various student groups: the gay rights coalition, proponents of ERA, consumerists and environmentalists. Each section of the speech began with the phrase, "And here is another point I'd like to make to the modern-day student," and was followed by a blistering attack on the folly of questioning the establishment. When the speech was over, the governor received a hugh ovation, and was praised in the press for taking a "vigorous position," which was a "clear message to the modern-day student."

At the commencement no one questioned the purpose of his message; everyone accepted the governor's word that he was speaking to the students. The governor seemed to be engaging in a legitimate persuasive attempt, that is, trying to *change the responses* of the student body. Remember that in the last chapter we defined persuasion as communicative behavior that reinforced, changed, or shaped responses. This speech would seem to fit this definition. However, the next day the campus newspaper polled some student leaders and discovered that few, if any, of them had any knowledge of the speech. In addition, at commencement time most of the students were gone. The governor's opposition to their activities was no news to them; he had already make his disapproval clear. But they had little or no knowledge concerning this speech. If he was really trying to persuade the student body, why did he choose this time and place for the message?

The nature of the commencement ceremony offers us a clue. Sitting behind the governor on the platform was the university's board of regents, a federal judge, and several legislators. In the audience were several thousand persons, mostly parents of the graduating seniors. Because of the advance publicity put out by the governor's office, several dozen reporters were present, as well as camera crews from two television stations.

Speaking to one of these reporters after the speech, the governor stated that he thought "it was time someone spoke out to the students, and that students needed to hear some common sense," but because the student body (other than the graduates) was unaware of the speech, it seems likely that the governor had some other audience in mind. The parents and the television crews, of course, were good candidates! His real purpose was not to persuade the students, but to enhance his own image. When the governor announced six months later that he was going to run for the U.S. Senate, no one was really surprised.

The governor's tactic, usually called *scapegoating*, is depressingly common in modern political communication. The procedure is to attack some person or issue (the scapegoat) that is unpopular with the audience, hoping that this use of the scapegoat will create your own advantage. For example, in 1978, Senator Frank Church of Idaho attacked the Russians for stationing a combat brigade in Cuba, and threatened that unless this unit was removed, he would be forced to vote against the SALT II agreement. His message to the Russians was actually a message to his constituents in Idaho that said, "I am not as liberal as some of you folks thought I was." The Russians were puzzled because the unit in question had been in Cuba for 20 years and had not been thought of as a combat unit. Church lost the campaign anyway.

These two examples demonstrate some of the problems linking *message* and *response* in communication. To be precise about what responses are designated in the persuasive interaction is quite important. In order to do that, however, we need to look more deeply into the nature of responses themselves.

COMMUNICATION: THE PROBLEM OF PURPOSE

It is easy to condemn the governor and Senator Church as self-seeking Machiavellians. But whatever we think of them, we must admit that they were both successful in what they set out to do. And part of their success stemmed from their ability to confuse their audience (and perhaps even themselves) about their purpose. Confusion about purpose is a common characteristic in much of modern communicative practice. Often it leads to real difficulties in message construction and evaluation. It is extremely important, in any study of persuasion, to be able to define precisely the purposes of the interaction.

Let us look at a somewhat more prosaic example of confusion of communicative purpose. In almost every rural county in the United States, there is a county extension agent. These agents' principal mission is to assist farmers in agricultural innovation. We might also say that their main activity is the communication of these innovations to farmers. When asked about their purpose, they typically report that they *inform* farmers about new developments in agriculture. They assume that an informed farmer will tend to adopt agricultural innovations more rapidly than uninformed ones. But a recent poll taken by agricultural editors showed that agents had preferred adoptive behavior over information. In the poll, the agents were asked, "If you had to choose the most important outcome of your work which would you choose: the *adoption* of modern agricultural techniques or the *understanding* of new agricultural techniques?" Over 80 percent of the agents responded in favor of adoption over understanding. In other words, they preferred that farmers would use new practices, even if the understanding of the background of the practice might be hazy. On one hand, they all pay lip service to the informative aspects of their job, but on the other hand, they felt that the persuasive purpose was more important. Their true purpose was probably to be both informative and persuasive.

This kind of confusion is found everywhere and illustrates the need for careful definitions of communication and persuasion. For if terms are not clearly defined, none of us can know what we are talking about or whether we agree or disagree with any given statements. If we examine more precisely the words *inform* and *persuade* we often see that it is difficult to distinguish between them. Sometimes we need to see a response in order to be satisfied that we have informed, and sometimes we believe that we have been persuasive even if we do not see an overt response.

If persuasion involves the kind of communication that shapes, changes, and reinforces responses, it seems logical to separate it from the kinds of communication that do not alter responses. But surely information shapes, changes, and reinforces responses! In fact, it is possible to use information alone as a basis for a theory of communication and attitude change (Saltiel and Woelfel, 1975). So how can there be communication that does not produce a response? More importantly, what kinds of alteration are involved, and even more basically, what do we mean by *responses*?

Typically most of us would agree that a response is manifested in *behavior*. But what exactly is behavior? Since you probably are tired of questions by now, let us try a few answers. Hull (1943) defined behavior as a movement of an organism. This is a very precise definition, but is not too useful in most practical analysis. A yawn, a stretch, or an idle twitch all fit into this classification. This has led others to use a more distinctive classification, instrumental behavior. Instrumental behavior is defined in terms of the effect a movement has on an environment (Spence, 1956, p. 42). Using this definition, we would classify door opening as a single unit of behavior, whether we used the right hand, the left hand, or even the feet to get the door opened. Instrumentalism is an extremely useful concept from general psychology. But it is not without its problems. For example, B.F. Skinner has shown that even though we may feel that the connection between behavior and the change in environment is a causal one—that is, before learning takes place, we must feel that our action causes the reinforcement—that, in fact, the learning connecting them does not necessarily follow this pattern (1948). Many behaviors merely precede the outcomes. Skinner showed how pigeons developed "superstitious" actions because they were reinforced at random intervals and not causally. Skinner called this kind of learning "operant condition" and further asserted that all instrumental learning was of this type.

This controversy among learning psychologists should not keep us from the common-sense view that it is possible to classify the many kinds of behavior that affect our environment. But that is only the beginning. Human beings respond in a great many more ways than simple instrumental responses. For example, we all engage in verbal behavior as well. This is something common to all of us and is quite different from instrumental behavior. The difference is not complicated; we all know the differences between actually doing something and talking about it. Further, we can subdivide this verbal behavior into different classifications (Skinner, 1957).

Instrumental and verbal behaviors are not the only types of behavior. We can also distinguish between these types and autonomic behavior, which is the internal responses that the body makes, often involuntarily. Perceptual behavior, which is discriminating among stimuli, is well known to psychologists and is actually a different kind of response from the other types. Persuasion could, in theory, elicit any one of these types of behaviors. We do not always assume, however, that communication produces one of these behaviors.

For example, we often assert that communication involves meaning (Pearce, 1976). But what exactly does *meaning* mean? It can refer to word-behavior relationships, printed definitions, or emotional responses to a set of words. Some have defined communication as "the transfer of meaning from one person to another." If we accept this definition, we probably believe that one can communicate without necessarily producing overt responses.

This kind of "communication" can best be illustrated with an example. Suppose that you watch one hundred repetitions of a television commercial extolling the virtues of Datsun cars. As a result, you may come to believe that Datsuns are really marvelous automobiles. You certainly do not necessarily jump up after each showing and shout "Datsuns are GREAT cars! They are DRIVEN!" You probably just sit there. But sometime later, in talking with a friend who has just bought one, you might say "Gosh, that's a nice car." In other words, the name *Datsun* acquired a meaning for you that was different than the meaning it had before you watched those hundred commercials. If a strict behaviorist told you that this really was not communication, you would disagree. Furthermore, the agencies that produced and sold these commercials would be offended. *Something* happened when you watched these ads, but no *overt response* was visible at the time.

However, we are all satisfied that communication took place, and many would further say that this communication was persuasive.

Traditional Communicative Purposes

Careful analysts of communication have distinguished between various types of responses and find it necessary to be quite specific in defining various forms that communication might take.

Aristotle was probably the first thinker to distinguish between types of communication. He felt that communication was divided into *deliberative, forensic*, and *epideictic* types.[1] Deliberative communication was principally concerned with matters of policy, such as what course of action the state should take. Forensic communication concerned matters of factual occurrence, especially questions of whether or not a specific action had taken place. Epideictic issues concerned values of that society, questions of praise and blame. Aristotle's distinctions seem to be based on subject matter, but if we look at them closely, we see that he was really distinguishing among types of responses. Matters of policy in the Greek city-state referred to action that was to be taken, that is, overt behavior. Questions of fact, the belief that a given act did occur, usually concerned "forensic" situations where the acts were punishable by law. The same was true of questions of praise and blame—if the Athenian believed that Pericles was a wonderful man, he did not necessarily have to march against Sparta to demonstrate his belief.

Aristotle's thinking has profoundly affected Western civilization and has had great effect on the assumptions about communication that most modern theorists make (King, 1969). From him we get the basic notion that communication often does not imply an overt response, and it is from this distinction that we get the basic delineation between *informative* and *persuasive* communication. Almost everyone believes that when we are informed, we store impressions and ideas in our memory, and when we are persuaded, we respond overtly, that is, visibly.[2]

When we study persuasion, then, do we eliminate all communication from which the receivers change only mentally and do not exhibit an overt response? Some have taken this point of view, distinguishing between persuasion, argumentation, and conviction (Zelko, 1939). But if we adopt this point of view, this means that the Datsun commercial mentioned above was not persuasive. On the other hand, if we feel that the Datsun commercial really did persuade, how do we know that without the response being visible or detectable in some systematic way? It is in

---

[1]Aristotle, of course, did not use the word communication—he was referring to persuasion. He entitled his principal statement of communication theory *rhetoric*, a common usage even today. There are, of course, important differences between rhetoric and communication (Bormann, 1980), but we will treat them at a later point.

[2]We will discuss this difference in greater detail in Chapter 3 when we examine attitudes.

these questions that we see some of the most troubling aspects of definition in communication theory today.

Response Potential

One of the biggest problems lies in the decision of what to call behavior because only *observable* behavior can be studied and analyzed. After a paleontology lecture, for example, you might believe that dinosaur eggs have been found in the Gobi desert. An independent observer, however, would have no idea whether you believed this statement or not. But once the observer asks "Have dinosaur eggs been found in the Gobi desert?" and you say "Yes!" there is some observable criterion of communicative result. This particular belief probably will not affect your day-to-day activities very much. But nonetheless, the belief is tucked away into your mental storage system somewhere, and can be retrieved when necessary. This is the result of "informative" communication. But if we accept only *observable* behavior as evidence of the effect of communication, then we will conclude that you were not affected. This is nonsense, of course. We do not apply such strict standards to most communication. However, you will remember that most persons define persuasion as communication in which a response was involved, which means that the strict standard is applied to persuasive communication but not to informative or "convincing" communication. This problem may be solved by considering another type of response, the *potential* as well as the actual response.

Let us consider another example. What happens when a stranger in town stops and asks for directions to the ball park? We may give her an elaborate set of directions, and after receiving them, she may say, "I understand," get in her car and drive off. Was the communication successful? We can only decide if we specify what we wanted in the interaction. If all we wanted was to get the stranger out of our hair so that we could go back to whatever we were doing, then the communication was demonstrably successful; she drove off instead of asking more questions and taking our time. But if we are less callous (for whatever reason) and have a sincere desire for her to get to her destination, we might present a good set of directions and a written map. Unfortunately, we will never know if we have been successful unless we leap on a motorcycle and follow her out to the ball park. Then, if she gets there, we can say that our communication was successful. This is pretty silly, but at least it is possible. Some other very meaningful types of communication are not so easy to analyze.

Consider, for example, a policeman who is taking a class in emergency medical treatment. The students are taught to perform the "Heimlich maneuver," a course of action designed to assist a person who is choking on food or some other object in the throat. After taking the course, the policeman goes about the job and for five years never encounters a person in distress from choking. Was the communication in the classroom a success? Most of us would say that as long as the policeman *knew* what to do, the communication was indeed a success.

But there is no observable way to tell if the policeman knows. He might wear a little badge telling us he passed that course, but that is the only external item that might offer us a clue. The instructors in the course probably asked the policeman test questions about the Heimlich maneuver and judged from the responses that enough was known about it to pass the course. However, in most communicative situations, we do not get to test the receivers except in very unusual circumstances. Even so, we are probably not willing to say that without some kind of external indication the communication was unsuccessful. We are willing to assume that some kind of change has taken place in the internal makeup of the receiver; tucked away somewhere in the receiver's repertoire of responses is the *potentiality* of responding a certain way.

If you take a first-aid class, you will not acquire new behaviors but the *potential* for new behaviors. When we gave the stranger directions to the ball park, what we instilled was a *response potential*, not a response. What the receiver does with it is her business. We could infer its presence by certain tests ("Tell me again, which way do you turn at the second stop light?") but we can only validate the response by following the traveler. Since most of the time we cannot do this, we infer the potential response by past performances in similar situations. In other words, we cannot observe these response potentials, we can only infer them.

Let us recapitulate a moment. It is easy to say that the goal of persuasion is a response on the part of the receiver, but the problem is more complex than that. Sometimes the persuader aims at potential behavior, not immediate behavior, and when this is the case, the success of the communication can only be inferred, not directly observed. We can try to infer the presence of the response by tests or questions, but most of the time we infer using past validations of similar persons in similar situations.

Now we can be more specific about the meaning of the responses that we will include in our definition of persuasion. They can be motor responses, psychobiological, verbal, and the like. Recall, however, that we must include in our definition of persuasion the influencing of *potential* behavior as well as overt behavior. This means that we will need to be as interested in the inner aspects of human experience as we are in the outer ones.

CLASSIFYING RESPONSES—
INNER AND OUTER

Knowledge about the inner, or hidden part of our existence has fascinated philosophers and psychologists for many years. When I have a toothache, its presence is obvious to me, but when you have one, I cannot tell where it is or how severe it is unless you make the inner event known by groans, shrieks, or other meaningful behavior. The reality of the toothache is different in each case. However, none of us will contend that the toothache is not real just because we do not experience it directly; we are usually willing to take the sufferer's word for it. Indeed, much of human experience consists of making instant inferences about the inner states of total strangers. When we drive in traffic, we usually assume that the other drivers have inner states similar to our own; for example, they see red and green lights, they believe in law and order, and they value their lives as much as we value ours. We bet our lives that these assumptions are good ones, and most of the time we are correct. But once in a while a driver gets on the road with an inner state vastly different from the rest of us, which sometimes has tragic results.

In addition, some persons have serious conflicts between their inner experience and their outer behavior. A few years ago in a small town in Iowa, the police arrested a motherly cashier at a local bank. She was a stalwart in the Methodist church, a Sunday-school teacher, a well-known clubwoman, and a friend to all. However, she had systematically embezzled over $1 million from the bank over a period of 20 years. The money went to deserving students for help with their educations, to churches for small projects, and as "loans" to persons who seemed deserving. For over 20 years, this lady lived with an inner and an outer life in dramatic conflict. Upon her arrest, she spoke of the relief that she felt, now that the secret was out at last. She was tried and found guilty, and a sympathetic judge noted that she had not enriched herself at the bank's expense and suspended her sentence.

Not many persons have this inner-outer conflict in the dramatic proportions experienced by this motherly embezzler. However, there is probably more inner-outer conflict in our society than many of us believe. In recent years we have seen many homosexuals come "out of the closet," expressing relief that they no longer have to lead dual lives in which they are heterosexual in public and homosexual in private.

We have all had the feeling at times that we would like to "tell it like it is," but were prevented from doing so by various restraints. This is such a common problem that one would expect more formal attention to be paid to it in studies of behavior. However, serious researchers have only recently begun to explore some of the dimensions of inner-outer conflict and its effect on our lives. Persuasion involves both inner and outer experience, and if we are to have a reasonable knowledge of the process, we will need to see how they are related to these two aspects of experience.

The Outer Responses— Observable Behavior

We have already discussed some of the classes of overt behavior, instrumental and verbal response, for example. Let us be more specific in the further classification of responses.

Instrumental responses.   Earlier in this chapter, we defined the instrumental response as a response that affected the environment in some systematic way. But the definition of a response is never easy. Is it an instrumental response if someone tries to change the environment and fails? What is it when a person *stops* doing something, rather than starts? Is this an instrumental response?

Most of the time, we use our common sense about what a response is, but sometimes responses are not easy to observe. Must someone engage in some kind of activity in order for us to say that they responded or can they change some ongoing activity, such as cutting down on smoking? Many of us would class this as a response or, at least, as a meaningful result of communication. We should consider instrumental responses quite broadly in the study of persuasion. Therefore, any change in the response pattern, such as starting or stopping (as well as attempting) an action would qualify here. In the next chapter we will examine the notion of behavioral intention as well as behavior, and this notion of change in response pattern will be useful there.

Verbal behavior.   All of us talk in some way or another. This talk usually consists of words arranged in specific patterns. We have no way of knowing exactly how many words there are in any one person's vocabulary, (there are approximately 500,000 words in a good unabridged dictionary). We know that many theorists have classified vocabulary into "active" and "passive" categories. Active vocabulary refers to words we use with some frequency, and passive vocabulary refers to words we only recognize. Verbal behavior is usually considered the active portion of our language use. Every person is capable of using words, grammar, and relationships.

Tests have been constructed that attempt to measure the hidden dimensions of language. In fact, such tests attempt to make the passive vocabulary manifest itself as observable behavior. Some of these tests are well known to all of us. We have encountered them in the ACT test, the SAT test, and other tests of academic ability. There are even tests of inflection, dialect, and phonology.[3] All of these usage elements can be considered aspects of verbal behavior.

Affects.   Almost all of us are sure that we can tell how a person feels by observing certain external signs of emotions. Frowns, laughter, crying, relaxation, and many others form visible symbols of inner states that we are accustomed to observing. However, in Western civilization, we are taught that suppression of the visible symbols of emotion is a good thing, and many of us try to do this. But even when we try, some of these inner states manifest themselves in nonverbal behaviors (Knapp, 1972). Nonetheless, it may be possible to completely hide the inner states behind a carefully trained exterior. Poker faces are not confined to poker games, unfortunately.

One way of getting behind the mask of Western culture is to measure the responses to the autonomic nervous system. The easiest ones are heart rate, respiration rate, and skin conductivity. Polygraphs, or lie detectors measure these responses, and when significant alteration appears the polygraph operator infers

---

[3]One of the most famous of these was the old NBC announcer's test, which assessed one's suitability to become a broadcaster. Unless an individual had good general american speech, he or she could not pass this test.

that the individual is lying. Unfortunately, this process is not always effective. Some other autonomic responses are pupil dilation, blood-sugar level, and muscle tension.

Lewis Donohew and his associates (Donohew, Parker, and McDermott, 1972; Donohew, Palmgreen, and Duncan, 1980) have shown that there is a strong relationship between information processing style and psychobiological factors. In other words, we respond emotionally more than we think. In Chapter 11 we will examine some of the important psychophysiological factors involved in persuasion.

Discriminating responses. There is a class of responses that could be easily categorized as one of the first three, but typically it is not because the response is determined by the nature of the stimuli that create it. These are *discriminating* responses, and by them we know that organisms can tell the differences present in external stimuli. It is quite useful to look at these responses separately because of the nature of the perceptual process that precedes them. Perception seems like a process that is almost entirely internal, but there are important external manifestations that we should consider: loud sounds make us jump, strong light makes us blink, and so forth. In addition, there are many responses associated with discrimination among stimuli, such as sounds, lights, and sensory input. The ability of an individual to tell when a guitar string is out of tune can always be manifested in an external behavior. If it were not, we would have no way of telling that the individual's inner perceptions were accurate. In the 1930s, Professor Seashore of the University of Iowa developed a famous test of musical ability, which measured individuals' abilities to discriminate between pitch, rhythm, and tempo. Although we are not accustomed to thinking of perception as having external manifestations, we can see that each perceptual response can be cast into external framework.

The Inner Human—
Nonobservable Behavior

Each of these outer responses can be thought of as having an inner component, an antecedent condition that causes the outer, or overt, response. Although it is true that these inner components are not strictly observable, it is nonsense to assert that they do not exist or that they are meaningless. In addition, it is important to note that they are responses in the strict sense of the word. Let us look at each of these more specifically to see how they are organized.

Behavioral intentions. Earlier in this chapter we discussed an individual who wished to go to the ball park but lacked the directions. After communicating the directions, we could tell if the person knew the way by asking questions about the route and observing the answers. Something exists in the mind of the person that enables her to perform the instrumental response. It is common in social psychology to speak of attitudes that are the precursors of action, or behavior.

Fishbein and Ajzen (1975) used the term "behavioral intention" to describe that inner response that immediately precedes instrumental response. You will remember that instrumental acts were defined by the effect they had on the environment. The acquisition of such acts was called instrumental learning. For example, when a rat learns to turn left in a T-maze, it has probably done so as the result of some reward for turning left, but turning left is not the only motion involved in the situation. The rat had to start moving down the maze, turn left, and then continue the motion to the end of the maze. We could get even more analytical and see that the rat had to move one foot, then another, and then another, and so on. Some psychologists have been concerned with these minute responses, calling them the "fractional anticipatory goal responses," and being concerned with the problem of reinforcing each of these to bring about a desired goal. The total response was the important thing, but what was it that was learned? Something inside the organism was changed, just as something inside a child changes when he or she learns to ride a bicycle.

Language.   The inner component of verbal behavior is usually called language. Language is usually very well organized, but no one seems to know exactly how it is accomplished. We know that simple vocalizations become associated with particular perceptions, and when this happens we call the vocalizations words. Then these basic units of language soon get expanded into more elaborate vocabularies; the words become more abstract and grammatical rules organize them into consistent and recognizable patterns. Our language system is acquired at an early age, and is well established before children start school. Throughout our school experiences, additions and refinements are made to the system. Mathematics is an example of a nonexperiential language system almost totally acquired through formal schooling. Although the basis of our language is perceptual, a great deal of it is abstract and transcends perception. We cannot find specific referents for abstract words.

Affects.   No one who has experienced a headache would contend that the experience is not real. Although none of us can experience another's headache or emotions or feelings, common sense tells us that feelings are an important part of our inner lives. Some of these inner experiences stem from emotional reactions, some arise from physiological conditions, such as hunger, thirst, and the like, and some others are related to totally different processes. Frustration, for example, produces a reaction totally unlike simple hunger or thirst. Friendship and love also produce responses that are emotional but are quite different from the deprivation responses. We are accustomed to using the word *emotion* for these feelings, but sometimes it is better to reserve this word for more intense responses. *Affect* is a better word because it may imply a very weak response as well as a strong one. Many of our affective responses are learned, but often they are acquired simply by chance. However they are acquired, they are extremely important aspects of our inner life. We will return to the discussion of affect in Chapter 3 when we discuss attitudes.

Percepts. The mechanism by which we receive information about our environment is usually called *perception* by most psychologists. Most of us do not simply respond to our environment, we actively participate in it. In other words, we seek out some stimuli and ignore others. This direction and organization of incoming stimuli gives us stability and balance, but it is often done so unconsciously that we are not aware of its processes. Our perceptions go through rather extensive filtering, sharpening, and other alteration, and when they are through with the initial stimulus, the end product is something we might call a *percept*. Percepts are stored in our memory, some for many years. Images of long-forgotten scenes or experiences can be recalled years later under special stimulation. No real agreement exists among neurophysiologists about the amount and kind of percept storage, but it is clear that percepts form an extensive base of inner experience, and they influence the communicative process significantly.

The Inner-Outer Transfer

The relationship between inner and outer responses in our daily lives is a complex one, and often it is purely arbitrary. For example, when we learned to read, we did so by seeing a printed word and then responding orally to that word. Most of us have memories of rooms full of children chanting "See Spot run!" when the words were held up by the teacher. But as we gained skill in reading, we were able to suppress the outer vocal elements in reading more and more. In the fourth and fifth grades, however, many children can be seen moving their lips as they read. Indeed, many adults still do this. Slow readers need to learn to transcend this response to read faster than they can speak. Most of us do this in high school. But even in very fast readers, physiological studies show that unconscious responses occur in the musculature of the larynx, especially in the cricothyroid muscles. In addition, these responses are going on when we *think*, even though we may not be aware of them. In other words, what we thought was an entirely inner response has an outer component that many of us were not aware of.

Let us review the inner and outer responses of behavior. The four inner behavioral types were behavioral intentions, language, affects, and percepts. Each of these also has an outer component: instrumental response, affect display, verbalization, and discriminatory behavior.

How do these categorizations help us understand the processes of persuasion and communication? First of all, they show that both inner and outer responses *can be legitimately categorized as behavior*. When we say that persuasion is communication that changes, reinforces, or shapes a response, we can reasonably include these inner responses as part of the persuasive goals. In other words, persuasion does not have to produce an observable response in order to be meaningful. Although it is true that the inner responses cannot be directly observed, the processes by which they are inferred are well known and represent well developed measuring techniques. A great deal of the difficulties in communication study arise because of the use of introspective methods, which have been assumed to be necessary because of the nature of communicative responses. The above framework shows how we can extend the behavioristic point of view to inner responses. Let us proceed to examine this point of view and see why it is particularly suitable for the study of persuasion.

BEHAVIOR AND BEHAVIORISM

Why do we need to classify persuasion as a behavioral study? Can we not include the typical definitions of communication where introspection and "meaning" kinds of theories are as important as the more strict observation of responses? What advantages do behavioral studies offer that other do not? In this section, we will examine some of the issues that delineate behavioral studies from more traditional formulations. In general, behaviorism seeks a more *scientific* approach to knowledge. As Bernard Berelson put it,

> The scientific aim is to establish generalizations about human behavior that are supported by empirical evidence collected in an impersonal and objective way. The evidence must be capable of verification by other interested scholars and the procedures must be completely open to review and replication. The search for broad propositions about human behavior and the effort to build knowledge cumulatively require that general categories descriptive of behavior be set up and used more or less systematically. . . . The ultimate end is to understand, explain, and predict human behavior in the same sense in which scientists understand, explain, and predict the behavior of physical forces or biological factors, or, closer home, the behavior of goods and prices in the economic market. (1963, p. 3)

Here we have articulated a fairly straightforward statement of principle, one with which few of us could disagree. The essential thrust is realistic and empirical, and the desire for general knowledge is both laudable and practical. Why should acceptance of Berelson's ideas be a problem?

Unfortunately, many modern communication theorists do not agree with this approach to knowledge. A dominant theme among recent writers has been a lack of enthusiasm for behaviorism and a desire for alternate modes of explanation. Most of these theorists view the problem as arising from the basic framework of the philosophical underpinnings of behaviorism.

Many have expressed a strong interest in an epistemology based on phenomenological principles, such as Williams (1973) and Grossberg and O'Keefe (1975). Phenomenology asserts that the reality of any event lies in the mental phenomena that the event creates in us. For a phenomenologist, the important part of experience is the percept and not the external manifestations of it. Putting it another way, the inner experience becomes the focus for all study to the exclusion of all else. Some have arrived at this preference out of concern for particular variables in communication, such as Deetz' concern for language (1973). Others, like Smith and Kearney (1973) yearn for more traditional rhetorical theories. Still others, like Phillips (1976) feel that communication needs its own philosophical system, arguing that both behaviorism and phenomenology are inadequate for a full explanation of philosophical events. Much of this concern, of course, represents a recent trend toward more humanistic themes in psychology especially those articulated by Rogers (1964), Mead (1956), and more recently, by Harré and Secord (1973).

It is important to note that in a recent book, *Communication Theory*, Ernest Bormann asserted that an integrated approach, using both humanistic and scientific approaches is a vain one (1980, p. 15). This would seem to indicate that in any communication study, a specific point of view is necessary. In this book, the point of view is scientific; we take the view that behaviorism is the most effective way to study persuasion. Although behaviorism has significant difficulties and certainly is not perfect, phenomenology is critically flawed in two important characteristics: (1) it relies on *introspection* as a source of data, and (2) it makes no serious attempt to achieve *objectivity* in its theoretical formulations. Let us look briefly at some of these problems.

Introspection as Method

One serious problem with the recent critics of behaviorism is that they have not dealt with the original arguments that led to its acceptance. Several factors contributed to the early popularity of behaviorism in social science, but probably the most compelling was the inadequacy of introspection as a source of legitimate data.

A brief example might be helpful at this point. When we observe a situation in which a persuasive message has been part of the interaction, evaluative responses are a common reaction to the message. People say things like "This was a great session. It influenced me a lot," or "That was very clearly put. Now I know exactly what to do." In each of these statements, individuals are describing a state of mind or an internal condition. We do this so often that we seldom, if ever, question the validity of these statements.

What happens, then, if someone does exhibit more than casual attention to these statements? What can we do when one observer says "That was swell. I'm going to adopt that approach," and another says "Boy, was that a terrible message. I'll never follow that plan." Can a message be both good and bad? Effective and ineffective? Hart and Burks (1973) assert that a "rhetorically sensitive" person would be tolerant of this kind of ambiguity. But how much ambiguity can we tolerate and have an acceptable theoretical system of communication? Every time we are asked a question, do we only respond "Well, yes and no. It depends." If we do this, people are going to stop asking us questions. If a physician tells us that we need a major operation, we might ask if this operation will cure what ails us. If the physician says "Well, yes and no. Sometimes it helps and sometimes it doesn't," we are going to go somewhere else.

At the heart of the problem lie the basic assumptions that we wish to make about what we know. Kaplan (1964) has characterized some of the styles of thinking in the social sciences, varying from the literary to the formal. What is at issue here is whether theories of persuasion are only literary ones, or if they can be advanced to what Kaplan calls the "eristic" (1964, p. 260). If we accept the aim delineated by Berelson, then we need to have some method of resolving conflicts in theoretical issues, that is, we need some kind of verificatory technique. Unfortunately, the private experiences of individuals cannot be verified, only accepted. Tolman describes the problem very well:

> Suppose, for example, I introspect concerning my consciousness of colors. All you can ever really learn from such instrospection is whether or not I shall behave toward those colors in the same way you do. You can never learn what those colors "feel" like to me. It is indeed conceivable that just as immediate "feels" (if there are any such things) of the colors may be something quite different for me than they are for you, and yet if I agree with you in behaving to them, i.e., in my namings and pointings to the colors, no amount of introspection will ever discover to you this fact of their uniqueness to each of us as immediate "feels." You will only discover what the colors are to me as behavior possibilities. (1961, p. 4)[4]

In other words, there is no way to verify the internal event unless there is some clear procedure linking the internal event with an external event.

The Need for Objectivity

Psychologists came to this position reluctantly, and only because reports of subjective experience in and of themselves, are notoriously inaccurate. Individuals lie, distort, and hallucinate. Many participants in behavioral studies bias their behavior toward what they think the experimenter wants (Rossiter, 1976). Perception itself is unreliable. Governments and churches impose standards for reality that often deviate wildly from simple observation. Not until we invoke some kind of verificatory principle can we entertain the possibility of a community of knowledge that meets the criterion of objectivity.

The danger inherent in subjective social science is clearly described in the work of Gunnar Myrdahl. He approaches the problem by delineating knowledge into "beliefs," which pretend knowledge, and "valuations," which do not. Beliefs are intellectual and cognitive, and valuations are emotional and volitive. Myrdahl's experience in writing *An American Dilemma* provided him with firsthand experience in the basic confrontations with beliefs and valuations concerning American

---

[4]From E. Tulman, *Behavior and psychological man.* Berkeley: University of California Press, 1961. (Reprinted from the *Psychological Review,* 1922.) Copyright © by the University of California Press. Reprinted with permission.

Blacks. Myrdahl argues that objectivity is the only way in which we can solve the pressing social problems that beset us:

> By increasing true knowledge and purging opportunistic, false beliefs in this way, social science lays the groundwork for an even more effective education; making people's beliefs more rational, forcing valuations out in the open, and making it more difficult to retain valuations on the lower level opposing those on the higher level. (1967, p. 41)[5]

Perhaps instead of the word *behaviorism* for the scientific study of communication behavior, we should substitute *objectivism*. What is objectivism? Cunningham provides perhaps the most current definition. It is possible for an inquiry to be objective if, and only if:

> a. it is possible for its descriptions and explanations of a subject-matter to reveal the actual nature of the subject-matter where "actual nature" means "the qualities and relations of a subject-matter as they exist independently of an inquirer's thoughts and desires regarding them," and b. it is not possible for two inquirers holding rival theories about some subject-matter and having complete knowledge of each other's theories (including the ground for holding them) both to be justified in adhering to their theories. (1973, p. 46)[6]

At this point you may be convinced that we ought to be objective and behavioral, but you are not totally sure what this implies for the study of persuasion. The implications are really quite simple: we should attempt to make our knowledge as replicable and general as possible, using direct observation as our principal datum, and controlling for as many extraneous factors as possible. To see how this works, let us look at an example of an experiment in persuasion, and see how the search for objectivity manifests itself in a specific instance.

Objectivism and Research Methodology

Did you ever wonder whether men or women were more persuadable? Dr. Thomas Scheidel of the University of Washington also wondered. Many persons feel that women are the "weaker sex" and that men typically are more independent thinkers. You can see the implications in either answer to the question.

Dr. Scheidel set out to answer the question systematically. First of all, he needed an operational definition of the word *persuadable*. He chose to study "attitude shifts resulting from the communication and the subsequent retention of the speech content." (Scheidel, 1963, p. 354) He devised a speech that could be repeated to many different groups of persons and a test of attitude that could

---

[5]Gunnar Myrdahl, *Objectivity in social research.* New York: Random House, 1967, p. 41. Copyright © 1967 by Pantheon Books, a Division of Random House, Inc. Reprinted with permission.

[6]F. Cunningham, *Objectivity in social science.* Toronto: University of Toronto Press, 1973. Copyright © 1973 by the University of Toronto Press. Reprinted by permission.

be replicated anywhere. In other words, if another researcher wished to do the same experiment, Scheidel could furnish that person with the materials so that the same stimuli could be repeated exactly.

Then he posed these questions:

> Is there a difference between the sexes with respect to the attitude shift which a short persuasive speech produces? Is there a difference between the sexes with respect to the extent to which they generalize persuasive appeal beyond the specific topic which the appeal covers? Is there a difference between the sexes with respect to the amount of the speech content which they retain? (p. 354)

You will notice that Scheidel is not talking about any specific group of men and women or any specific topic; he uses the words *men* and *women* generically, that is, to refer to all men and women. Naturally there is no way that he can test all men and women, so he must take certain steps to make his results as generalizable as possible. Let us look at some of these steps.

Selection of a sample. If you wanted to get an idea about how much salt was present in sea water, no one would expect you to measure *all* of the oceans! A sample of sea water would suffice, as long as certain rules were observed about its selection. We would not select our sample close to the Mississippi delta, for example. We would also be careful to store our sample where it could not be rained on or where it could not freeze, or where any number of other things could not happen to it. Similarly, in a persuasion experiment, we take as much care as we can to make the persons in the sample as representative as possible, and guard them from as many extraneous influences as possible.

How did Scheidel obtain his sample? At the time that the study was conducted, he was a faculty member at the University of Washington at Seattle. In that university, there are thousands of students enrolled in freshman-level classes. Scheidel chose speech classes, since his membership in the speech faculty made this more convenient. No important differences are present in these classes from freshman English, history, or any one of a number of classes available. We can also assume that the University of Washington is not very different from other universities like it. There are some differences in college students (see Chapter 3, p. 000), but these differences probably do not affect Scheidel's problem. University freshmen are indeed more intelligent than the general population, but this difference would tend to make the differences between the sexes decrease, not increase. Scheidel chose 242 of these students and proceeded with his study.

Preparation of materials. Scheidel's next step was to prepare a short speech that advocated less federal power in the areas of health and education. Having selected the topic, he was then ready to measure the students' general attitudes toward the topic. He prepared a number of statements such as "Government power has already been extended too far," and "The government should build hospitals for those persons who cannot afford medical coverage." Some were positive, and some were negative. The statements were put together in the form of an attitude test in which the students could indicate whether they agreed or disagreed with the statements and how strongly. The tests were then scored; each student was assigned a number that represented his or her attitude about federal power and education. Then he let everyone listen to the speech, and then again gave them the test.

Statistical treatment.   Scheidel found that women changed more than men. However, if you are an ardent supporter of ERA, you might say "Wait a minute! This could have happened by chance! The next time Scheidel gives that test, the results could very well be in the opposite direction. This group of women that Scheidel tested are nothing but a bunch of shrinking violets. Most women aren't like that." Your argument would have force, except that Scheidel subjected his results to a test of *statistical significance*, a method that determines exactly how likely the outcome could be. Scheidel's test proved that the outcome, if it happened by chance alone, would have only occurred one time out of a hundred. This is so unlikely that we are probably justified in accepting the conclusion that women persuade more easily than men.

Extrapolation of results.   Of course, we cannot extrapolate with any precision exactly how any other group of women will behave with respect to a given persuasive speech. In Chapter 11 you will read that the "sex" differences in Scheidel's study are really personality differences. Males and females differ in many characteristics, but one important characteristic is world-view, or outlook. Males in our culture tend to be more independent, less caring, and less helping than females. Men who are caring, less independent, and more helping are usually called androgynous males, in that their personalities are similar to females. Note that an androgynous male is not feminine, only similar to women in some important personality factors. Scheidel's study is what persuasion researchers consider *hard evidence* because it was gathered with great care and reported without prejudice. If you read Scheidel's study (and we hope that many of you will), you will not read any statement like "I'm glad these stupid women are at last shown up for what they really are—spineless." What you will see is a straightforward account of his procedures and how the results came out. You may not appreciate the outcome, but *you cannot dispute the data presented or the level of probability associated with it.* Introspective accounts are subject to such disagreement, and as such are not as compelling in the descriptions of hard facts.

Throughout this book, you will be reading the results of studies like Scheidel's. This kind of objective data is the foundation of the study of persuasion, and is the root of the behavioristic style of thought. As you read further in the text, you will see statements like "Miller (1965) discovered. . . ." This only means that a researcher named Miller published a report in 1965 that demonstrates the point in question. You can look up the study in the bibliography of this book, and then read Miller's specific procedure. By looking up some of these research reports, you will appreciate the techniques of persuasion research, and you will know what it means when we say that we know something about persuasion.

SUMMARY

Persuasion is defined as the shaping, reinforcing, or changing of responses. But most communications are extremely fuzzy about the responses that are aimed for, or indeed, even who the correct audience is. Many traditional theories of communication have been founded on the concept of *meaning* or effects not related to a visible response. This has led to confusion about the nature of communication and especially about the nature of persuasion.

This confusion can be eased if we examine the kinds of responses available to persons: instrumental, verbal, affective, and discriminative. Each of these responses has an inner and outer component, both of which are clearly *responses* as used in the definition of persuasion. Since all of the responses can be objectively studied, the behavioristic approach is probably the best framework for persuasion study.

QUESTIONS FOR FURTHER STUDY

1. Read an inaugural address by any recent president. Can you pick out the ostensible purpose? The real purpose?
2. What is the principal purpose of a university professor—persuasion or information? Defend your answer.
3. Do you know anything that does not affect your behavior? If so, what is it? Why does knowledge affect (or not affect) you?
4. How many of your actions are learned and how many can be accomplished by a simple set of directions? (Hint: We must *learn* to type.)
5. Try to remember specific scenes from your childhood. Can you remember them clearly? Organize these in terms of percepts. Take the percepts and try to put them into words. Why is it difficult to capture them this way?
6. Remember a specific time when you were angry or agitated. Can you remember it without becoming angry again? What does this tell you about affects?
7. Go to the library and look up Dr. Scheidel's study in *Speech Monographs*. Would you have conducted the study the way he did? Why or why not?

SUGGESTIONS FOR FURTHER READING

BERELSON, B.   *The behavioral sciences today.* New York: Harper and Row, 1963.
MYRDAHL, G.   *Objectivity in social science.* New York: Random House, 1967.
PEARCE, B.   The coordinated management of meaning: a rules-based theory of interper-

sonal communication. In G. Miller (Ed.) *Explorations in interpersonal communication.* Beverly Hills: Sage, 1980.

ROGERS, C.   Toward a science of the person. In T. Wann (Ed.), *Behaviorism and phenomenology.* Chicago: University of Chicago Press, 1964.

SCHEIDEL, T.   Sex and persuasibility. *Speech Monographs,* 1963, *30,* 353–358.

SKINNER, B. F.   Behaviorism at fifty. In T. Wann (Ed.) *Behaviorism and phenomenology.* Chicago: University of Chicago Press, 1964.

CHAPTER THREE
ATTITUDES, ATTITUDE CHANGE, AND BEHAVIOR

In the first chapter we examined the nature of persuasion and its place in our daily life. There persuasion was defined as communication that reinforced, shaped, or changed responses. However, in Chapter 2 we saw that the word *response* was more complex than this simple definition seems to indicate. Responses have inner and outer components and they may be of at least four different types: instrumental, affective, verbal, or discriminatory. In other words, a persuasive communication could aim at any one of three levels of alteration (reinforcing, shaping, or changing), and affect any one of four different kinds of responses. Here we see 12 different kinds of persuasion, the results of which could occur either as overt or covert behavior. For example, one form of persuasion would be at attempt to shape the discriminatory response, and another might be an attempt to change the instrumental response. A strict classification system might be very useful. This would mean that there are at least 24 different kinds of behavioral outcomes of persuasion. However, most social scientists, in the interest of simplification, have used a more general word, *attitude*, to stand for most of these responses. This has been very useful, in that strict distinctions among responses are not really necessary in many given social situations. At the same time, the usage of a broad term like *attitude* sometimes creates definitional difficulties that are inherent with trying to make one word stand for too much.

In this chapter, we will examine some of the definitions of attitudes. We need to do this for three main reasons: First, many social scientists have used this term in a variety of ways, and students of persuasion need to be familiar with this usage. Second, a substantial amount of the research done in this field in the last 20 years has sprung from an attitudinal framework that defines attitude change as the principal end of persuasion. In order to understand this research, we need a basic familiarity with this terminology. Third, *attitude*, as a broadly defined construct, can be extremely useful in describing commonalities in a number of social and political situations, and can simplify their descriptions. Let us, therefore, turn our attention to the way that most researchers use the word and further examine how persuasive communications and attitudes are related.

When we hear a term like *attitude statement*, it probably brings to our minds "On to the Bastille!" or "A house divided against itself cannot stand!"—utterances that had enormous effect in bringing about change in societies. Statements like these are certainly attitudinal, but few of us in our daily persuasive activity have occasion to advocate revolutions or to start a civil war. However, most of us do wish our communications to have some effect. In addition, many times we cannot settle for extremely small effects in language or percepts.[1] If asked, most persuasive communicators assert that they want change in "real" attitudes. Furthermore, we would like these attitude changes to predict behavioral changes. We need to look at the ideal definitions and the usage that researchers have made of these terms in the past.

This chapter will examine the problem in detail. First we will discuss the current definitions of *attitude* in social science. Then we will examine *attitude change* and explore various explanations for the process of alteration. Then we will look into the relationship of communication to this process of change, and we will consider that relationship as it applies to the kinds of behavioral classifications set out in the previous chapter.

THE NATURE OF ATTITUDES

Attitudes have always been of interest to social psychologists. Gordon W. Allport expressed this interest in 1935 when he wrote

> The concept of attitude is probably the most distinctive and indispensable concept in contemporary American social psychology. No other term appears more frequently in experimental and theoretical literature. It has come into favor, first of all, because it is not the property of any one psychological school of thought, and therefore serves admirably the purposes of eclectic writers. . . . The term likewise is elastic enough to apply to the dispositions of single, isolated individuals or to broad patterns of culture. Psychologists and sociologists therefore find in it a meeting point for discussion and research. (Allport, 1967, p. 3)

The word *attitude* is used in many ways: a high school principal may mention a student's *attitude* when deportment is being discussed, an historian may speak of Ghandi's *attitude* about Britain, and the Harris poll may sample *attitudes* about a

---

[1]Not all changes in language are small ones, even though they may seem so. Consider the implications of the use of *he* as a generic pronoun, and the persuasive task that was necessary to eliminate sexist classifications in simple writing.

raise in taxes. It is hard to imagine that all of those uses could be made of the same word.

The word is derived from the Latin term *aptus*, which originally meant "suited" and from which also come our words *apt* and *aptitude*. One of the original meanings for *attitude* concerned orientation or position in space; you will remember that one of the tasks astronauts had in steering the space shuttle was to keep the "attitude" controls working. *Position, orientation*, and *attitude* are still used synonomously to represent an approach to an idea.

Generally we take the word *attitude* to mean a particular predisposition to respond in a given social situation, such as the propensity to express a prejudice, to buy a product, or to attend a football game. Most previous research has assumed that attitudes represent the inner behavior that will have the greatest influence on outer behavior. It is a common assumption that these inner and outer responses will correspond in a causal way, one leading to the other.

However, attitudes and behaviors do not always correspond. In a classic study, Richard LaPiere (1934) toured around the country with a Chinese couple. LaPiere kept careful records of the hotels and eating places that they visited. After the trip, LaPiere wrote to the places that they visited and asked if they accepted Chinese persons as guests. A great majority who wrote back responded that they did not! LaPiere concluded that the social attitudes of the hotel managements had little correspondence with their actions. LaPiere assumed that the mail response accurately reflected attitudes. It is difficult, however, to determine which index does show the real attitude. Which response best expressed the proprietor's attitude about Chinese, the written "I don't serve Chinese here" or the behavior of giving service when a Chinese person appeared at the establishment and requested it? The two different responses are obviously distinct behaviors that resulted from different kinds of stimuli. Isn't it possible for an individual to have an attitude that leads to consistent behavior, such as the avoidance of Chinese in all situations, no matter what stimuli were involved? Most of us would assume that if there is any meaningful way to use the word *attitude*, then the proprietor would have an attitude about Chinese that we could see operating in both sets of responses. Is it useful to say that one has an attitude only when a given question is asked, and that it changes when another circumstance arises?

Let us take another tack and look at some responses to an attitude-related question. In his national newspaper column on January 21, 1968, William F. Buckley Jr. reported the results of a survey that his magazine, *The National Review*, had conducted some years earlier. In this survey, students on different college campuses were asked the question Which do you prefer, nuclear war or surrender to the Russians? Students from different colleges and universities showed a good deal of variety in their responses. Table 3-1 illustrates these responses. Here we have a fairly straightforward report of different responses to an identical question. We assume that the different students had different verbal responses because of some different internal structure. To describe these differences in general, we assume that each group of students was possessed of different attitudes. All

TABLE 3-1

COLLEGE OR UNIVERSITY	PERCENT OF STUDENTS RESPONDING "SURRENDER"
Reed	60
Brandeis	48
Sarah Lawrence	45
Williams	39
Harvard	33
Stanford	27
Howard	21
Boston University	17
Yale	16
Davidson	14
Indiana University	7
South Carolina	4
Marquette	3

we have to do now is to decide exactly which attitudes are involved. But here the process gets more difficult. Mr. Buckley concluded that "A striking aspect of the poll was the tendency of the poorer students to be more firmly anti-Communist, more gratefully American than the wealthier students. This tendency, as we see, crystallizes in the near-identity of the five poorest schools in the survey (Howard, Indiana, South Carolina, Marquette, and Davidson, in that order) with the six schools most willing to go to war rather than surrender to the Communists."

In other words, Mr. Buckley sees in these responses anti-Communist attitudes among the poorer students, and he assumes that these persons exhibit "gratefully American" attitudes. Does this response reflect the attitude that Mr. Buckley attributes to it? There is no doubt that if we are anti-Communist to a strong degree, this attitude will influence our verbal behavior. But at the same time, there could be other attitudes that could be invoked by the response to the question. Obviously, any attitudes we may have about nuclear war are triggered by this question. A student who has a particular horror of nuclear war or a strong antiwar attitude might have chosen surrender, even if this student also hated Communism. The geographical locations of the students who preferred war are of interest: it is much easier to advocate nuclear war from Davidson, North Carolina or Bloomington, Indiana than it is from New York City, Washington, or anywhere on the Eastern seaboard. Of the hawks, only Marquette is close to a metropolitan center (Milwaukee) and this particular student body has a religious orientation that makes it atypical.

It is as possible then, to argue another interpretation for Mr. Buckley's poll and say that geography influenced the responses more than did the pocketbook, since fear of atomic attack is related to where one lives. We could easily say that the poll shows prudence more than anything else, and that the attitude measured concerned nuclear war, not anticommunism. The point is that any kind of social response can be importantly influenced by more than one attitude, and no social stimulus can ever be said to elicit only one. This is especially true when we ask the kind of question that Mr. Buckley and other journalists often prefer, those that produce newsworthy dilemmas that he can use to suit his own purpose. We could always find other factors that are at work to produce the responses that we use to determine our comparisons.

If we wish to make any sense at all out of data like those in Mr. Buckley's poll, we need to be much more specific about what we mean by *attitude* and how we wish to connect it with whatever behavioral goals of conflict resolution and social change are involved.

How has the word *attitude* typically been defined? Let us look at some representative definitions:

> . . . predispositions to respond, but are distinguished from other such states of readiness in that they predispose toward an evaluative response (Osgood, Suci, and Tannenbaum, 1957).
>
> . . . a disposition to act favorably or unfavorably to a class of objects (Sarnoff, 1960).
>
> . . . the Attitude-Reinforcer-Discriminator system (Staats 1968).
>
> . . . evaluative responses (O'Keefe, 1980).

Though each of these definitions seems considerably different, there is actually much common material in them. Let us try to explore the definitions of attitude more analytic fashion.

Operationalism in Definitions

Attitude, as we generally use the word in psychology today, is a construct or a descriptive word for a class of observations. To illustrate what a construct is, let us first examine the relationships that are studied in behavioral science. The most typical relationship studied is between what goes in and what comes out. This is often called the stimulus-response relationship. The laws that result from such study are called $S \rightarrow R$ laws. Another way to study behavior is to see what relationships different responses have with one another, and these are called $R \rightarrow R$ laws. If we feel that a given organism will respond differently to stimuli, we might introduce a new factor between the stimuli and the responses, and the result will be $S \rightarrow O \rightarrow R$ laws. These relationships are operational, because each of these terms can be specified by the operations that are performed to create the relationship. As long as we can observe each element in the process no serious problems occur, and the construction of lawful relationships is a relatively simple one (Bergmann and Spence, 1941).

With a concept like attitude, however, the process is not so simple. For example, when we give two different persons a stimulus question like Do you think male and female college students should live together if they are not married? we may get quite different responses, even though the organisms are quite similar (in other words, they are roughly the same type of persons, from generally similar backgrounds.) The stimuli are the same, the organisms are the same, but we are sure that there is a difference somewhere that causes one to respond, "Hooo, weee!" and the other to respond "Goodness, no!"

One way of describing the difference is to say that one person has a liberated attitude about sex and the other a negative attitude. What we have done is use a word to describe a difference we cannot see but is manifested in the difference in the responses. We realize that the differences may lie in language, percepts, or affects, but we simplify by lumping all of these constructs into a new one. Then the construct of an attitude is inferred to exist in the respondents, mainly from the different behaviors they both exhibit. The construct intervenes between the stimulus and the response. Now we have an $S \rightarrow X \rightarrow R$ law, and the X is merely a term of convenience to describe the relationship or to make it appear more sensible. X has its fundamental meaning in the S and the R of the law. The operations performed to arrive at X are the operational definition of X, which is a construct.

What is this thing called a construct? Certainly nothing mysterious. Our language is full of them. If it were not, all of what we call science would disappear. Consider the word *mass*, as it is used in physics. When we examine a cube of lead with a volume of 1,000 cubic centimeters, we might have difficulty distinguishing it from a cube of tin the same size. However, we can place each cube on a scale and see that the two cubes have different effects on the scale; the lead makes the needle point to a larger number than the tin does. The two are different, so to describe the difference we use the word *mass* and say that the lead has more of it than the tin does. *Mass* is the result of a class of operations called weighing. *Space, time, velocity,* and other constructs in physics are similarly defined. We use them so often, however, that we feel that they have objective reality. The meaning of these constructs lies in their operations, and without the operations no meaning is present.

Since attitude is a construct, the only meaning it can have is in the operations that we perform to infer its existence. Therefore, our task in examining attitudes is going to be to examine the kinds of operations that we can sensibly include or omit in the construct. The behavioral sciences do not exhibit the unanimity of usage apparent in the physical sciences, however. Some researchers are fond of one kind of operation, others feel that another operation should be used. Our purpose, then, will be to examine some of the principal points of view about the definition of attitudes and attempt to look at them all in terms of their usefulness for persuasion. In addition, we will try to make sense out of them as they use different inner and outer components of behavior.

A Derivational Approach— Doob's Definition

One way that we might define attitude is to use some well-established constructs from general psychology, much as a physicist defines *velocity* by using the words *distance* and *time*. Such an approach is used in Leonard W. Doob's classic definition of attitude:

1. an implicit response (inner)
2. which is both (a) anticipatory and (b) mediating in reference patterns of overt response
3. which is evoked by (a) a variety of stimulus patterns (b) as a result of previous learning or of gradients of generalization or discrimination
4. which is in itself cue- and drive-producing
5. and which is considered socially significant in the individual's society (Doob, 1947, p. 135).

This definition of attitude specifies a completely nonobservable kind of response that is the result of prior learning. Doob's definition is derived from the behavioral system of Hull (1943), which in turn was derived from well-established concepts in general psychology. If we return to the four classifications of response from Chapter 2, we can see that Doob has specified a complex inner component of an instrumental response that has inner connections to percepts and to affects. The learning that Doob refers to is the result of reinforcement. In other words, this response is acquired in the same way as the more simple instrumental responses are acquired.

Important factors in this definition are the cue- and drive-producing aspects of attitude. According to Doob, an attitude cues other responses in much the same fashion as the word *four* is a cue for the word *five*. There is another sense in which attitudes are cue-producing, however. We now know that prior attitudes have great influence on the way that we perceive the outside world. In a sense, we see what we want to see. Most of this research has been done since Doob's article appeared, but it seems reasonable to include these perceptual effects in his notion of the cue-producing process of attitude.

The drive-producing properties of attitudes are the most distinct characteristics that attitudinal responses possess as opposed to those acquired in ordinary learning. *Drive*, as Doob uses the word, is synonomous with *affect* and is the basic energizing function of an organism. The primary drives were once considered to be the main motivators of our behavior—hunger, thirst, sex, and others—but researchers have shown that secondary drives have just as great a capability of energizing behavior. The affect produced by an attitude is a secondary one; it is learned much the same way as a new skill, or any other response.

Judson Brown (1953) has described the process of learning secondary affect rather well. He uses the example of money as a typical motivator. When we are out of money, we are conscious of many out-of-money cues. A flat wallet or a low number in the checkbook, or even creditors calling on the telephone produce emotional responses. These cues have been established in the presence of other kinds of anxieties, such as the fear that one may be evicted from an apartment or the presence of hunger. The drive for money is the result of the anxiety-producing cues attendant on the lack of money and the subsequent anxieties about the more basic needs of the organism. Thus an individual comes to value money and have an attitude about its presence or absence in a wallet, purse or bank account. This attitude is drive-producing in the sense that it produces behavior and its reduction is reinforcing.

As we look at typical attitude-related behaviors in our society, we find it easy to see the drive-producing capability, that is, the dimension of social significance. Doob states that our attitudes toward cream cheese or new hats are trivial, and hence are not of enough importance to be considered attitudes under his definition. It is admittedly difficult to decide what is socially significant and what is not; attitudes about Bo Derek may be trivial when compared to attitudes concerning the Palestinian Liberation Organization, but a sociologist may consider predispositions concerning Miss Derek of great social significance! Doob did not specify what he would call social significance, since this factor differs from society to society. He suggests that one way of approaching the dimension is to ask if a given response is generally labeled good or desirable in any society.

Perhaps a better way might be to consider to what extent a given attitude is generally drive-producing in any society and how intense the drives are. To be sure, there is no eminently defensible way of separating the socially significant from the trivial; each of us can make a case for our own interests. But in spite of the problems involved, Doob's distinction seems to be a good one, and we should limit ourselves to discussing attitudes of social significance only. For students of persuasion, judgments of social significance are very important ones, for we typically feel that persuasive communication about trivial subjects is a waste of time.

Cognitive Approaches to Attitude

Another way that has been used to approach the definition of attitude is to confine it to the perceptual and linguistic inner functions, ignoring any possible instrumental functions. Many persons who have done this have labeled this approach the cognitive aspect of attitude. Indeed, some have even asserted that this is the only way that attitudes should be studied. A cognition is knowing, a connection between a specific percept and linguistic use. For example, you might know that pizza is round, at least most of the time. You might also associate a number of other things that you know about pizza, such as spicy, Italian, hot, tasty, and the like. Each of these elements is a cognition. Our cognitions about pizza may largely determine our behavior toward it. If you also link *fattening* with pizza, you may behave differently than if you link *delicious* with it (but not necessarily!)

Pizza and its associated cognitions may not be a world-shaking issue, but when we look at significant social concepts we may see how the cognitive approach may be useful. A phrase like *women's liberation* may be associated with cognitions like fair, honest, modern, and worthwhile by one person, and aggressive, pushy, left-wing, and stupid by another. It is not hard to see how these two persons would differ with respect to the Equal Rights Amendment.

There are a number of approaches to attitudes as cognitions, and language plays an important part in most of them. Let us examine a few of these.

The semantic differential.   The largest question is how to decide which cognitions are important and which ones to use. In an attempt to solve this problem, Charles Osgood proposed a meaning-centered approach to the study and definition of attitudes. Working with a test of his own invention called the semantic differential, Osgood found that it is possible to relate concepts to general qualitative reactions expressed by bipolar adjectives. For example, we can look at the word *abortion* in terms of the way it could be described on a series of scales like this:

valuable ____ : ____ : ____ : ____ : ____ : ____ : ____ : worthless
stupid ____ : ____ : ____ : ____ : ____ : ____ : ____ : smart

We could use almost any set of adjectives that we liked, such as good–bad, hot–cold, rough–smooth. In Osgood's research he discovered that almost all concepts were generally responded to in terms of three distinct dimensions: evaluation, potency, and activity (Osgood, Suci, and Tannenbaum, 1957). These dimensions are thought to represent the structure of the inner linguistic structure. The evaluation scales were generally of the value type, such as good–bad, valuable–worthless. Potency scales generally described qualities of power, such as strong–weak, brave–cowardly. The activity scales were generally defined by adjectives like fast–slow, active–passive, and the like. This predisposition to rate most concepts three ways seems to be fairly general, both in terms of the persons who do the rating and the kinds of concepts that are rated. Because three dimensions are present, Osgood hypothesized that each concept has a "semantic space" and its meaning can only be defined in terms of these three dimensions. To know what a concept means for Osgood is to know what power it has along each of these three dimensions of semantic space.

Our attitude about anything, says Osgood, is defined by the way in which we react to it in the evaluative portion of the semantic space. He cites the close relationship between the semantic-differential measuring technique to other measuring techniques, and he reasons from this that the evaluative dimension is indeed the best measure of attitude. Many more contemporary writers still use Osgood's definition. O'Keefe (1980) represents the best example of this modern usage, and the case he makes for this scheme is logical. But it is important not to confuse O'Keefe's notion of attitude with other more comprehensive definitions. Woelfel, Cody, Gillham, and Holmes (1980) have examined other methods in constructing multidimensional models of attitudes. They argued that to work with a unidimensional system was to ignore many interesting aspects of attitude structure. They advocate the use of geometrical models in the construction of attitude models.

Osgood's definition is, of course, centered around a specific measuring instrument and has the weakness of being conceptually unrelated to other kinds of responses that might indicate attitude on a given subject. More interesting dimensions might be discovered using Woelfel's technique, but there is nothing in their definition of attitude that differs fundamentally from Doob's. Both Osgood and Woelfel have specified a given operation that defines attitude and can be said to indicate it. Doob specifies what elements have gone into the formulation of attitude. Operationalism, if followed strictly, leaves us with definitions that center around specific measuring techniques.

Attitudes and beliefs.   Many writers are convinced that conditioning theory or a learning approach to human behavior is counterproductive, and instead would substitute an entire psychological system based on cognitions (Brewer, (1974). While their claims may be overstated (Dulany, 1974), there is some good reason to apply some of the cognitive approach to the general problem of attitudes and their formation. What does it mean to say that an individual has a belief about a particular issue or problem? For example, in 1981, *Scientific American* (Nowak, 1981) reported that 34 percent of Polish youth believed that a sensible government for Poland would involve state ownership of basic heavy industry. The relationship between this belief and other fundamental beliefs about socialism, government, and individual liberties cannot be ignored. The entire structure of the belief system must be examined. It may be possible that these cognitions and their attributes have little to do with specific perceptions or specific behaviors. Further, it may be as important to study the cognitions in and of themselves as it is to study the other aspects of the attitudinal problem.

Some writers have held that there is an important distinction between beliefs and attitudes, that beliefs are really not attitudes at all, and should not be treated in the same way. Fishbein (1967) has articulated this point of view fairly well. He has stated, for example, that individuals can have the same attitude about segregation because of entirely different sets of beliefs. One individual may believe that blacks are athletic but lazy, while another may believe that blacks have a natural sense of rhythm and a childlike sense of humor. These two individuals may give identical responses to the question Should blacks and whites share the same school?" The two have different beliefs but the same attitude. Fishbein goes on to add that the structure and change in attitude can be explained by the "summation" of beliefs in a number of ways. In other words, attitudes are the sum total of a number of beliefs. Infante (1973b), Cronen and Conville (1973), King (1975), and Jaccard and King (1977) have all shown that the Fishbein formulation can have some utility in predicting how attitudes are formed and changed.

However, Cronen and Conville (1975) find a number of problems with the general adaptation of belief theory to attitude theory. They see difficulties with the notion of belief strength or weights. One belief, it would seem, could be stronger than another. Cronen and Conville showed that this simplistic approach led to a number of problems. In addition, they believe that the summation explanation of the creations of attitudes ought to be viewed with some suspicion. However, Cronen and Conville did not discuss one of the most important problems with the definition of beliefs, namely, their valence. Beliefs can take on positive or negative connotations to the user. In the statements about blacks cited above, blacks are characterized as possessing negative attributes in the belief statement. To say, as Fishbein does, that an attitude must include an evaluative statement is to beg the question as to which is the attitude and which is the belief. When I say that blacks are athletic, I am implying something good or bad about blacks, depending on how I feel about athletic individuals. It is difficult to imagine a belief that is entirely free from evaluation. If I am as objective as I can be about some of my beliefs about blacks—for example, blacks are dark-skinned human beings—then I have a statement that has little psychological or sociological utility for me. The phrase *dark-skinned* is not neutral for a prejudiced person, and so my idea of neutral becomes nonprejudiced, which is most definitely an attitudinal position. For that matter, almost any attribute that I would use to single out blacks takes on evaluative connotations because it is a belief held about blacks and not some other class of people. Even if I go so far as to say, Blacks are absolutely indistinguishable from whites, I am revealing something about my attitude structures. In short, the hoped-for distinction between attitudes and beliefs is probably not defensible.

Comprehensive Approaches to Attitude

The inner (or implicit) responses that we call attitudes obviously can be manifested in a number of ways. There are many other ways to define attitudes, and theorists have postulated more than a single dimension in measurement. Katz, for example, has defined attitudes as the "predisposition of the individual to evaluate some symbol or object or aspect of his world in a favorable or unfavorable manner" (1960). He goes on to define opinions as the verbal manifestation of attitudes, and sets out two basic components that attitudes possess, the cognitive component (or beliefs) and the affective component (or feelings). For example, we might know that unbalanced budgets bring inflation, but we might have no cares about it one way or another. A state penitentiary inmate has little involvement in the economy, and might not care if the rest of us have inflation or even a full-scale depression. On the other hand, if the inmate had some emotional involvement with our economy, he or she would then be opposed to recessions, and consequently opposed to balanced budgets. Katz defines the intensity of the attitude in terms of the degree of affective arousal involved in it. If this is acceptable, we might conclude that when no affective arousal is present, the attitude would have zero intensity and, therefore, would not exist. Katz does not make this point in his definition, but it seems a reasonable interpretation.

Dichotomous approaches. The dichotomous approach to attitudes has been manifested in the distinction between logical and emotional discourse, which has been a standard of rhetorical criticism for centuries. However, Katz' characterization of the two approaches as different manifestations of a unitary concept of attitude is quite different from the rhetorical approach, and so is the interpretation offered here that without emotional intensity no attitude exists.

Another problem arises from the distinction that is made between the attitude and the symptoms or characteristics of it. According to Katz' definition, attitudes have two components, affective and cognitive. But we might well say that these two components are simply two different kinds of manifestation of a single attitude, that what I feel and know about an object in my environment are merely two different ways of responding to it. The cognitive elements of this definition would be found in the percept portion of the inner responses and would often be coupled with the language. Most individuals who use the word *cognitive* in the attitude problem are not specific about whether cognitive or linguistic definitions are meant. For example, one can know that the Brooklyn bridge connects Manhattan and Brooklyn without a visual percept of the bridge's appearance, how it feels to walk across it, and so on. We will return to this problem when we discuss cognitive dissonance in Chapter 5.

Let us now turn to another more comprehensive approach to attitudes, this one by Rosenberg and Hovland (1960). These writers have defined attitudes in terms of three different kinds of manifestations: the affective, the cognitive, and the behavioral. For example, they would distinguish between an emotional response to birth control, knowledge about birth control devices or results, and the actual practice of birth control in a family situation. If we take this approach, it makes little sense to ask which of the three represents the real attitude, since all three are different manifestations of the construct. Whether we can meaningfully group all three kinds of responses together is another question. Many writers are fond of pointing out that little research has been done concerning the relationships between what we have called attitudes as opposed to what we call real behavior. As Arthur Cohen put it, many investigators make

> ... the broad psychological assumption that since attitudes are evaluative predispositions, they have consequences for the way people act toward others, for the programs they actually undertake, and for the manner in which they carry them out. Thus attitudes are always seen as precursors of behavior, as determinants of how a person will actually behave in his daily affairs. In spite of the wide range of the assumption, however, very little work on attitude change has dealt explicitly with the behavior that may follow a change in attitude (1964, pp. 137–138)[2]

Cohen went on to say that unless such linkages are established, attitudes will have little significance in psychology. However, if we accept the view of Rosenberg and Hovland, attitudes cannot be contrasted with behavior, because behavior merely reflects a dimension of attitude.

There is some evidence to show that the three approaches to attitudes may have some consistency, that is, the three manifestations of attitude may spring from some implicit response. Cooper and Pollock (1959) demonstrated that affective responses, in the form of psychogalvanic skin response, were closely associated with cognitive measures of attitudes toward blacks. DeFleur and Westie (1958) demonstrated a similar effect with attitude measures and volunteering behavior. A good deal of the problem involved in the demonstration of these relationships lies in the measuring instruments involved. Cook and Selltiz, in discussing this problem, state that "an attitude cannot be measured directly, but must always be inferred from behavior—whether the behavior be language in which the individual reports

---

[2]From *Attitude Change and Social Influence* by Arthur R. Cohen. © 1964 by Basic Books, Inc. By permission of Basic Books, Inc., Publishers, New York.

his feelings about the attitude-object, performance of a task involving material related to the object (for example, recall of statements that take a position with respect to the object), or actions toward a representative of the object-class" (1964, p. 36). They might have added that the behavior could be responses on affectively-oriented measures such as skin conductivity or eye-pupil dilation.

If these kinds of indicators are to be considered behavior in the sense that Rosenberg and Hovland use the word, then there is no problem. The use of such terminology would also eliminate the necessity for separate categories of behavior. What Rosenberg and Hovland seem to be discussing is the outer portion of behavior. Many call this overt. But the use of the word *overt* with *behavior* does not improve the definition much, for the "overtness" of a given response is capable of a wide range of interpretation. When an individual is wired up in a polygraph, a heartbeat becomes an overt behavior, although normally we would consider heart rate an inner or covert response. If a professor is interviewing his dean and the dean notices the professor wiping his hands on his trousers, shifting his position frequently, and glancing about the room, the dean may correctly conclude that the professor is nervous. Is the response that the dean observes an overt or a covert one? If the dean looks very closely she may see a fine coat of perspiration on the professor's forehead. Is this a covert response, or, since the dean was able to see it, was it overt? Because this question is not capable of being answered, the distinction may not be a good one. We might want to add the word *ordinarily* to our definition of overt and let it go at that.

There is one more consideration in examining the overtness of a given behavior. The object of the attitude may make an important difference in the kind of response. For example, an attitude about jet air travel requires a different orientation than an attitude about space travel; we use jets a good deal, but few of us have taken a trip in the space shuttle. Overt behavior is just not possible in many kinds of attitudes. For example, we seldom, if ever, are asked to perform overt behaviors on issues like the devaluation of the pound or our foreign policy toward the Israeli government. It might be possible to construct overt behavioral consequences on some of these issues, but none of the consequences would involve the actual decision process.

Attitudes and behavior.   We have seen that it is possible to define attitude (and, indeed, many theorists have) as a behavioral predisposition. But so often attitude measures are strictly verbal in nature, and so the question arises about the nature of the relationship of the attitude and the behavior that might accompany it. It has become fairly typical to view these relationships as the attitude-behavior problem, assuming, first, that a problem exists (Cushman and McPhee, 1980) and, second, that one's new theoretical orientation will solve the problem (O'Keefe, 1980). LaPiere's study of the Chinese couple (1934), cited earlier, was an example of two different approaches to attitude. LaPiere defined one response as an attitude and another as an action. Dillehay (1973) has effectively demonstrated the pitfalls inherent in taking LaPiere too seriously. However, recently Larson and Sanders

(1975) do just that, without the cautions, and they suggest that it is widely known that attitudes and behavior do not necessarily correspond. Steinfatt and Infante (1976) have dealt effectively with some of Larson and Sander's misconceptions. The distinctions between inner responses and outer behavior are a useful method of solving this pseudoproblem. In addition, the inclusion of the concept of potential behavior is helpful. Further, Bostrom (1980) has drawn a distinction between the *predisposition* to respond, and the *opportunity* to respond. In the 1980 presidential election, for example, many persons may have wished to vote for Anderson but were prevented from doing so by the fact that only Carter and Reagan were on the ballot. The predisposition may have been there, but the opportunity certainly was not. To argue that the attitude did not correspond with the behavior is just silly. Unfortunately, a good bit of the attitude-behavior controversy has some of that flavor. Ajzen and Fishbein (1978) have done an exhaustive review of this issue and conclude that when four important factors—action, context, target, and time—are controlled, there is a rather good configuration between most measures of attitude and subsequent behavior.

A great many of the problems involved in the attitude-behavior difficulty are clearly definitional. Siebold (1975) has defined the problem differently by delineating verbal reports about attitudes and subsequent behavior. His path analysis model is an extremely clear and useful explication of these relationships.

Attitudes—
A Comprehensive Model

If students read all of the attitudinal research diligently, they would be thoroughly confused at this point! Many researchers use confusing terms, few are willing to build on others' work, and often the research seems to be designed to advance a specific theoretical orientation, rather than to shed light on this important psychological and social problem. The best way to make sense out of the general confusion is to construct a comprehensive model and show how each of the general views of attitude fit into it. In constructing such a model, we need to refer to the types of behavior (both inner and outer) designated in Chapter 2. Let us look at these behavioral elements and see how they fit into the general attitude problem.

Let us examine Fig. 3-1. Here we see several elements of attitudes as they relate to one another. The boxes on the left-hand side of the figure represent different internal elements of attitudes, much as the internal types of behavior were defined in Chapter 2 (see pages 26-28). The difference is that now we assume that various internal elements cause other internal elements as well as the outer responses. For example, the use of a word can cause both a physiological response as well as an affect. The arrows in the diagram represent these causal paths. If someone whispers, "let's get married" to you, you might well experience an affective internal response as well as a physiological response, such as breaking out in a cold sweat.

There are many possible connections between elements. Saltiel and Woelfel (1975) have added factors such as age and sex to the elements presented in Fig. 3-1

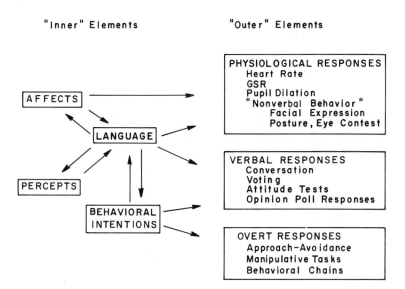

FIGURE 3-1

to construct a theoretical model of attitude change. What we often forget is that sometimes we respond using as simple a path as possible. If we return to the example of LaPiere and the Chinese couple, you will remember that in one situation the actual couple was present and elicited one response, and in the other situation, a card or letter elicited a quite different response. Figure 3-2 represents what might have been going on in the first instance. Both a verbal response and an overt response are created by language, percepts, and affects.

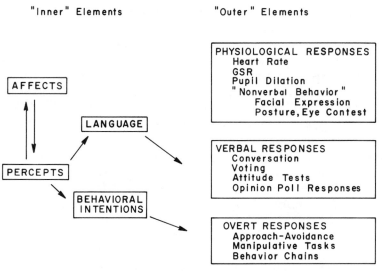

FIGURE 3-2

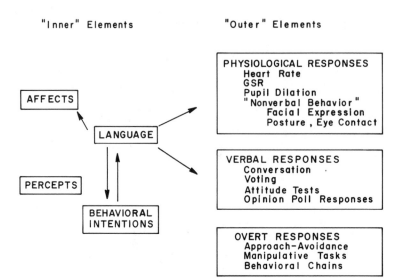

"Inner" Elements   "Outer" Elements

PHYSIOLOGICAL RESPONSES
Heart Rate
GSR
Pupil Dilation
"Nonverbal Behavior"
Facial Expression
Posture, Eye Contact

AFFECTS

LANGUAGE

PERCEPTS

BEHAVIORAL INTENTIONS

VERBAL RESPONSES
Conversation
Voting
Attitude Tests
Opinion Poll Responses

OVERT RESPONSES
Approach–Avoidance
Manipulative Tasks
Behavioral Chains

FIGURE 3-3

In Fig. 3–3, however, quite a different process is invoked. No direct perception of the Chinese couple is indicated. Instead the process starts with language—the card or letter. In addition, the end product is only verbal, rather than overt. In other words, in Fig. 3–3 we see only a linguistic response toward an unknown person, rather than an overt response toward an individual who is present in the restaurant. All of the elements of the process are present both times. In other words, just because different results occurred, it does not necessarily imply a different fundamental structure. The system is simply not activated the same way each time. It makes no sense at all to claim that Figure 3–2 represents attitude and Figure 3–3 represents behavior, but that is precisely what many persons have done.

Part of the problem represents a natural desire to explain inconsistencies between verbal behavior and other kinds of behavior. This is an old problem in psychology, and needs our attention. Deutscher (1973), for example, wrote a thoughtful book, *Why Do They Say One Thing, Do Another?* The old popular song goes "Your Lips Tell Me No-No, But There's Yes-Yes In Your Eyes!" But these dichotomizations are not as frequent as many persons believe. We can easily detect behavior-behavior inconsistencies, as well as attitude-attitude inconsistencies. No human being is entirely consistent all of the time. In addition, these kinds of inconsistencies can frequently be explained more easily by some other type of behavior, such as the absence of self-monitoring (Snyder, 1981).

So when we use the word *attitude*, we must be very sure that we know exactly what we mean by this term. In addition, when we read that a researcher studied attitude change, we must also be sure we know how this attitude was defined. What, then, can we conclude about general usage of the word? There are, surprisingly, some common elements in most definitions. Let us list some of these:

1. Attitudes control kinds of social behavior, that is, they may be said to be determinants of what different individuals will be likely to do in similar social situations. Although little research shows strong relationships between attitude tests constructed to measure them and the actual behaviors in a social situation, this is largely because observation is difficult in most cases. When writers define attitudes in terms of the tests they use, they set up artificial meanings for the word *attitude*.

2. Attitudes are closely related to our emotional life; they produce affective responses and they are centrally related to what we value, desire, or are emotionally attracted to.

3. Attitudes can be inferred from a variety of responses, not all of which are consistent. Most social situations involve many attitudes, any one of which can be said to be predominant at a given time.

4. Attitudes are dynamic, changeable, and shift from one situation to the next. Some kinds of attitudes are more stable than others, but all are subject to various influences.

The general question of what creates attitude change is our next topic.

THE DYNAMICS OF ATTITUDE CHANGE

If we have committed ourselves to the idea of changing attitudes with persuasive communication, we owe it to ourselves to examine the process involved in attitude change. Not only would we want to change attitudes more efficiently, we might wish to look at the process to see if communication has any effect at all. What makes us change our attitudes as we interact with other individuals in our society? Do we really change in a significant way or do our basic attitudes remain the same and do the manifestations of them vary from time to time? The answers to these and other questions will significantly influence the kind of theories we have about the roles of communication for the purpose of attitude change, that is, the processes of argumentation and persuasion.

Causes of Attitude Change

We have all had the experience of changing our mind about something, and the process may have been accomplished by many different social circumstances: new information, new group attitudes, or new reward structures. This experience may have convinced us that others change their attitudes in the same way. The process of change, if it does take place, is not something that happens every day. Here is how Muzafer Sherif puts it:

> To say that a person has an attitude toward some objects, persons, groups, institutions, or ways of living means that he already has his own yardstick for evaluating these things as desirable-undesirable, as good-bad, as acceptable-objectionable in some degree. His evaluation of his family, his religion, his politics, his standard of living, or his country—and those of others—do not shift easily from day to day. He does not take these matters lightly. To an important extent, these evaluations are constituents of his picture, not snap judgments or transitory opinions on his part. To

this extent, change in his attitudes is not a discrete event of shifting one single item in his psychological make-up. Changing his attitude means changing him as a person, changing a part of himself as he has come to know himself relative to his social world. (Sherif, Sherif, and Nebergall, 1965, p. 13)

We might say, based on Sherif's statement, that we all resist being changed as a person in this way.

At the same time, we must recognize that change does take place. Theodore Newcomb's study of the changing attitudes of undergraduates at Bennington College is a classic demonstration of the effects of time and experience on attitude structures (Newcomb, 1958). But not all changes are this gradual. Sometimes a change is dramatic and can be called *conversion*. The sinner finds religion, the former bachelor decides on marriage, the inveterate gambler swears off horses, and so on. This kind of change is not as uncommon as we might suppose.

So while attitude change is not an easy process or something that is undertaken often, we must recognize that a good deal of change does take place and that we can usually observe its occurrence.

Measurement problems and change.   How much must an individual change before we can term the change a significant one? One important difficulty in attitude change is the demonstration (in a measurable fashion) that change has taken place. Attitudes can manifest themselves through a variety of responses, sometimes affective, sometimes cognitive, and sometimes behavioral. Whatever responses we choose as the indicator of attitude will be the result of some social stimulus that we apply to the individual being measured, and in order to measure change, we must apply the stimulus again. In other words, if I wish to see if you are changing your attitudes about migrant workers' schools in Florida, I might ask you this week, "Do you agree that federal funds should be allocated to the establishment of schools for migrant workers in Florida?" Your response, affirmative or negative, would be an indication of how your attitude is at this moment. But if I should come around again in two weeks and ask the same question, you might well remember the earlier question and wonder why I was still interested in it. At the same time, the original question may have stimulated you to do some thinking on the subject. In addition, you might remember your original response and might not wish to appear wishy-washy by exhibiting too much change from time to time.

In other words, most of the time attitude change is difficult to measure unless some more subtle method is employed and care is taken to mask the purpose of the questioning. The process of measurement affects the end product, and so when we speak of the measurement of attitude change, we are dealing with an inferential process at best and an experimental artifact at worst. Although care should be taken in evaluating data that purport to show attitude change, these methodological reservations do not preclude change itself.

Functionalism and the question of change.   Daniel Katz (1960) has taken an entirely different approach to the problem of attitude change based on the *functional* characteristics of attitudes. Katz has seen that attitudes are used by individuals to (1) adjust to problems and situations that our lives thrust upon us, (2) act as an ego-defense in threatening situations, (3) express values appropriate to personal identification, and (4) provide knowledge and structure to the universe. Whether or not an attitude will change will depend upon whether the situation changes, requiring a different function at the different time. Katz' formulation is quite interesting and provides a good framework for analysis.

Attitude change and reinforcement.   Obviously, the manner in which we define attitude will influence the way that we define attitude change. If attitudes are defined as functions, they will be altered as functional needs arise. Doob's definition, however, is quite different, resting on a different set of principles, which in turn rest on the assumption that changes in response are the result of *learning*. Doob's definition, since it rests on Hull's behavioral system, would imply that attitude change is the result of drives, cues, responses, and rewards. Attitudes are learned, then, in the same way that other kinds of responses are learned, namely, by being reinforced. There is some evidence for this view: Janis and King (1954) in a study of role playing found that attitude change was apparently caused by role playing that was more improvised, and the experimenters felt that the improvisation was more rewarding than the other conditions. Hence, a rewarded response produced the attitude change. Scott (1957) provided a little better evidence for the rewarded response theory; he placed subjects in a situation where they were asked to debate a particular topic, and then randomly designated some as winners of the debate and others as losers. The winners exhibited more attitude change in the direction of their arguments than did the losers.

While Scott demonstrated that his two conditions were different, he did not demonstrate whether he was using reward or punishment. In other words, the winners may have been neutrally reinforced and the losers may have been punished, or the losers may have been neutral and the winners reinforced positively. To explore this relationship, Bostrom, Vlandis, and Rosenbaum (1961) placed students in a situation where they were asked to write essays advocating positions that they did not believe in. Some of the group was rewarded, others were punished, and a third group was given no rewards or punishments. This study demonstrated that both rewards and punishments were instrumental in affecting attitude change; the rewards added to attitude change, and punishments detracted from change. Further evidence for the efficacy of reinforcement is provided by Infante (1976). In his study, he provided feedback to speakers telling them that they had succeeded in a persuasive task. Those who had this kind of feedback showed more attitude change than those who received no feedback or those who were told that they had failed.

In the studies cited here, attitudes have been demonstrated to be a function of a response offered by an individual, coupled with some kind of reinforcing contingency. The interaction of the responses and the reinforcements is the apparent cause of the attitude change, and so we should be justified in calling the change in attitudes *learning*. Many other studies have shown attitudes to be affected by reinforcing contingencies, and since the more simple learning situations have been extensively studied, it seems reasonable that we might wish to apply the results of such study to attitude change. When we do this, we are doing the same kind of theorizing that Doob did in the construction of his definitions of attitudes. The appeal of fitting the attitude construct into well-established construct systems is a strong one. However, it is considerably more complex than has been presented here. A comprehensive review by Burgoon, Miller, and Sunnafrank (1981) shows that the learning problem can be approached from a classical conditioning approach, an instrumental conditioning point of view, a contiguity point of view, a cognitive point of view, and a mathematical point of view. Certainly a complex process!

Attitudes and cognitive processes.   One way of looking at attitudes and their structure is by examining the cognitive elements—the percepts and language—that go into their formation. As we mentioned earlier in this chapter (p. 46) Fishbein (1967) demonstrated that attitudes could be built up out of separate cognitive elements. In addition, Cronkhite (1969) showed that the building up of many smaller units of cognitive structure is an adequate explanation of the attitude change process over larger periods of time. Infante (1972) has furnished further evidence of the usefulness of Cronkhite's hypothesis. But the specific nature of cognitive elements as opposed to other explanations is a rather important question in current psychology. The question, simply put, is whether circumstances create human behavior *and* cognitions, or whether circumstances create the cognitions and the cognitions create the behavior. Cronen and Conville (1973) argue that immediate situations create evaluations without cognitive mediations. Delia and others (1975) argue against this interpretation, citing Brewer (1974) who examined hundreds of research studies in which cognitive awareness and reinforcement were coupled. Brewer concludes that there is no convincing evidence that reinforcement *per se* causes responses without cognitive mediation, but an examination of the data cited by Brewer reveals that, at the same time, there is no real evidence that mediation occurs first in reinforcing situations. The question of which causes which is of great interest to theoreticians, and could have substantial implications to the study of persuasion.

Attitudes and Social Influence

Unfortunately, the typical paradigms of the laws of learning are difficult to observe and interpret in our social systems, and many other kinds of conceptual schemes have been suggested that may make our understanding of this process difficult.

Kelman's approach.   One such interpretation is that by Herbert C. Kelman (1961), who has proposed a theory of social influence that is also a theory of attitude change. Kelman hypothesizes that behavioral and attitudinal influences are the result of three kinds of social processes: "compliance," "internalization," and "identification." We respond to others in a compliant fashion, says Kelman, when we are influenced to do something when another person (an agent) has control of means or ends that are important to us. This resulting behavior persists only so long as we are under the surveillance of the agent. This influence explains the attitude that we have only as long as the boss is around. Whether or not we would wish to call these real attitudes is unimportant, the important thing is that they do occur.

Kelman's second kind of influence, identification, occurs when we are influenced by an individual who we find socially attractive (outstanding or admirable). As long as we find the individual's attitude a salient factor in the attractiveness or social desirability, then we will adopt the attitude. This is the process that occurs when we believe in an issue because the president of our fraternity believes in it—a fairly common kind of attitude change.

The last process hypothesized by Kelman is internalization. We are moved by internal influence when we are affected by individuals who we consider to be credible and whose credibility is relevant to the situation in which we find ourselves. This is a so-called rational process and occurs when we take the advice of experts or individuals who have established believability in some important way.

The three processes as defined by Kelman have been demonstrated to affect the opinions of individuals a good deal. Kelman is not the only social-influence writer; social influence is of great interest to most social psychologists. In Chapter 4 we will examine in more detail Kelman's processes and other theorists who have contributed to our understanding of social influence. Kelman does typify the social-influence writers and is used here as a good example of thinking on this subject.

It is interesting to note, however, that the social-influence processes are not inconsistent with a learning-theory approach to attitude change. The mechanisms of social influence could be easily interpreted as the response-and-reward contingencies most often appearing in our social framework. Kelman's contribution may be the unique manner in which he organizes this response-reward repertoire, so that we can look at the whole process in a meaningful way.

All of these theories concerning the mechanism of attitude change have experimental evidence to support them and are not necessarily inconsistent with one another. We have already seen that Kelman's theory may be interpreted as the response-reward contingencies that spring from the most common social interactions. The balance theories may describe a drive that prior learning may have created out of situations in which consistency was rewarded. Attitudes do change, and these changes are a function of the social actions that individuals perform. But how much of this change can be attributed to communicative activity is another matter, indeed.

Theories of role enactment. Charles Berger (1972) has suggested that persuasion can be fruitfully examined from the point of view of role-enactment, rather than a strict communication point of view. Most communication theories emphasize the nature of the message, source, and situations in interpreting the attitude change that takes place in the persuasive situation. Berger presents evidence that when individuals are called on to take an active role for or against an issue, this role enactment has a strong effect on subsequent attitudes.

Counterattitudinal advocacy is a special kind of role enactment. It refers to the process that occurs when an individual must, of necessity, take a position *counter* to his or her own; that is, when one advocates something that, deep down, one does not believe in. Many students express shock that psychological researchers find this process interesting, arguing that, first of all, honest persons do not do this, and second, that the whole process smacks of brainwashing. The sad fact is that often honest persons find themselves in situations in which they must take a position somewhat different from their own. Congressmen often adopt positions to represent their constituency, and administrative officials often need to represent the view of the entire administration rather than their own. The secretary of state, for example, may attend an international conference on disarmament with official instructions from the president and the rest of the government to take a particular position. The secretary may have had a strong voice in the formulation of that position, but whether the position is his or not is irrelevant—his job is to represent the government, not himself. This situation is not uncommon in labor negotions, in legal pleading, and in many other "real life" persuasive settings.

What happens to a person when he or she must argue against his or her own feelings? The answer is a complex one. Perhaps the best review of the relevant issues here can be found in Miller (1973). The issues underlying the various theoretical positions are too complex to be reproduced here, and as Miller notes, "no one position can claim hegemony over the others" (1973, p. 145). The important facts are that counterattitudinal advocacy is a strong source of a kind of persuasion, and a socially significant phenomenon.

Communication

When we say that an attitude has been changed, are we speaking of permanent, long-term effects? It seems unlikely that communication will produce them, although many communicators seem to desire this as a result. The word *conversion* is often used to describe the dramatic effect that can happen when communication produces well established, long-term effects. Some writers equate conversion with the word *persuasion*. This would seem to imply that when we have persuasion the result is a completely new life style, or an entirely changed individual.

As we examine the typical effects of persuasive communications however, we must recognize that this kind of result is rare. For example, when the Federal Communications Commission chairman tells radio and television broadcasters that they should be more public spirited and work for more high-quality programs in the public interest, the immediate effect among the broadcasters is largely that of indifference. When almost anyone in public life speaks in favor of higher taxes, there is seldom a rush to the tax office to volunteer more funds for the operations of government. Do these speeches, therefore, produce no attitude change? We would probably not go that far in describing their effects.

How much attitude change is actually brought about by communication? Are some attitudes changed, while others are left alone? Can a communicator sensibly plan to change an attitude structure if he or she feels that it is important? Several researchers have examined the structures of attitudes in a way that might help answer (at least partially) these and other questions concerning the relationship of attitudes and communication.

Central or peripheral?   One way of examining the nature of the changes that communication can achieve is an approach taken by Milton Rokeach (1960). He has proposed an interpretation of attitude structures that he calls belief theory, and hypothesizes that there are many levels of beliefs that guide our day-to-day activity. Some of these beliefs are central, or core beliefs that are important to our very identity. Such beliefs are concerned with our individual worth, the innate value of the group memberships that we hold, and the like. For some persons, religious identity is the most important part of the belief system that they hold. For others, national identification is primary. All of us believe that we exist, and that the maintenance of life systems is important, and so on. Lack of strength in these central beliefs might be an indication of lack of ego, as Freud put it, and a possible sign of neurosis or psychosis.

Often we call these central beliefs *values*, because they seem to be more important in the general psychological makeup of individuals than mere beliefs or attitudes. There is some evidence that individuals do hold those ideas more strongly and adapt slightly to situational considerations. Heath (1976) showed that central value systems remained stable in an interactive situation, and that persuasion could be thought of as the application of value systems as a decision-making process.

Along with these central beliefs, we also hold more peripheral beliefs, which are not essential to our identity. These peripheral beliefs are more amenable to change and more subject to negotiation as far as the individual is concerned. This characterization does not imply a lack of importance to these beliefs; it only indicates that these beliefs can be given up without serious loss or change of identity of the individual. For example, a belief about the habit-forming qualities of marijuana is certainly important in our society, and may be of great importance to a given individual, but he or she may alter this belief without serious psychological consequences. This would then be a peripheral belief.

The circles in Figure 3–4 will help us understand the notions of centrality and peripherality. You will notice that the center circles are the inner beliefs about nature and reality. We all *know* that the earth is here and that it will be here tomorrow. Similarly, we know (second level) that we are who we are, and that others are similarly equipped with such feelings. As we progress outward toward the periphery, we find that the beliefs are less strongly held. Milton Rokeach has used this "central-peripheral" interpretation of attitudes and attitude change in any given society. He has demonstrated that some persons have a more rigid system of central-peripheral beliefs, and in theory would change less than others. We will

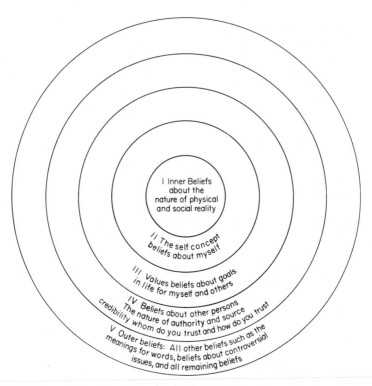

I Inner Beliefs
about the
nature of physical
and social reality

II The self concept
beliefs about myself

III Values beliefs about goals
in life for myself and others

IV Beliefs about other persons
The nature of authority and source
credibility whom do you trust and how do you trust

V Outer beliefs: All other beliefs such as the
meanings for words, beliefs about controversial
issues, and all remaining beliefs

FIGURE 3-4 From T. Steinfatt, Human Communication: *An interpersonal introduction.*
Indianapolis, Indiana: Bobbs-Merrill Educational Publishing, 1977.

return to this notion in Chapter 11 when we discuss the nature of the receivers and
attitude change. However, it is no small problem to discover what these central
beliefs are.

The process of persuasion. If communication is to affect attitude, we
would infer from the material presented earlier in this chapter that the attitudes are
affected through learning processes, through the social-influence processes, or
through the positive valences of cognitive consistency—three processes that have
been shown to be operative in the changing of attitudes. If it is indeed possible for
the act of communication to elicit these three processes, then we would have no
difficulty in ascribing attitude change as the dependent variable in our interaction.

In order for learning to take place, the learner must interact with the environment in such a way that there is a reward for performing a response that
constitutes the learning. Many communicative interactions seem to fit into this
category. Conversation, for example, typically involves responses from both
members of the interaction, and attitudinally related responses, if certain conditions are present, can be rewarded by one of the members of the dyad. The difficulty
lies in eliciting the responses to be rewarded—if the responder does not choose to

perform as predicted, the result is not going to be attitude change. In addition, certain important conditions have to be met before a verbal reinforcer such as Yes, or Good is efficacious. The situations presented by Burgoon and others (1981) illustrate how difficult this process might be to bring about in a typical communicative interaction. Nonetheless it does take place and needs to be considered. Most persuasive interactions probably operate on congruity-balance-dissonance principles.

As the number of receivers of a given communication increases, then the possibility of the source adjusting to individual responses and giving specific rewards to individuals diminishes drastically. An audience of ten is almost too bulky to respond overtly and to receive verbally administered rewards by the source. This, of course, means that most typical audiences for most speeches are constituted so that attitude change through the learning processes is unattainable. We might, therefore, conclude that attitude change typically found in most persuasive situations did not occur because of the juxtaposition of responses and rewards.

Kelman's three-part social influence process seems to offer a better explanation of the influencing of attitudes through communication. A communicator with whom an individual can identify is one who can exert a good deal of influence, and a speaker who has credibility in the Kelman sense will bring about attitude change. Some speaker-audience situations conform to the situations hypothesized by Kelman, and those, of course, can be interpreted in Kelman's terms. However, the most useful theory for most persuasive attempts is probably the theory of cognitive consistency.

The most common occurrence in persuasion is the connection of a highly valued source and a less highly valued attitude object. That connection contains certain inconsistent elements. The fashion in which this inconsistency is resolved is the core of the model of persuasion that will be presented in a subsequent chapter.

Communication, then, can affect the attitudes of receivers, but not in the typical ways that these attitudes are discussed in much of the literature on attitude change. Communication makes use of the processes of social influence and cognitive consistency, and generally it does not use response and reward to a great degreee.

In the chapters that follow, we will examine some of the details of this process. Elements that constitute the process, such as the source of the communicator, the receiver of the message, and other important characteristics, will be treated separately.

SUMMARY

Though it is possible to define behavior as instrumental, verbal, affective, and discriminatory, most social scientists use broader terms. Probably the most popular one is *attitude*. Attitude is used by many to describe a number of psychological responses. Most persons use the word to describe differentiation, which often has led to an excessive emphasis on operationalization.

Doob's approach has been derivational, using well-known concepts from general psychology. Cognitive approaches focus on linguistic and perceptual elements. Some writers have preferred more comprehensive approaches, and the attitude-behavior controversy has resulted from too stringent an interpretation of causal links in verbal and instrumental approaches.

Attitudes are thought to change in a number of ways. Measurement is a difficult problem here. Change can be attributed to functions as well as reinforcement. Social influence is a special case of this, and uses role enactment as well as counterattitudinal advocacy. Communication, of course, is involved in this process, and persuasion is usually the result of linking highly valued sources with attitudes.

QUESTIONS FOR FURTHER STUDY

1. How do you tell when someone is prejudiced? Can you always tell for sure?
2. In an election, is it more important to a candidate to be a good candidate or to belong to the correct party?
3. Do you ever have to argue for a position that you don't believe in? How does it feel?
4. What was the last *significant* change of attitude you experienced? What brought it about?
5. Do you smoke cigarettes? What is your attitude about this habit as opposed to your behavior?
6. How would you respond to Buckley's questionnaire? Why?
7. Look back at Chapter 2 and the distinctions among behavioral intentions, percepts, language, and affects. How can these fit into various definitions of attitudes?

SUGGESTIONS FOR FURTHER READING

AJZEN, I. & FISHBEIN, M.   Attitude-behavior relations: A theoretical analysis and review of empirical research. *Psychological bulletin*, 1978, *84*, 888–912.

ALLPORT, G.   Attitude. In M. Fishbein (Ed.). *Attitude theory and measurement.* New York: John Wiley, 1967, pp. 3–34.

CRONEN, V. & CONVILLE, R.   Belief salience, summation theory, and the attitude construct. *Speech Monographs*, 1973, *40*, 17–26.

KELMAN, H.   Compliance, identification, and internalization: three processes of attitude change. *Journal of Conflict Resolution*, 1958, *2*, 51–60.

MILLER, G.   Counterattitudinal advocacy: a current appraisal. In D. Mortenson & K. Sereno, *Advances in communication research.* New York: Harper and Row, 1973, pp. 105–151.

OSGOOD, C., SUCI, G. & TANNENBAUM, P.   *The Measurement of meaning.* Urbana, Illinois: University of Illinois Press, 1957.

ROSENBERG, M. & HOVLAND, C.   Cognitive, affective, and behavioral components of attitudes. In M. Rosenberg & others (Eds.), *Attitude organization and change.* New Haven: Yale University Press, 1960.

CHAPTER FOUR
THE SOURCE OF PERSUASION—WHO SAYS IT?

Almost every theory of persuasion since Aristotle's has recognized that communicative sources are as important in changing attitudes as the content of the messages that they impart. Probably the first statement of this common-sense idea was made by Aristotle, who said, "As a rule we trust men of probity more and more quickly about things in general, while on points outside the realm of exact knowledge, where opinion is divided, we trust them absolutely."[1] This statement is generally confirmed by our experience, which is the case with most common-sense statements. When a prominent juvenile court judge speaks about juvenile delinquency, it seems ridiculous to hypothesize that the judge might not have the same effect as a former juvenile delinquent speaking on the same subject. In practice, they seldom present the same messages; their experiences are too different. But if they did, what then? What if both the judge and the juvenile delinquent said that juveniles who have been convicted of serious crimes should receive heavier sentences because research has shown that lighter sentences produce more repeating offenders, and they said it to similar audiences? Most of us would agree that the juvenile delinquent might be at least as effective as the judge, given this kind of message. In other words, both would be credible, but obviously for very different reasons.

Credibility is a complex topic, and has received a great deal of attention from researchers in persuasion. In this chapter, we will explore the factors that make up credibility, and see how they work in persuasion.

[1] *Rhetoric*, i, 1356a.

FIGURE 4-1

WHY DO SOURCES DIFFER?

A rational model of attitude and opinion change would assume that messages would have the same effect, regardless of who presents them. However, we might also assume, just as rationally, that our experience in dealing with different types of people has formed certain habits of evaluating them as message sources, based on a success-failure pattern of reinforcement.

The necessity of evaluating message sources seems so transparent that some of the early research in this area looks like documentation of the obvious. Obvious ideas have a way of turning out to be wrong, however, and it was with this end in mind that researchers began to study the differential effects of varying communicative sources in producing attitude and opinion change.

"Message" Effects
vs. "Source" Effects

One of the first systematic tests of a credibility hypothesis was done by Hovland and Weiss (1951), who set about to define sources of high credibility as opposed to sources who were likely not to be believed. Their construction of sources was largely *a priori*, drawing from Hovland and Weiss' own notions of what factors would make a source believable. For example, in a message concerning atomic submarines, they contrasted Robert J. Oppenheimer (the physicist who led the Manhattan project, and was well known as the father of the atomic bomb) with *Pravda*. To no one's surprise, Oppenheimer proved to be a more effective source in producing attitude change. Only one of Hovland and Weiss' source pairs turned out not to be different, showing that the subjects participating in the study had pretty much the same ideas about source credibility as did the experimenters.[2] The results of the study were probably not as interesting as the techniques em-

[2]In addition to contrasting Oppenheimer to *Pravda*, they also compared the *New England Journal of Biology and Medicine* with a mass circulation picture magazine, the *Bulletin of the National Resources Planning Board* with a well-known right-wing newspaper columnist, and *Fortune* magazine with a famous female movie gossip columnist. This last pair was not to prove different. One wonders how Hovland and Weiss could have missed, since their audiences were mainly composed of Yale University undergraduates (primarily Eastern and primarily male).

ployed and the willingness on the part of the experimenters to adopt operationalism in the study of credibility. Hovland and Weiss used the device of repeating the same message for different audiences, that is, holding the message constant, and varying the introduction or the attribution of the message to a source. Their operationalism is evident in their willingness to let credibility be defined in terms of the results of the communication, not hypothetical attributes of the sources.

The definition of *credibility* as an attribute of the source that existed prior to the communication is not new. Aristotle wrote of this as one of the modes of rhetorical proof, and used the term *ethos* to describe the effect. However, it is not necessary for us to restrict the effect to precommunication factors alone. Anderson and Clevenger (1963) have characterized credibility or *ethos* as a variable existing either prior to the communication or as part of it. The source who, as part of the message, introduces personal material, makes use of what Anderson and Clevenger called intrinsic source effect. Its opposite, extrinsic credibility, occurs as a result of nonmessage factors. This distinction, while sensible, seems to have attracted little attention outside the field of communication. No evidence exists to indicate that extrinsic credibility is any better or worse than intrinsic credibility.

It seems clear that credibility resides in the attribution of characteristics about the communicator, whether the communicator reveals these attributes or someone else reveals them. These attributes are made important only by the effect that they have on listeners, and nothing else. And while the word credibility is used here to designate these attributes, it is artificially chosen—ethos would serve as well, as would source effect and several other terms. The word is not important as long as we remember that credibility refers to any effect resulting from the characteristics of the communicator in an argumentative or persuasive situation.

Why different sources are evaluated differently is not an easy matter to decide. Many areas of human experience contribute to credibility. In their book *Communication and Persuasion*, Hovland, Janis, and Kelley hypothesize the effect as being the result of

> . . . attitudes toward him, the communicator, which are held by members of the audience. Any number of different attitudes may underlie the influence exerted by a given communicator. Some may have to do with feelings of admiration and stem, in part, from a desire to be like him. Others may involve awe and fear of the communicator, based on perceptions of his power to reward and punish according to his recommendations or demands. Still other important attitudes are those of trust and confidence. (1953, p. 20)

These attitudes, they go on to say, are created by learning on the part of the receivers. Almost anything that contributes to this influence is part of credibility, but the major portion of their explanation concerns two main factors called trustworthiness and expertness. Communicators have trustworthiness when they are not assumed to be lying for one reason or another, and they have expertness when their training, experience, and intelligence have been demonstrated to be relevant for this problem.

There is probably no question that trustworthiness and expertness do indeed function in communicative situations to produce attitude change. It would be rather rash, however, to assume that all credibility is a function of these two factors. Trustworthiness and expertness are the two factors implied by the rational model of communication reception, and that model may not state the case as well as a model that includes other kinds of influence. Our approaches to credibility have been importantly influenced by the assumption of rationality on the part of the receivers, and we have probably not dug deep enough into the process to fully understand what goes on when one individual influences another through a persuasive communication.

Sources as Interpreters of the Environment

Our perceptions of our environment are importantly influenced by the perceptions of others or at least by the verbal reports of such perceptions. All of us know this influence to one degree or another, but the degree to which it operates is dramatically illustrated by a famous experiment performed by Asch (1956). In this study, individuals were asked to judge how long a line was in relation to several other lines on a stimulus card. Then they were asked to wait until several other individuals reported their judgments. Those individuals were confederates of the experimenter and coached to give responses that were clearly wrong. In other words, each individual in the test situation saw a line almost exactly the same as the test line, and heard many other members of the group respond with a wrong answer. Here the individual's eyes gave one message and the ears gave another through the perceptions of others.

In this situation, over 30 percent of the total responses given were errors in the direction of the group response. When Asch interviewed the respondents following the experiment, many of them indicated that they had actually perceived the line to be as the group had said it to be. It is, of course, impossible to determine just what the respondents saw; it may have personally been difficult for them to admit to Asch that they had been influenced by a group judgment that much. It is always difficult to admit that you have been fooled. But we can say with certainty that these persons modified their behavior as a result of the group's response in the experiment and that many of them persisted in stating that their behavior (even while being influenced) was correct and desirable.

Admittedly this laboratory experiment is quite different from what we usually consider as persuasive communication. But it does have two of the basic elements of persuasion, namely, messages from an influencing agent and the modification of a response by the receiver. The receivers even indicated that they believed the responses to have been correct. It is true that Asch found that a majority of at least three was necessary to bring about the change desired, but the stimuli used in the experiment were so clear and well defined that it seems unlikely that any effect at all would have been apparent.

In another earlier experiment by Sherif (1958) a highly ambiguous stimulus was used, the so called autokinetic effect. This is produced by having individuals sit in a dark room and look steadily at a pinpoint of light. The light appears to move, although in reality it is standing still.[3] Sherif showed that subjects experiencing the autokinetic effect in pairs were strongly influenced by each other and together established a norm of response that was a fairly permanent characteristic of their subsequent responses. So here we have influence as a result of communication that clearly does not result from expertness in the sense discussed by Hovland, Janis and Kelley, although trustworthiness may be involved.

Deutsch and Gerard (1955) hypothesized that at least two kinds of influences are present, normative influence, which stems from group membership, and informative influence in which others serve as sources of information about the real world. Deutsch and Gerard correctly deduced that normative social influence is present when an individual is aware of group membership and the group in turn is aware of the individual's responses. When individuals were allowed to respond privately, only informative influence persisted, and when prior commitment was asked for, it had a mitigating effect on responses. So in one case, an individual was influenced by others acting as mediators of fact; in the other case an individual was influenced by others as establishers of norms. Thibaut and Strickland (1961) used the terms *group set* and *task set* to describe these processes. And so, while trustworthiness is involved in this kind of influence, it is hard to attribute all of the influence demonstrated by Deutsch and Gerard this way. Normative social influence is probably another factor in the influence one individual has on another in the communicative situation.

Sources as Models

Herbert Kelman (1961), whose theories of influence were discussed in Chapter 3, has proposed that another dimension be added to the possibilities of social influence. Kelman admits the importance of normative influences and calls it identification. He describes this as a result of certain prior conditions, namely, the agent that brings the influence to bear must be attractive (or the group membership involved must be attractive) and the behavior that will result from the influence must be salient to the agent or the group. You will remember that the informative social influence was characterized by Kelman as internalization, and corresponds closely with what Hovland, Janis, and Kelley (1953) called expertness. Kelman adds a third dimension to influence, calling it compliance. This form of social influence is brought about through the application of power in a situation where the agent has control over the means and ends of the influenced person. The influencer mediates the rewards and punishments and must depend on surveillance in order for the power to be effective. This kind of power was briefly mentioned by Hovland,

---

[3] The autokinetic effect is familiar to all of us who have tried to look at objects in the dark. For centuries it plagued astronomers who could not be sure whether a light in the sky moved. The invention of astronomical instruments changed all that.

Janis, and Kelley's discussion of credibility, but no examples appear in the research they report. Kelman demonstrated the effect of compliance in bringing about opinion change, and showed that it was indeed subject to the conditions he described. Although these conditions (means-ends control and surveillance) limit the influence severely, it would be difficult to examine the whole problem of credibility without it.

French and Raven (1962) have approached the problem from a slightly different theoretical framework; they discuss social power. *Power* is a word with connotations quite different from *social influence* as used by writers mentioned so far. It is interesting, however, to see that French and Raven were led to almost the same conclusions about the sources of power as others have been about the sources of influence. They arrived at five descriptive terms: attractiveness, expertness, reward, coercion, and legitimacy. The first two seem to correspond fairly well with Kelman's identification and internalization; the last three seem to be different methods of achieving compliance. Although French and Raven use the word *power*, the manner in which it is manifested for them is in opinion change. Power seems, then, to be power as an influencing agent in communication, and it has almost perfect correspondence with credibility as we have been using the word here.

THE FACTORS OF CREDIBILITY

If we continued to look through significant theories of interpersonal influence, we could undoubtedly add several other different names for the kinds of influence that interact in the persuasive process. Here we have included only a few, primarily because they seem to be the most important for describing the communicative interaction and because they seem representative of the field in general. We started with the pioneering research of Hovland and Weiss who asserted that credibility was composed of trustworthiness and expertness, and then we looked at some of the representative research in small-group studies that demonstrated normative pressures, which are quite different from the factors discussed by Hovland and Weiss. Then we examined a few theorists who have been interested in power as a factor in social influence. Each of us can probably remember when we have been influenced by a person who has one or more of these characteristics (a teacher, for example, may have power over us by giving a grade, and at the same time can be considered credible by his or her expertise). But are these the real characteristics of sources? Do people in general evaluate sources from different points of view?

The Factor-Analytic Approach

When a preconceived theory is tested in an experiment, the choices of the respondents are limited to the options presented by the experimenter. If there are any other dimensions involved but not tested by the particular experimental situation, those dimensions will be overlooked.

In an attempt to create a more open-ended approach to influence, Berlo, Lemmert, and Mertz (1969) asked a group of individuals to write down names of high- and low-credibility sources, and then describe the characteristics of each of the sources written down. From the descriptions furnished, they constructed bipolar adjective pairs describing the sources, such as experienced-inexperienced, interesting-boring, and the like. These pairs were used to construct semantic-differential type scales to use in judging sources. These judgments were subjected to factor analysis to determine what characteristics tended to group together and form factors that could be said to be the dimensions of source credibility. Factor analysis is a statistical technique that groups measurements together to form factors. This analysis yielded three factors: *safety*, *qualification* and *dynamism*. Safety seems to be similar to what Hovland, Janis, and Kelley called trustworthiness, and qualification comes very neatly under the classification of expertness. It is surprising to see a distinctly different approach providing evidence that similar sources of evaluation of sources are at work in the communicative situation. Even the last factor named, dynamism, is not so different from the hypothesis proposed above, and it bears a strong resemblance to what Kelman called compliance.

The Berlo, Lemmert, and Mertz data, then, seem to offer corroborating evidence that source credibility is composed of different types of influence, and these factors are at least similar to the kinds of influence that have been discussed separately by other theorists.

Other researchers have studied credibility from a factor-analytic point of view. Probably the best of these studies is that of McCroskey (1966), whose analysis produced two factors, expertness and trustworthiness. Whitehead (1971) essentially repeated the Berlo, Lemert, and Mertz study with almost exactly the same effect, and Baudhuin and Davis (1972) showed that factors can vary widely with different sources and situations. (They called their factors *authoritativeness*, *attractiveness*, *esteem*, and *personal integrity*.) Tucker (1971) has demonstrated that the use of these scales will vary from situation to situation and that we should not blandly assume that each source will have these characteristics in equal or even comparable degrees. This, of course, is an eminently sensible view. Many of us get our information from persons who are not expert in a particular topic but are only relaying this information to us from other more expert sources. Sometimes we accept influence from persons who might not be at all credible in the usual sense. But all in all, the factor-analytic studies seem to present convincing evidence that social influence in general and credibility in particular are generated by a variety of factors.

Alternatives to Factor Analysis

Unfortunately, the factor-analytic studies do not always hold up under close scrutiny. Smith (1973) tested evaluations of credibility dimensions in varying contexts and showed that the contexts were important influences on individual's credibility evaluations. Applbaum and Anatol (1972) showed that some scale values changed as a function of the situation and the speaker. However, Lewis

(1974), Steinfatt (1974), and Hensley (1974) all have found deficiencies in Appl-baum and Anatol's analysis.

More serious doubts about the factor-analytic approach come from Cronk-hite and Liska (1976) and Liska (1978). They are troubled by what they see as serious methodological and statistical problems in many of the factor-analytic studies. Some of the specific problems are worth looking at in more detail:

> Factor analytic . . . scales were generally selected haphazardly, sometimes from the researcher's own imaginations, but more frequently from previous studies. They were seldom generated by the subjects themselves. The danger with this approach is that the array of factors may, in fact, use factors of judgment which go undetected because they are given no scales representing these factors. . . . We found that, in the search for generalizable factors of source credibility, factor structure differences among rater populations, among sources rated, and among topic/communication situations. (Cronkhite and Liska, 1980, p. 102)

These authors go on to urge that we examine credibility from the point of view of the attribution process in the communicative interaction: which will be especially influenced by the goals, the situations, and especially the utility of the information that is being transmitted. In other words, probably no single set of factors is going to be an exhaustive one for all situations and all sources, and we may occasionally run into a situation in which a source who is low in every credibility characteristic persuades better than the best source possible.

The basic question, of course, is whether credibility is indeed a multivalued concept, with different kinds of sources of influence, or if it is more of a single, global evaluation. If deficiencies in the factor-analytic technique are the main problem, it might be useful to examine the work of McLaughlin (1975), who showed that factor analysis is not the only methodological tool in discovering the structure of credibility judgments. She used nonmetric multidimensional scaling in an attempt to discover credibility structures, and showed that public figures were evaluated on three clearly different factors: ideology, seriousness, and image. These have a certain rough correspondence to the results of factor analysis, but it should be remembered that McLaughlin's sources were universally politically active and had had a good deal of media exposure, so they were certainly not comparable to more ordinary message sources. There are other ways of demonstrating that credibility is a multivalued concept. Addington (1971), for example, was able to show that varying types of vocal variations produced substantially different varia-tions in credibility judgments. Infante (1980) has examined the credibility factors from the point of view of their construct validity, that is, whether these factor structures fit into a cogent scheme of judgments about sources. Infante concludes that the scales are valid as credibility judgments. Pearce (1971) also showed that delivery style affected different factors in different ways.

McCroskey and Young (1981) have raised an entirely different question concerning the general idea of credibility: the distinctions between person percep-tion and source perception, or true credibility. All of us are accustomed to thinking of persons in set ways, but we cannot always consider these ways of person perception to operate when we think of someone as a source of persuasive messages. McCroskey and Young are especially suspicious of the dynamism factor.

Kaplan (1976) analyzed source evaluations from an entirely different perspective, that of attribution. He found that distinctiveness, consistency, and consensus were important underlying factors in this evaluation. In other words, Kaplan feels that we ought to look at more fundamental processes rather than the more superficial aspects of factor analysis. King (1976) has shown that source perceptions vary widely with the needs of the receiver and with the kind of topic. He correctly observes that

> . . . current source perception research is creating a conceptual and an empirical quagmire. This result is primarily due to the emphasis placed on perceived source attributes and the lack of concern with the communication needs of the receiver or the potential function served by sources. Perceived source appropriateness . . . was offered as a potential alternative to the person perception approach currently dominant. (1976, p. 225)

Does this mean that credibility is not a factor in persuasion, and that we ought to abandon it? Far from it. Most of the time, the factors of credibility will be important in predicting how receivers will accept messages, and quite often the general characteristics from the factor-analytic studies will be important. Cronkhite and Liska are certainly correct, in that the factor-analytic studies do not offer a comprehensive view of social influence. Where, then, do we seek these other factors? Earlier in this chapter, we discussed the clear effects of normative and compliance effects, as demonstrated by two separate sets of independent research. Could we not incorporate these with some of the results of the factor-analytic studies and arrive at a useful picture of credibility? Such an attempt may be hopelessly general, but might also give us a broad set of guidelines to use in the analysis of persuasion.

THE COMPONENTS OF CREDIBILITY

Let us try to summarize some of the general directions that this thinking about credibility factors has taken. Each of the approaches has certainly been logical and offers new insight about how persons might be perceived in a communicative situation. Table 4–1 illustrates how these factors might be compared. Hovland and Weiss, our first credibility researchers, are listed on the left. Their two factors were expertness and trustworthiness. Berlo, Lemmert, and Mertz are listed next. Their qualification factor is the same as Hovland and Weiss' expertness, and, therefore, it is listed on the same line. Safety, as defined by Berlo, Lemmert, and Mertz, is the same as trustworthiness, and so those two are listed on the same line. But Hovland and Weiss did not include a characteristic like dynamism, and so this factor is listed below on the third line.

Kelman's approach to social influence is next. His internalization factor is

TABLE 4-1 Approaches to the Credibility Concept

HOVLAND & WEISS (1951)	BERLO, LEMMERT & MERTZ (1972)	KELMAN (1961)	DEUTSCH & GERARD (1955)
Expertness	Qualification	Internalization	Informative
Trustworthiness	Safety	—	—
—	Dynamism	Compliance	—
—	—	Identification	Normative

clearly the same as expertness and qualification, and so it is listed first. Kelman does not include anything comparable to safety or trustworthiness, but he does include compliance. Those who can demand compliant behavior may typically be more dynamic as defined by the scales, and so those are listed on the same line. No identification factor was reported by Hovland and Weiss or Berlo, Lemmert, and Mertz. Deutsch and Gerard are placed on the right of the table. They proposed only two factors—informative and normative responses to other persons. The first seems to be clearly identified with the top line, and the normative factor is almost exactly the same as Kelman's identification.

This table would seem to indicate that there are at least four identifiable credibility factors. Let us take a four-factor approach to credibility as a working hypothesis. How would each of these work in typical communicative interactions?

Qualification-Expertness

This is one of the most clearly identified components of credibility. This factor operates when listeners are convinced that the source has training, ability, and experience enough to bring about belief. This factor, when manipulated, is positive in nature; low qualification-expertness is only the absence of the factor. For example, a college sophomore doing a term paper on radioactivity would probably be low in this component, not because of any given stupidity or propensity to misunderstand radioactivity, but only because of training and experience. Hewgill and Miller's study (1965) is probably the best example of the experimental manipulation of this variable. They contrasted a professor of nuclear research with a high school student. There is a possibility that certain kinds of qualification-expertness might be negatively evaluated by certain groups. For example, an Air Force general speaking on the subject of foreign policy might not be too successful with a group of environmentalists, but the lack of influence hypothesized here would probably be the result of group membership, not qualification-expertness.

Safety-Trustworthiness

This is the factor that operates when the source is believed to be telling the truth and not dissembling in any way. Most sources are assumed to be truthful, and so when the factor of credibility is manipulated, it is basically negative. The information about the source who has low safety-trustworthiness is usually information about prior falsehoods in verbal behavior, or the attribution of ulterior motives to the communicative purpose. It is likely that this factor is differentially effective for many of us; individuals with a pronounced tendency toward paranoia seem generally to assume that all communicative sources are unsafe and untrustworthy. We could interpret this as a result of learning histories as well; the question of cause is a difficult one to resolve. The "low" credibility in the Greenberg and Miller (1966) study is a good example of the operation of this component in an experimental setting. Their source was introduced as a self-styled expert on fallout shelters who made money from the sale and installation of shelters to communities.

Compliance-Dynamism

This is the name for the kind of influence possessed by the source who has either a real or implicit power relationship with his receivers. In identifying this factor, we are assuming that the dynamism of Berlo, Lemmert, and Mertz shares common characteristics with the compliant behavior of Kelman or the coercive influence of French and Raven. The scales that defined this component for Berlo, Lemmert, and Mertz seem to describe behavior similar to the behavior of persons in power situations. These scales will be discussed in greater detail in the next few pages. Kelman's study (1958) manipulating compliance as an opinion influence is a good experimental example of this kind of credibility in operation.

Normative-Identification

Here we have the type of social influence that arises out of a persuader being identified with a particular group membership that has salience for the receiver. This membership may be actually held by the receiver or it may be a group with which the receiver identifies. This component of credibility could be either positive or negative, since the communicator could hold membership in a group that elicited hostility in the listeners. A good example of this influence was demonstrated by Haiman (1949), in which one source was identified as a member of the Communist party and another was a normal American. Many different terms have been used instead of normative-identification. Rogers (1962) used the term *homophily* and cites many instances in which the innovation of technology failed because the source was not homophilious.

Each of the components of credibility can be thought of as having a different anchorage, or starting point.[4] Normative-identificatory credibility is anchored in the listener's perception of group membership and to the group membership of the source. Qualification-expertness is anchored in an entirely different fashion because it relates to the listener's perception of his or her own qualification-expertness on the topic of the argument. If I feel that I have just as good a background on a particular topic as the source, it will be hard for qualification-expertness to be operable in my case. Baseheart and Bostrom (1972) illustrated this kind of compar-

---

[4]I am indebted to Gerald Miller for the notion of anchorage in qualification-expertness. It would seem that his concept is general enough to extend to other forms of credibility.

ison. Individuals who felt that they were at least as expert as the communicator were not as affected by a communication attributed to that source.

Safety-trustworthiness is anchored in an entirely different fashion, namely, the perception of the outside world that is typical of the receiver. This perception has been studied extensively under the rubric *Machiavellianism* and may be basic to many other kinds of credibility. If the listener has a paranoid reaction to the communications of others, then the safety-trustworthiness factor will not be anchored at all, and probably it would not be manipulable. In other words, some of us feel that everyone is trustworthy, others say trust nobody, and the rest of us fall in between.

The anchorage of compliance-dynamism is not simple because more is involved than mere power. If power were the only consideration, the factor would anchor well in the receiver's perception of his power in relation to the power of the arguer. This factor could anchor negatively, because the arguer may be in a social situation in which he or she has less power than his listeners—a teacher speaking to a school board, for example. But this factor seems to be broader than the power relationship, because persons seem to adopt life styles that relate to their general outlook toward other persons. Aggressive persons, for example, generally assume a type of relationship similar to a power structure even when such a structure is not formally present. The individual's self-image might be the best description of the anchorage of the factor of compliance-dynamism.

In addition to anchorage, each factor has its own valence. Some factors are positive, some negative, and some both. Table 4–2 illustrates the specific valences of each of the factors. Normative-identificatory credibility is both positive and negative, qualification-expertness is positive only, safety-trustworthiness is negative only, and compliance-dynamism is positive only. It is clear that each of these factors operates in communicative interactions. But do they occur purely, by themselves in each situation? For example, a factory production worker may be influenced by the foreman, who has power to produce compliance-dynamism, and who may also hold membership in several groups that might produce normative-identificatory influence on the worker. Indeed, the group membership of the group foreman might simultaneously have normative-identificatory and compliance-dynamism opinion effects. However, simultaneous occurrence in communicative situations should not be construed as evidence that the factors are not separable as distinct sources of influence in communicative situations. An examination of some previous research in credibility seems to indicate that these factors are distinct enough to warrant separate definition and conceptual treatment.

RESEARCH AND THE COMPONENTS OF CREDIBILITY

A considerable body of research has been conducted concerning credibility and persuasion, and if the four components delineated above are meaningful at all, we would reasonably expect them to be exhibited in some of this research. In observing

TABLE 4-2   Means, Anchorages, and Valences of Credibility Components

CREDIBILITY COMPONENT	SOURCE	ANCHORAGE	VALENCE
Normative-identification	Group membership	Perception of own membership	Positive and negative
Qualification-expertness	Training, ability, experience	Perception of own membership	Positive
Safety-trustworthiness	Honesty, lack of self-interest	Authoritarianism or dogmatism	Negative
Compliance-dynamism	Vigor, strength, power	Self-image	Positive

instances of each of these factors in operation, however, some problems in classification inevitably crop up. Part of this is due to the tendency of experimenters to treat credibility as a single factor, often confounding two forms in one experiment. Part of it is due to the experimental method itself; certain strictures are necessary before control of variables is possible.

Normative-Identification

As cited earlier, Deutsch and Gerard offer evidence of the normative-identificatory credibility effect, but the details of this experiment are rather far from what is usually studied in a communication experiment, and probably cannot be said to be as good an indicator of this credibility factor as we might wish. Lefkowitz, Blake, and Mouton (1955) offer good examples of normative-identificatory social influence, but in their study, no communication was employed at all; they examined the behaviors of individuals at street corners when varyingly dressed individuals crossed the street against the light. Well-dressed individuals produced more followers than did poorly dressed individuals, and it is hard to attribute this to anything other than a normative influence on behavior. Basset, Staton-Spicer, and Whitehead (1979) illustrated the effects of attire directly on credibility. They showed that well-dressed persons were evaluated as more credible. Reasonably, we could assume that since normative-identificatory behavior occurs in a wide variety of situations, it probably also occurs in communication. Strodtbeck, James, and Hawkins (1958) demonstrated how status influences jury deliberations, which seems to be an instance of normative-identificatory credibility in a communicative society.

All of this seems to indicate that the normative-identificatory credibility is not as familiar to researchers in communication as it might be, and this is exactly the case. It could well be reasoned that since group members are comfortable with their own group, this really represents safety and can be identified as such without loss of theoretical power. However, there is enough evidence in the literature concerning normative-identificatory credibility that it is probably not an exaggeration to assert that safety represents fully the operation of this component.

Some studies do report a rather clear normative-identificatory effect. Haiman, for example, used as one of his sources a speaker who was supposedly a member of the Communist party. While it is true that the Communists have never been noted for truthful utterances, it is probably also true that they represent a definite negative group in our society. Haiman, found, of course, that the Communist speaker was not as believable as the other speaker. Walster, Aronson, and Abrahams (1966) may have involved a normative-identificatory credibility effect when they contrasted a public prosecutor with a criminal as sources. Once again, however, we see an element of safety-trustworthiness in the credibility involved.

Kelman's study does represent a clear-cut normative-identificatory effect. Kelman used as a source an outstanding student from a black college, speaking to an audience of black college students. In this case the group membership was highly salient, and this salience understandably was shown to be critical in demonstrating the effect. Kelman used attitude change as his dependent variable, and this operational approach is an especially strong demonstration of the effect involved. This was not the case in Harms' experiment involving status and voice (1961). Harms tape recorded speakers whose voice and diction would classify them as high status, low status, and middle status. Harms then asked listeners of high, middle, and low status to rate the voices in terms of their credibility, and found uniformly that high-status speakers also were accorded the most credibility. Whether or not these speakers would have actually brought about more attitude change is not reported, but the assumption that individuals are affected more by persons they consider to be credible would seem to be a pretty good one. Several other studies have shown some correspondence of credibility ratings and attitude change, giving support to this assumption. Harms also demonstrated the characteristic of identifying with group membership; the low-status respondents rated high-status speakers better than low-status speakers. This illustrates that normative-identificatory effects are operable, not only when speakers and listeners share the same group membership, but also when listeners perceive that a source is a member of a group the listener finds attractive.

In another approach to credibility, Winthrop (1965) compared the effects of sources that the receivers liked and disliked. This manipulation produced a difference in the amount of attitude change exhibited by the listeners, and it is difficult to interpret these data in any other fashion other than normative-identificatory credibility. Those whom we like may be expert, safe, and dynamic, but there is certainly no reason to expect them to be so; in fact, we may even have an opposite expectation. What is foremost in the perceptual system of these listeners is the group membership and interpersonal attraction involved, and although we might make a case for this manifesting a safety dimension, it seems to be stretching the interpretation a good distance. Winthrop's data probably can be best interpreted as a clear example of normative-identificatory effect.

Weiss (1957) has reported some interesting data that may also represent a normative-identificatory source effect. He showed that when a source agreed with the listeners on a particularly salient attitude, then this source had more effect in bringing about change on a different attitude. In other words, if I point out that you and I are in close agreement on the evaluation of capital punishment, then I can have more effect on you when I attempt to influence your attitude about farm price supports. Logicians have called this flogging a dead horse and have railed against it, apparently because practitioners of persuasion have sensed its effectiveness and like to practice it. The theoretical explanation that is invoked in interpreting these data is a congruency hypothesis, which asserts that congruency on one issue leads to congruency on another. If this were true, then the congruency effect should operate at all levels, and in fact, it does not. Brehm and Lipsher (1959) demonstrated that opinion congruency is a factor in producing attitude change until the speaker advocates a high degree of change from the listener, at which point the congruency fails to be effective. It seems much more reasonable to assume that opinion congruency establishes a minimal normative-identificatory effect initially that is destroyed by asking for too much change. In other words, the listeners may perceive the arguer as a member of their group when he or she shows the opinion congruency, and when the position on the advocated issue gets too extreme, the source becomes too much of a deviant to hold group membership any more. Further evidence for this point of view is furnished by the study done by Byrne (1961), which showed that opinion congruency is associated with attractive persons. We might recall that *attractiveness* is the term Kelman used to define identificatory effects. The data on opinion congruency seem to indicate that congruency studies are demonstrating a normative-identificatory source effect.

Not all of the evidence about homophily is positive. King and Sereno (1973) found that similar sources were effective only when their effectiveness was subjective, not objective. But Cantor, Alfonso, and Zillman (1976) showed that peers were a more effective source than experts.

In spite of the evidence of research studies, there is still a serious argument to be raised concerning the normative-identificatory source credibility, and that is the failure of the factor-analytic approach of Berlo, Lemmert, and Mertz to demonstrate such a factor. Let us look at the safety factor as extracted by this analysis. Table 4–3 lists the scales utilized. There is probably no question that we might apply these scales to individuals whom we like and who are members of our reference groups. As a matter of fact, in examining the scales closely, we only see a few (ethical-unethical, fair-unfair, objective-subjective) that relate to safety-trustworthiness as defined above. Even those are low in factor purity and probably are not being used in the sense of safety-trustworthiness. The only conclusion that can be reached from these data is that *safety* as defined by Berlo, Lemmert, and Mertz is not the kind of safety implied by Hovland, Janis, and Kelley's *trustworthiness*. Berlo, Lemmert, and Mertz imply as much in their discussion of the safety factor:

> Safety, then, is more than just another name for Hovland's concept of trustworthiness. The Safety dimension is more general than a simple intent-oriented notion of trustworthiness. It includes a general evaluation of the affiliative relationship between source and receiver, as perceived by the receiver. (1969, p. 571)

TABLE 4-3   Scales Employed in Defining the "Safety" Factor

FACTOR PURITY	SCALE	SAFETY	QUALIFI- CATION	DYNAMISM
64	Kind-Cruel	84	19	−01
59	Safe-Dangerous	80	19	−02
59	Congenial-Quarrelsome	82	20	03
58	Friendly-Unfriendly	82	18	06
58	Agreeable-Disagreeable	81	22	01
57	Pleasant-Unpleasant	82	19	06
54	Gentle-Harsh	82	18	−10
53	Unselfish-Selfish	80	15	−02
51	Just-Unjust	81	26	04
50	Forgiving-Unforgiving	76	20	−06
48	Fair-Unfair	80	25	03
42	Hospitable-Inhospitable	75	25	08
41	Warm-Cool	67	15	11
39	Cheerful-Gloomy	74	17	18
39	Sociable-Unsociable	74	25	10
38	Ethical-Unethical	73	30	05
37	Calm-Upset	68	23	08
33	Patient-Impatient	69	26	−10
−09	Objective-Subjective	28	13	24

It should be fairly easy to design an experiment in which the normative-identificatory safety as defined by the factor-analysis study could be compared with the safety-trustworthiness dimension. Here we would need to combine a source from the receiver's group, with strong liking and positive identification—and present the source as having a strong selfish interest in the outcome of the message. An example of this might be a college professor arguing for higher salaries in colleges or a physician arguing against government medicine. Most of the hardline persuasion that is done in our society is of this type, that is, strong normative-identificatory credibility with negative safety-trustworthiness. Television advertising is only one of many examples. Many political figures have been discredited over and over again as truth-telling sources, but they continue to have a strong effect on the opinions of many members of our society. When social problems are debated, the social worker pleads for more social work, the teacher pleads for more education, the police chief pleads for more policemen, and the government agencies want another federal program. Each of these sources is untrustworthy in Hovland's sense of the word, but it would be foolish of us to assume that they are without effect for this reason. The normative-identificatory effect simply seems to override the negative safety-trustworthiness.

This illustrates once again the danger of constructing rational models of receiver behavior as models of persuasive communication. Rokeach described the process involved as compartmentalization, which consists of keeping one kind of belief conceptually separate from another kind of belief (Rokeach, 1960, 55). A credibility model based on rationality could not account for this kind of compart-mentalization, which Rokeach has shown to operate in a good bit of human behavior.

Homophily is probably one of the best ways to describe the normative-identificatory effect. McCroskey, Richmond, and Daly (1975), in a comprehensive analysis of homophily, found that it was composed of factors labeled attitude, morality, appearance, and background. This gives us a good comparison to the Berlo, Lemert, and Mertz scaling.

Qualification-Expertness

In examining the research done with qualification-expertness, we find little of the ambiguity present that was observed in the research dealing with normative-identificatory source effect. Early definition of this component of credibility by Hovland and his associates has stimulated a good many research reports examining this factor. Unfortunately, the tendency to look on credibility as a single factor or characteristic has led to a good deal of intermixture of the factors in experiments. In Hovland and Weiss' study (1951) (see page 64) the contrasting of *Pravda* with Robert Oppenheimer represents many different factors at work, but it seems apparent that Robert Oppenheimer was credible because of his expertise in nuclear research. Another early study with variables that are confounded is that of Kelman and Hovland (1953). These researchers utilized a judge for their high-credible source and a juvenile delinquent for their low-credible source. These two are different in qualification-expertness, normative-identificatory, and safety-trustworthiness credibility factors, and we might even add a little compliance-dynamism to the total picture, since a judge has real power in our society. These two early studies in credibility are admirable examples of credibility in operation, but it is difficult to say just what kind of credibility is being tapped in each case.

One of the few clear examples of qualification-expertness operating by itself is a study done by Hewgill and Miller (1965). The source pairs used to contrast credibility by these researchers were a professor of nuclear research and a high school sophomore doing a term paper on fallout. The topic was related to the desirability of certain types of fallout shelters. A clear demonstration of qualification-expertness was evident in their results. In addition, Hewgill and Miller showed that this factor interacted with high fear appeals in such a way as to invalidate a good many early research conclusions concerning persuasive commu-nication. High fear appeals are thought of as being largely ineffective, but Hewgill and Miller showed that high fear appeals are effective when coupled with high credibility in the source.

Qualification-expertness emerges as a clear factor in the Berlo, Lemmert, and Mertz factor analysis. Table 4-4 illustrates the scales used in this factor. These scales are clearly related more strongly to safety-trustworthiness than the safety-trustworthiness scales were related to other components. So the factor analysis shows some ambiguity that might lead us to conclude that qualification-expertness partakes generally of safety-trustworthiness.

TABLE 4-4   Scales Employed in Defining the Qualification Factor

FACTOR PURITY	SCALE	SAFETY	QUALIFI- CATION	DYNAMISM
41	Trained-Untrained	27	82	14
41	Experienced-Inexperienced	25	80	14
30	Qualified-Unqualified	37	76	09
26	Skilled-Unskilled	33	77	18
22	Informed-Uninformed	34	74	18
12	Authoritative-Unauthoritative	21	67	34
03	Able-Inept	44	65	18
−03	Intelligent-Unintelligent	42	62	23

Aronson, Turner, and Carlsmith (1963) studied the interaction of this factor with the amount of opinion change advocated by the arguer, and they found that there was a point at which qualification-expertness was no longer effective. We might conclude that qualification-expertness can take a listener a certain distance but no farther. However, the similarity of this study to the Brehm and Lipsher study discussed above seems to indicate that qualification-expertness and safety-trustworthiness have similar dynamics in the communicative interaction, and they probably work in much the same manner. Whether or not this represents a characteristic typical of all manipulations of credibility is not yet clear.

Tompkins and Samovar (1964) varied credibility in their experimental study by using high qualification-expertness for the credible source and low safety-trustworthiness for the noncredible source. It is not clear in their study which produced which or which of the two was significantly different from neutral. So when an experiment varies credibility in this way, it is impossible to say that it is clear evidence for either effect, only that the two are significantly different from one another.

In studying another variable, namely, the nonfluencies, or instances in which a speaker makes some kind of departure from perfect delivery, two experiments have shown that credibility is significantly affected by this kind of manipulation. Miller and Hewgill demonstrated a close relationship between nonfluencies and qualification-expertness as measured by three of the scales from the Berlo, Lemmert, and Mertz data: experienced-inexperienced, expert-ignorant, trained-untrained, and competent-incompetent. Sereno and Hawkins (1967) report a similar finding, and it is interesting to observe that in these studies, unlike the Harms study discussed above, the credibility of the source is compared with measures of attitude change. However, the nonfluencies that were manipulated in these instances were also coupled with listeners' ratings of compliance-dynamism, and once again we cannot be sure which factor produced the attitude change. We have, in these two studies, a new manner of manipulating "intrinsic" credibility, and one that cannot be ignored.

In another study dealing with intrinsic credibility, Ostermeier (1967) wrote communications in which the source referred to personal experience with the topic being discussed. Self-references were compared to prestige-reference in which the source mentioned an expert source from which the argument was drawn. The self-reference was found to be highly superior in producing attitude change. These self-references took this form: "As a former undergraduate college student, I personally studied under both the honor system and the faculty-proctor system. During this speech I will draw upon some of my first-hand experiences that I believe are pertinent to the point I am making in the speech." We might conclude that the establishment of personal qualification is superior to the citation of high-prestige evidence in a persuasive communication, but one other factor indicates caution: the experimental subjects were college students and the identification of the arguer in this case as a college student drawing on his experiences as a college student seems to indicate that normative-identificatory credibility played some part in the results shown in this study. This conclusion is supported by the fact that Ostermeier reports greater safety factor as identified earlier in these pages seems to reflect normative-identificatory credibility more than anything else. This study, although seemingly an example of one kind of intrinsic credibility, probably represents at least two credibility components. Cantor, Alfonso, and Zillman (1976) report a similar finding.

Kelman (1961) has reported a clear demonstration of the qualification-expertness component operating in a persuasive communication, but he identified it as internalization. His source, as presented to this audience of students, was a professor expert in the topic. Kelman contends that for internalization to take place, the credibility of the source must be relevant, that is, related to the topic that is being discussed. This relevance has not always been necessary to bring about attitude change, however. We are all familiar with television commercials in which individuals of great qualification-expertness testify about some product or another. Mickey Mantle has been most expert at the game of baseball, but his expertise certainly does not extend to the quality of steel used in a particular razor blade, or the germicidal qualities of a particular ingredient in a given soap product. Mickey continues to sell soap and razor blades with great success, however, and we might be a little harsh in assuming that all qualification-expertness needs to be relevant. The fantastic success of the "lite" beer commercials that use aging athletes testifies to the power of this factor.

And while we may be able to explain away the above examples by referring to other intervening variables, a study by Aronson and Golden (1962) demonstrated that the qualification-expertness of a source does not need to be relevant to produce significant attitude changes in listeners. A source who is introduced as being qualified on one subject seems to carry this qualification to many subjects. It is hard to attribute Aronson and Golden's finding to a normative-identificatory interpretation of credibility.

Safety-Trustworthiness

The next major credibility characteristic of sources is the safety-trust-worthiness that operates negatively when individuals are convinced that a source is speaking for some ulterior motive or personal profit. As in qualification-expertness, this factor is frequently manipulated experimentally but not always by itself; it is usually confounded with another factor. The Kelman and Hovland study cited earlier contrasted judge and juvenile delinquent, and the juvenile delinquent is probably considered to be seeking personal gain in the communication. Tompkins and Samovar (1964) also presented audiences with a source that was negatively evaluated in safety-trustworthiness, but as in the case with Kelman and Hovland, the factor was confounded with qualification-expertness. The belief behind the use of safety-trustworthiness as a factor in credibility is that all audiences believe an honest and sincere speaker more than someone that does not tell the truth. This may certainly be the case. However, all audiences do not always know if the source is honest and sincere. Safety-trustworthiness as it is discussed here refers to a characteristic as perceived by the audience; it does not refer to the honesty or sincerity of the speaker. It is a powerful factor, however. Smith (1973) illustrated that when safety-trustworthiness is low, it matters little how high the other factors are.

The basic mechanism that seems to be involved in this dimension seems to be the attribution of motive to the source. If an audience feels that there is an ulterior motive to the persuasive communication, they are likely to assign the speaker low credibility. Pastore and Horowitz (1955) studied communication situations in which the communicators' motives were described in two ways, selfishly and unselfishly. The attribution of the selfish motive diminished the persuasive effect of the communication a good bit. Allyn and Festinger (1961) showed that when a communicator informs the audience that the purpose is to change them, this motive seems to affect the outcome of the speech. Walster and Festinger (1962) contrived a situation in which subjects overheard a communication, and the overheard communication (that is, the communication that was supposedly not intended for the subjects) was shown to be more effective than the communication that was intended for them. The implication seems to be that the overhearing of a communication insures the absence of suspicious motives. An interesting finding in this area was reported by Mills (1966). When a persuader was introduced who did not care whether the audience was affected and did not like the audience, the persuader was more effective. However, when the persuader did like the audience and did care about the outcome, the message was less effective. Apparently not liking the audience seems to influence the attribution of suspicious motives, at least it seems to have done so in this particular instance.

What sort of mechanism is involved in this attribution of motive in the safety-trustworthiness credibility component? Greenberg and Miller (1966) provide at least a partial answer to this question by varying the time when the motives of the source were identified. When the low credibility was known before the speech was heard, the speech produced little opinion change. But when the lack of safety-trustworthiness was delayed until substantial parts of the communication had been received, then the effect of the negative safety-trustworthiness was reduced. This seems to indicate that this kind of low credibility has the effect of a kind of forewarning, and it is probably similar to other forewarnings effects in communication. McGuire and Papageorgis (1962), for example, have shown that

TABLE 4-5   Scales Employed in Defining the Dynamism Factor

FACTOR PURITY	SCALE	SAFETY	QUALIFI-CATION	DYNAMISM
60	Aggressive-Meek	−08	09	77
55	Emphatic-Hesitant	01	14	70
41	Frank-Reserved	05	−09	55
33	Forceful-Forceless	−03	25	61
25	Bold-Timid	−31	−08	64
19	Active-Passive	17	25	61
16	Energetic-Tired	24	24	63
08	Fast-Slow	11	31	50

forewarning interacts with the type of message that is presented, and their findings lead one to believe that a true source credibility is involved in this process.

Compliance-Dynamism

When we turn to examination of the compliance-dynamism source credibility, we are faced with fewer studies that show this component in action. The Kelman study is an exception because clear compliance was demonstrated with a source that had power over means and ends of his audience. Kelman's condition of surveillance was also shown to be necessary for the operation of the influence. But whether or not this factor is the same factor referred to in the Berlo, Lemmert, and Mertz scales is another question. We can best answer the question by looking at the scales as defined in Table 4-5. Many of these scales seem to be definitely describing the behavior of individuals in power situations. Energetic-tired and fast-slow seem to be exceptions to this, but they are low in the arbitrary ranking of factor purity and do not have as much of the factor as do the other scales.

Some interesting research has been done concerning factors that seem closely related to this component of credibility. The studies cited above concerning nonfluencies (Hewgill and Miller, 1965, Ostermeier, 1967) seem to have some definite relationship to compliance-dynamism. Nonfluencies seem to diminish the factor, at least as the factor was measured in those two studies. In another instance, however, Bowers (1965) examined dynamic or extroverted delivery and failed to observe any differences between it and introverted or less dynamic delivery. Baker and Redding (1962) used a measurement of perceived tallness and showed a significant difference in favor of tall speakers. Whether one tends to comply with tall persons can only be conjectured. It is not, however, impossible that size is a factor in this component of source credibility.

THE ORIGINS OF CREDIBILITY

Most of the naive research presented at the beginning of this chapter seemed to indicate that credibility was an important factor in bringing about attitude change. But not all research shows that credibility is universally important for all audiences and for all kinds of messages. Lashbrook, Snavely, and Sullivan (1977), for example, showed that with apathetic listeners, credibility was only effective at certain information levels.

Which of the credibility factors is the most effective in bringing about attitude change? If we had to choose between being competent and dynamic, which would we pick? Unfortunately, not too many researchers have interested themselves in this problem. Wheeless (1974) adopted a regression approach to the problem, and showed that competence and sociability were significant predictors of attitude change, but that extroversion composure, and character were not.

Situational Factors

You will remember that King (1976) argued that specific situations call for particular types of credibility. Personal decisions, for example, do not call for the same kind of qualification-expertness that we would want in deciding what kind of engine is best for a compact car. Cantor, Alfonso, and Zillman (1976) illustrated that peers are more effective in personal choices than are experts. The implication of this view is that the given situation creates the credibility that will be used, and that no two situations are alike. This argument is similar to that offered by Cronkhite and Liska (1980). In other words, no consistent credibility factors can be said to be meaningful in every persuasive situation.

The difficulties with such an approach lie in the position that nothing can be known generally about credibility and that each interaction is different. Of course, each situation *is* different, but there are many similarities among situations. Some of these are important enough to make a general discussion of credibility worthwhile.

Consider a typical persuasive situation: an engineer from a local power company is invited by the garden club to speak about the future of electrical energy. The engineer can safely assume that qualification-expertness is high, that compliance-dynamism is irrelevant, that normative-identification is in doubt, and that safety-trustworthiness is low. This configuration may be different in another situation, but without knowledge of the credibility factors, there is no way to know how the situations are different and what to do about them. While King might argue that each situation is unique, we need a yardstick to tell us in what way they are unique. Yardsticks are all general in nature.

Cultural Factors

Many times our culture determines credibility. In a monarchy, the sovereign is usually highly credible. Consider the esteem with which the British regard Queen Elizabeth. In Hollywood, movie producers are highly credible (if their latest movie made money), and in New York it is stockbrokers. In Iran the clergy is held in much esteem, and in the Soviet Union technologists are highly regarded.

Delia (1975) illustrated how regional dialect (Southern in this case) has a strong effect on the evaluation of a political figure. Miller and McReynolds (1973) showed that in our culture males are perceived as being more credible, especially by females. Widgery (1974) added attractiveness to the list. Many cultural factors influence this judgment, and our culture seems to regard good looks and power as two of the most important. It should not be surprising that Walter Cronkhite, heavily made up and representing a powerful television network, was one of our most credible public figures.

Message Factors

One would hope that a good message would produce, or at least enhance credibility. Carbone (1975) demonstrated just this, that good style (listenability, human interest, diverse vocabulary, and realism) created credibility. Goss and Williams (1973) reinforced this finding, examining the effects of equivocal message structures. They found that equivocation produced low credibility. We cannot always separate message from culture, which was the case in Delia's study, where for example, Southern speech produced the credibility effect, but we could term it a message effect or a culture effect.

Attribution and Credibility

Eagly and Chaiken (1975) and Kaplan and Sharp (1974) have explored the role of attribution processes on credibility. For example, an astronaut who advocates increases in the NASA budget could be evaluated in one of two ways: the message, or the nature of NASA itself, or in terms of the astronaut. Whichever attribution is made would determine the kind of credibility that is used. This is certainly similar to King's situationalism. Kaplan (1976) showed that these attributions are made on the basis of distinctiveness, consistency, and consensus cues. Kaplan concludes that a person is considered credible about an object if his or her response is distinctly associated with that object, is constant over time, and is in agreement with the responses of other persons (1976, p. 195). The relationship that Rosenfeld and Plax (1975) discovered between personality structure and credibility fits nicely into this explanation.

Social Learning

These diverse theories are of great interest, but hardly explain the underlying mechanism for the acquisition of credibility judgments. For such an explanation, we will have to rely on the concept of social learning. Hovland, Janis, and Kelley, you will remember, interpret all credibility as the result of each individual's learning history (1956, p. 21). This is a pervasive explanation, in that it is not possible to refute in any single instance or finding. However, no real test of this explanation has been offered. Prior learning has been studied as a mediating process in almost every form in psychology, save this one. Experimental testing of this type would simply reinforce the "acceptance" response when it is offered after a given type of source offers it. Whether or not the concept of credibility is subject to this kind of reinforcement would then be settled. Ware and Tucker (1974) demonstrated that heckling changed an audience's credibility evaluations of the speaker being heckled. Goss and Williams (1973) tested equivocation as a possible influence on credibility and found that equivocal statements only affected a character dimension, whereas agreement with the listener's initial positions had a strong effect on evaluations of credibility. Ragsdale and Mikels (1975) found that a good performance in a question period enhanced credibility but did not test for persuasive effect. Schweitzer (1970) found that dynamic delivery did increase evaluations on a dynamism scale, but these scales were not exactly the same as those we examined above in the compliance-dynamism discussion. None of these findings, however, gives us any cue to the exact nature of the way in which credibility is created.

We could say that we learn to respond the way we do in any other learning situation, that we soon learn which message to associate with credible persons, and what kind of appearance credible persons are likely to have. The attribution process can also be attributed to learning. In fact, many persons have believed that culture is not innate, but learned.

Therefore, social learning as an explanation still remains as the most plausible hypothesis. It may be likely that different processes are involved, but until experimental evidence is forthcoming that demonstrates this conclusively, we must depend on learning histories for our "rationale" for this form of suasive discourse. But no matter how we interpret this, it is clear that students of argumentation and persuasion can ill afford not to examine the source as a highly effective force in the process of changing attitudes through communication.

SUMMARY

Credibility is obviously one of the most important features of any persuasive interaction. Early research found an expertness and a trustworthiness factor in credibility. Sources can be viewed as mediators of stimuli about the environment and as behavior models.

The factor-analytic approach to credibility has dominated communication research for a number of years, and has extended our knowledge of the ways that persons evaluate sources. But there are a number of conceptual and methodological problems associated with the factor-analytic studies. But nonetheless, it seems to be true that persons do evaluate other persons from a variety of points of view. At least four factors are considered central: qualification-expertness, safety-trustworthiness, compliance-dynamism, and normative-identificatory.

A number of interpretations can be offered as explanations for the origins of credibility: situations, social learning, culture, messages, and attribution.

QUESTIONS FOR FURTHER STUDY

1. Who do you recognize as a high-credibility source? Why?
2. Who do you label as a low-credibility source? Why?
3. Is group membership important? Why? How does one become a

member of a group? How does one remain a member of a group? Relate this to normative influence and identification.

4. How do internalization, informative influence, and expertness relate to each other?

5. Review the various factors of credibility with regard to the coercion-free choice quadrants in Chapter 1. What form of credibility belongs where?

6. How does each credibility factor relate to its component; for example how does safety relate to trustworthiness?

7. Can a source be a high qualification-expertness source and a low safety-trustworthiness source? Explain.

8. Write a letter to the editor of your local newspaper. How can you make yourself credible?

SUGGESTIONS FOR FURTHER READING

ANDERSEN, K. & CLEVENGER, T.   A summary of experimental research in ethos. *Speech Monographs*, 1963, *30*, 59–78.

APPLBAUM, R. & ANATOL, K.   Dimensions of source credibility: a test for reproducibility. *Speech Monographs*, 1973, *40*, 231–237.

BAUDHUIN, S. & DAVIS, M.   Scales for the measurement of ethos: another attempt. *Speech Monographs*, 1972, *39*, 296–301.

BERLO, D., LEMMERT, J., & MERTZ, R.   Dimensions for evaluating the acceptability of message sources. *Public Opinion Quarterly*, 1969, *33*, 563–576.

CRONKHITE, G. & LISKA, J.   A critique of factor-analytic approaches to the study of credibility. *Communication Monographs*, 1976, *43*, 91–107.

DELIA, J.   A constructivist analysis of the concept of credibility. *Quarterly Journal of Speech*, 1976, *62*, 361–375.

McCROSKEY, J. & YOUNG, T.   Ethos and credibility: The construct and its measurement after three decades. *Central States Speech Journal*, 1981, *32*, 24–34.

CHAPTER FIVE
COGNITIVE CONSISTENCY—
BALANCE, DISSONANCE
AND CONGRUITY

Sometimes we can learn a great deal about human nature by listening to others' conversation. Have you ever heard a conversation like this one?

HOWARD: The trouble with the oil companies today is they want it both ways. They want a shortage so that they can contrive an artificial price hike so that they can get more for less effort.

BEVERLY: How can you say that? They have to get their crude oil from the OPEC countries! The Arabs are the ones raising the prices, not the oil companies. We get over half of our crude oil from overseas.

HOWARD: That's their story. Maybe that is what they do, but I'm not convinced that they have to. They're saving the American oil for later and using the overseas oil because it's more expensive and we can be forced to pay more for it.

BEVERLY: I read last week that a U.S. Department of Energy survey showed that the oil companies were not making an unusual profit, but were only getting a normal return on their investment. Recently the profits have been high, but we should remember that oil companies have sometimes gone in the red.

HOWARD: That shows that the Department of Energy is run by politicians who have bought off the administration. Everyone knows that the oil companies are running the government right now.

In spite of what Beverly says, Howard has an answer. If Beverly's next example was an oil company that gave all its profits to hospitals, Howard would undoubtedly assert that it was all a plot. Beverly is trying hard, but there is something going on in Howard's consciousness that prevents the information about the oil companies from making an impact. He is maintaining a *consistent* stance about oil companies today. Having taken this stance, new information is rejected because it is *inconsistent* with his position. Many of us know all too many Howards who do this constantly. What is going on in their consciousnesses? How do people get this way? And most important, when people have this kind of inner information processor, how can persuasive activity modify them?

The study of this phenomenon has led to a number of interesting theories of social behavior that are generally called the *consistency theories*. These theories are applicable to the process of persuasion. If everyone who takes a position on some issue is like our mythical Howard in the dialogue, then persuasion would be impossible. Yet we know that persuasion does occur and that it follows certain rules. The purpose of this chapter is to explore this consistency phenomenon and see how it can help us understand the process of persuasion.

In recent years, a number of writers, notably Heider (1946), Osgood and Tannenbaum (1955), and Festinger (1957), have proposed differing theories of the way in which consistency might affect attitude change. Most of them use the term cognition as a basic unit in these theories. You will remember how cognitions were defined in Chapter 3. A cognition was, you will remember, an object plus an attribute. However, the consistency theories have not confined themselves to cognitions solely; they have also included affects and behaviors as well.

The fundamental basis of all theories of consistency is that most persons wish to keep their cognitions as balanced as they can. Many writers have used the term *homeostasis* to describe this tendency. Homeostasis, of course, is the name for the general tendency of our bodies to maintain physical and chemical equilibrium. When we are too hot, for example, our skin manufactures perspiration, which has a cooling effect. When our system is short of salt, we develop a craving for salty foods, which then ought to produce a balance in the blood. If our bodies do this automatically, say the consistency theorists, why not our minds?

Using this approach, most theorists predict that attitudes will be organized as consistently as possible in the system. Inconsistency in the cognitive structure will result in change that will be in the direction of consistency. In other words, attitudes are changed to bring cognitive elements into balance. For example, I may learn that the surgeon general says that smoking is harmful to my health and I may also know that I enjoy smoking. These cognitions are inconsistent with each other, and I may change some of my cognitions to produce a more consistent view. In the example given, I might change my attitude about smoking and drop the habit. There is no reason why I might not also change my attitude about the source of the communication, the surgeon general, and decide that he or she really hasn't all of the evidence.

This theory of attitude change generally states that a situation where cognitions are inconsistent creates a drive (motivation) toward attitude change, which then results in more psychological comfort. Whether this feeling is really a motivation as the learning theorists speak of it is not known. Most of the time, when a learning psychologist speaks of motivation some physical deprivation is meant—hunger, thirst, or pain. Brown (1960) has shown how these "primary drives" can operate to produce secondary drives, such as tension and anxiety. If inconsistency is truly motivating, then we would expect it to be at least similar to the imbalances displayed when the physical system is upset in some way. We will return to this question later in this chapter. But for now, it is helpful to think of cognitive imbalance as a condition that leads to internal tension and provides the push that is needed to make persuasion work.

BALANCE THEORY

One of the first theoretical statements of this type was Heider's balance theory (1946). Heider postulated that there were a number of elements in each person's "phenomenological world": a Person (P), an Other person (O), and some object (X). Each of these elements has within it some characteristic of approach or avoidance, called by Heider "liking" or "disliking." For example, P could like O, O could like X and P could also like X. Given this structure, then each of the elements can be incorporated into a system in which a set of relationships can be generated and inferred.

You will remember our old friends, Howard and Beverly. Beverly likes the oil companies, but Howard does not. But Howard likes Beverly, and values the relationship. This system is now in *imbalance*. If Howard would change his orientation about oil companies, the system would once more be in balance. But note that Howard can also change his orientation about Beverly and achieve the same result. Depending on how the individual elements are structured in this triad, the system will be at rest or unstable.

There are a number of ways that the systems can be constituted. Figure 5-1 shows eight of these. You will see that half of them are in balance and the other half are out of balance. When a triad is out of balance, Heider assumes that it is unstable and pressure is applied to bring it into a balanced state. In the example cited at the beginning of this chapter, Howard could not simply live with the relationship when it is unstable. He must either change his opinion of Beverly or his opinion of the oil companies.

FIGURE 5-1   Adapted from C. Kiesler, B. Collins, and N. Miller. Attitude change: A critical analysis of theoretical approaches. New York: John Wiley, 1969.

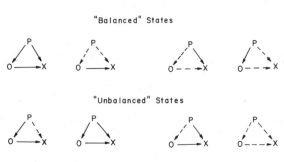

The implication is clear with regard to persuasion: the receiver must be positively oriented about the source, and the source must communicate a relationship toward an object different from the one that the receiver holds. This produces an unstable state that will be resolved in some fashion. We would hope that the receiver would change about the object or the source.

We all know, however, that sometimes these imbalanced states remain stable inspite of their inconsistency. For example, we all know of Isaac Asimov and enjoy his writing. Most of us also like air travel. We might be shocked to hear that Dr. Asimov dislikes traveling by air. In theory we might change our opinion of air travel to dislike, but we might also simply attribute the dislike of air travel as one of Dr. Asimov's charming eccentricities. However, if enough instances of these eccentricities take place, we might then alter our opinion of Dr. Asimov. Heider, unfortunately, did not mention the *amount* of imbalance necessary to bring about opinion change of one kind or another.

Other theorists have attempted to extend Heider's model. Cartwright and Harary (1956) attempted to handle some of the nonsymmetric situations that Heider ignored, be more specific about how balance and imbalance are created, and handle more complex relations. Unlike Heider, Cartwright and Harary specify that sometimes one situation is more or less balanced than the other. In this alone, their theory is much more useful.

Ableson and Rosenberg (Abelson and Rosenberg, 1958; Rosenberg and Abelson, 1960) also have suggested a variation on the basic balance model. They emphasize that there are a number of possible ways in which balance can be restored, and hypothesize that in any imbalanced situation, one could rank the probability of the various means to restore the balance.

Feather (1965) proposed a balance model that was highly specific for communicative situations. Feather used concepts of source, receiver, communication, and issue as the basic four elements of a four-part balance system. In his model, the receiver could have a separate cognition concerning the communication, which would be different from the cognition about the issue. Feather's model, like Heider's, does not provide for relative strengths in any of these relationships. Peterson and Frandsen (1979) argue that indexing these strengths would be a useful extension of Feather's model, and the model might have great utility in predicting the kinds of arguments generated in a persuasive interaction.

All in all, theories of balance are interesting but not as useful for persuasive interactions as we might wish. Let us turn our attention to another one of the consistency theories, that of cognitive dissonance.

COGNITIVE DISSONANCE

In a fascinating book entitled *When Prophecy Fails* (1956), Leon Festinger, Henry Riecken, and Stanley Schacter examined the events surrounding the unsuccessful prophecy of a religious cult that had predicted the end of the world. They found that the cult, instead of dissolving after the unsuccessful prophecy, had grown stronger because the members began to proseletyze and try to gain new members. This fascinating phenomenon led Festinger to the articulation of a general theory of cognitive organization that was expressed in the *Theory of Cognitive Dissonance* (1957). Festinger's definition of dissonance goes as follows: "x and y are dissonant if not-x follows from y" (1957, p. 13). Festinger felt that persons in dissonant situations will seek consonance and avoid dissonance.

The Causes of Dissonance

What are these things that are dissonant? They can be a number of things. Table 5-1 illustrates some of these. Four cases are presented. In the first, the source of dissonance arises from principles of logic. Obviously if one pencil costs 5 cents, then a dozen pencils ought to cost only 60 cents. If the college bookstore wants 98

TABLE 5-1   Possible Consonant and Dissonant Relationships

CASE	COGNITION A	CONSONANT COGNITION B	DISSONANT COGNITION B'
1. Consistent or inconsistent with principles of logic	If one pencil costs 5¢, a dozen pencils will cost 60¢.	The college bookstore wants 60¢ for a dozen nickel pencils.	The college bookstore wants 98¢ for a dozen nickel pencils.
2. Consistent or inconsistent with social mores	According to the campus honor code, thou shalt tell the truth, the whole truth, and nothing but the truth.	I told the instructor frankly that I didn't take her exam because I wasn't prepared for it.	I told the instructor that I didn't take her exam because my grandmother died— but I didn't mention that it happened on October 3, 1951.
3. Consistent or inconsistent with encompassing rules or principles	The less you eat, the more you lose.	I cut out bread, beer, potatoes, pie, and butter and lost 20 pounds.	I cut out bread, beer, potatoes, pie, and butter and still gained weight.
4. Consistent or inconsistent with past experiences	I've found exchange students from Samaria to be selfish and inconsiderate.	At the conference some Samaritan students parked their car in such a way that I couldn't get mine out of the lot.	At the conference some Samaritan students gave my car a push after the battery went dead.

Source: From Individuals and Groups, by A.A. Harrison. Copyright © 1976 by Wadsworth Publishing Company, Inc. Reprinted by permission of the Publisher, Brooks/Cole Publishing Company, Monterey, California.

cents for a dozen pencils, we are upset because of the inconsistency. The other examples presented by Harrison also lead to psychological discomfort.

One of Festinger's original demonstrations of dissonance occurred in post-decision situations. For example, before the purchase of a new car, one may be able to clearly see the pros and cons of an American versus a Japanese auto. Although the decision is in the offing, no real discomfort takes place. But once one decides one way or the other, the information favoring the not-chosen alternative becomes dissonant. Having chosen an American car, for example, one might then be made uncomfortable by the knowledge that the Japanese import looks better or that it gets better mileage. In order to reduce this feeling, one seeks information about the American car in order to make it seem even better as the chosen alternative. Brehm (1956) did indeed find that persons who made a choice about an appliance tended to seek information about their choice rather than the nonchosen alternative.

One interesting aspect of Festinger's theory is that it offers a good explanation of the situations in which we are forced or coerced to behave in a manner inconsistent with our real feelings or cognitions. You will recall that one of Kelman's principal types of social influence was compliance. How do persons react when forced to comply in a fashion inconsistent with their original feelings? This, of course would seem to produce a great deal of dissonance.

Festinger hypothesized that compliant persons would justify their behavior by changing their perceptions of the desirableness of the behavior. A graduate student, for example, who is forced to take statistics will, as a result, tend to feel that statistics is desirable. Aronson and Mills (1959) tested this hypothesis by varying the severity of initiations for membership into groups. Groups that required a severe initiation were valued more highly than those that did not require an initiation at all. We might call this the fraternity effect.

Some other source of justification might also reduce the dissonance brought on by the compliant situation. For example, Festinger and Carlsmith (1959) asked undergraduates to spend time performing a boring task. At the completion of this task, they were asked to persuade another undergraduate that the task was actually quite interesting. In one condition, each student was given $1 for the job, and in another condition, each was given $20. Those students who were given only $1 rated the task as more interesting than those who were given $20. Festinger and Carlsmith reasoned that the description of the boring task as interesting was a producer of dissonance; that is, each student had to engage in behavior that did not fit the facts and, in addition, had to perceive themselves as liars. But those who received $20 were able to reduce the dissonance by the attribution of the large reward. Those who only received $1 were presumably still dissonant, and, as a consequence, tended to change their attitudes (or their perception) of the task as a result.

Self-Perception or Dissonance?

In an interesting test of the generality of the dissonance phenomena, Daryl Bem (1967) suggested that the principal reason why the individuals in the $1 situation reported that they liked the task better was that they observed themselves making the statements without attendant reward. Bem felt that persons could experience the same effect without actually going through the responses. Accordingly, he designed a study in which individuals heard a tape of another individual in the Festinger and Carlsmith situations. Bem's subjects reported the same outcomes that Festinger and Carlsmith did, leading to the interpretation that *self-perception*, not dissonance was the principal source of this change. Bem's conclusions have led to an interpretation of dissonance phenomena called attribution theory, in which individuals are said to attribute characteristics to themselves and others based on the information that they perceive.

Serious questions should be raised about the attributions in Bem's study, however. Dillehay and Clayton (1970) repeated Bem's tapes in a direct replication and failed to find the same results. In Dillehay and Clayton's study, the individuals in the $20 condition perceived themselves as enjoying the task *more rather than less*. Since they used Bem's tapes and materials, one would conclude that the differences could only be attributable to the individuals in the separate studies, or to the inherent instability of the idea of attribution in this situation. Dillehay and Clayton conclude that the size of the reward was seen as the most important factor in the interaction.

Dissonance in Free Choice Situations

We have seen how dissonance is created when an individual is forced to take a position counter to his or her own. In this situation, a good deal of attitude change follows. Miller (1973) called this problem counterattitudinal advocacy, and he illustrated the many ways in which this phenomenon occurs. Miller and Burgoon (1973) proposed that researchers in persuasion consider this approach to persuasion.

But what about situations in which the receiver has free choice whether to listen or to turn away from the interaction? In the bulk of the interactions that we call persuasive, listeners are entirely free to do what they like. Does dissonance theory operate in this circumstance?

Probably the best answer to this question can be found in a comprehensive investigation undertaken by Gary Cronkhite (1966). In this study, he set out to discover if dissonance was indeed created by a situation in which receivers were presented with information that was not consistent with their original attitudes. Individuals who opposed the admission of Communist China to the United Nations, but who felt strongly that John Glenn (one of our original astronauts) was a good person, were exposed to a message in which Colonel Glenn advocated that the Chinese be given a seat in the United Nations. This situation contains all of the elements of dissonance—a cognition of worth in the source and a negative cognition for the concept advocated. Cronkhite reasoned that if these persons were really going to experience dissonance as defined, then there would be some significant disturbances in their heart rate and in their GSR (skin conductivity). Most individuals who are anxious do indeed exhibit changes in heart rate and GSR, and so if dissonance produced any real anxiety, these physiological measures should show it.

Individuals who experienced dissonance as defined did indeed show some differences in GSR response, but did not exhibit any differences in heart rate. Following the speech, an attitude test was given to the individuals, and during this test no differences were exhibited. The amount of GSR response was unrelated to attitude change. Cronkhite concluded that

> There is some indication that extremely "dissonant" subjects were more aroused than their mildly "dissonant" counterparts, there is evidence that "dissonant" subjects in general were *less* aroused than "consonant" subjects. (1966, p. 399)

In other words, no real evidence for the dissonance phenomenon as predicted by the theory was apparent.

In another study by Donohew, Palmgreen, and McDermott (1972), persons were tested to see if the dossonance aroused would depend on the personality of the individual as measured by the dogmatism scales. The dissonance prediction was shown to work only with listeners who were high in dogmatism. It may be that if Cronkhite had examined the dogmatism of his receivers, a different finding would have occurred.

These ambiguities show rather plainly that some kind of consistency phenomenon is present in these interactions, but perhaps the dissonance interpretation is not the best one. But in spite of the ambiguity about dissonance theory, a number of interesting studies have been generated by it. It is probably safe to say that some sort of dissonance occurs in socially ambiguous situations, but that the dissonance explanation is too overgeneralized and as a consequence, untestable, to be of much real use to persuasion explanations. In addition, Larson (1973) suggests that the experiments used probably did not add enough information to actually create dissonance. However, if we confine ourselves to situations in which forced compliance is involved, the dissonance explanation is probably quite useful. The counterattitudinal advocacy phenomenon, of course, is of great theoretical and practical importance (Miller, 1973). Miller and Burgoon's (1973) approach to the forced compliance situation is a challenging approach to persuasion. But the forced compliance situation is probably not as useful to most practical persuaders. In communicative situations, most receivers have a substantial amount of free choice: they can listen or not, believe or not believe, or make up new data to handle any discomfort that they might experience. Some other approach to consistency must be found if we are to describe the persuasive interaction with any utility.

CONGRUITY

Of all the theories of consistency, the one that is the most relevant for the study of persuasion is congruity theory, since it predicts a specific interaction between source and object. This theory was originally proposed by Osgood and Tannenbaum (1955). In their statement, they hypothesized certain very specific interactions between communicative sources and the objects of the communication. Osgood and Tannenbaum hypothesized that evaluations of source and object, when connected by a positive assertion, would affect each other and would move to a position of equilibrium. In other words, the object would affect the source and the source would affect the object. In all cases, they hypothesize that judgments would move toward a position of equilibrium. They went on to cast their theoretical statements into a well-developed mathematical scheme.

A mathematical statement is capable of exact testing, because it makes precise predictions about the outcomes of the interaction. Unfortunately, Osgood and Tannenbaum added two *ad hoc* corrections, one for incredulity and the other for assertion strength. Of these two, Chester Insko has written "Neither of these corrections follow from the congruity principle and both are simply introduced in an attempt to patch up and make more reasonable some of the congruity implications" (1967, p. 112). Nonetheless, Osgood and Tannenbaum's congruity predictions are widely admired by many communication theorists, and have had a significant influence in the development of thinking about persuasion. Congruity is one of the more important theoretical notions advanced in cognitive psychology in the last 20 years. For example, it was considered one of the 11 major topic areas to be discussed in a recent important collection on cognitive psychology (Berkowitz, 1978). Because it is the only cognitive theory to concern itself with the interactions that produce attitude change as a result of communication, it certainly deserves our attention.

Congruity theory, as articulated by Osgood and Tannenbaum, contains two basic elements, or forces: pressure and reluctance. Pressure is the result of the distance of one object of judgment from another, when they are linked together by a communicative assertion. In other words, if a source is positively valued, and an object is negatively valued, their linkage (by a communicative act) should produce pressure. Conversely, when a negatively valued source advocates a positively valued object, it should create the same amount of pressure. In Osgood and Tannenbaum's system, pressure is represented by P.

The second force, reluctance is derived from the distance each object of judgment is from a neutral point in judgment. The theory states that objects of judgment close to neutral will be more susceptible to change, and objects of judgment far from neutral will resist change. Both pressure and reluctance are illustrated in Fig. 5-2. In this illustration, the scale along the left edge represents evaluations of the object of judgment. A $+3$ is extremely positive, -2 is somewhat negative, and 0 is neutral. OJ_1 (object of judgment number one) is at approximately $+2.5$ and OJ_2 is at approximately -1. This means that pressure is equal to 3.5. Reluctance of each OJ is expressed by the absolute value of the OJ divided by the sum of the absolute values of each OJ. Osgood and Tannenbaum's equations are shown below. In these equations AC_{OJ_1} represents the attitude change in the first object of judgment, and AC_{OJ_2} is the attitude change in the second object of judgment. The d represents the distance of each object of judgment, and the P

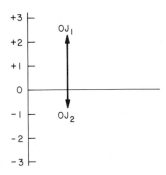

FIGURE 5-2

represents pressure. These two equations were the basis for the predictions made in Osgood and Tannenbaum's study:

$$AC_{OJ_1} = \frac{\left|\, d_{OJ_2}\,\right|}{\left|\, d_{OJ_1}\,\right| + \left|\, d_{OJ_2}\,\right|} P_{OJ_1} \tag{1}$$

$$AC_{OJ_2} = \frac{\left|\, d_{OJ_1}\,\right|}{\left|\, d_{OJ_2}\,\right| + \left|\, d_{OJ_1}\,\right|} P_{OJ_2} \tag{2}$$

Even if the equations represent real relationships, they are unduly obtuse and use symbols that are unnecessarily abstract. Furthermore, when Osgood and Tannenbaum added the incredulity factor and the assertion constant the theory became murky indeed.

If all the deficiencies are present in this theory, then why should we bother with it? Let us look at some of the research that has been done with this theory.

Research Concerning Congruity

There has not been as much research done to test the congruity principle as some of the other consistency theories, such as cognitive dissonance. Nevertheless, some experimental evidence is available.

Balancing phenomena have been observed in hundreds of careful tests. In addition, specific congruity effects have been observed by Kerrick (1958), Tannenbaum and Gengel (1966), Gulley and Berlo (1956), Bettinghaus (1961), and Bowers (1963). All these studies used source-concept interactions. However, there is some evidence that the Osgood and Tannenbaum description of congruity simply does not explain this balancing.

Triandis and Fishbein (1963) and Anderson and Fishbein (1965) demonstrated that a summation model was better than a congruity model in predicting impression formation. A summation model is nothing more than a statement that says that attitude will be built by summing up the total of a number of other attitudes. In other words, if you have a communication where positive attributes are piled on another attitude or individual, you would expect them to have a cumulative impact. On the other hand, congruity predicts that when a positively evaluated source is coupled with a positively evaluated attitude object, the situation will be in balance. As a consequence, pressure will be zero and no change will occur. Fishbein's summation model predicts that the positive attribution will "add to" (hence, *summation*) the value given to the source. However, in Fishbein and Hunter (1964), the first two instances of adding positive adjectives did not increase the positive evaluation of the individual. Only when the adjectives numbered four and eight did the summation effect take place. Nonetheless, congruity would have predicted that no change at all would have taken place, even with the additional adjectives, because pressure would have equaled zero. We can take these studies as evidence that congruity probably is not a good predictor for situations where both source and object are evaluated positively, or both are evaluated negatively. Insko (1967) has called this the most damaging evidence against congruity theory. In other words, as a general principle congruity theory probably does not hold up, but in situations where the two concepts are opposite in sign, balancing does not work as well as a simple summation.

This means that the congruity principle does not predict well when source and object are both positively valued. What is the implication of this finding for the use of congruity in persuasion? When source and object are both positive, we have a situation in which persuasion does not take place. What is the point of a highly valued source advocating something that the audience already believes in? The example of the governor in Chapter 2 shows how futile this process can be. One important persuasive situation is the one that occurs when a highly valued source advocates something that an audience dislikes. In other words, if the audience is positive about a concept, the speaker asks them to think more negatively; and if the audience is negative about it, then the source asks them to be more positive. This is the *change* of response as specified in our definition of persuasion in Chapter 1. Other forms of persuasion, such as reinforcement probably follow other principles. If congruity is to be a valuable theory in predicting persuasive interactions, then it must relate to that most important of receiver-source attitudes, namely, credibility.

Credibility and Congruity

You will remember from Chapter 4 that credibility is another word for the receiver's attitude about the source. This should indicate that if congruity operates in a communicative interaction, it ought to also affect credibility, just as it was predicted to affect other judgments of the source. However logical, this prediction is a little hard for some to swallow. If a source is, let us say, "competent," the fact that he or she advocates something we do not like should certainly not influence our evaluation of the source's competence. After all, the source will not change at all in the interval during which we receive the message.

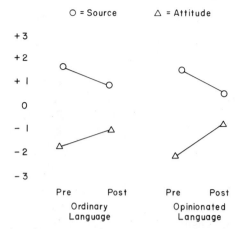

FIGURE 5-3   Interactions of Opinionated Language, Attitude Change, and Credibility in Miller and Baseheart.

This rational model of persuasion is essentially Aristotlelian and ignores the dynamics of the communication process. Credibility is not fixed at all. In fact, Brooks and Scheidel (1968) and Brooks (1970) report that credibility evaluations of individuals change markedly in the first few seconds of listening to the person speak. This reported change took place *before* any significant content could be introduced. In one instance, the speaker was Malcom X, a black power leader whose initial credibility with the white audience was low. The credibility shift took place after Malcom X offered a short prayer and a short introduction of another speaker. Both high and low credibility evaluations were affected. Brooks suggests that the results are due to defense mechanisms, but he does not suggest *why* persons would wish to defend against both high- and low-credibility persons. Ordinary statistical regression is probably as good an explanation as any other.[1] But other than regression, should credibility change as a result of a persuasive communication?

A study done by Miller and Baseheart (1969) provides good evidence for congruity in the interactions of sources and objects. In this study the principal object of investigation was opinionated language as it interacted with high and low credibility. Figure 5-3 presents the findings of this study. The congruity effects are highly visible.

We can see that this study produced rather dramatic evidence for a congruity effect, one that certainly cannot be considered a summation or some other type of effect. The telling point of Miller and Hewgill's data is that the opinionated language heightened the effect and produced more incongruity. This study, together with the earlier studies demonstrating congruity effects, seem to indicate that

[1] Statistical regression means that when a group of persons makes any kind of judgment that is extreme, the second measurement of that judgment will generally tend to slip, or "regress," toward a more moderate position.

the interaction of credibility and attitude change is going to follow some kind of congruity model.

Unfortunately, there are real limitations on the general principle of congruity. In most of the studies observed, sources that were low in credibility simply failed to show any effects whatever. Congruity theory would predict that when a low-credibility source advocated a highly popular idea, the source would gain in credibility. These studies do not seem to show this. Another study by Greenberg and Miller (1966) may shed some light on this problem. In this study, the experimenters delayed the identification of the credibility of the source until the message was over. In other words, the receivers heard the message, and after the message was over they were asked to evaluate their attitudes abut the topic. When the low-credibility source was not identified till the end, the messages provided some persuasive effect. However, when the low-credibility source *was identified before the message*, no attitude change took place at all. Apparently what happens when we get ready to listen to a low-credibility source, we simply turn off, invent counterarguments throughout the communication, and generally do not allow the message content into our cognitive system. Roberts and Maccoby (1973) showed how counterarguments concerning sources are generated throughout a persuasive message. The implication of this, of course, is that *congruity theory must be limited to those interactions in which sources are evaluated positively and attitude objects are evaluated negatively, when source and object are connected by a positive assertion.* Obviously, if the source is connected to the attitude object with a negative assertion, then the object must be positive. What happens to the congruity predictions in this situation? Are Osgood and Tannenbaum's original ideas of any value?

The recasting of the congruity idea forms the basis of a revised version of the congruity theory called the *RSO* theory (Bostrom, 1981). *RSO* stands for receiver-source-object interactions. This simplified congruity formulation has been shown to have wide application for persuasive interactions. In addition, it takes into account many factors originally overlooked by the authors of the congruity statements. Let us look at this basic theory and see how it applies to persuasion.

"RSO" THEORY AND COMMUNICATIVE INTERACTIONS

It may be helpful to review some of the contentions of the original congruity theory. First, let us cast (1) and (2) in different terms. If we do this, Osgood and Tannenbaum's two equations look like this:

$$rs_2 - rs_1 = \frac{|\,ro_1\,|}{|\,rs_1\,| + |\,ro_1\,|}(ro_1 - rs_1) \tag{3}$$

$$ro_2 - ro_1 = \frac{|rs_1|}{|rs_1| + |ro_1|} (rs_1 - ro_1) \tag{4}$$

ro_1 means the receiver's attitude toward the object, and rs_1 means the receiver's attitude toward the source. The subscripts refer to the precommunicative and postcommunicative attitudes. If rs_1 is positive, then we know that there will be very little pressure if ro_1 is also positive. In addition, this does not meet the conditions set out above, because it describes a high-credibility source advocating something that the receivers already agree with.[2] If we confine ourselves to this situation, then the equations simplify themselves somewhat. If

$$\frac{|ro_1|}{|rs_1| + |ro_1|} = \frac{ro_1}{rs_1 - ro_1} \tag{5}$$

and

$$\frac{|rs_1|}{|rs_1| + |ro_1|} = \frac{rs_1}{rs_1 - ro_1} \tag{6}$$

then the values from statements (5) and (6) can be substituted into statements (3) and (4), giving us

$$rs_2 - rs_1 = \frac{ro_1}{rs_1 - ro_1} (rs_1 - ro_1) \tag{7}$$

$$ro_2 - ro_1 = \frac{rs_1}{rs_1 - ro_1} (rs_1 - ro_1) \tag{8}$$

These two statements allow considerable simplification, because they are exactly the same as:

$$ro_2 - ro_1 = rs_1 \quad \text{or} \quad ro_2 = ro_1 - rs_1 \tag{9}$$

$$rs_2 - rs_1 = ro_1 \quad \text{or} \quad rs_2 = rs_1 - ro_1 \tag{10}$$

[2] If the assertion is negative, of course, the ro can certainly be positive. This, however, is exactly the same as the situation in which a negative attribute is advocated.

Now to these expressions must be added the correction for incredulity and the assertion constant. When these two expressions are added to (9) and (10), they produce:

$$ro_2 = ro_1 - rs_1 + 0.025\,(rs_1^2 + 1)\,(ro_1^2 + ro_1) + 0.17 \tag{11}$$

$$rs_2 = rs_1 + ro_1 + 0.025\,(rs_1^2 + 1)\,(ro_1^2 + ro_1) + 0.17 \tag{12}$$

No mention is made in Osgood and Tannenbaum about whether the incredulity factor should be reversed for each expression. Their previous practice would seem to indicate that this should be done, but when this factor is calculated, the above expressions seem most apt for both kinds of change.[3]

We have lost the adjustment for reluctance and pressure has been assumed to be the evaluative judgment of the other factor in the expression. Some correction is needed, of course, and the corrections for incredulity do modify the astonishing predictions made by the original expressions. Readers can recheck the calculations of the congruity expressions in Insko (1967, pp. 115–116.).

But in spite of the inelegancies in the original congruity principle, we should not lose sight of the fact that source-receiver interactions *do* produce congruity effects. And the two major elements used by Osgood and Tannenbaum to describe congruity, pressure and reluctance, are probably responsible for the balancing that occurs in these situations.

Basic Elements

RSO theory starts out with pressure, as does congruity theory. This is defined as the distance between the evaluations of the source and objects. But RSO theory asserts that the pressure is distributed between *both source and object,* and it would be unrealistic to expect the same amount of pressure to be exerted on each one. A more logical value for pressure for both sets of changes, then, should be the distance between the two, divided by two. Pressure, then, is

$$P = \frac{rs_1 - ro_1}{2}$$

The second main idea (also used by Osgood and Tannenbaum) is reluctance. Reluctance is a little more difficult to define because there is no generally accepted model for this kind of resistance. In addition, there is certainly no strong theoretical reason for using the statement Osgood and Tannenbaum hypothesized, or a linear

---

[3]If the value in the second parenthetical term is positive, this term grows unrealistically small. Because the system described here has assumed that rs will always be positive and ro will always be negative, the incredulity expression postulated above in (11) must be altered to $(0.025\,r + 1)\,(ro-\mathrm{ro}) + 0.17$.

function based on the scale value only. Why should an individual that is farther out on the scale resist scale movement more than one closer to neutral? RSO theory utilizes response latency for a foundation of the reluctance function:

$$rel\,(ro_1) = \frac{2}{2 + 0.1667\,ro_1^2}$$

and

$$rel\,(rs_1) = \frac{2}{2 - 0.1667\,rs_1^2}$$

These two expressions give a good approximation of latency based delay of response (Bostrom, 1981).

RSO theory then combined the two expressions. (Note that pressure is described the same in both, because the values of rs_1 will always be positive and the values of ro_1 will always be negative.)

$$ro_2 = ro_1 + \frac{(rs_1 - ro_1)}{2} + \frac{2}{2 + 0.1667\,ro_1^2} \tag{13}$$

and

$$rs_2 = rs_1 - \frac{(rs_1 - ro_1)}{2} - \frac{2}{2 + 0.1667\,rs_1^2} \tag{14}$$

These two statements express the basic relationship between sources and receivers that might take place in any communicative interaction.

However workable these two statements may seem, they only represent the basic relationships described by Osgood and Tannenbaum. We now know that persuasive interactions are importantly related to another concept, namely, the strength with which the source links him/herself with the attitude object. This is a message effect, and is clearly illustrated in Miller and Baseheart. It is not a constant, as Osgood and Tannenbaum assumed, but a variable, and it ought to be included in the description of the strength of the interaction. Using the original notational scheme, this factor can be labeled so_1.[4]

If the strength of this factor is related to pressure, then its value ought to be inserted in the expressions so that pressure will be increased when so_1 is increased.

[4]Because this variable is subscripted, the implication is that the source might change his/her value of the object when the communicative interaction is over.

In other words, so_1 adds to pressure, and is distributed across both receiver and source. It, too, will have to be divided by 2 to express its effects. When this value is put into (13) and (14), they now look like this:

$$ro_2 = ro_1 - \frac{(rs_1 - ro_1)\, so_1}{4} + \frac{2}{2 + 0.1667\, ro_1^2} \tag{15}$$

and

$$rs_2 = rs_1 - \frac{(rs_1 - ro_1)\, so_1}{4} + \frac{2}{2 + 0.1667\, rs_1^2} \tag{16}$$

How well does the RSO theory predict in actual communicative situations? Let us examine the data provided by Miller and Baseheart. To assess a value for "so_1" in these interactions, Bostrom took a sample of the language used in Miller and Baseheart and submitted it to a group of persons similar to the individuals used as subjects in Miller and Baseheart's study. After reading the samples, these individuals were asked, "If you heard someone make a speech using the following paragraph, how strongly do you think they would feel about the topic of the speech?" They then marked a semantic differential scale ranging from +3 to −3. For the opinionated language, the value obtained was 2.6, and for the nonopinionated language, the values were 2.1. Using these values for so_1, and applying the statements in (15) and (16), there was a fairly close approximation to the values actually derived by Miller and Baseheart.

Involvement

Another factor is extremely important in any general expression of source-receiver interactions, namely, that of involvement in the issue. The importance of this factor has been demonstrated by Sereno (1968), Sereno and Mortenson (1969), Sereno and Bodaken (1972), and many others. Basically involvement inhibits attitude change. However, most research in involvement has only measured the effect on attitudes and not on judgment of sources. Both of these should logically effect the process.

Sereno (1968) has probably the best demonstration of the effect of involvement on the persuasive process. He measured involvement using the "own-categories" procedure set out in Sherif, Sherif, and Nebergall (1965). This is based on a concept called "latitudes of acceptance and rejection," in which an individual is asked to judge how acceptable each position on a scale is to them. Some persons find a wide range of positions acceptable, and others find only a narrow range acceptable. Those with a narrow range are those that are highly involved, and those with a broad range are those who are less involved.

How can involvement fit into the congruity formulation? The basic way that involvement works is to reduce the amount of change that a highly involved person experiences in a persuasive situation. *RSO* theory assumes that it does the same thing for the judgments of persons, and the predictions should contain some measure of involvement for each attitude. If we call involvement in the attitude I_O and the involvement with the source I_S, then we would write (15) and (16) as follows:

$$ro_2 = ro_1 - \left(\frac{I_S}{I_O} \right) \left(\frac{(rs_1 - ro_1)\, so_1}{4} + \frac{2}{2 + 0.1667\, ro_1^2} \right) \quad (17)$$

and

$$rs_2 = rs_1 - \left(\frac{I_O}{I_S} \right) \left(\frac{(ro_1 - rs_1)\, so_1}{4} - \frac{2}{2 - 0.1667\, rs_1^2} \right) \quad (18)$$

If involvement in the attitude is greater than the involvement in the source, then the attitude will change less than the source, and vice versa.

Figure 5-4 shows the nature of the changes in Sereno's data. We can see that involvement has a strong effect on the outcome of the persuasive interaction. Can this be quantified in the same fashion as the other factors?

Units of involvement, like many other concepts in the behavioral sciences, are not easy to measure. In Sereno's study, one level of involvement was compared with another but no actual measurement took place. Exactly what *quantity* each of these

FIGURE 5-4   Interactions of involvement, attitude change and credibility in Sereno.

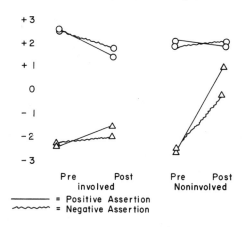

levels represents is another matter. We might examine the measurement technique for any clue it might offer. Since the latitude of acceptance of the low-involvement individuals is approximately four times greater than those in the high-involvement group (Sherif, Sherif and Nebergall, 1965, p. 52), we could easily set the low value to 1 and the high value to 4. However, what is important as well is the degree to which the individual is involved in the judgment of credibility of the source, and possibly the source him/herself. How involved were Sereno's subjects in the judgments of the source's credibility? Because the source was Dr. Jonas Salk, the inventor of the polio vaccine, we can be sure that the source was very credible, and probably the confidence with which these students made that judgment was relatively high. If the highest unit is 4 and the lowest 1, let us estimate the value at 4.0 for both high involvement in the attitude and in the judgment of Salk's credibility. Then I_S/I_O will be 4 for attitude change; I_O/I_S is 0.25 for source change if the involvement in the attitude is low. If the involvement in the attitude is high, then both values will be 1.

Probably the most important aspect of the RSO theory is the use of credibility scales for the source evaluations. Older theories of congruity utilized general evaluative scales, and in persuasion, these may not be as interesting as the credibility evaluations. Because credibility is composed of safety-trustworthiness, qualification-expertness, normative-identification, and compliance-dynamism, we might expect each of these to be affected in the same way if RSO is a perfect predictor. A test of this idea is found in Bostrom (1981). The safety-trustworthiness scales and the qualification-expertness evaluations are indeed affected. The normative-identificatory scales are affected also, but the prediction is not as strong. The last factor tested, the compliance-dynamism factor, does indeed predict attitude change, but it does not reflect the post-observation change in credibility that the other scales do. In other words, the RSO theory seems to be valid for the first three credibility factors but not for the fourth.

SUMMARY

The general notion of consistency has been an important force in psychology in general and in attitude change in particular. Three main types of consistency theories have been proposed: balance, cognitive dissonance, and congruity.

Balance theories are the earliest examples of the consistency theories. As such, they were relatively simple, involving two persons and external objects. Dissonance theory, on the other hand, is more complex, extending to a wide variety of objects and attitudes. Dissonance is probably more useful to predict forced-compliance behavior than free responses, and, consequently, it is probably not as useful for students of persuasion.

Congruity is the only set of consistency theories directly aimed at the communicative interaction, since congruity uses sources and receivers as elements. However, Osgood and Tannenbaum's congruity theory is internally inconsistent and predicts poorly. A newer version of congruity theory, called RSO theory, has been shown to be a good predictor of communicative interactions. RSO theory is useful since it utilizes credibility judgments in its basic data. Research with RSO theory indicates that all of the credibility scales except compliance-dynamism follow the basic congruity configurations.

This generally means that congruity is an important factor in the interaction of source credibility and object attitudes. Credibility is *reduced* by successful persuasion. The implication of this is that persuaders ought to choose their issues carefully.

QUESTIONS FOR FURTHER STUDY

1. Can you remember how you reacted when someone last presented you with information with which you did not agree? Describe the internal sensation.
2. Find a close friend that smokes cigarettes. Question your friend closely on the knowledge about the connection of smoking and lung cancer (emphysema or heart disease). What balancing phenomena can you observe?
3. What do you do when you and a close friend disagree? Do you or the friend change positions or do you ignore the fact that you disagree?
4. Can you remember a personal example of counterattitudinal advocacy? Describe it specifically.
5. What issues are you involved in? How do you know?
6. When did you last read an editorial that upset you? How do you feel about that editorial now?

SUGGESTIONS FOR FURTHER READING

BOSTROM, R.   The interaction of sources, receivers, and objects: *RSO* theory. In M. Burgoon (Ed.) *Communication yearbook V.* New Brunswick, New Jersey: Transaction Press, 1981.

CHAPANIS, N. & CHAPANIS, A.   Cognitive dissonance: five years later. *Psychological Bulletin*, 1964, *61*, 1–22.

DILLEHAY, R. & CLAYTON, M.   Forced-compliance studies, cognitive dissonance, and self-perception theory. *Journal of Experimental Social Psychology*, 1970, *6*, 458–465.

FESTINGER, L.   *A theory of cognitive dissonance.* New York: Harper and Row, 1957.

FEATHER, N.   A structural balance model of evaluative behavior. *Human Relations*, 1965, *18*, 171–185.

HEIDER, F.   Attitudes and cognitive organization. *Journal of Psychology*, 1946, *21*, 107–112.

OSGOOD, C., & TANNENBAUM, P.   The principal of congruity in the prediction of attitude change. *Psychological Review*, 1955, *62*, 42–55.

CHAPTER SIX
THE PROCESS OF
PERSUASION: MODELS

Up to this point in this book, you have been presented with a good deal of general information about persuasion, about attitudes, credibility, and cognitive consistency. We have seen that these terms can all be used with precision and that they all have some impact on the persuasive process. However, what we have not seen is precisely how they all fit together. *Persuasion*, you will remember, was defined as the changing, shaping, or reinforcing of responses on the part of the receiver. We further asserted that this changing could include both inner and outer responses. We know that the receiver is not a passive participant in the process; a great deal goes on inside the receiver's cognitive system that contributes to the changes in response. You will recall (from Chapter 3) that thought alone has been shown to significantly affect attitude change during and after a persuasive message. Clearly, this indicates that the receiver's internal processes are as important as the messages and other external factors are.

In this chapter, we will examine some of the general theories about the mechanisms of persuasion, that is, some of the explanatory schemes that have been offered as an interpretation of the inner processing that leads to changes in attitude and response. Two of the most important elements to be considered are the attitudes to be changed and the credibility of the persuader. Credibility is nothing more than the receiver's attitude about the source. Although these attitudes may be quite complex, the whole process may be thought of as the interaction of attitudes about sources, messages, and attitude objects. In this chapter, some general models of these interactions will be presented. Then, a more detailed process model will be presented that integrates the processes involved.

HOW DOES PERSUASION
WORK?

Part of our thinking about how persuasion works is inextricably tied up with our thinking about how communication works. Let us review this thinking about persuasion with a discussion of some of the more important models of communication.

Models of Communication

One good way of adding to our understanding of anything complicated is to use *models*. A model is a construction of the interrelation of all the parts involved in a process. Thus, in constructing a general model of communication, David Berlo (1960) used a four-part structure, consisting of source, message, channel, and receiver. Although the four elements seem to be fairly firmly grounded in common sense to many of us, the utility of Berlo's model is immediately apparent if we look at a practical example. In most communicative interactions, different sources almost always present different messages; one person never says exactly the same thing as another person, even if the circumstances are exactly the same. Nonetheless, it is important to be able to know what part of the communicative effectiveness was due to the source and what part to the message, because if a problem exists, we need to know which part to change. Berlo's model asks us to examine the separate elements as different processes, at least *conceptually* for the purposes of analysis. In other words, the model gives us the ability to look at the separate parts of the whole, and to analyze these parts when something goes wrong and when a new design is needed.

Engineers find it useful to construct mathematical models of physical events, to see what will happen under many different circumstances. These models are nothing more than a series of "if-then" statements that describe various contingent events. For example, a dam that is being proposed for a given river will be modeled under various conditions of water flow and saturation to see if the proposed design will hold up. Problems, if any, can be detected before the dam is built.

The general purpose of a model is to present an overall understanding of the interrelationship of elements in a larger process and to show how these elements effect the entire system.

Models of Persuasion

Some familiar models of the communication process are those of Westley and MacLean (1957), Shannon and Weaver (1949), and Barnlund (1970). These models were all designed to illustrate, in general, the communicative process. None of them tells us specifics about the complex form of communication we call persuasion. However, because persuasion is communication, we will need to use general models of communication as the basis for our persuasion model. Let us examine some models that have been used to describe persuasion.

The motivated sequence.   An early model of the persuasive process was the "motivated sequence" of Alan Monroe (Ehninger, Monroe, and Gronbeck, 1978). Monroe's basic design was borrowed from John Dewey (1933), who had attempted to analyze basic problem-solving as a form of thought. Monroe reasoned that if people really organized their thoughts the way Dewey described them, then that organizational pattern probably was good for a persuasive effort. His motivated sequence was the result, and it looked like this:

1. Attention
2. Need
3. Satisfaction
4. Visualization
5. Action.

You can see that this is an extremely logical way for a receiver to proceed: to first pay attention to the source, then recognize a need that exists and should be met, to match the solution proposed by the source to produce satisfaction, to visualize the solution in action, and to arouse oneself to action. If this is the process that is used, then the source's general strategy should also follow this as a plan. We will return to this plan later in this book in the chapter on organization (Chapter 9). Monroe originally constructed his motivated sequence in 1935, and it still remains a useful model of persuasion. In addition, it is an extremely sensible way to organize a persuasive communication. There are, however, some serious questions that must be raised about the adequacy of the model.

First of all, the motivated sequence model depends on a number of assumptions that cannot always be made. One is that the listener is a rational person. If everyone were rational and used rational thought processes in decision making, then Monroe's model would hold for many persuasive situations. However, we know that many persons do not use rational processes in their decision making, and in fact, many otherwise rational individuals form their attitudes and beliefs through cognitive processes that are automatic and nonrational. Many times simple association of the sources with the persuasive act may suffice, without even resorting to messages. For example, if we hear that Walter Cronkhite once advocated increased use of nuclear energy, we are likely to be moved to that position, even though we did not hear Mr. Cronkhite's reasoning on the subject. Also, there is evidence to indicate that nonrational messages are at least as effective, if not more effective, than rational ones. (We will examine this phenomenon more exhaustively in Chapter 10 when we discuss evidence.) In addition, there is some evidence to indicate that some aspects of persuasion are mindless (Roloff, 1980). In other words, persons are sometimes persuaded to change their attitudes or positions on an issue, but they do not know why they have changed or sometimes even that they have changed.

Another assumption that Monroe made was that one could begin with the attention step and then proceed logically. We now know that attention is often a function of need (the second step) and that without it, listeners "tune out" the source.

In examining the motivated sequence, we are presented with the difficulty of distinguishing between a prescriptive and a descriptive approach to persuasion (and, indeed, to communication in general). When we take the prescriptive approach, we tend to look at what the persuasive process *ought to be*, and when we take the descriptive approach, we emphasize what persuasion *is*. If we take the prescriptive approach, we would say that the motivated sequence is the best way for persuasion to proceed. If we take the descriptive approach, we would ask if this sequence is really the way it happens. Let us, therefore, look at some other models of attitude change and see if we can find alternatives to supplement the original hypothesis expressed in the motivated sequence.

General-Systems Models

In a thoughtful analysis of persuasion, Raymond Tucker (1971) has proposed that we look at the process of persuasion from a general-systems approach, in other words, that we examine the persuasive system *as a whole*. This means that the boundary of the process should be broadened to include considerations of many different elements rather than attention to achieving only the persuader's goal. Tucker's model is more aptly termed a process with the following elements: (1) component selection, (2) system objectives, (3) system inputs, and (4) outputs. Tucker's model, like Monroe's, assumes a rational process at each of the steps and does not necessarily predict what will happen in a given persuasive interaction. Like Monroe's model, this model is prescriptive rather than descriptive.

Another model similar to Tucker's is Cegala's, which is a general approach to interpersonal persuasion (1980). All interpersonal systems, says Cegala, are determined by: (1) knowledge of rules pertinent to context of persuasion, (2) selection of a strategy, (3) instructional orientation, and (4) self-esteem. These four elements are a system in the same manner as Tucker's system approach. The system is, of course, grounded in interpersonal relationships rather than the organizational terms of Tucker's, but the system analogy is a useful one.

Florence's evidence model. Florence (1975) has proposed a model of attitude change that integrates the message elements of evidence and the credibility of the source. Unlike Monroe, however, Florence attempts to explain how receivers come to believe in the specific portions of the message (such as the need and plan offered by Monroe's ideal persuader). Florence asserts that two important factors are involved, the credibility of the speaker (source) and the evidence that is contained in the message. Figure 6-1 illustrates how these elements interact in Florence's model. In the model, the solid lines represent direct causal links, and the dotted lines represent contingent causal links. Here we see, then, that the credibility of the source creates a belief in the desirability of the solution, which, in turn, directly affects the attitude about that solution as well as the belief in the truth of the solution. The evidence contained in the message also affects the desirability of

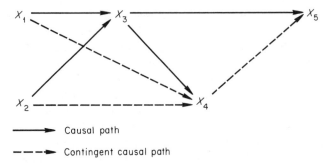

Causal path

Contingent causal path

FIGURE 6-1 Diagrammatic representation of posited relationships where: X_1, credibility of the source of evidence, X_2, evidence usage; X_3, desirable belief; X_4, truth belief, X_5 attitude. From T. Florence, An empirical test of the relationship of evidence to belief systems and attitude change. *Human Communication Research and the International Communication Association,* 1975, *1*, pp. 145-158.

the solution. In addition, the credibility and the evidence can affect the belief in the truth of the solution, which can affect the attitude without the desirability being affected. Florence's data, however, did not support the contingent link between credibility of the source with the truth of the proposed solution.

Florence presents an interesting alternative to the classic Monroe paradigm, however. By integrating the concepts of truth (is it so?) and desirability (should we take action?) along with the credibility of the evidence source and the evidence itself, he has advanced our general thinking about the fundamental nature of the internal processes involved in persuasion. The model makes several definite statements about input and output, that is, the relationships between cause and effect in persuasion, and subjects those relationships to careful test.

Reardon's superordinate construct model. In Florence's model, the attitude (and, by implication, the resulting behavior) was the result of two intervening judgments: the truth of the proposition and the desirability of its adoption. Reardon (1981) has proposed a similar model of the internal processes that describes these judgments as constructs. In her model, she focuses on the interpersonal persuasive tasks exclusively, and she derives her constructs from the dimensions proposed by Cody and McLaughlin (1980). These researchers asked a number of persons to assess the nature of a number of interpersonal persuasive tasks, such as persuading your professor that a test item was ambiguous or persuading a bartender to let an underage person buy a drink. These assessments were made in terms of general characteristics, such as formality/informality, friendly/unfriendly, and the like. Cody and McLaughlin found that the persuasive tasks were described in terms of five main factors: intimacy, personal benefits, resistance, dominance, and consequence. Reardon integrated these into the comprehensive model of interpersonal persuasion presented in Fig. 6-2. Here we see each of the constructs presented

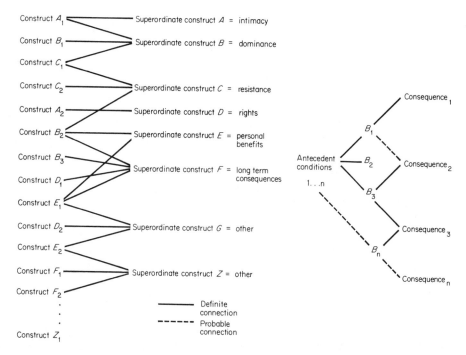

FIGURE 6-2 Construct-Rule Linkage for Persuadee Logic. Reprinted from *Persuasion: Theory and Context*, by K.K. Reardon. © 1981 Sage Publications, Beverly Hills/London. With permission of the publisher.

in relation to one another. Cody and McLaughlin's main factors are called superordinate constructs and the more specific constructs that go into each of these are listed on the right side of Fig. 6–2 as A_1, B_1, and so on. Each of these superordinate constructs is then hypothesized to create a number of behavioral repertoires (B_1, E_1, and so on) represented on the right of the model, which in turn are believed to be linked with a set of consequences at the far right of the model.

Reardon's model is an extremely interesting approach to the problem of describing persuasion through the intervening constructs that all of us typically use in determining our day-to-day behavior. She further hypothesizes that these constructs (together with behavioral rules) form their own internal logic (1981, p. 111). To make Reardon's model clearer, let us examine the process through an example or two.

Suppose that a college student who works at a fast-food chain wishes to have the manager increase the food allowance. (Most of these chains do not allow employees unlimited hamburger privileges!) The student will approach the task from some combination of initial constructs that determines the nature of the student's relationship with the manager. If the manager and the student have a more or less intimate relationship, the intimacy may become one of the superordinate constructs in the choice of the persuasive task. Because one of these persons is

113

clearly dominant, dominance will probably be involved. The student will present each of the elements of the construct system as a set of antecedent conditions, for example, how much more efficiently the student might work if the hamburger ration were increased, how much better the morale in the store will be, how much better the employer-employee relationship might be, and so on. In addition, the manager will be integrating those constructs with long-term consequences of the act, personal resistance, and the like. The result of this integration is the set of possible behaviors from which the manager will choose. Exactly which behavior will be chosen will be determined by the perception of the general consequences as perceived on the far right of the model.

Here we have a fairly detailed generalization about the persuasive process, bringing together a number of specific predictions about the interaction between two persons. Reardon goes on to suggest that we discover how these are interrelated by the accounts, or rationalizations, that individuals give after the specific interactions take place (1981, p. 106). In other words, if the manager decides that the student worker can have more hamburgers, we can only discover the rationale by asking the manager why the rule was suspended. The manager can then presumably relate an account of what was involved in the decision to suspend the rule.

Reardon's model, while extremely interesting, has a number of specific problems. The first, and probably most important, is that there is no specific prediction about the general effectiveness of any of the specific superordinate construct systems in bringing about any specific response. In other words, there is no way for us to tell which construct system would be the most effective in designing a persuasive appeal to the manager. Indeed, one real difficulty in using psychological constructs is that no possible prediction can be made about any *group* of persons in any communicative interactions. In other words, if we take the position that the evaluation of any communicative situation will depend on the constructs used, we have said that each persuasive interaction is unique and no more general statements can be made about it. The implication is that each interaction is phenomenologically unique (Delia, 1977), which denies knowledge of communicative situations in general. To put this another way, we have a system in which we can only describe how the interaction between the student worker and the manager happened this particular time, and we cannot further use this information in another setting. When someone asks us what strategy to use in a future situation of this type, we can only answer, "It depends."

The second important problem with Reardon's model is the dependence on accounts for the validity of the rule structure that is involved. From Chapter 2, you will remember some of the problems inherent in introspection as a psychological method. The accounts that Reardon depends upon are totally introspective, and are subject to the problems of that method. The manager may present an account of subsequent behavioral choice that emphasizes harmony among employees, the long-term benefits of treating everyone alike, how fairly the manager usually has been in other relationships, and so on. This account, however, will usually omit items about how much fun it is to put down a college student, how good it is to have power over others, and how frightened one might be by possible transgressions of company rules. In other words, we must face the disagreeable facts that persons often lie about their behavior and their "accounts" are usually nothing more reliable than face-saving devices. In short, the predictive value of the Reardon model at its present stage of development, is not very high. This does not mean that the model is not useful or that we will not someday have specific information about the interaction of constructs that can be usefully applied. But at this point we have only two sets of interactive principles to base a model of persuasion on, namely, credibility evaluations and message effects. We could term these as specific source or message constructs in the Kelley model. However, one other factor that was ignored and that is extremely important is the general balancing, or consistency judgments that are typically made in anyone's internal evaluative system. Any model of persuasion will have to include consistency principles as part of its basic structure.

Consistency or alignment?   One of the central questions in the choice of models for persuasive communications is the role of consistency judgments. Larson and Sanders (1975), in their analysis of persuasive effects, assert that persuasion results from alignment, in that individuals are persuaded when they move to a closer evaluation of the source. In other words, to persuade someone, they say, it is necessary to get receivers to be more closely aligned with the source. This is an interesting hypothesis, and it is true that many individuals, when making choices about persuasive strategy, do indeed rate alignment with the receiver as one of the desired outcomes of the communication (Roloff and Barnicott, 1976). Steinfatt and Infante (1976) have effectively detailed some of the shortcomings of the Larson and Sanders approach. We are more than justified in asserting that consistency theory is probably the better predictor for source-attitude interactions. Consistency theory in general, however, predicts that as a result of a successful persuasive interaction, evaluations of sources will be less positive. Larson and Sanders cite a study by Miller and Hewgill (1966) in which the posttest evaluations of credibility are less when the message was successful. However, in that study, no evidence was presented as to the evaluations of credibility *prior to the persuasive communication*. In the last chapter, data from Tannenbaum (1955), Miller and Baseheart (1969), Sereno (1968), and Bostrom (1981) all show significant attenuation of credibility judgments following a successful persuasive interaction. Bostrom (1981) showed that of four factors of credibility, only one was not affected by the congruity effect (compliance-dynamism). These data demonstrate that not all kinds of credibility are affected, but that most credibility factors are involved. In the case of the data cited by Larson and Sanders, the most logical explanation is that the groups that were assigned to the most effective condition happened by chance to have more positive evaluations of the source. This is a common occurrence in almost any experimental study involving individuals. The lack of pretest data in that study means only that the conclusion that Larson and Sanders draw cannot be maintained. The overwhelming evidence is for some sort of congruity effect to be operating in the persuasive situation. Our models, therefore, will have to include a systematic provision for congruity (such as RSO theory) before they can be complete.

You will remember, however, that our definition of persuasion included shaping and reinforcing responses, as well as changing. RSO theory indicates that not all of these effects can be explained by a congruity-type theory. Therefore, a complete model of persuasion must include more types of interaction. In the next section, a more detailed account of persuasion is presented.

A MODEL OF PERSUASION

There are many elements that must be considered in a model of persuasion, and all of them cannot be fitted into any one model that we might construct. Because most of the process is probably sequential, at least in its major elements, a model should contain a series of sequential steps, much as a computer programmer constructs a flow chart for a computer program. This certainly does not mean that persuasion is programmable, or that individuals are persuaded in a mechanical fashion, like a computer is programmed. It only means that there are enough similarities to make the flow-chart technique a useful one for us. Some of you are familiar with computer simulation, which is an analytic technique that analyzes any human activity and then tries to construct the steps that a computer would have to take in order to perform the same activity.

This kind of simulation is not new in communication. Bodaken, Lashbrook, and Champagne (1971) constructed a simulation model for small group interactions, and Donohew and Tipton (1973) constructed another for information processing in general. Recently Colby (1973) and Abelson (1973) have constructed simulation models for the processes inherent in attitude change.

Flow Charts

If you are not familiar with flow-chart technique, it may be useful to look at some of the symbols used. A flow chart is constructed from a series of steps, or operations, that take place in a given order. The flow from one part to another is represented by arrows that give the direction. The various processes in the chart are represented by different symbols. For example, a diamond-shaped step represents a decision. After the decision, the flow follows the direction indicated by the decision characteristics. Input and output functions are usually represented by a trapezoid, and storage is represented by IBM cards. The small circles represent "go to" statements, that save a lot of complex lines on the chart. When you come to a circle with a number in it, you need to find a step that has that number in it, and go to that step from the circle. No one has any trouble with the go-to statement when playing Monoply, and the concept is exactly the same in a flow chart.

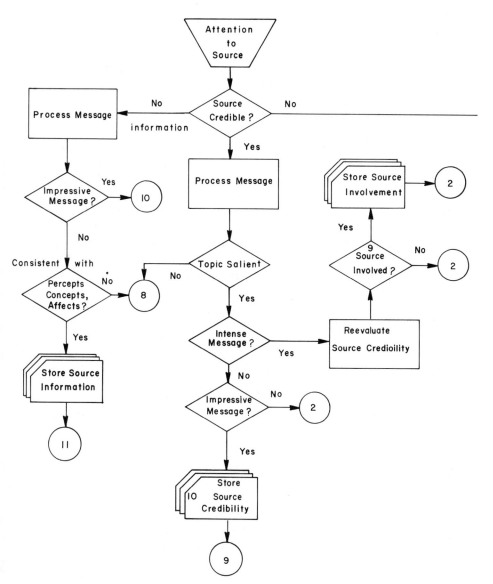

FIGURE 6-3

Let us now construct what probably happens in a persuasive situation. Figure 6–3 illustrates the beginning of the persuasive interaction. You will notice that each element is connected to other elements by lines and arrows. The diamond-shaped elements represent choices made and the direction one takes from each of these is determined by the nature of the decision made. Let us go through this first part of the model and examine each of its elements in turn.

Initial Steps

The first step in the persuasion process is attention to the source. Notice that this is a deliberate act, a legitimate step by the receiver. This does not mean that the persuader should not attempt to use attention-getting devices in the communication, and that a communicator or an advertiser cannot get attention by shouting "HEY!" at the receiver. It only means that the *continued* attention of the receiver is the first act in the persuasion process. This underscores the fact that this model is drawn from the point of view of the receiver, and the options and internal processes available to the source are not part of this sequence. We will see in later chapters how the source can be responsive to varying decisions and actions on the part of the receiver. However, for now, it is useful to model only the receiver's activity and look at persuasion from the point of view of the receiver's internal activity.

The next step is a judgment of the source's credibility. Here this decision is represented as a "yes-no-no information" option, but actually the real judgments are of greater complexity. However, when an initial judgment of "not credible" is made, the receiver stops listening to the source as an opinion influence. You will remember that in the study done by Greenberg and Miller (1966) receivers that had no information about a low-credibility source went ahead and processed the message, resulting in attitude change. Those that did know in advance that they were dealing with a low-credibility source had hardly any attitude change. These data show that credibility is probably the first step in all of the judgment processes. If the receiver judges the source to be totally noncredible, the flow proceeds to step 8 in Fig. 6-4. Here the first judgment made is whether the source has any intrinsic interest to the receiver. If not, the receiver withdraws from the interaction. If the source is of interest, then the receiver goes on to process the message as information about the source, and if the source is salient to the receivers' life, then the information will be stored. This branch, which takes place at the initial processing of the message, certainly happens a lot, and it could be called a model of nonpersuasion.

Let us return to Fig. 6-3 for a moment. We might call the principal axis in this figure the mainstream of the persuasive process. When a source is judged to be credible, then the message is processed. A decision is made about the salience of the topic, and if the topic is found nonsalient, the flow proceeds to 8 on Fig. 6-5, the same loop that was used for noncredible sources. The flow then proceeds as above. However, if the topic is salient, then the next step is the evaluation of the message. You will recall that in the Miller and Baseheart study already cited (1969), one of the conditions was opinionated language. In this condition, a judgment would be made that the message was intense, and the flow would proceed to reevaluating source credibility. Then if the source was judged to be involved, the flow could move to the first processing related to consistency.

Consistency Judgments

The content of the communication is usually composed of one or more of the elements mentioned in Chapter 2, namely, percepts, concepts, or affects. Each of these could be judged to be consistent or inconsistent with the percepts, concepts,

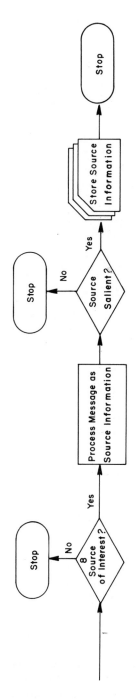

FIGURE 6-4

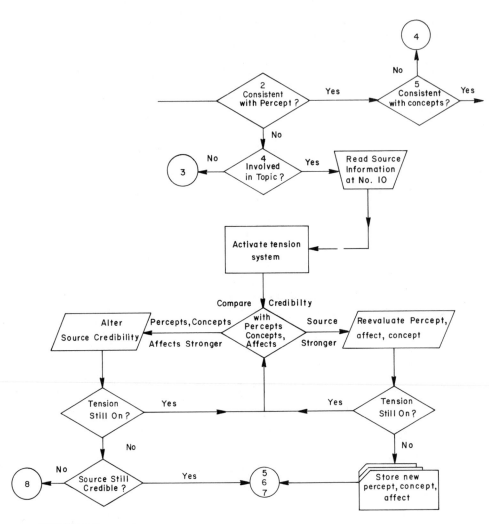

FIGURE 6-5

and affects contained in the receiver's storage system. So the first judgment of consistency would be one of these. We have no idea whether one or the other goes first, and in truth, they probably all go on at the same time. However, the model is only illustrative, so let us take it in a linear fashion. This process is diagramed in Fig. 6–5, beginning with the diamond-shaped choice labeled "2—Consistent with percept?" You will see that we got here from Figure 6–4 from the diamond-shaped box labeled "9—Source involved?" If the message is not consistent with an existing percept, then a decision about involvement is made (see Sereno, page 000) and the source credibility is reread. Now we proceed to the bottom of Fig. 6–5, which could be called the consistency loop. In this loop, the first thing that happens is that the tension system is activated, since we now have a high-credibility source advocating something that is inconsistent with a receiver's internal system. The amount of this tension, you will remember, is directly related to the pressure generated by the incongruity and the strength of the source's attitude about the percept.

The next step is to compare the credibility with the existing percepts. (In the flow chart, the decision step reads "compare credibility with percepts, concepts, and affects" because the flow will go through this consistency loop three times.) If the source is stronger, then the percept is altered, and if the percept is stronger, then the source is altered. In fact, both will be altered a little, depending on the predictions of the model in the preceding section. Then a reading will be made of the tension system, and if the tension is off, the flow will proceed out of the consistency loop to the rest of the process. Unfortunately, if, in the midst of this loop, the source's credibility is seriously damaged, the flow will proceed to step 8, and then out of the process. The other way to get out of the consistency loop is in the circle (go-to statement) that has three addresses in it, 5, 6, and 7. These steps are represented in Fig. 6-6. This means that the first time through it will go to 5, the second time through to 6, and the third time through to 7. The first two, 5 and 6, are decisions about concepts and affects, but 7 proceeds on through the flow. Then further action can be taken.

Often one communicative interaction is not enough for a receiver to make a decision or to take any action. In this step, the flow chart has shown the process going back to the first step. In actuality, the receiver might well seek out another source, or engage in any other information-seeking behavior.

But assuming that no more information is needed, we can then proceed to a decision about whether action is required or not. If so, then behavior results. The next step on Fig. 6-6 reads "Overt behavior." If overt behavior is not required, the next step is to judge whether some potential action will be needed, and if so, a plan will be filed. This corresponds to the internal plans that were discussed in Chapter 2. You will remember that in that chapter, several situations were described where potential behavior was as important or even more interesting than immediate behavior. The last step, of course, if the communication does not require action, is to store the message and stop the system.

Message Effects

You will recall that in Fig. 6-4, a decision was made about whether the message was intense. If the decision was yes, you will remember, the flow proceeded through some steps modifying source evaluations. But the no decision is also important, because it leads to the decision about the message. Here is where all the message effects described in Chapters 8, 9, and 10 take place. This model asserts that the messages are effective because they raise the source's credibility. This is probably true in its broad outline, but in our later chapters, we will see how complex the modifications on this process can become. For example, in the chapter on evidence, we will see how secondary credibility plays an important part in the whole process. In some cases, a persuader is merely a channel in which the real

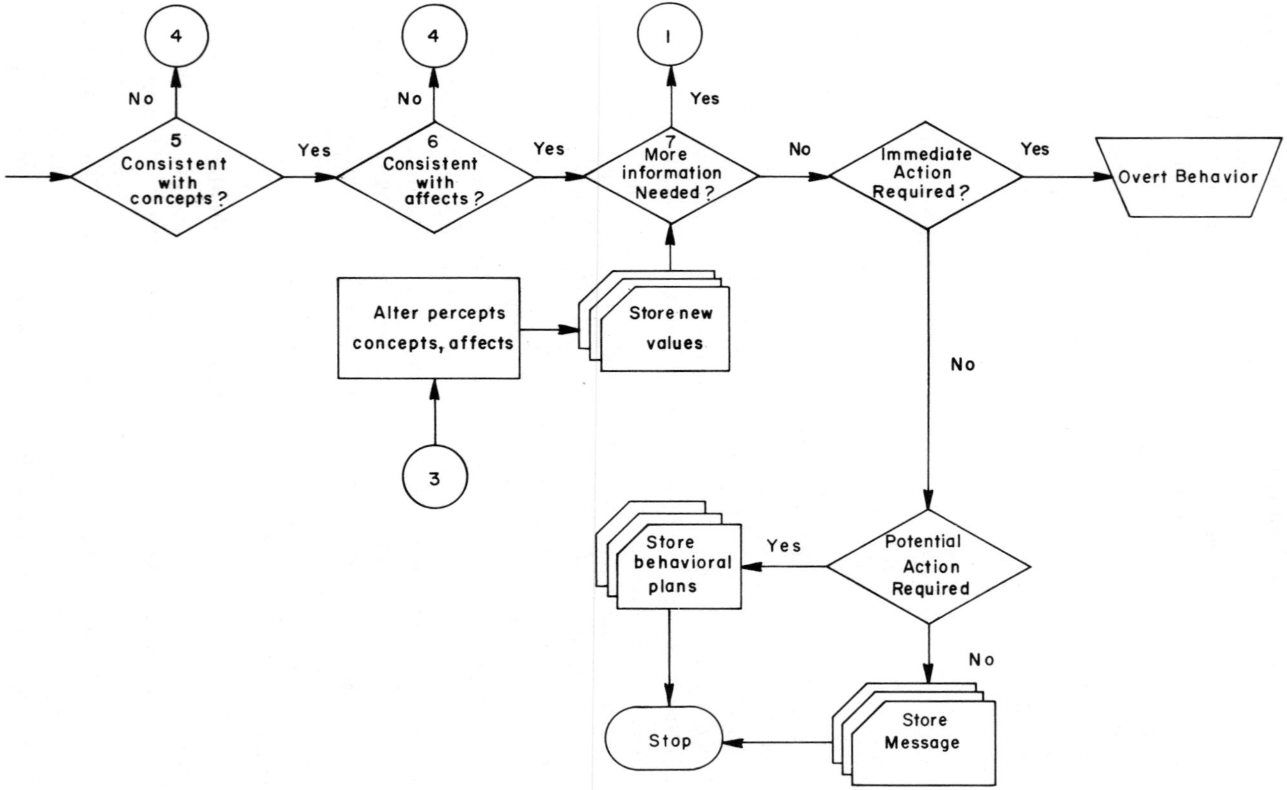
4
4
I
No
No
Yes
5
Consistent
with
concepts?
Yes
6
Consistent
with
affects?
Yes
7
More
information
Needed?
No
Immediate
Action
Required?
Yes
Overt Behavior
Alter percepts
concepts, affects
Store new
values
3
No
Store
behavioral
plans
Yes
Potential
Action
Required
No
Stop
Store
Message

FIGURE 6-6

persuader is the expert who is being talked about in the communication. In other cases, the source is minimally credible, but through impressive message construction, which can consist of linguistic and logical elements, gains credibility. Messages, of course, can heighten some of the other internal steps in the process. Spillman (1979), for example, tested the process of making listeners *aware* of inconsistency in the message. She found that this awareness was approximately the same as self-esteem threats in another message, offering evidence for the motivating character of an inconsistent message. This implies a connection between the message steps and the activate-tension-system step. For simplicity's sake, complex interactions of this kind have been left out of the model. Message effects can be complex. Armstrong, Fink, Bauer, and Kaplowitz (1981) have detailed how message discrepancy can have a complex effect on retention of a message. So our model is a bit over-simplified for the message portion.

Sometimes there is no information available about the source. When this happens, a different process is followed. No information about source leads to judgments about the message, and if the message is impressive, the source can gain in credibility, and the process can proceed as if the source had been credible in the first place.

The entire model is presented in Fig. 6–7 on pp. 124–125. Each of the elements fits together and forms a unified process.

We will return to the various segments of the model in later sections of the book. One thing that the model can do for all of us is to help us keep the various portions of the persuasive process in mind when we discuss particular elements. The entire process is interrelated, and to discuss one element without thinking of its relationships to the others is misleading.

SUMMARY

Modeling is a useful process that brings elements together when a total system is involved. A visual representation is useful in that it depicts the total system in a way the verbal models cannot. Models of persuasion depend on assumptions made for models of communication.

A number of models of persuasion have been utilized in the past. The motivated sequence was an extremely popular model that served not only to describe the persuasive process, but also to prescribe the organization of persuasive messages. Systems models are also useful, because they related the elements of persuasion to larger processes. Reardon's model of superordinate constructs is quite interesting but lacks generality.

A model of the intrapersonal processes in persuasion is detailed using flow charts to give a visual representation of the many steps involved in persuasion. This model illustrates that the receiver is quite active throughout the entire process, rather than passive.

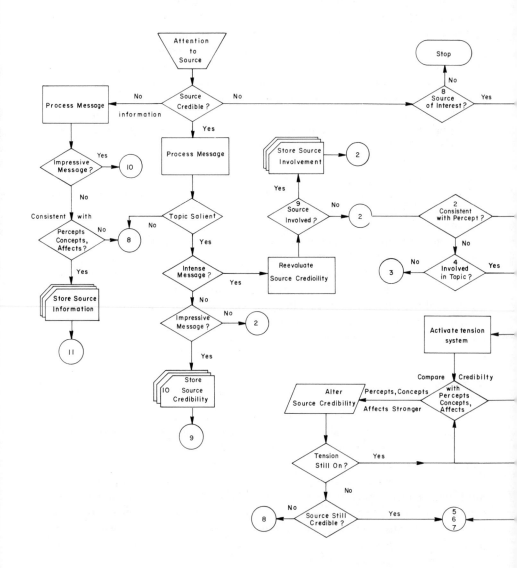

FIGURE 6-7

124

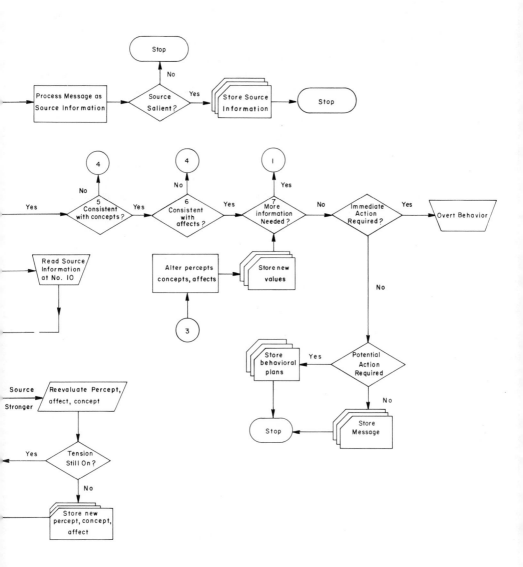

QUESTIONS FOR FURTHER STUDY

1. Examine a newspaper editorial, and look for attention, need, satisfaction, visualization, and action steps. Are any missing? Why?
2. Would you accept a source's message, if it seems to support your ideas and values in his introduction, but then seems to be so ego centered that it later ignores the audience? Why or why not?
3. Are you easily persuaded? Why? Are you a credible person?
4. Study the flow chart in this chapter, and then go through it again substituting a specific message of your own.

SUGGESTIONS FOR FURTHER READING

COLBY, K. Simulation of belief systems. In R. Schank & K. Colby (Eds.) *Computer models of thought and language*. San Francisco: W.H. Freeman, 1973.

FLORENCE, T. An empirical test of the relationship of evidence to belief systems and attitude change. *Human Communication Research*, 1975, *1*, 145–158.

REARDON, K. *Persuasion: theory and context*. Beverly Hills: Sage, 1981.

CHAPTER SEVEN
STRATEGIC CHOICES: SITUATIONS AND TOPICS

Our preceding chapters have given us a comprehensive look at the process of persuasion including the way in which receivers process attitudes in general, as well as attitudes about sources. One might say that all of this background is part of the preconditions of persuasion, that which is necessary before the process can begin. The next logical step is to plan the task more specifically.

The first decision that a persuader must make is the choice of issue, that is, where to persuade and where not to. After the issue is chosen, the next task is to choose a strategy to achieve the change desired. You will remember that Doob (1947) defined attitudes as those structures that affected issues of *social significance* only. Doob's recommendation about attitudes is a good one for choice of issue as well. Just as it makes little sense to discuss attitudes that determine preference for green IBM cards over blue ones, it also makes little sense to attempt to persuade others to change attitudes of that type. Students of public speaking are familiar with the injunction to be relevant, and writers of editorials are familiar with the problem of finding significant material every day for the opinion page. The question of social significance, is, of course, a highly subjective one. Nonetheless the persuader must deal with the issue or face the possibility of wasting the time of the persuader and the audience. How, then, can we decide if an issue is significant or relevant?

One answer is to examine what others find significant in our society. Often the media are seen as the arbiters of significance. The agenda-setting hypothesis (McCombs, 1976) states that newspapers and television news coverage is extremely effective in creating judgments of importance in given audiences. This means that the mass media are probably not effective in telling us what to think, but they are extremely effective in telling us what to think about. Palmgreen and Clarke (1977) found that television news was the strongest influence in agenda setting for national issues, and newspapers were the strongest influence in agenda setting for local issues. However, given all the input from the news industry and other sources, one must eventually make the decision oneself and at some point decide that one issue is worth the trouble that persuasion causes, and another is not. Factors such as the audience, the setting, and long-range goals are all important in this decision.

We must be especially careful in our choices of these issues when we recall that every successful persuasive interaction causes us to lose credibility. We might like to think that each of us has an unlimited amount of this commodity. However, the reality is that our credibility resources are not unlimited, and, therefore, we must be selective in our choice of times and topics for persuasive attempts.

Having decided on a general issue on which to construct a persuasive appeal, the persuader must then decide on the precise goal that will represent success. You will remember that persuasion was defined as communication aimed at changing, reinforcing, and shaping responses. The nature of the audience and the situation will determine whether shaping, changing, or reinforcing is called for. But more important, the particular type of attitude that is to be changed, shaped, or reinforced is vital. You will recall that behavior can be generally classified into perceptual, linguistic, affective, and instrumental responses, each of which was preceded by a particular inner attitude structure. Which of these kinds of responses should be the goal of persuasion? Can a persuader be satisfied with the very small change that is made by the reinforcing of a percept, or the shaping of an affect? It might be useful to look at some representative thinking on issue choice by some of the writers in argumentation. They classify issue choice as one of the main tasks in argumentative theory. These writers might offer a good bit of help with the choice of task and subject.

TYPES OF ISSUES

Typical theories of argumentation classify subject matter into types of propositions. A proposition is the verbal manifestation of the attitude that a persuader might want the receiver to accept. These statements have traditionally been considered to be of three types: fact, value, and policy (Crocker, 1962, 23–25). This system of classification is fairly well accepted by most theorists of argument, though minor variations appear. King (1969), for example, classifies discourse into three types: influencing, inspiring, and entertaining. Ehninger (1974) classified propositions (claims) into four categories: classificatory, declarative, evaluative and actuative (claims of fact for Ehninger could be subdivided into classificatory or declarative tasks). The divisions of fact, value, and policy are closely related to other classifications of behavior that were presented in Chapter 2. Facts are defined as empirically verifiable events, values concern choices of good and bad, and policy concerns questions of future action. These, of course, are closely related to the

TABLE 7-1 Classification of Persuasive Tasks

ARISTOTELIAN	ARGUMENTATIVE THEORIES	ATTITUDE CLASSIFICATION	INTERNAL PROCESS
Forensic	Fact	Belief	Percept
Deliberative	Policy	Behavioral intention	Plan
Epideictic	Value	Evaluative	Affect

general classifications of persuasion proposed by Aristotle, and are quite similar to some classifications of attitude that we already have examined. These general classifications are compared in Table 7-1. We see that the Aristotelian classification of forensic persuasion is almost exactly the same as factual issues, and this in turn is quite similar to Fishbein's (1967) definition of beliefs. We recognize all of those as almost the direct equivalent of the percept from Chapter 2. The second classification, that of epideictic persuasion, is the same as the value category. Attitude researchers have typically used the word *evaluative* to describe this kind of attitude structure (O'Keefe, 1980). These, of course, are the same as the affective responses. The last category, deliberative, is the same as a policy category; the deliberative issue affects what a given government, group, or person ought to do in a particular circumstance. This is the same as Fishbein's behavioral-intention construct (Fishbein and Ajzen, 1975) that precedes instrumental behavior in the system. In other words, the general categories of fact, value, and policy discussed by argumentative theorists are pretty much the same as the category system proposed here and elsewhere by behavioral theorists. The last column in Table 7-1 is taken directly from the categories of behavior in Chapter 2. Let us look at some of these categories in more detail and see how they can each be of help to the persuader in the choice of subject matter.

Persuading to Alter Beliefs: Factual Issues

It seems to be a contradiction to think about persuasion that concerns facts. If something is a fact, how can we change our minds concerning it? The answer lies in the nature of facts and their verification.

Empirical verification, as everyone knows, is verification through one of the many senses. When there is correspondence between the sense experience and the classification implied by the statement, we say that the statement is verified. If we say, "The Washington Monument is 169.2941 meters high" then we can verify this statement by actually visiting the monument and performing the measurement. Anyone can do it who knows where the monument is and who has a ruler that is at least 170 meters long. The actual measurement is a lot of trouble, but it is certainly possible and no one is going to dispute our measurements if they are carefully done.

Because this operation gives the Washington Monument a certain quality, in a sense we have added to the linguistic store about the monument. We have classified linguistically. This has led Mills to reject the terminology of questions of *fact* and to use the word classification in its place (Mills, 1964; Ehninger, 1974). No one tries to persuade another about this kind of statement when direct empirical verification is possible.

Unfortunately, however, a good many of us pay no attention to this sensible position, and we attempt to persuade on these kinds of topics anyway. Interminable hours are spent wrangling about which year it was that Babe Ruth hit 60 home runs, whether Alan Alda has ever missed appearing in an episode of M*A*S*H, and whether a Mustang will go faster than a Cougar (cars, not animals). The sensible thing to do is to verify the statement: the baseball record book can be found, we can examine the M*A*S*H tapes (or telephone the producer), and we can take the cars out on the track and see how they do. Verification, however, involves some effort, and it is often easier to argue. It should be clear that persuasion of this kind is inproductive because the result means little. Even if we persuade a friend that George Herman Ruth hit 60 home runs in 1935, the "victory" would mean little because it simply is not true.

Does this mean that questions of fact should not be utilized in persuasion simply because they can be settled by empirical verification? The problem is not that simple. The verification of statements is not as easy as it sounds. If I assert that the grass is green, you have only to look at it to decide whether it fits into the classification you are accustomed to referring to as green. This is a broad classification, as any decorator or painter will tell us; "green" means all kinds of colors, which can range from very light pastels to unusual dark shades that can barely be differentiated from black. But let us look at the grass another way, by asserting that the grass is "bluegrass." I may now be using classifications that you cannot make easily. When we perceive events (or stimuli), we vary a good deal in the way that we attend to those stimuli and the way in which we discriminate between those stimuli. For many of us, stimuli tend to become generalized. For example, many of us tend to respond to *bluegrass* about the same way that we respond to ryegrass, or bentgrass, or any other plantlife we find in our lawns (even dandelions and crabgrass). Each of us has been taught different kinds of verbal categories, and the landscape gardener and the suburbanite probably classify grasses with much more efficiency than the average resident of Manhattan. So it may not be possible to verify anything empirically unless a special set of learning experiences is shared with the statement maker and the statement receiver. So if a friend tells you that your serratus anterior is larger than your thyrohyoideus, you may find yourself completely unable to respond, let alone verify the statement to see if you need a doctor, a priest, or a club to hit your friend.

Another problem with verifying factual statements lies in the differences in the perceptual process itself. Our attitudes influence our perceptions. In a classic experiment, economically deprived children perceived stimuli associated with money as being much larger than more neutral stimuli (Bruner and Goodman, 1947). Apparently, we all do this. In addition, social psychologists claim that perceptual distortions are caused by our group membership. In our discussion of the normative-identificatory credibility effects, we looked at a study by Asch (1962). You will remember that in this experiment, Asch demonstrated that when a majority of a group pretended to misperceive a stimulus, a lone individual in the group who did not know of the prearranged plan tended to go along with the verbalization of this misperception. They later reported that they had, in fact, really misperceived the stimulus. So it is likely that our group memberships affect the way we see and hear, and that verification of outside stimuli is correspondingly difficult.

Another problem seems to arise when we are asked to verify a statement, and we have, on some other occasion, publicly committed ourselves one way or another concerning the nature of the statement (Deutsch and Gerard, 1955). An unreasoning insistence on consistency seems to lie behind the desire not to appear wishy-washy. Candidates for public office are very careful not to commit themselves to statements or positions they may have to reverse later on. For example, in order not to appear inconsistent, a prominent national politician once alleged that some of the apparent inconsistencies between his earlier statements and his later statements were due to having been brainwashed by the administration. This foolish admission provoked gleeful howls from the press, some of whom professed great delight to learn that this particular candidate at least had a brain, washed or not.

Still another difficulty arises from the structuring process inherent in our language itself. The way our language works seems to influence our perceptions of the way the world is—our language determines, to a great extent, the kind of perceptions we have of outside stimuli. Whorf (1954) has pointed out that the way a Navaho perceives is greatly different from the way we perceive, and these differences seem to be the result of the differences in our languages. It would be difficult to verify a statement if we did not have the linguistic concept implied by the statement, and if, furthermore, we were not in the habit of relating linguistic events in the same manner implied by the other language.

So there are four main reasons why the verification of factual events is not as easy as it sounds: (1) our verbal learning varies, (2) our attitudes influence the way we perceive stimuli, (3) our prior commitments influence our responses to stimuli, and (4) our linguistic habits tend to force us into habits of perception that may be quite different from the patterns of another cultural group. When we say we know something, we are talking about degrees of uncertainty, and it is difficult to support the notion that there is any certain knowledge of any kind of event. This, of course, is not a common sense approach to knowledge, but common sense told us for years that the earth was flat, that women had fewer teeth than men and that blacks are less intelligent than whites. We know now that all of these statements are false. Common sense is still telling us things that we know are distortions of reality. It tells us, for example, that the sun rises in the east and travels around the earth until it sets in the west. We know, however, that the sun stands still (relatively) and that the earth is rotating on its axis, producing an illusion of motion from the sun. Doubt is a useful tool, and sometimes a skeptical examination of even the most commonplace knowledge can turn up difficulties that are quite important.

Up to this point, we have been talking about first-hand knowledge only, the process involved when we actually witness the event ourselves. Most of what we know has not come to us this way, but has been transmitted by the verbal reports of others, who represent to us that they have experienced the event and are now passing it on to us. The four difficulties mentioned above are now multiplied by the distinct possibility of deception and deceit.

They may also depend on the importance of the statement. Most of us can recall with great clarity the moment of hearing the news that President Reagan had been shot and was believed to be in serious condition. Some mistake was possible, of course, or perhaps someone was playing an elaborate prank. However, for most of us the belief did not wait for elaborate verification; it followed in a sickening rush after hearing of the news. It seems possible that if the news had been presented in a less convincing way or with cues present that suggested some alternative explanations, a different reaction might have followed. It seems clear that if a report of a factual event is presented in a manner that our learning histories suggest to be accurate, we tend to accept it rather quickly.

Many critics cite this tendency as an indication of the natural stupidity of the human race, but if we think about it a minute, we must admit that civilization as we know it depends on the acceptance of knowledge that is not only second-hand but third, fourth, and indeterminate-hand. We read in the newspaper that New York City is perilous at night, we read in a textbook that hominid skulls have been found in the Olduvai gorge in Africa, and we are informed by a highway sign that the road curves ahead. We accept this reporting with little consideration of the possibility that some of these reports might be false, and our acceptance is so rapid and complete that we consider it second nature. This acceptance involves an inferential process (as a logician would describe it), but we need not consciously refer to the process to understand it. Society has given us an elaborate set of reward contingencies, and behaving as if we believed these reports has been rewarding in our past experience. To behave otherwise—especially in the case of highway signs—is to invite disaster. In other cases, to behave differently from our fellows is to invite a good deal of social disapproval. So learning seems to affect the acceptance of statements in important ways.

Given this process, we must recognize that certain kinds of factual statements are not as certain as others, and we are sometimes justified in persuading others about them. This varies with the importance (social significance) of the fact and with the amount of uncertainty associated with the verification. If a doctor told you that you had a stomach ulcer, you would certainly not wish direct verification, because that would involve an operation so that the doctor could actually inspect the lining of the stomach. However, if the doctor tells you that you have cancer in the stomach, the expense and upset of the operation may be justified. If it is vital to our national interest to know about Jupiter or Saturn, then we will justify the expenditure that it takes to obtain this information.

In short, there are many times when we cannot verify factual statements, and there are times when we should not try to verify them. The decision as to which time is which is usually described as a common sense decision, which is just another way of saying that it is made of the basis of what sensible people consider to be valuable. Almost any factual statement is uncertain, but we only have so much time and energy in our short lives, and so we must be selective about what we expend effort for. As long as we retain the adversary system in our courts, we will probably continue to treat certain classes of factual statements as if they were debatable. Each of us has a different idea of what constitutes a socially significant issue. The judgment of a significance and the commitment to spend time on it and attempt to verify it becomes a decision based on values alone.

Values and Beliefs

The second traditional type of subject matter for persuasion has been termed propositions of value (Mills, 1964, p. 44). These topics relate generally to questions of the value or inherent worth of any given event. Many of us, sore and smarting from an argument over religion or politics, might feel that we should avoid questions of value entirely. There is some real justification for this. Look at what happens when we discuss the question of birth control, for example. Many church leaders have asserted that birth control by artificial means is immoral, because it leads to licentiousness, which, by their definition, is sex without the express intent of procreation. Other church leaders have taken a different position, contending that overpopulation is a greater danger to the human race than licentiousness, and that sex in and of itself is not an evil thing. Now if any of us were participants in this debate, how would we go about persuading someone else that sex is immoral or evil unless accompanied by specific intent to procreate? It is futile to look for verified factual statements that relate to this statement. If we cite statistics that seem to indicate that there is a greater tendency for childless couples to be divorced, we would still not have proved which was the cause and which was the effect; birth control and childlessness may both be the result of a poor marriage, not the cause of it. Even if we did prove that the two are causally related, we have still not made any statements about the inherent evil of sexual behavior, because we depend for this assumption on the belief that divorce is inherently evil. Many persons believe this, but we must recognize that whether or not divorce is inherently evil is another question of value that is just as difficult to prove as was the first one about sex.

A value statement has no external reality but is the expression of a private, internal event. When I assert that capital punishment is immoral, I am describing my reactions to capital punishment, which involve a private set of relationships that has led me to use the word *immoral* when I use the term *capital punishment*. I also have other internal reactions: When I consider the victims of capital punishment my blood pressure may rise, I may get more adrenalin in my bloodstream, and if anyone would ask me what is wrong, I would probably say that I was angry. My reaction is pure affect. At the same time my neighbor or my colleague may have similar reactions, but believes that capital punishment is justified. She gets angry when a criminal is let off with life imprisonment rather than execution. Our discussions of this issue are likely to be fairly unproductive, since what each of us usually ends up saying is "I believe this way, and when you don't believe this way you are different from me and, therefore, mistaken." Our problems stem from our different learning histories that have taught us, in one way or another over the past years, to react this way. Each of us has been rewarded or punished for different kinds of statements and reactions, and now we find them difficult to unlearn. Threat to them only causes us to react more strongly, and to solidify our positions. This seems to be a perfect place for persuasion. However, if you will recall the hierarchy of beliefs presented in Chapter 3 (Fig. 3–4), you will remember that the centrally located beliefs are particularly resistant to change.

Whatever kind of genetic theory we hold about values, we still must admit that value statements do not, by definition, have any built-in mechanism for verification the way a factual statement has. Value statements are verified by their utterance only, for when I say that capital punishment is morally wrong I am referring to my internal state; my statement, to be wholly accurate, should be "I feel that capital punishment is morally wrong."

The only way we verify our values is simply by asserting them, and we utilize values in argument by referring to commonly held values in our society. This is the well-known argument by authority. For example, the science of aesthetics has been an attempt to put together rational systems that will separate good art from popular art, good ideas from popular ideas, and generally introduce an elevation of value statements that popularity does not achieve. Usually their arguments are authority-centered, apparently assuming that one becomes an authority independently of other people's judgment. L. L. Thurstone, writing about the measurement of commonly held values, reported:

> It was an illuminating experience to discover that some of my friends in the humanities were hostile to the very idea of subjecting questions of aesthetic theory to empirical inquiry. On one of these occasions, a friend showed me a quotation from Aristotle that settled the matter for him. It was heresy when I suggested that we know more about this problem than did Aristotle. (1959, p. 36)

Clearly we could construct persuasive communications using authority on value questions. On the other hand, we may be more accurate if we examine values from an empirical point of view and go on from there.

Questions of Policy

Questions of policy, as Miller (1966, p. 37) has correctly pointed out, are really only questions of value in another form. The traditional definition of a debate over policy centers on some future action, such as Let us abolish capital punishment in our state. This seems to mean that we are going to contend that no one should henceforth use the electric chair, the rope, or the firing squad in our state, and we are apparently talking about the future because we cannot amend past actions. Clearly, a question of value is implied by the statement, which is that capital punishment is immoral. This assertion ought to be enough to create a behavioral intention—to need more is to say that we often hold values that do not influence our actions. However, you will remember (from Chapter 3) that very often that is exactly the case.

There is another important point that we must consider in discussing questions of policy. Few of us have the opportunity to make any meaningful responses on questions of national policy. We may have strong feelings about capital punishment, but the decision is still going to be made by the state legislature. Their decision will be made almost solely on the basis of what they consider the values of their constituency to be. Edmund Burke and Abraham Lincoln may have written with eloquence about the legislator's conscience, but it would be naive to believe that conscience is the principal motivator of most legislators. What this means is that most political persuasion does not aim at real behavior change from the electorate, but changes in value. You might remember the governor in the beginning of Chapter 2. How common might this be in your state? Debate in the legislature might serve as a model for policy debates if we thought that legislatures were influenced by argumentation and debate. High school civics books report how legislatures and their committees talk over the issues and decide them on their merits, but anyone who has observed a legislature at close range knows that there is no issue more influential in swaying votes than the exercise of power. A useful view of persuasion should examine the real possibilities and effects of the process, not an elaborate myth about the rule of the people and social action by the populace.

CHOICE OF STRATEGY IN PERSUASION

The theoretical framework presented above is, of course, quite valuable in working out general methods of choosing one's ground in persuasion generally. But often persons in given interpersonal interactions react differently than the "ideal" structures might predict. Recently a number of researchers have examined the process of strategy choice in persuasive interactions, and have discovered that usually a number of outcomes are involved in the strategy choice. Let us examine some of these choices.

Potential Audience on Strategy Choice

Hazen and Kiesler (1975) performed an extremely interesting study, in which they examined the effect of potential audiences on the choice of subject for persuasive attempts. Groups of students were asked to prepare persuasive communications. One group was told to assume that their audience is a group of women who are *very opposed* to the topic. Another group was told that their audience was moderately in favor of the topic. Others were told that their audience was moderately opposed, and still others were told that their audience had no opinion. The members of the group who thought their potential audience was going to be opposed to their speech used more problem-centered arguments than did the other groups. When the potential audience was perceived as more friendly, the persuaders chose more solution-centered communications. Potential feedback from the audience increased this tendency. Hazen and Kiesler conclude that persuaders need to consider potential audience's range of acceptability, in designing persuasive communications (1975, p. 68).

Of course, one of the typical choices everyone has in the persuasive situation is the long-term problem of who is served, the communicator or the audience? Persuaders are often so interested in their short-range goals (sell the product, win the vote) that they forget the ultimate good of their audience, their community, and other social groups. One way of terming this kind of choice is a simple one: prosocial versus antisocial communication. It may indeed be much easier to persuade when one does not have to worry about the rightness or wrongness of the decision. On the other hand, narrow self-interest is not always a good choice either.

Prosocial and Antisocial Strategy Choices

How does one decide whether a choice is ethical or unethical? The classification is not that simple, of course. Marwell and Schmitt (1967) listed 16 compliance-gaining techniques that might be used in a family situation. These are listed in Table 7-2. You will notice that it is difficult to group these into prosocial (ethical) or antisocial (nonethical) categories. Marwell and Schmitt used a factor-analytic technique to group these 16 strategies into categories. Their factor names were: rewarding activity, punishing activity, expertise, activation of interpersonal commitments, and activation of interpersonal commitments. Whether these categories actually reflect ethicality or nonethicality is not certain. In one situation, a rewarding communication strategy might be ethical, in another, a rewarding strategy might be unethical.

TABLE 7-2 Sixteen Compliance-Gaining Techniques (Examples from Family Situations)

1.	Promise	(If you comply, I will reward you.)
		"You offer to increase Dick's allowance if he increases his studying."
2.	Threat	(If you do not comply, I will punish you.)
		"You threaten to forbid Dick the use of the car if he does not increase his studying."

3.	Expertise (positive)	(If you comply, you will be rewarded because of "the nature of things.") "You point out to Dick that if he gets good grades he will be able to get into a good college and get a good job."
4.	Expertise (negative)	(If you do not comply, you will be punished because of "the nature of things.") "You point out to Dick that if he does not get good grades he will not be able to get into a good college or get a good job."
5.	Liking	(Actor is friendly and helpful to get target in "good frame of mind" so that he will comply with request.) "You try to be as friendly and pleasant as possible to get Dick in the 'right frame of mind' before asking him to study."
6.	Pre-Giving	(Actor rewards target before requesting compliance.) "You raise Dick's allowance and tell him you now expect him to study."
7.	Aversive stimulation	(Actor continuously punishes target making cessation contingent on compliance.) "You forbid Dick the use of the car and tell him he will not be allowed to drive until he studies more."
8.	Debt	(You owe me compliance because of past favors.) "You point out that you have sacrificed and saved to pay for Dick's education and that he owes it to you to get good enough grades to get into a good college."
9.	Moral appeal	(You are immoral if you do not comply.) "You tell Dick that it is morally wrong for anyone not to get as good grades as he can and that he should study more."
10.	Self-feeling (positive)	(You will feel better about yourself if you comply.) "You tell Dick he will feel proud if he gets himself to study more."
11.	Self-feeling (negative)	(You will feel worse about yourself if you do not comply.) "You tell Dick he will feel ashamed of himself if he gets bad grades."
12.	Altercasting (positive)	(A person with "good" qualities would comply.) "You tell Dick that since he is a mature and intelligent boy he naturally will want to study more and get good grades."
13.	Altercasting (negative)	(Only a person with "bad" qualities would not comply.) "You tell Dick that only someone very childish does not study as he should."
14.	Altruism	(I need your compliance very badly, so do it for me.) "You tell Dick that you really want very badly for him to get into a good college and that you wish he should study more as a personal favor to you."
15.	Esteem (positive)	(People you value will think better of you if you comply.) "You tell Dick that the whole family will be very proud of him if he gets good grades."
16.	Esteem (negative)	(People you value will think worse of you if you do not comply.) "You tell Dick that the whole family will be very disappointed in him if he gets poor grades."

Source: G.R. Miller, F. Boster, M. Roloff, & D. Siebold. Compliance-gaining message strategies: A typology and some findings concerning effects of situational differences. *Communication Monographs*. 1977, 44. Reprinted by permission of the Speech Communication Association.

In an attempt to examine the effects of the situation on these kinds of persuasive choices, Miller, Boster, Roloff, and Siebold (1977) placed individuals in hypothetical situations in which compliance from another person would be desired. The experimenters presented these persons with Marwell and Schmitt's options and asked them to choose which technique they would use. The hypothetical relationships were varied: some were interpersonal in nature and others were noninterpersonal, some were short-term relationships and others were long-term. For example, the noninterpersonal, long-term-consequence situation was described like this:

> You have been living six months in a house that you purchased. You learn that your next-door neighbors (the Smiths, persons with whom you have had only limited contact since moving in) plan to cut down a large shade tree that stands near your property in order to construct their new two-car garage. However, in the long run, loss of the shade tree will adversely affect the beauty of your home, your comfort, and, perhaps, the value of your home. How likely would you be to employ each of the following strategies in order to get the Smiths to leave the tree standing? (1977)

Then each person was asked to mark each of the 16 choices in terms of the probability of choice. These researcher's results are expressed in Table 7-3. You will see that in the interpersonal situation, the short-term strategy choices were altruism, altercasting, and liking. But in the noninterpersonal situation, these same choices were threat, promise, liking, and expertise. Miller, Boster, Roloff, and Siebold conclude that probably source traits, message choices, situational effects, and their interactions are better predictors of the correct strategy choice than traditional reliance on source-oriented or message-oriented factors (1977, p. 51).

What kind of influence on strategy choice would an individual's personality have? Roloff and Barnicott (1978) attempted to answer this question by repeating the Miller et al. study with persons of different personality patterns. They chose to study Machiavellianism in this setting. Machiavellians are those whose personalities tend toward manipulation and control of others. They found that the high Machiavellians were more likely to employ psychological-force techniques than the low Machiavellians. They did not find that the strategy choices at different levels were affected by Machiavellianism.

In another study of persuasive techniques, Cody and McLaughlin (1980) examined a large number of potentially persuasive interpersonal situations, and asked individuals to evaluate them using a number of evaluative scales. They then grouped these scales into a number of factors. These factors are presented in Table 7-4. This table contains six factors: intimacy, dominance, resistance, rights, personal benefits, and long-term consequences. Cody and McLaughlin conclude that these six dimensions ought to play an important part in the evaluation of interpersonal persuasive activity, rather than the simplified personal-interpersonal and long-term–short-term dimensions used in Miller et al. and Roloff and Barnicott.

In a later study, Cody, McLaughlin and Jordan (1980) used cluster analysis to further study the types of interpersonal strategies chosen by individuals. Rather

TABLE 7-3   Strategies Likely and Unlikely to be Used in Each of the Four Situations

	INTERPERSONAL	
	SHORT TERM	LONG TERM
Likely strategies	Altruism (M* = 5.95) Altercasting+ (M = 5.81) Liking (M = 5.29)	Threat (M = 5.88) Altercasting+ (M = 5.82) Altruism (M = 5.59) Liking (M = 5.45) Promise (M = 5.28)
Unlikely strategies	Moral appeal (M = 2.42) Aversive Stimulation (M = 2.42) Esteem− (M = 2.45) Threat (M = 2.51) Pre-giving (M = 2.85)	Esteem− (M = 2.17) Self-feeling− (M = 2.25) Aversive Stimulation (M = 2.51) Debt (M = 2.74) Esteem+ (M = 2.94)
	NONINTERPERSONAL	
	SHORT TERM	LONG TERM
Likely strategies	Threat (M = 5.83) Promise (M = 5.79) Liking (M = 5.62) Expertise+ (M = 5.36)	Expertise+ (M = 6.15) Expertise− (M = 5.86) Altruism (M = 5.52) Promise (M = 5.23) Liking (M = 5.21) Debt (M = 5.17) Altercasting+ (M = 5.08)
Unlikely strategies	Moral appeal (M = 2.98)	Aversive Stimulation (M = 2.28)

*M = "Mean Score"

Source: G.R. Miller, F. Boster, M. Roloff, & D. Siebold. Compliance-gaining message strategies: A typology and some findings concerning effects of situational differences. *Communication Monographs*, 1977, 44. Reprinted by permission of the Speech Communication Association.

than the six dimensions found earlier by Cody and McLaughlin, these researchers found eight clusters: threat, hinting, simple statement-question, altruism, deceit, disclaimer, simple statement, and reason. Quite an assortment! This illustrates some of the inherent values we seem to hold about the type of strategical choices that we think is reasonable in ordinary situations.

Topoi

It is interesting to note that one of the more important precepts in classical rhetoric was the choice of the places where arguments lurk (Clark, 1957, p. 75). Because one of the principal tasks in ancient rhetoric was the invention of arguments, it was logical to treat the process of invention as a separate step. Arguments were to be found in places, and because the Greek term for place was *topos*, these argumentative places were called *topoi*. From this we get our English word *topic*.

TABLE 7-4   Cody and McLaughlin's Factors of Interpersonal Persuasive Situations

ITEM	FACTOR
I.	*Intimacy*
1.	This situation involves a personally meaningless relationship-This situation involves a personally meaningful relationship
2.	This situation involves a shallow relationship-This situation involves a deep relationship
3.	This situation involves a superficial relationship-This situation involves an intimate relationship
II.	*Dominance*
4.	The person in a situation like this situation controls many of my behaviors-The person in a situation like this situation does not control many of my behaviors
5.	The person in a situation like this situation usually dominates me-The person in a situation like this situation usually does not dominate me
6.	I am usually submissive to the person in a situation like this one-I am not usually submissive to the person in a situation like this one
III.	*Resistance*
7.	I could talk the person in this situation into doing this very easily-I could not talk the person in this situation into doing this very easily
8.	I think the person in this situation would be very agreeable to this persuasion-I think that the person in this situation would not be very agreeable to this persuasion
9.	I feel that the person in this situation would not be resistant to my persuasion-I feel that the person in this situation would be resistant to my persuasion
IV.	*Rights*
10.	I have no reasonable grounds for making this request-I have strong reasonable grounds for making this request
11.	I have no justification for making this request-I have every justification for making this request
12.	I do not have a right to make this request-I have a right to make this request
V.	*Personal Benefits*
13.	I personally would get a lot out of it if I were successful in this situation-I personally get nothing out of it if I were successful in this situation
14.	I personally gain if successful in this situation-I personally do not gain if successful in this situation
15.	It would be to my personal advantage if I were successful in this situation-It would not be to my personal advantage if I were successful in this situation
VI.	*Long-term Consequences*
16.	This persuasion has future consequences for the relationship between the person in the situation and myself-This persuasion does not have future consequences for the relationship between the person in the situation and myself
17.	This persuasion has long-term consequences on the relationship between the person in the situation and myself-This persuasion does not have long-term consequences on the relationship between the person in the situation and myself
18.	This persuasion would improve the relationship between the person in the situation and myself-This persuasion would not improve the relationship between the person in the situation and myself

Source: M. Cody & M. McLaughlin. Perception of compliance-gaining situations: A dimensional analysis. *Communications Monographs*, 1980, 47, 132–148. Reprinted by permission of the Speech Communication Association.

Aristotle's list of *topoi* was extremely long, but Cicero's was more manageable. He listed places like definition, contrast, similarity, consistency, cause and effect, and the like (Clark, 1957, p. 77). The similarities between the classical approaches and the results of the Cody and McLaughlin study are striking, to say the least. Whether we say that we are choosing our ground or choosing a place for argument is probably only a difference in emphasis.

Cognitive Complexity and Persuasive Strategy

An interesting approach to the study of strategy choice centers on another personality variable, that of cognitive complexity. Persons who are cognitively complex typically elect a different set of strategies than those who are less complex. Studies by Delia, Kline, and Burelson (1979), O'Keefe and Delia (1979), and Applegate (1981a) show differential selection of persuasive strategy by differing levels of cognitive complexity. To see how these strategy levels are studied, let us look at one study in some detail.

Applegate (1981a) examined both cognitive complexity and concept abstractness on the choices persons made in persuasive interactions. The individuals were asked to play persuasive roles in situations closely corresponding to real interactions. For example, one situation was described like this:

> Suppose that you had been hired as an assistant office manager. The manager often leaves you in charge. Imagine that a friend of yours is an employee. His/her work is satisfactory in most respects but s/he is continually five or ten minutes late in getting to work. You know that other employees have noticed this lateness and that it occurs when you have been left in charge. What would you say to this person in this situation? (p. 42)

This and one other task were used to measure cognitive complexity. Then the students were placed in dyads and were shown a five-dollar bill, and assured that one or the other of them would get the five dollars at the close of the session. They were told that their task was to persuade the other person that he or she should receive the bill. In other words, each person was trying to persuade the other to give up the money. These interactions were videotaped and responses analyzed. These videotapes were scored for ten separate persuasive strategies, including level of strategies employed and number of strategies employed. Both construct abstractness and complexity were shown to have a strong effect on the strategy choice. In other words, the more complex persons had a great many more strategies at their disposal, more listener-adapted strategies, and more concern for creating and preserving a positive interpersonal relationship. No evidence was available to see which of these persons were the more successful, but it is hard to see how the more complex persons could not have been successful with these strategy choices.

In general the literature concerning the persuasive strategy choice is limited, in that interest in this topic is comparatively recent. We can expect a good deal of interesting findings in this area in the future.

SUMMARY

The choice of the persuasive strategy is an extremely important one. We can look at these choices in two different ways, from a prescriptive point of view and from the point of view of what persons tend to do in persuasive interactions. Both are valid in their own way.

Prescriptive statements have centered around the Aristotelian divisions of fact, policy, and value. These divisions are very closely related to the kinds of behaviors categorized in Chapter 2. General orientations to these behaviors can be thought of as attitudes or beliefs (in the case of factual issues). Different social situations call for quite different approaches to choice of issue and topic.

In many interpersonal situations, persons choose strategies and issues in interesting ways. Both prosocial and antisocial strategies are employed. Many factors affect this choice, including cognitive complexity.

QUESTIONS FOR FURTHER STUDY

1. Cite examples of various types of forensic, deliberative, and epideictic persuasion.
2. How can epidiectic persuasion be used to a speaker's advantage? Be specific.
3. Do questions of value and/or policy always lead to a behavioral intention? Are our actions always affected by our values? Explain.
4. Is Sherif and Sherif's latitudes of acceptance, neutrality, and rejection helpful in knowing your audience?
5. Which of the persuasive strategies discussed seem to describe your own techniques?

SUGGESTIONS FOR FURTHER READING

EHNINGER, D. *Influence and argument.* Chicago: Scott, Foresman, 1974.
KING, R. *Forms of public address.* Indianapolis: Bobbs-Merrill, 1969.
MILLER, G., BOSTER, F., ROLOFF, M. & SIEBOLD, D. Compliance-gaining message strategies: a typology and some findings concerning effects of situational differences. *Communication Monographs,* 1977, *44,* 37–51.
ROLOFF, M. & BARNICOTT, E. The situational use of pro- and anti-social compliance-gaining strategies by high and low Machiavellians. In B. Ruben (Ed.) *Communication yearbook II.* New Brunswick, New Jersey: Transaction, 1978.

CHAPTER EIGHT
THE MESSAGE I: MATERIALS

When we examined the general choice of topics for persuasive communications, it may have come as a surprise that many factual questions were not considered as good topics for persuasion. From that, you may have concluded that facts were not important. Nothing could be farther from the truth. Facts are highly important; it is only certain types of factual *issues* that are usually not considered persuadable. Facts often form a vital part of the content of the message. But facts are not the only aspect of message content. We also consider illustrations, examples, quotations, and other materials. For most of us, our credibility will be determined by what we put in our message. Though it is interesting to examine other aspects of messages—called "paramessages" by Rosenthal (1972)—sooner or later we need to pay attention to message content.

Therefore, we need to consider the question of basic materials, that is, the content of messages. In this chapter we will explore this content. The principal focus will be on *evidence*, because this concept has received a good deal of attention from those who have studied persuasion. Then we will look at some other approaches to content, specifically the notions of fear appeals in messages.

EVIDENCE AND PERSUASIVE COMMUNICATION

When you hear the word evidence you may immediately think of a detective looking for clues or an attorney trying to defend a client in courts. That image is not far fetched because evidence is closely related to the process of belief. Indeed, Miller

(1966) has defined evidence as anything that contributes to belief. Other writers have been more specific about what evidence should be.

Traditionally, evidence has been classified into *facts, testimony, and authority*. It might be helpful if we looked at each of these in turn to see how each could fit into the process of constructing a persuasive message. Traditional theories of rhetoric and argumentation stressed the value of documentation for materials in the production of attitude change. However, there are reasons to believe that this emphasis on evidence, although desirable from a social and logical point of view, may not be as important from a practical point of view.

We would all like persuaders to know what they are talking about. This may be one of the rules that governs communicative interactions (Higgins, 1981). But from our study of the effects of credibility, we know that often it is enough only to know that a given source has taken a given position on an issue. The content of the message may only serve to heighten the effect, as the model of persuasion in Chapter 6 indicated. You will remember that the intensification effect was part of the role of language, but at the same time, part of the model of persuasion involved the role of thought and rational consideration of the message content. This is where evidence comes in. It might be helpful, then, to begin our exploration of evidence with the basic question of whether evidence is usually effective in most persuasive situations or if evidence could be profitably ignored by persuasive communicators. Indeed, some researchers have questioned whether evidence actually has much, if any, impact in persuasion. Let us examine some of these studies and see how these authors arrived at their conclusions. First, however, it may be helpful to make sure that we all are using the term evidence in the same way.

What is Evidence?

In its broadest sense, evidence is data that can be used to establish a conclusion. But evidence is usually defined as factual statements or empirical data containing "verifiable information on the occurrence, existence, classification, or character of phenomena," or opinions "of persons other than the advocate which are offered in support of claims"; or "objects not created by the speaker or writer" (Mills, 1964). In most persuasive situations, real evidence is limited, but sometimes, documents, photographs, and objects can be used as evidence. In the dispute about the teaching of evolution as opposed to "scientific" creationism, the existence of fossils has been cited by the proponents of evolution as compelling evidence, in that their physical existence is hard to deny and the proponents of creationism must find another explanation for their existence rather than the evolutionary hypothesis. Therefore, in a practical sense, we might conclude that evidence is something that cannot be disavowed as easily as the unsupported opinion of the persuader.

Given that view of evidence, then, we could say that evidence is anything that would assist the communicator in the persuasive task. But it is not that simple. The traditional writers in argumentation assert that there are many different types of evidence: direct, indirect, negative, reluctant, real, or created. The type of evidence available, of course, depends on the topic and the source. The persuader may have to depend entirely on external sources if the topic concerns foreign policy, but if the topic is community needs, personal experience might be just as useful.

For example, consider the task of an undergraduate who attempts to persuade the university athletic board that students should get better seats at football games. In this persuasive task, the student's own knowledge and experience is a perfectly appropriate body of material for the message. But if this same student attempted to persuade the city council to grant special parking facilities for students, a different kind of evidence would be called for: financial data, studies of space available, the opinions of the police chief, and so on. The student would have been considered an authority on student opinion and student life, but not on traffic and parking. Therefore, the evidence requirement would be different. Most of us, unfortunately, are usually faced with the second situation in which we must find our evidence.

Most students of persuasion care little for the form that evidence may take; they wish evidence to be effective. Again, several criteria may be employed to judge the evidence's worth. Traditional writers in argumentation have studied these criteria in depth. Most agree with Minick (1968) that evidence should meet the test of relevancy, reliability, and availability. In addition, they stress two aspects of evidence, namely, personal and public. In creating the message, the persuader should have an open mind and be willing to let the evidence speak for itself. Suppose, for example, you set out to advocate busing for racial balance in a given school system. After examining all the available evidence, you conclude that your original idea was a little too strong and now you are going to take a position that is a little less dogmatic. This is the personal aspect of evidence. The public use is the effect on the chosen audience.

Traditional writers, of course, treat evidence from a prescriptive point of view. In most studies of persuasion, however, evidence is treated from a descriptive point of view. Although most traditionalists would feel that any persuasive attempt should contain evidence, the compelling effects of high credibility alone might lead us to ask if evidence is necessary at all.

Is Evidence Necessary?

If source credibility alone is enough, then a persuader need not utilize evidence. You will recall that in our model of persuasion, message content could be used to enhance the persuader's credibility. Is it absolutely necessary to have evidence to persuade? An intriguing study by Tucker and Ware (1971) suggests that perhaps nothing more is needed for persuasion than familiarity with the name of the topic. They arranged for individuals to be exposed to a neutral name under the guise of an experiment designed to test the ability to remember names. The test name was evaluated as good if there had been a substantial number of mere exposures to it. In other words, simply the familiarity of the word seemed to cause respondents to evaluate it better. We see this effect in political campaigns where an individual runs on the strength of name recognition, and astronauts and movie stars defeat better qualified candidates in elections. The differences discovered by

Tucker and Ware are not large, but they certainly are large enough for us to take the effect seriously.

Surely, we might think, even if some messages are effective in and of themselves, evidence would add to the persuasibility of messages. Can we find any direct tests of evidence as a persuasive device?

Let us look at an early attempt to study evidence. Cathcart (1955) demonstrated significant results favoring inclusion of evidence in a message designed to achieve attitude change. Cathcart designed messages that advocated abolition of capital punishment. One message contained no evidence at all, and a second had evidence that supported most of the assertions in the message. A third was similar to the second, but each of the citations of evidence was given a source documentation. The fourth was the most elaborate of all; it contained evidence, documentation of the source, and some indication that the source was a valid one. Cathcart found that the first and third messages were approximately the same, whereas the second and fourth were significantly better. However, the fourth message—the overkill message with sources, documentation, and source credibility—was no more effective than the citation of sources alone. We must take Cathcart's findings very seriously, because they have been exactly replicated by Bostrom and Tucker (1969). In other words, traditional notions about evidence and its structure do not necessarily produce attitude change.

In another study, Bettinghaus (1953) asked individuals to reveal persons who they believed to be most expert on a given topic. Two forms of an experimental message were then developed. One form contained six instances of evidence clearly identified with the name of the individual quoted. The authorities cited were those most often named as experts by the experimental subjects. The other form of the speech included the quotations used in the first form; however, the citation of sources was omitted and the quotations appeared as statements originated by the speaker. The first form was found to be significantly more effective in changing the attitudes of the subjects.

These studies seem to indicate that the inclusion of evidence in messages produces attitude change, though in a nontraditional fashion. However, other studies report conflicting results.

Anderson (1958), Costley (1958), Gardner (1966), and Wagner (1958) found no significant superiority in the production of attitude change for a message with high-quality evidence over a message including either no evidence or low-quality evidence. All of these experiments presented three or four forms of a persuasive communication to three or more experimental audiences. In none of the tests was there found any significant differences in attitude shift among the three or more forms.

The McCroskey Studies

James McCroskey of the University of West Virginia is responsible for one of the most comprehensive set of investigations concerning the use of evidence in persuasive communications. In a detailed summary of evidence effects (1969), he noted that previous evidence research had produced no definitive answers concerning the effects of evidence on attitude change. To provide some of these answers, he set out to conduct a number of related experiments to explore evidence.

McCroskey suspected that a number of variables interacted with evidence in producing either attitude change or resulting source credibility. These variables include source credibility, credibility of sources of evidence, delivery and medium of presentation, and prior knowledge of the audience of the evidence presented. McCroskey defined credibility as "perceived authoritativeness and character as measured by either Likert or semantic differential instruments" (1969, p. 171). In other words, only qualification-expertness and safety-trustworthiness were included in his definition of credibility.

Credibility and evidence.   The first variable that McCroskey suspected of interacting with evidence in the production of attitude change was source credibility. Specifically, he hypothesized that a message with evidence would be more successful than one without evidence when credibility was low, but that evidence would have no effect when credibility was high. McCroskey's hypothesis seems logical. First, the use of opinions or facts attributed to a source other than the speaker is a direct attempt to enhance the speaker's credibility. When the speaker's credibility is already high, bringing in even more credibility to bear on the case may be unnecessary. In short, there may be a point beyond which increasing credibility does not increase attitude change. Second, the *RSO* (congruity model) predicts that the greater the inconsistency between attitude toward source and attitude toward concept, the greater the pressure to change attitude. When the source's credibility is initially high, the fact that other high-credibility sources are in agreement is consistent and, thus, unlikely to have much effect on the source's credibility. The initially low-credibility source, on the other hand, has much to gain in credibility by demonstrating that high-credibility sources agree. In short, the initially high-credibility source has little to gain from evidence, and the low-credibility source may increase credibility by citing evidence that, in turn, may increase the amount of attitude change produced. McCroskey's studies bore out these conclusions. Evidence was only differentially effective for sources that were medium to low in initial credibility.

Traditional theory insists that for evidence to have a favorable impact on an audience it must come from sources the audience accepts as credible. Because of some conflicting results across topics in two earlier McCroskey studies, he suspected that evidence included in the messages employed may not have been the best available. Several writers have asserted that unbiased evidence is better than biased evidence, and that reluctant evidence (a biased source testifying against what appears to be his or her interest) is the best of all. Therefore, McCroskey conducted four more studies but found no support for this theory. In each study, biased sources were perceived to be less credible than unbiased or reluctant sources, but unbiased sources were found regularly to be more credible than reluctant sources.

Delivery and evidence.   McCroskey found in two earlier studies relating to the effects of evidence on attitude change and perceived source credibility that his results were conflicting across topics when the message was attributed to a moderate-to-low-credibility source. In both of these studies evidence had its predicted effect when the message topic was federal control of education, but in neither study did evidence have its predicted effect when the topic was capital punishment. Postexperiment interviews indicated that the receivers perceived the delivery of the speaker on federal control of education to be very good, but the receivers perceived the delivery of the speaker on capital punishment to be dull and monotonous. Therefore, McCroskey suspected the quality of presentation of a message to be a variable that could interact with evidence usage and, in turn, could produce the conflicting findings across topics.

Delivery long has been thought to be a significant variable in oral communication. Poor delivery theoretically distracts from the content of the message by drawing the attention of the audience to poor delivery characteristics and by reducing the clarity of the message. Because poor delivery might cause an audience to miss evidence as it is presented by causing them to attend to something else, and because it might prevent the audience from clearly understanding evidence they do hear, poor delivery could interact with evidence usage in persuasive communication.

With this idea in mind McCroskey conducted two more studies to test the hypothesis that inclusion of evidence in a persuasive speech increases attitude change and perceived credibility when the speech is well delivered, but it has no effect on either attitude change or credibility when it is poorly delivered. Both studies found support for this hypothesis. The first study showed that greater attitude change and higher perceived credibility were produced by the condition that included evidence and good delivery than any of the other three conditions that were used. The second study manipulated four variables, namely, evidence, delivery, initial credibility, and media of presentation. The results indicated that inclusion of evidence increased immediate attitude change only under conditions of good delivery accompanied by initial low credibility. Results were consistent across media of transmission that included audio-tape and video-tape.

The results of these two studies, taken together, support the conclusion that poor delivery can inhibit the effect of evidence on immediate attitude change, but it does not inhibit its effect on credibility. Because the results of these studies were consistent for live, audio-taped, and video-taped speakers, McCroskey had no reason to believe that the medium of presentation was related to the effect of evidence in persuasive communication.

Novelty of evidence. Because of the conflicting findings across topics mentioned in the two previous sections, McCroskey also considered another variable (prior familiarity of the audience with the evidence cited by the speaker) as possessing the capability of interacting with evidence in producing attitude change. In the post-experiment interviews he found that the evidence cited by the speaker of capital punishment was old hat. On the other hand, the evidence cited by the speaker of federal control of education was one of interest and surprise at what was described by several subjects as the "shocking facts."

Therefore, McCroskey conducted a study to test whether presenting evidence to people who previously have been exposed to that evidence will have any effect on either attitude change or credibility, and whether presenting the same evidence to people who are not familiar with it will significantly increase attitude change and credibility if the message is initially from a medium-to-low credibility source.

The results of the study were precisely predicted by the hypothesis. Moreover, the results indicated that evidence must be new to the audience before it can have an impact on their immediate attitude change or their perception of the message source. This, of course, is what would be predicted by the model presented in Chapter 6. Old evidence has already entered the cognitive system of the receiver. If it had created tension, that tension would have already been resolved or defense mechanisms constructed to avoid the recurrence of the tension. The representation of that evidence to the receiver would, therefore, have no effect.

Long-term effects.   McCroskey also examined long-term effects to see if evidence had any effect on sustained attitude change. Most of the studies were for periods up to seven weeks. In four out of five cases the inclusion of evidence was found to increase significantly the amount of attitude change sustained over time. In the fifth case, the effect was present, but it did not achieve statistical significance. No interactions between evidence usage and other communication variables were found relating to sustained attitude change.

McCroskey did not explain this sustained effect. Because all the messages produced significant immediate attitude change, one possible explanation is that evidence may interfere with the process of selective recall. The evidence included in the experimental messages in the studies that measured sustained effect was, for the most part, quite vivid and memorable. Such material may have been more memorable than other elements of the messages. Whether less striking evidence would have a similar impact is not known.

McCroskey listed six generalizations concerning the effect of evidence in persuasive communication. These generalizations were obtained from his research as well as other studies conducted prior to his:

1. Including good evidence has little, if any, impact on immediate audience attitude change or source credibility if the source of the message is initially perceived to be high-credible.
2. Including good evidence has little, if any, impact on immediate audience attitude change if the message is delivered poorly.
3. Including good evidence has little, if any, impact on immediate audience attitude change or source credibility if the audience is familiar with the evidence prior to exposure to the source's message.
4. Including good evidence may significantly increase immediate audience attitude change and source credibility when the source is initially perceived to be moderate-to-low credible, when the message is well delivered, and when the audience has little or no prior familiarity with the evidence included or similar evidence.

5. Including good evidence may significantly increase sustained attitude change regardless of the source's initial credibility, the quality of the delivery of the message, or the medium by which the message is transmitted.

6. The medium of transmission of a message has little, if any, effect on the functioning of evidence in persuasive communication. (McCrosky 1969, pp. 175–176)

More Recent Research on Evidence

What has been done to explore further the effects of evidence since McCroskey completed his research program? A number of researchers have explored some specific variables that give us more information on this interesting problem.

How does evidence work? This may seem like an unreasonable question, but most researchers are not at all sure exactly how evidence works. Although Cathcart (1955), Bostrom and Tucker (1969), and Kline (1969) demonstrated relationships between the use of evidence and subsequent attitude change, the relationship is not a simple one. Whitehead, (1971), for example, failed to find a significant difference between evidence attributed to authority and evidence simply introduced as part of the speakers' own knowledge. Harte (1976) failed to find differences between evidence-no-evidence conditions, but he did find some differences between topics. McCroskey (1970) tested whether evidence would be an inhibitor of counterpersuasion, and showed that evidence did work in this fashion as well.

How do we explain these findings? The answer will not be a simple one. Part of the explanation might lie in the interaction of evidence and credibility of the source, but once again, the research findings are somewhat equivocal. You will remember that Cathcart (1955) and Bostrom and Tucker (1969) showed that the use of evidence attributed to qualified authorities was more effective than unqualified assertions, whereas Ostermeier (1967) and Whitehead (1971) found no such relationship. In an attempt to solve some of these difficulties, Florence (1975) designed an interesting study in which he was able to demonstrate that evidence's effects are principally in the belief system, and that we might need to distinguish between beliefs and attitudes in examining evidence effects. Florence's model is discussed more fully in Chapter 6 (p. 113). Some evidence is aimed toward beliefs and some is aimed toward specific behavior in this model. However, King and Sereno (1973) found little difference between belief messages and value messages.

Games receivers play. Another interesting explanation of evidence is proposed by Collins (1970) and Harte (1976). Collins views the communication situation from the standpoint of five broad theoretical principles that he calls games receivers may play. These games were hypothesized to affect credibility. They are the problem-solving game, the consistency game, the identity game, the economic game, and the authority game. We may not agree with Collins' use of the term game to describe the source-receiver interaction, but his categories may be helpful in studying evidence.

According to Collins, when an individual is playing the problem-solving game, the goal is to get truthful, factually correct information that is relevant to the problem. In this framework, evidence may assume the role ascribed to it by traditional theory, that is, the chief material of proof. A receiver playing the problem-solving game would presumably be interested in the extent to which a persuader supports the message. Credibility and other factors are used in the problem-solving game only insofar as they aid decision-making. Information from some sources is more useful and more likely to be correct than information from other sources.

An individual playing the consistency game, on the other hand, operates on the premise that, as Collins put it, "good guys are supposed to say good and useful things and bad guys are supposed to be inept and wrong." Thus, for such persons the credibility of the communicator may overshadow the evidence or lack of it. The high-credibility source is persuasive regardless of the presence of evidence. If the source is not credible, then evidence cannot help. As Anderson and Andersen (1980) point out, "It seems possible that the source's constant reliance on external sources may make him seem less knowledgeable—and hence, lower his perceived ethos." Two of the studies mentioned earlier, Bostrom and Tucker (1969) and Ostermeier (1967) also suggest this. In any case, the player of the consistency game is more influenced by what a speaker's evidence or lack of it says rather than how well the evidence proves the speaker's contentions. Source-evidence interaction takes place during the problem-solving game, of course, but such interaction is at the heart of the consistency game.

When receivers change their attitudes in order to become more closely allied with a positive reference group or individual, they are playing the identity game. Within this framework evidence may be of little value to the communication except, perhaps, insofar as the evidence serves to make the source a more attractive object of identification. Similarly, evidence may be of little value to the source when the auditors are engaged in either the economic game or the authority game. Attitude change results from the economic game because the communicator is able to reward compliance and punish resistance. In the authority game, attitude change is produced by communicators who, in the view of the audience, are legitimately able to prescribe behaviors and opinions. Elected or appointed officials and leaders, for example, may wield influence in this manner. Evidence, thus, would be unnecessary when auditors are engaged in either the economic or authority games. Indeed, the presentation of evidence may be detrimental in that it might suggest to auditors that the source is willing to exercise his power or authority.

Thus, Collins' analysis suggests that in some communicative situations evidence may be of little value, in others it may be useful but for widely varying reasons, and in still others its employment may be counterproductive. The analysis does not suggest which game an auditor or group of auditors might play at a given time, but several variables would appear to govern that choice. Personality factors of the receiver, the nature of the communication source, the structure of the persuasive message, and the communication channel are but a few of the factors likely to influence whether one game will predominate over another.

Collins' games are similar to Kelman's classifications of influence (1961) and

French and Raven's notions about power (1962). The various types of credibility factors discussed in Chapter 4 also relate importantly to the games proposed by Collins.

To test these game notions, Harte (1976) investigated the effect of the communication topic and receiver attitudes toward the use of evidence. Harte selected two topics, British royalty (neutral) and a balanced U.S. budget (favorable). Two versions of a message for each topic were constructed, one with maximum evidence and another with none. The minimal evidence versions of the messages were created by systematically omitting evidence statements from the original maximal evidence versions. Harte found that the receiver's initial attitudes influenced the way in which evidence affects attitude change. When receiver attitudes were extreme, evidence produced significantly greater long-term (but not immediate) attitude change regardless of the initial credibility of the source. But this was not the case when the receiver's attitudes were initially neutral. When receivers held initially neutral attitudes the inclusion of evidence in the message produced no significant persuasive advantage either immediately following or three weeks following exposure to the message. Thus, this study seems to suggest that the use of evidence may aid long-term attitude change regardless of the initial credibility of the source and particularly if the auditors hold initially extreme attitudes. In the language of the game analysis, then, auditors with initially extreme attitudes appeared to be playing a different game at the end of three weeks than auditors with initially neutral attitudes.

Collins' analysis may help to explain why evidence was observed to occasionally have negative immediate effects during this investigation. Though not statistically significant, the finding that evidence may be detrimental to attitude change is somewhat novel. McCroskey (1969), for example, was emphatic in noting that in none of his studies was evidence ever observed to *decrease* attitude change. This was consistently the case in the McCroskey investigations, but not in the Harte study.

The results of the Harte study, then, suggest that the nature of the communication topic may be significantly related to evidence effectiveness, and perhaps to the process of attitude change (or game) employed by auditors.

Probative potential.   Probative potential is the term used by Dale Hample (1977, 1978) to define the power of evidence, or its strength. Sometimes evidence works and sometimes it does not. Hample has developed a method for measuring the basic power of relative evidential structures. He shows that this power can be one of the most important predictors of attitude change in a persuasive situation. He has refined this concept of evidence into a fairly sophisticated theory of argument (Hample, 1979) and has demonstrated the vital part evidence plays in argument. Probative power may be a more descriptive term for what Wall (1972) termed more simply evidential attitudes. Wall demonstrated that much of what we think of as evidence must be related to what receivers think about the source of the evidence.

Hample has cast his theoretical predictions into a well-developed mathematical scheme, but he has observed that Wyer's model of averaging characteristics (1974) fits his data slightly better than weighing units "probabatively" (Hample, 1981).

The overall picture about evidence is far from clear. Almost everyone seems convinced that evidence is necessary for persuasion. We have seen, however, that this simple statement is not true; evidence may or may not be effective, depending on what kinds of communicative tasks are involved.

FEAR APPEALS

Now that we have examined some of the theories of evidence, let us look at another specific issue that has been of great concern to researchers in persuasion, that of fear appeals. When one is motivating the receiver, how intense should the message be? It would seem logical to state that a message that used a little threat, that is, fear appeal, would be more effective than one that did not. Motivational factors play a prominent role in attitude change. The amount of tension present in the system will determine how much change is needed to achieve comfort, but there are a number of methodological problems in using fear-arousing communications (Higbee, 1969; Leventhal, 1970). This problem, as others, has proved to be a complex one.

The first attempt to study fear in persuasive situations was that of Janis and Feshbach (1953). They concluded that fear appeals actually inhibited persuasion. These results were confirmed in a later study (Janis and Terwilliger, 1962). These researchers concluded that high fear appeals led to receivers forming defenses against thinking about the message, and as a result, a fear-arousing message actually produces less effect than a milder message. More recently, however, Insko, Arkoff, and Insko (1965), Leventhal and Niles (1965), and Leventhal, Watts, and Pagano (1967) showed fear appeals to be effective. How can these conflicting findings be resolved? Typical attempts to answer this question have centered on the other variables present in the communicative interaction. Let us look at a few of these.

The importance of the topic is one logical factor that we might examine. Sereno's studies (Sereno, 1968, Sereno and Bodaken, 1972) suggest that involvement is crucial to the result of a persuasive message. Berkowitz and Cottingham (1960) and Leventhal and Niles (1964) predicted that the topic of the persuasive message interacts with fear arousal. In other words, the more important the topic was to the receiver, the less effective a fear appeal was for that receiver. These researchers suggested that the principal explanation for these results was simply higher arousal in the receivers who deemed the topic important, thus inhibiting processing of the message. Involvement effects (Sherif, Sherif, and Nebergall, 1965), however, would seem to explain these data better.

After fear is aroused, it would seem logical that the source would attempt to show that adopting the recommendations in the message would reduce the receiver's fear. Cope and Richardson (1972) showed that fear appeals *with* reassuring recommendations are much more effective than fear appeals without the reassurance. But Dabbs and Leventhal (1966) and Moltz and Thistlethwaite (1955) found that these reassuring recommendations did reduce anxiety but did not necessarily produce the attitude change recommended in the communication.

The nature of the receiver may play an important part in the way fear appeals are processed. We will examine a great many receiver characteristics in the next chapter. However, fear appeals ought logically to be related to the receivers' self esteem. Leventhal and Perloe (1962) found that persons high in self-esteem were more influenced by optimistic communications, and persons low in self-esteem were more influenced by threatening communications. Dabbs and Leventhal (1966) found that high-esteem persons were more influenced by high-threat communications, and low-esteem persons were more persuaded by low-threat communications. This seems consistent with the hypothesis advanced by Janis and Feshbach, which asserts that too much anxiety inhibits attitude change by creating cognitive dysfunctions.

Probably the most useful explanation of the role of fear appeals was provided by Hewgill and Miller (1965), who studied the interaction of fear appeals and credibility. They found that high-credibility sources were able to utilize fear appeals, whereas low-credibility sources were not. In other words, fear appeals were effective if and only if the source was credible. Hewgill and Miller's finding explains all of the other contradictory data about fear appeals: when a source is not sufficiently credible, there is probably only so much motive that the source can provide for the receivers. When the message is fear producing, it is easier to tune out the message than it is to change attitudes. With a high-credibility source, however, this effect cannot take place.

MISCELLANEOUS MESSAGE CHARACTERISTICS

Let us now look at some of the characteristics of messages that do not fit neatly into the two categories above.

Logical Content of Messages

Many writers would like to characterize messages as emotional and logical. A fear appeal is one example of an emotional message, but others would be appeals to self-interest, to chauvinistic motives, and the like. A logical message, on the other hand, would be more in line with the prescriptive view of evidence mentioned earlier in this chapter. Scott and Hurt (1978) approached this problem in an interesting fashion, defining *logical* as a belief-producing message and emotional as a message that expresses a relationship between emotional feelings and cognitive categories. They found that homophilious sources (persons who were perceived as belonging to the ethnic, social, and geographic groups similar to the receivers) were more effective when they used emotional messages. On the other hand, heterophil- ious sources (those who were perceived as ethnically, socially, or geographically different from the receiver) did better when they used logical messages. You will probably remember that homophily was one of the characteristics in defining sources high in normative-identificatory source credibility in Chapter 4. In other words, normative-identificatory credibility makes logical message content superfluous.

This study is useful, in that it not only distinguishes between types of source credibility, but further distinguishes types of attitude change requested in the message. Beliefs as defined by these researchers involve only perceptual and linguis- tic responses, whereas emotional attitudes add affective responses as well. You may wish to review these categories in Chapter 3.

Supportive or Refutational Material

Burgoon and Chase (1973) examined the interaction between supportive material and language intensity on the effectiveness of a message aimed at inducing resistance to persuasion. They found that with supportive material, it was better to have low language intensity, and that with refutational material, it was better to have high language intensity. Both high and low intensity were better than moder- ate intensity. Supportive material was that kind of evidence that bolstered the persuader's conclusion, whereas refutational material was that which attacked the opposite point of view. This study is useful if one does have an opponent in the persuasive task or if there is a clear-cut opposite point of view, such as the dispute between the evolutionists and the creationists. However, it does not answer the main question about which material to use. If one is to use supportive material, high language intensity is probably not the best choice.

Humor in Persuasion

Many times humor is recommended as an indispensable part of communica- tion. Everyone likes to laugh, and it would seem logical that if an audience is pleased by the humorous content of a message, then the message ought to be more persuasive. Charles Gruner (1965) attempted to measure the effect of a satiric speech about censorship, but he found that the satire had little or no effect on attitudes about censorship. Gruner found that the receivers involved had not perceived the message as a persuasive attempt, but had only evaluated it as humor. He then tried alerting receivers to the persuasive purpose of satire and found that receivers whose attitudes were not intense about the topic were indeed affected by the humor. In a later study (1967), Gruner examined the effects of two columns by a nationally syndicated humorist, Art Buchwald. Gruner found that when the read- ers were told initially that the columns were by Buchwald and were further reminded of Buchwald's purpose, then the columns were effective. When individ- uals read the columns without this cueing, no attitude change took place.

Gruner (1970) also attempted to see if humor would enhance the effects of informative communication. No effects were observed. More recently, Munn and Gruner (1981) studied the effects of "sick" jokes and found that they had little effect on the receiver's evaluation of the source's credibility. Chang and Gruner (1981) found that self-deprecating humor was effective for high-credibility sources only.

All in all, the effects of humor are problematical. It may well be that receivers are affected by humor in persuasive communication, but the research evidence is equivocal. Persuaders ought to consider carefully before humor is used as a persuasive device.

Self-Esteem Messages

Spillman (1979) constructed messages that contained attacks on the receivers' self-esteem. In her study, she designed messages that asked undergraduates at the University of Utah to participate in activities to improve minority relationships on campus. The attack on self-esteem took the form of asserting that Utah students were far behind other campuses on this issue, and were, in fact, bigoted. This message was more effective than a values-comparison message alone or than a combination of the two. The receivers' self-esteem was not affected by the message content. This factor may not be extremely useful in most persuasive interactions, but if the source has some idea about the possible self-esteem of the potential audience, it may be worth using.

Importance of Content to Receiver

Chaiken (1980) examined the effects produced by messages that contained either two or six arguments. When receivers felt that the subject had consequences for them, then the messages with the higher number of arguments produced more change for an unliked source, but not for a liked source. Chaiken calls this importance involvement, but in view of the more precise way in which involvement has been used in past research (Sherif, Sherif, and Nebergall, 1965; Sereno, 1968; Sereno and Bodaken 1972), the word *importance* is much more descriptive. Chaiken's finding is similar to that of Luchock and McCroskey (1978), which we will discuss below under Defective Evidence.

Self-Description by the Persuader

Often a source may illustrate a message by slipping in hints to the audience about personal experiences, specific credibility references, and so on. For example, a political candidate may say, "When I was head of the CIA, I found that . . ." and it does seem to make sense. If the audience does not know that you know about the topic, then you should let them know why you are qualified to speak on this topic. Ostermeier (1967) found that reference to personal experience on an issue was highly persuasive, and Wheeless (1973) found the same effect. In addition, Wheeless discovered that the lack of explicit references helped a low-credibility source. Mills (1977) discovered that when another person sponsors a speaker, then higher credibility results, but evidence in the situation does not produce high credibility. So perhaps a persuader is better off using the self-referential technique.

Defective Evidence

We have spoken a good deal about the various types of evidence, but we have not examined the use of evidence that has some logical or reasonable defect. As we observed earlier in this chapter, traditional thinking about persuasion asserts that there is a right and wrong way to persuade. But what happens when a source uses the wrong method?

In an interesting study by Luchock and McCroskey (1978), defective evidence was found to interfere with subsequent attitude change. A low-credibility source was helped by the inclusion of good evidence, but a high-credibility source was not significantly aided by the inclusion of good evidence. For the high-credibility source, bad evidence was not significantly different from good evidence. This seems to indicate that if one is credible, one can get away with irrelevant and poor evidence in persuasion. This, of course, has significant ethical implications.

SUMMARY

The raw materials of a persuasive message may well be the content or the materials utilized. Typically this has been called evidence. Early studies of evidence in persuasive communication were equivocal in their findings. The McCroskey studies detailed a number of significant finding concerning evidence:

1. Including good evidence has little, if any, impact on immediate audience attitude change or source credibility if the source of the message is initially perceived to be highly credible.
2. Including good evidence has little, if any, impact on immediate audience attitude change if the message is delivered poorly.
3. Including good evidence has little, if any, impact on immediate audience attitude change or source credibility if the audience is familiar with the evidence prior to exposure to the source's message.
4. Including good evidence may significantly increase immediate audience attitude change and source credibility when the source is initially perceived to be moderate-to-low credible, when the message is well delivered, and when the audience has little or no prior familiarity with the evidence included or similar evidence.
5. Including good evidence may significantly increase sustained attitude change regardless of the source's initial credibility, the quality of the delivery of the message, or the medium by which the message is transmitted.
6. The medium of transmission of a message has little, if any, effect on the functioning of evidence in persuasive communication (McCroskey, 1969, pp. 175–176).

Evidence can also be examined from the point of view of the games receivers play and probative potential.

Fear appeals are a particularly interesting form of persuasive content. Early research concluded that high fear appeals resulted in receivers forming defenses against the fear message. However, high-credibility sources were effective in using fear appeals.

Many other aspects of material have been studied. Most conclude that message content is too important a factor to be ignored.

QUESTIONS FOR FURTHER STUDY

1. Consider a persuader who uses Ostermeier's intrinsic credibility only. Does this convince you? Why or why not?
2. Have you been aware of conservation messages designed to get you to conserve energy? Would you classify these as fear appeals?
3. Do you know anyone who has been warned by a physician to lose weight (stop smoking, exercise)? What kind of evidence did the doctor use?
4. How do you react to scare messages?
5. Visit a university debate tournament or a practice session. How does the evidence used convince you?
6. What system of evidence does this book use? Is it convincing?

SUGGESTIONS FOR FURTHER READING

BOSTROM, R. & TUCKER, R.   Evidence, personality and attitude change. *Speech Monographs*, 1969, *36*, 22-27.

COLLINS, B.   *Social psychology*. Menlo Park, California: Addison-Wesley, 1970.

GRUNER, C.   Editorial satire as persuasion. *Journalism Quarterly*, 1967, *44*, 727-730.

HAMPLE, D.   Testing a model of value argument and evidence. *Communication Monographs*, 1977, *44*, 106-120.

HEWGILL, M. & MILLER, G.   Source credibility and response to fear-arousing communications. *Speech Monographs*, 1965, *32*, 95-101.

JANIS, I. & FESHBACH, S.   Effects of fear-arousing communications. *Journal of Abnormal and Social Psychology*, 1953, *48*, 78-92.

CHAPTER NINE
THE MESSAGE II: LANGUAGE

In 1893, William Jennings Bryan spoke to the U.S. Congress about those who are enterprising enough to start businesses and produce wealth. According to Bryan, the producer of wealth "goes forth into a night illuminated by no star; he embarks on a sea whose farther shore no mariner may find; he travels on a desert where the everlasting mirage makes his disappointment a thousandfold more keen" (Wood, 1961). Bryan, of course, did not mean that enterpreneurs actually made these impressive journeys; he wanted to say that people in business did not always know whether they would make money or not. Why the elaborate language? Clearly, Bryan felt that if he dressed his sentiments up in elaborate language, he would be more persuasive.

Times have changed, and Congressmen, thank goodness, do not sound like *that* anymore. But even so, we all know that language is an important aspect of communication. The right word may be more important than any other part of our messages. How does language fit into persuasion? In the past chapters, we have examined attitudes, source credibility, cognitive consistency, models of persuasion, and choice of strategy and basic content. But none of these topics helps us in the actual construction of a persuasive message.

Messages, obviously, are of extreme importance in persuasion. At times, some persuasion might occur simply because an individual who is well liked is associated with a given attitude. This endorsement phenomenon occurs often in politics and advertising. Pollsters estimated that in 1976, President Carter received at least 100,000 votes due to the endorsement of Charlie Daniels (a country singer)! However, most of us must rely on messages to implement whatever change is desired in the persuasive interaction. In the next three chapters, various approaches to messages will be discussed, namely, language, organization, and materials. Language, or the choice of words, seems to many of us to be the most basic of message elements. Let us, therefore, look at language first.

Study of language is of particular importance to communication. Michael Burgoon (Burgoon, Jones, and Stewart, 1975) has written that communication theorists have tended to borrow theories from other disciplines such as psychology and sociology (you might reexamine all the references from Chapters 3 and 4 for confirmation of Burgoon's statement). However, says Burgoon,

> ... the theories advanced by other disciplines do not seem to be adequate explanations for much human communication activity. Over the past five years, a program of message-related persuasion research has at the very least called into question specific psychological explanations of persuasion. Several studies using language intensity ... suggest that this one message variable may significantly mediate predictions of dissonance, social judgment, inoculation, incentive, and other psychological theories of attitude change. (1975, p. 241)[1]

Language may be one of the most persuasive parts of a message. The right slogan, a particular identification, an appropriate symbol can all be crucial keys to persuasion. Symbols have great power. In the late sixties, an instructor at a midwest university was prosecuted for burning the U.S. flag in a class. The instructor had intended to demonstrate that the flag as a symbol had great affective power. His arrest and the subsequent loss of his job bear eloquent testimony to his point. Symbols sometimes are the principal means by which we all achieve our identity.

How do we use symbols in persuasion? Many would say that the creation of symbolic associations is the principal means of persuasion and the most powerful. For example, if a persuasive message links energy saving with patriotism, it will certainly be much more effective than a message linking energy saving to a more mundane concept like saving money. Many successful advertisers believe that the right word (especially in the naming of a product) is more important than any other factor in merchandising. Sometimes this concern with names seems a little silly. Tubbs (1978) reports interesting discussion of the problems that General Motors executives had in implementing a decision to manufacture and market a small Cadillac. In many of their minds, the terms small and Cadillac simply could not go together!

You will remember that many theories of attitude center on words as the principal elements of the construction of attitudes. Successful persuasion, from these theoretical points of view, involves change in *meaning*, or the way in which we use our language. However we approach it, we recognize that all of us construct our messages out of words, and so the nature of words becomes of crucial importance

---

[1] M. Burgoon, S. Jones, and D. Stewart, Toward a Message-centered theory of persuasion: Three empirical investigations of language intensity. *Human Communications Research*, 1975, *1*, pp. 240–256. Reprinted by permission.

to our task. Let us, therefore, examine the role that language has in the persuasive process.

THE NATURE OF LANGUAGE

How does language work? You will remember from Chapter 2 that language has two principal aspects, overt verbal behavior and covert inner experience. The inner components are stored and consist of our vocabularies and knowledge of rules, grammar, and usage. The outer components consist of the actual behavior that each of us performs while using language. However, the nature of language is a great deal more complex than Chapter 2 indicated. Language has many functions, each of which are highly specialized. In order to understand the role that language plays in persuasion, it might be helpful to examine some of them in detail.

Charles Morris and the Theory of Signs

One of the important early theoretical analyses of language was *Signs, Language, and Behavior*, by Charles Morris (1946). In his theory, Morris focused on what he called "the theory of signs," because he felt that signifying was the principal function that language performs for us. In other words, he looked at language principally from the denotative approach. According to Morris, signs are *perceptive, evaluative*, and *prescriptive*. To understand which function a sign has at which time is crucial to the understanding of the nature of language. Morris felt that his approach would provide some much-needed precision to the way in which we think about language.

Language and perception.   The perceptive function is served by those signs that denote classes of stimuli, or percepts. When we merely identify someone by his or her name, when we designate a street by a street sign, and when the social security administration assigns us a number, we are utilizing the perceptive function of language. This enables us to relay the sense of the object without the object itself being present. You will remember that early languages contained actual pictures of objects as their symbol systems. The letter A evolved from a picture of an ox, because the word for ox sounded like "ah." Egyptian hieroglypics and Chinese ideographs (picture writing) all shared this characteristic. This function of language is performed best when it is most specific, and performed worst when it is highly abstract.

If you will review the types of behavior in Chapter 2, you will remember that percepts are an important inner response. These experiences are the basic elements that make up stored knowledge. When language is used perceptively, it acts as a joiner for these percepts to an external symbol, which serves to define and make them useful.

Consider what happens when we pick up the telephone and order a pizza from the corner pizzeria. We have a picture in our mind of many different types of pizza topping and what we like. But our knowledge of the various types of pizza topping would be of little use to us if we were not able to accompany this knowledge with words like *anchovies, green pepper,* and *pepperoni.* This perceptive function may be one of the most important functions that language has in our day-to-day use.

Once we have established the percept-language links, we can form concepts. A concept is a *class* of percepts, like *tree.* We have stored percepts that are images of fir trees, birch trees, and Christmas trees. But we can use the word *tree* without having to deal with each individual percept. As concepts get more abstract, the less accurately they can serve the perceptive function.

Language and evaluation.   Morris' second category was called the evaluative function, and it is quite different from the perceptive function. Here we react to a word in an emotional manner. Whether the word has any relationship to our actual experience is irrelevant. Sometimes the word may acquire its meaning through experience, but at other times the word itself suffices. Hardly any of us have actually known anyone that could be called a communist, but most of us have a strong reaction to the word itself.

The distinguished speech scientist, Wendell Johnson, was fond of regaling his students with a particularly interesting example of the link between symbols and affect. According to Dr. Johnson, he was serving rattlesnake meat as an hors d'ouvre at a cocktail party, and guests were trying this delicacy somewhat tentatively. One woman, however, found the snack particularly delicious, and had eaten several. Dr. Johnson found that she had not been told what the source of the meat on the snack was. On hearing that she had been eating rattlesnake, she promptly threw up. The physiological reaction of her stomach to the meat was acceptable, but the mental reaction of her mind to the meat was strongly unacceptable. In other words, the *word* made her sick, not the rattlesnake meat.

Most of the evaluations you and I make are not this extreme. However, we need to be aware of the possibilities in the evaluative functions of language. Persuaders especially will use words to trigger emotional responses.

Prescriptive functions of language.   The prescriptive function of language might seem to have great value for students of persuasion. Morris has defined this as the process that occurs when a word elicits action in and of itself. This action need not be an elaborate response; it may be only a simple response, like the salivation of Pavlov's dogs. Most of us have some of these word-action linkages in our behavioral repertoire. When language follows a prescriptive function, then words and sentences are directly linked with instrumental responses. The reaction to the Chinese couple in Figure 3–4 (p. 52) was a prescriptive use of language. Most animals have their instrumental responses directly stored in terms of percepts and perceptual links, but the distinctively human characteristic of our species is our ability to store plans in terms of language. Morris felt that might have been one of the most important developments in the evolution of humanity.

Utilitarian (Procedural) Approaches
to Language

George A. Miller and Phillip N. Johnson-Laird (1978) have proposed an entirely different approach to language, namely, the functional approach. They believe that the meaning of words lies in the operations (procedures) persons follow when they employ the word and try to understand its use by others. Their system is similar to Morris' but they have been extremely specific in the construction of a system to show how language and perception function together to form the various kinds of linguistic functions. For example, in discussing the meaning of the sentence *The book is blue*, Miller and Johnson-Laird focus, not on the truth or falsity of the sentence, but on the functions one would have to employ to determine the truth or falsity of the sentence.

This approach is fairly complex but seems to have great utility. For example, in discussing Morris' perceptual function of language, Miller and Johnson-Laird analyze the separate processes involved in perceiving objects, surfaces, colors, space, time, changing motion and events, causes and relationships. All of these lead to an extremely detailed picture of the interactions between language and perception, and a more precise theory of language.

Miller and Johnson-Laird's research has been extremely valuable. First, it presents a defensible scheme in the empiricist tradition to account for the complexities of language behavior. A popular idea recently has been that language is one of the primal mysteries because behavioristic tradition does not provide an adequate explanation for it. "No one," writes Chomsky, "has succeeded in showing why the highly specific empiricist assumptions about how knowledge is acquired should be taken seriously" (1968, p. 53). It is certainly true that language is complex, but to assert that structure alone can explain it is probably a mistake. In addition, Miller and Johnson-Laird provide a specific set of explanations that do what Chomsky asserted could not be done.

The second valuable contribution of Miller and Johnson-Laird is their stress on the *functional* approach to language. In examining these functions, we see complexities that we would have missed had we taken a simpler approach to language. Therefore, we must turn to the functions that language performs in the persuasive interaction.

How have traditional theorists treated the problem of language and persuasion? Clearly, all have felt that language was important, because style was one of the original canons of classical rhetoric. However, style has never been easy to define. Thonssen and Baird (1948), in discussing style, stated, "surely no term has been bandied about more freely or has produced a fuller measure of controversy" (1948, p. 405). Their discussion of the general utility of style in persuasion is an extremely useful one. They summarize a great deal of the important thinking in persuasion about style, which has focused on clarity, appropriateness, and level. Much thought has gone into notions of brevity, coherence, figurativeness, and ornateness, all of which could be used to analyze style.

Primarily, however, the traditional approach has been to analyze the use of language from the prescriptive point of view, that is, looking at style from an abstract standard of quality rather than effectiveness. When one begins to construct a persuasive speech, the task is not to discover what will sound pleasing to the ear or look correct but what will do the job. Much of what traditional stylists have proposed have borne up rather well under empirical tests of effectiveness.

STYLE OF THE MESSAGE

Style was one of the most important elements in ancient rhetoric. By *style* rhetoricians generally meant the kinds of word choice, composition, and general level of the message. Cicero thought that persuaders should use three general levels of style: plain, middle, and grandiloquent (Clark, 1956). The most grandiloquent should only be used when the occasion was weighty and the persuaders' purpose was lofty. Consider these words from Abraham Lincoln's second inauguaral address:

> With malice toward none; with charity for all, with firmness in the right as God gives us to see the right; let us strive on to finish the work we are in; to bind up the nation's wounds; to care for him who shall have borne the battle, and for his widow, and for his orphan—to do all which may achieve a just, and a lasting peace, among ourselves and with all nations.

This certainly would not have been so effective if Lincoln had simply said, "Let's not be so beastly to the South."

The Problem of Style

Sometimes style is so dominant in the persuasive interaction that it serves to persuade on its own merits. Brown (1972) has done a masterful job in analyzing the persuasive impact of Will Rogers, which was accomplished by the *irony* (both dramatic and Socratic) in his messages. For example, during an American foray into Nicaragua in 1927, Rogers wrote:

> I see where our bombing planes down in Nicaragua bagged fifty natives yesterday. The natives put up a pretty good fight. They threw rocks and knives at the planes, but our forces were too cunning for them. They wouldn't fly low enough to be hit. Strategy has won us many a war and may pull us through this one. (Brown, 1972, p. 186)

The irony in this message made it totally unnecessary to continue with Will Roger's opinions of assaulting helpless persons in Nicaragua. Unfortunately, most of us do not have Rogers' talent and knack for irony. But there are a number of stylistic elements that we can use in the composition of persuasive messages. Carbone (1975) studied some of these.

In this comprehensive approach to style, Carbone defined style as listenability, vocabulary diversity, human interest, realism, and verifiability. These were defined in this way:

Listenability was measured by the number of words per sentence, the average number of simple sentences, and an "easy listening" formula score, which is derived from the count of polysyllabic words.

Human Interest was measured by the average number of personal words and the average number of personal sentences.

Vocabulary Diversity was measured by the "type-token" ratio, which is calculated by dividing the number of "types" (the number of times the same word is used) by the number of "tokens" (the total number of words used). Thus, in the sentence *George is George's best friend and George's worst friend*, there are six types: *George, is, best, friend, and, worst*. There are nine tokens. The type-token ratio is 6/9 or 1:1.5.

Realism was measured by a technique called the *r* count, which is the lack of abstractness and the average number of verifiable statements.

Verifiability was measured by the average number of clear empirical sentences and the average number of verifiable sentences. This means that a sentence can have only one unambiguous meaning.

Then Carbone measured the credibility of a number of messages on qualification-expertness, safety-trustworthiness, and compliance-dynamism. She found that the high credible messages were different in *all five* categories. In other words, listenability, human interest, vocabulary diversity, realism, and verifiability all made for a more persuasive message. Unfortunately, Carbone did not analyze what happens when one element of style is good and another is bad. This kind of interaction occurs fairly often among communicators, but her study does show a strong connection between a simple style and believability of a persuasive message. Her findings were borne out by Bradac, Konsky, and Davies (1976), who found that lexical diversity led to higher message evaluation.

Brevity of the message.   Ragsdale (1968) examined speeches in which brevity of style was compared to various kinds of verbosity. Although his results were not particularly significant, in general brief speeches were more effective. The listeners in this study also responded favorably to compound sentences, perhaps because they felt that this kind of sentence indicated "good oral style."[2]

Figurative language.   Classically, language that is decorative, that is, that uses metaphorical comparisons, alliterative constructions, and balanced periods, has been recommended to the persuader. But Carbone and Ragsdale found that

---

[2]Ragsdale's term. We may not always feel that compound sentences represent good style.

simplicity seems to be more desirable. What is the role of figurative language in persuasion?

Bowers and Osborn (1966) and Reinsch (1971) tested the effect of brief metaphors on the persuasiveness of a message, and found that the metaphors were more effective than a message without them. Reinsch also found that a metaphor was more effective than a simile. Credibility, however, was not affected. In a subsequent study, Reinsch (1974) found that an extended metaphor enhanced a source's credibility. Reinsch apparently assumed that if one is credible then persuasion is bound to follow, in spite of the fact that in his earlier study attitude change occurred without credibility being higher. Jordan (1972) has constructed an interesting interpretation of metaphorical usage, arguing that metaphors are reinforcing. In other words, the combinations of the language associations may have been inherently pleasing to the receiver.

Wheeless and McCroskey (1973) examined the effects of syntactical choices within a sentence (normal order, antithesis, inversion, omission, question, repetition, and combined choices). They failed to find a difference in these variations on attitude change, credibility evaluations, or subsequent behavior. As these authors put it, the results raise doubt about the significance of these language variables in the persuasion process.

Specifity of language.   One of the most common kinds of advice students receive in writing courses is to be clear and to avoid vague language. But often we see professional persuaders deliberately avoid specific references, apparently to avoid offending audiences. Should a persuader's language be highly specific and perhaps offend some persons or be slightly vague and offend no one? Goss and Williams (1973) showed that vaguely stating issues with which an audience disagrees could positively affect a communicator's character evaluation. In other words, speakers who were vague were perceived to have a higher character than those who were specific (when they disagreed with the audience). However, this effect was not apparent on the competency ratings of the same speaker. Williams and Goss (1975) replicated these findings. Feezel (1974) also studied vagueness of the message by adding terms like "probably" or "it is possible" to messages. This softened any offensiveness the statements might have had, but at the same time, reduced the acceptance of the message. In other words, the qualifiers made the source less effective. In a more comprehensive study, Williams (1980) examined the effects of vagueness on receiver recall and agreement with the message. He found that the recall of vaguely stated disagreeable issues was significantly worse than the recall of clearly stated disagreeable issues, but unlike Feezel, Williams found that the vaguely stated communication had greater effects. Williams concluded that vagueness might be a useful tactic when disagreeable issues are going to be presented (p. 40). Feezel, of course, did not differentiate between disagreeable and agreeable issues.

Most of these interpretations of figurative language could be interpreted as evidence of source intensity in the process. Intensity is of central importance because it explains a good many characteristics simply. Let us look at intensity more closely.

INTENSITY OF LANGUAGE

You will recall in the model of persuasion in Chapter 6 that one of the central processes was the judgment of how intensely the source held the position. If this is indeed the case, then language intensity is probably one of the most important aspects of language as it affects the persuasive interaction. How do we define *intensity*? It is easy to talk about intense language; it is less easy to define it. "You are mistaken," is clearly less intense than "You are a damn fool!" but in a sense the message is also different. Probably we cannot differentiate strictly between different content and different language. Nonetheless, it is certainly possible, within reasonable limits, to perk up the language in a persuasive speech with more vivid metaphors, with more interesting expressions, and with some stronger expressions about the subject. Miller and Baseheart (1969) and Infante (1973a) defined this variable in terms of opinionation. The simplest explanation of intensity is that it enhances the inconsistency effect and creates attitude change.

Are there other evidences of the importance of intensity? Mehrley and McCroskey (1970) showed that language intensity was significantly dependent on the attitude intensity of the individuals listening to the message. A number of other studies have also shown that intensity was extremely important.

Intensity: The State of the Art

Bradac, Bowers, and Courtright (1979) constructed a comprehensive review of the important variables that affect language in communicative interactions. They suggested that language should be analyzed from the point of view of three main variables: intensity, immediacy, and diversity. These three variables form the basis for a comprehensive theoretical statement about language in all communicative settings. This theoretical background was expressed by a set of 26 generalizations about language. Of these generalizations, intensity is the principal method in which language affects attitude change. Twelve of the generalizations can be constructed to summarize the effects that language has on persuasive interactions:

1. Cognitive stress is inversely related to the language intensity of sources. In other words, the more internally stressed the source is, the less intense the language will be. This, of course, is not how the receiver is likely to perceive the source.
2. Language intensity is directly related to receiver's attributions of internality to sources. In other words, when we perceive a person using highly intense language, we tend to judge that person as being more internally motivated than externally motivated.
3. Obscenity is inversely related to the amount of attitude change produced by messages and to postcommunicative ratings of source competence.

4. Language intensity of a nonobscene type in attitudinally discrepant messages is inversely related to postcommunication ratings of source competence.

5. For highly aroused receivers, language intensity is inversely related to attitude change.

6. Language intensity and initial receiver agreement with the proposition of a message interact in the production of attitude reinforcement or change in such a way that intensity enhances the effect of attitudinally congruent messages but inhibits the effect of attitudinally incongruent messages.

7. Language intensity in an initial message that supports receiver attitude is inversely related to amount of attitude change produced by a subsequent persuasive attack of moderate intensity.

8. Language intensity and initial source credibility interact in the production of attitude change in such a way that intensity enhances the effect of credible sources but inhibits the effect of less credible sources.

9. The relationship between initial source credibility, intensity, and attitude change is strengthened when receivers are high in need for approval.

10. Language intensity and maleness interact in such a way that intensity enhances the effect of male sources but inhibits the effect of female sources.

11. Language intensity and target participations in encoding are positively related to attitude change.

12. Language intensity and initial agreement with the proposition of the message interact in the production of receiver attributions in such a way that intensity in congruent messages enhances but in discrepant messages inhibits attributions of source similarity.

These statements express the state of the art as far as language intensity and the effects of messages are related.

Other intensity effects have been demonstrated but are not as general as these 12 principles. For example, Baseheart (1971) showed that need for social approval influenced the way that language intensity was effective. Burgoon and Chase (1973) examined the interaction between supportive material and language intensity on the effectiveness of a message. They found that with supportive material, it was better to have low language intensity, and that, with refutational material, high and low intensity were better than moderate intensity. Supportive material was that kind of evidence that bolstered the persuader's conclusion, whereas refutational material attacked the reverse of that position. Chase and Kelley (1976), however, failed to replicate this effect. These authors suggest that methodological variables may have contributed to this lack of a significant finding. Burgoon and King (1974) also demonstrated the utility of intense language, especially in a situation where active participation was taking place. Burgoon, Jones, and Stewart (1975) showed an inverse relationship between intensity and receiver expectations. All of these findings illustrate the complexity of this language element.

The Special Case of Obscenity

Many of us might feel that no one should ever use obscene language in a persuasive speech, and we would be surprised if we heard much of the rhetoric of the streets in which obscene language plays an important part. Bostrom, Baseheart, and Rossiter (1973) found that obscenity lowered appraisals of speaker competence, but did not lower appraisals of dynamism or safety, and it did lower the effect of a persuasive speech. However, male listeners who heard females using sexual profanity were affected positively and strongly. We might call this a titillation effect. Mulac (1976) also found that obscenity in a message reduced an individual's evaluation of a communication source. Obscenity is often considered a good way to intensify a message, but clearly, its use should be moderate.

Rhetorical Questions

The *rhetorical* question is a question that is not designed to be answered but is posed only to elicit an immediate response. In facing a partisan crowd, a political candidate may shout "Are you ready for four more years of doubt, hesitancy, and indecision?" If the crowd shouted "Yes!" the candidate would know that the speech has not gone well.

Many persuaders use rhetorical questions, but are they really of any use? Zillman (1972) provided one of the first tests of their usefulness. He asked individuals to assign a prison sentence to a juvenile who was charged with second-degree murder. First the individuals received information about the defendant that would lead them to adopt a favorable, a neutral, or an unfavorable opinion about the defendant. Then they heard a communication from a defense attorney that used either straightforward language or rhetorical questions. The rhetorical-question version of the speech was universally more effective (i.e., receivers recommended shorter prison sentences) than the version in which the information was presented more straightforwardly. Petty, Cacioppo, and Heesacker (1981) attempted to explain this finding by studying the use of rhetorical questions in strong and weak messages, and with issues in which audience involvement was varied. These researchers felt that the rhetorical questions were effective because they allowed individuals to respond covertly and apply their own cognitive systems to the persuasive message. They found that with topics of low involvement, rhetorical questions enhanced the effectiveness of strong arguments. However, when receivers were highly involved, the opposite finding was observed. It seems clear that when the receivers are highly involved rhetorical questions should be used only with weak arguments. Petty, Cacioppo and Heesacker interpret their findings as offering support to a cognitive-response model of language. In low-involvement situations, receivers are not motivated to respond cognitively, and so the use of rhetorical questions produced a more effective message. In high-involvement situations, they hypothesized that the receivers were already motivated to think about the issues, and that the rhetorical questions were then a distraction.

Language and Resistance

Resistance to persuasion will be discussed at length in Chapter 16, but because language has some effect on this phenomenon, we might examine this briefly before we leave the topic. Infante (1973a) examined the effect of opinionated language on the forewarning effect (so called because it occurs when someone warns a receiver in advance that the source is not a good one). An intensely worded forewarning reduced the credibility and the effectiveness of a less competent source, but not of a competent source. A nonintense forewarning was more successful when it preceded a competent source. In other words, intense language is acceptable when applied to the derogation of a noncompetent source but not to a competent source.

In a similar study, Infante (1975b) examined the effectiveness of language intensity in messages that were attitudinally congruent and noncongruent with the receivers. The nonintense language reduced the persuasiveness of the congruent usage in a subsequent message. In other words, the use of less intense language in that situation served as a mild inoculation to the subsequent messages.

SUMMARY

Language was traditionally ornate in the age of oratory. Though times have changed, we can still see important language effects in eliciting responses to persuasive communication.

Language can be examined from a number of points of view. Morris explained language functions in terms of perceptive, evaluative, and prescriptive acts. Miller and Johnson-Laird have proposed a detailed empirical account of language functions that is more comprehensive and more interesting than most.

Style has been shown to have a number of effects on credibility and message evaluations. Brevity and specificity are especially helpful, but metaphors are more persuasive. They probably gain their effect from an intensification of the language. Intensity is probably the most significant linguistic variable employed in persuasion.

QUESTIONS FOR FURTHER STUDY

1. Often emotionally-filled words are used to persuade; for example, "get for your money." Cite examples of commercials using emotionally charged words.
2. Is it necessary to distinguish between connotative (emotional definitions) and denotative (dictionary definitions) meanings in order to persuade? Explain.
3. What is the functional approach as described by Miller and Johnson-Laird?
4. Discuss examples of the following types of style: dramatic, nonchalant, lazy, flippant, and casual.
5. What role does language intensity play in the process of persuasion?
6. Which works better for you, low or high language intensity? Explain.

7. Are rhetorical questions always appropriate? Why?
8. How do you feel when a serious source uses profanity? Why?

SUGGESTIONS FOR FURTHER READING

BOSTROM, R., BASEHEART, J. & ROSSITER, C.   The effects of three types of profane language in persuasive messages. *Journal of Communication*, 1973, *232*, 461–475.

BRADAC, J., BOWERS, J. & COURTWRIGHT, J.   Three language variables in communication research: intensity, immediacy, and diversity. *Human Communication Research*, 1979, *7*, 257–269.

BURGOON, M., JONES, S. & STEWART, D.   Toward a message-centered theory of persuasion: three empirical investigations of language intensity. *Human Communication Research*, 1975, *1*, 240–256.

CLARK, D.   *Rhetoric in graeco-roman education.* New York: Columbia, 1957.

MILLER, G. & JOHNSON-LAIRD, P.   *Language and perception.* Cambridge: Harvard University, 1976.

MORRIS, C.   *Signs, language, and behavior.* New York: George Braziller, 1946.

CHAPTER TEN
THE MESSAGE III: STRUCTURE

After the selection of language, the next step in message construction is to order the language and materials into a meaningful whole. A jumble of sentences in no particular order is hardly persuasive. In addition, the task of organizing messages is complicated by our feeling that some organizational plans are more persuasive than others.

You will remember that in the chapter on models, we examined the motivated sequence, which was both a model and a plan for organizing messages. When receivers are using this thought sequence, it would make sense to use a step-by-step plan of the same kind in organizing the message. Then we would be justified in beginning the message with an attention step, proceed to a need step, a satisfaction step, a visualization step, and conclude with an action step.

On the other hand, we have seen abundant evidence to convince us that many times receivers do not think that way. Even when the process is entirely rational, there are other cognitive structures that may organize the incoming information. We should, nevertheless, organize the messages we present if for no other reason than to make them look good. Is organization a waste of time? Certainly the street rhetoric of the late sixties and early seventies in the United States was persuasive, but no one would have called the speeches of H. Rap Brown organized, in any sense of the word. In this chapter we will examine organizational principles to see if they can be demonstrated to have persuasive effects.

There are a number of reasons for organizing messages. Individuals organize their own thoughts to keep them useful and available. For example, a standard lecture in the U.S. Army basic training series made use of a code word for retention. The code word was designed to help trainees to remember the six characteristics required of good intelligence reports. The word was SELDOM, which stood for Strength, Equipment, Location, Disposition, Organization, and Movement. Few trainees who remembered the code word would ever forget the six characteristics needed in the intelligence report. Similarly, a popular course in memory teaches people to associate telephone numbers and addresses to word association schemes. These devices are called mnemonic in that they train individuals to remember things. One important outcome of an organizational scheme, therefore, would be retention of the message.

Scott, Osgood, and Peterson (1979) have examined the individual differences apparent in persons from the point of view of cognitive structure. Each of us seems to use structural schemes to some degree in our storage of beliefs, percepts, language, and affects. Scott, Osgood, and Peterson define these structures as the associative methods we use to organize and integrate these mental events. In other words, we need some internal plan to keep everything straight so that we can use our knowledge. Cognitive differentiation is one of the important activities that helps us do this.

We need to be able to differentiate between beliefs about traffic, for example, and beliefs about our families. Each of these sets of beliefs has its own structure and its own rules. Scott, Osgood, and Peterson have hypothesized that this differentiation is of three types: object complexity (the number of attributes on which an object is projected), attribute precision (the number of categories into which an attribute is subdivided), and dimensionality (the number and distinctness of the attributes available) (1979, pp. 180–181). This means that these characteristics of cognitive structure are importantly related to our abilities to store and use information. Therefore, it would seem to follow that structure is one of the most important aspects of information processing, and that if structure is not provided in the message, attitude change would be importantly affected. There is abundant evidence that structure assists in retention, and there is also some (less abundant) evidence to associate structure and persuasion. Delia (1976) has suggested a close connection between individual cognitive complexity and credibility, and O'Keefe (1980) has shown partial support for an interaction between cognitive complexity and attitude change.

But our principal interest here is in the effect that structure has in the message. Structure within the receiver is of great interest, but persuaders can hardly control this phenomenon. However, the message can be organized or disorganized, and it can be organized in a number of ways. In other words, sources can attempt to supply in their messages the cognitive organization necessary for retention and use of information.

EFFECTS OF ORGANIZATION

Comprehension and Retention

In one of the earliest studies of organization, Kenneth Beighley (1952) constructed messages following the motivated sequence (Chapter 6, p. 110). Then Beighley reconstructed the same messages, mixing them up in not-quite random order. To Beighley's surprise, the organized messages produced about the same effect as the disorganized ones. In other words, Beighley could not demonstrate any differences at an acceptable level of significance. However, Bettinghaus (1980) cites another study by Beighley in which this difference was proved. The problem may have been that Beighley used cognitive units that were rather large, and which may have contained enough structure within them to enable receivers to retain the information.

Gulley and Berlo (1956) performed a fairly comprehensive analysis of structure in messages. They examined inductive and deductive form, and compared climactic, anticlimatic, and pyramidal organization. No differences in retention were observed. Each of these three cognitive schemes produced about the same amount of retention. Many have interpreted Gulley and Berlo's results as evidence that organization makes little difference. But before we arrive at that conclusion, we must remember that each of the messages in Gulley and Berlo's study were organized; their interest was to detect any differences among types of organization.

Darnell (1963) and Kissler and Lloyd (1973) demonstrated that a sequential organizational plan resulted in better retention of a message. In Darnell's study, the message was completely disorganized on a sentence-by-sentence basis. These sentences were drawn out of a hat in order to create a random pattern rather than an organized pattern. Darnell's receivers did more poorly when they heard the disorganized messages. In this study we have the first clear-cut evidence that organization causes better retention. However, you will note that Darnell had to resort to complete disorganization in order to find these differences.

Whitman and Timmis (1975) investigated the influence of verbal organizational structure and verbal organizing skills on recall of facts, ability to pattern, and ability to solve problems. Receivers were tested on their ability to solve problems. Receivers were tested on their ability to organize verbal material. Then they heard recorded communications that consisted of either a high-structure sequence or a low-structure sequence message. Whitman and Timmis found that a high-structure sequence message produced more learning than a message of lesser structure; high-ability organizers learned more from a verbal message than did organizers of lesser ability; and the degree of structure and ability to organize interacted in learning tasks that required more than the recall of specifics contained in a learning stimulus.

Some caution must be observed, however. The test used to measure organizational ability has been strongly associated with intelligence, and it may have been that the finding in Whitman and Timmis' study is more attributable to receivers' IQ than any native cognitive structure.

Petrie and Carrel (1976) also demonstrated that verbal organizational ability (in addition to initial information and listening ability) positively affected the level of listening comprehension. However, Petrie and Carrel's study suffers from some of the same problems exhibited in Whitman and Timmis's investigation, namely, they confound the ability tests with intelligence.

Spicer and Basset (1976) also investigated the effect of informative message organization on listener learning. Two message versions were utilized. The organized version consisted of a chronologically ordered description of the rules of a game called Risk. The disorganized version consisted of the rules rearranged in nonsequential fashion. Results indicated that receivers hearing the organized version of the rules achieved significantly higher scores on a subsequent learning measure than subjects hearing the disorganized version of the rules.

Daniels and Whitman (1981) examined the effects of introductions, structure, and verbal organizing ability on learning message information. They felt that introductions would provide a cognitive scheme for assisting in retention. In other words, they attempted to provide receivers with cognitive structure that would help in the sorting, storing and use of subsequent information presented. "Subsumption theory," according to Daniels and Whitman, "suggests that the 'advance organizer' should be superior in learning effects to an introduction of message main points and that the 'advance organizer' should be superior in learning effects to an introduction of message main points and that the 'advance organizer' should interact with message structure and verbal organizing ability" (1981, p. 147). However, they found no overall "advance organizer" superiority to other introduction conditions. Simple interactions, which were analyzed to interpret a significant three-way interaction on one of two independent variables, provided qualified support for first-order interaction hypotheses. These hypotheses predicted that the superiority of an advance organizer to other introduction conditions would be greater for a low-structure message than for a high-structure message and greater for low-ability subjects than for high-ability subjects. They also included a prediction that the superiority would be greater for high-ability receivers than for low-ability receivers. Analysis of serial position effects indicated primacy in recall under high-structure message conditions.

Baird (1974) found that summaries inserted into a message increased retention, and Thompson (1960) also showed that message structure could increase comprehension. All in all, it must be concluded that organization has some effect on message comprehension and retention, but that these effects are not very precise. In other words, we know that it is good to organize the message, but we certainly are not ready to say for sure which kind of organization is superior.

Attitude Change

Gulley and Berlo (1956) also investigated the effects of their various organizational types on attitude change. In the deductive condition, climactic order produced a great deal more change than did pyramidal order. Their data, however, was so variable that the differences observed could easily have been attributed to chance. However, if organization leads to retention, then it also ought to lead to attitude change, since we conclude that it is the message that changes attitudes. You will recall, however, the many evidences we have seen that sources by themselves often have a persuasive effect, and that messages may only serve to enhance this effect. Therefore, the strict cause-effect interpretation of organization–retention–attitudes-change model may have to be modified.

In an attempt to answer this question, Thomson (1960) studied organizational structure and shift of attitudes. This study varied organizational structure in oral communication while controling the listeners' level of ability in organization. The results indicated the importance of organizational structure and listeners' level of ability in organization in retention, but the measurement of the shift of opinions was inconclusive. However, on the immediate shift of opinion test, the mean shifts were considerably less for those subjects who had a relatively high ability in organization when they were exposed to an inadequately structured communication. In other words, the organization assisted in the retention of the messages but not in the subsequent attitude change. In addition, intelligent persons did not have as much attitude change as others.

In a review of the literature concerning attitude change and organization, McCroskey and Mehrley (1969) note that several research studies seemed to indicate the following low-level generalizations about message organization: (1) a disorganized message will lower the credibility of a highly credible source, (2) an organized message will increase the credibility of a moderately credible source (possibly also a less credible source). However, McCroskey and Mehrley demonstrated that both fluency and organization are important variables affecting credibility. The experimental stimuli included two versions of a speech developed by Thompson advocating a guaranteed annual wage for all industrial employees. One version of the speech was presented by a highly credible source, and the second was presented by a person whose credibility was extremely low. The organized, fluently presented persuasive message produced a significant attitude change, whereas a disorganized fluently presented message, an organized nonfluently presented message, or a disorganized nonfluently presented message did not produce an attitude change. The latter three conditions did not differ significantly from each other. Also, the source who presented an organized version of the message was perceived as more credible than the one who seemed disorganized. Also, the source who presented a fluent version of the message was perceived as more credible than the less fluent speaker.

One real contribution that we can see in McCroskey and Mehrley's study is the first really defensible theory of organization and persuasion: *organization may produce greater attitude change through a process that leads receivers to perceive sources as possessing greater credibility because of the message characteristics.* The retention of information alone is usually not enough to bring about a great deal of attitude change, but the attribution of credibility is a powerful force in persuasion. A truly interpersonal theory of persuasion is person centered, rather than message centered. Both are important, and they interact. For a possible explanation of this interaction, you might wish to review the model presented in Chapter 6.

KINDS OF ORGANIZATION

In some of the earlier studies of organization, little was discovered that would help an individual write a persuasive message. Let us examine some specific variables that do have some effects on receiver attitudes.

Logic as a Basis for Message Structure

One of the obvious patterns that one might adopt for structuring a persuasive argument is one that follows logical sequences. A logical message will generally be more persuasive than an illogical one. However, Miller (1969) has shown that people frequently accept arguments that fail the usual tests of logical acceptability. However, there is good evidence that people do have some general idea of what should be logical in the messages that they accept (Stewart, 1961). However, Bettinghaus, Miller, and Steinfatt (1970) demonstrated that logic is of greater force when it is attributed to a high-credibility source than when it is attributed to a low-credibility source. In other words, the logical structure by itself does not produce the attitude change; the logical structure plus the source credibility is responsible for the effect. This reinforces McCroskey and Mehrley's findings about the interactions of credibility and organization.

However, this finding must be tempered by persons' inability to cope with complex logical structure. (Steinfatt, Miller, and Bettinghaus 1974). When the logical content in the message gets too involved, persons simply cannot process it well. Cronen and Mihevic (1972) explain that persons listening to an illogical argument with which they are in agreement may well be supplying a logical structure of their own to justify their acceptance.

Implicit or Explicit Conclusions?

Sometimes we can have a message in which the conclusion is not explicitly stated: we might present statistics that upholds the fact that capital punishment does not deter crime, and we might assert that capital punishment ought to be abolished. In this kind of message, we are using an implicit conclusion. An explicit conclusion, on the other hand, would be something like: "You can see from all of the moral, legal, and social reasons that I have given you that capital punishment ought to be abolished." Which of these two methods is the better?

Hovland and Mandell (1952) studied this problem and found that speeches in which the conclusions were explicit were more effective. However, Thistlethwaite, deHann, and Kamenetzky (1955) demonstrated that Hovland and Mandell's data could be explained on the basis of the listener's understanding of the message, and when understanding was held constant, drawing conclusions was not as much of a factor. In an attempt to retest this problem and examine another possible influencing agent, the commitment of the listener, Stewart Tubbs (1968) designed two forms of a message about the draft. In one form, conclusions were explicitly stated. In the other form, these conclusions were not present. Tubbs found that, regardless of the audience's degree of initial commitment, the explicit conclusion was more effective.

Sometimes grammatical form can affect the impact of a persuasive message. Joanne Cantor (1979) used four different forms of a message in a door-to-door appeal for funds. They were (a) polite-imperative, (b) agreement-question, (c) information-question, and (d) statement. The polite imperative seemed to be the most effective.

Order Effects

You will remember that Gulley and Berlo examined several different kinds of arrangement: climactic, anticlimactic, and pyramidal. Although they found no significant differences among those three, one might wonder where in the presentation the strongest argument ought to go, at the beginning, the middle, or the end of the message? This question is usually discussed under the subject of order effect because it asks in what order information ought to be presented. The basis for the answer to the question will depend on whether we believe in primacy (material will be remembered best, and most effectively, if it is presented first), and recency (material will be remembered best, and most effectively, if it is presented last). In one of the earliest studies of this type, Franklin Knower (1936) provided evidence for a primacy effect. However, Hovland and others (1957) investigated the primacy-recency question with ambivalent results. They showed both primacy and recency in their studies. In an attempt to explain some of the primacy-recency problem, Rosnow and Robinson (1967) felt that material with strong inherent interest, as well as materials quite familiar to the receivers, might well show a primacy effect, whereas uninteresting topics might produce a recency effect.

Kanouse and Abelson (1967) conducted an interesting study that was designed to test the use of positive and negative statements in persuasive communication. They also varied the strength of these statements. They found no overall effects as to strength and direction of the statements, but they did discover that the order in which the statements were presented was important. When a message has a strong negative argument and a weak positive argument, it was better to put the strong negative argument first. However, when the message combined a weak negative argument and a strong positive argument, it was better to put the strong positive second. In other words, where to put strong and weak statements depended heavily on the direction of the statement, whether positive or negative. This would be an important point when considering whether to use climactic or anticlimatic order. Kanouse and Abelson's finding is typically overlooked in the examination of organization because they were principally testing language effects. A great deal of the thinking concerning primacy and recency can be resolved by looking at their results.

SUMMARY

Organization has several functions, the most important of which is to provide cognitive schemes for the retention of information. Early research provided little general support for the need for organization in messages, but later work showed specific interactions between organization and retention. However, the question of organization and its subsequent effects on attitude change is less well demonstrated. It is probably safe to say that organization helps demonstrate the credibility of sources, but that organization in and of itself may not be as persuasive as early theorists assumed.

QUESTIONS FOR FURTHER STUDY

1. Why do we use the word disorganized as criticism of persons or structures? What is implied here?
2. There are many ways of organizing communications. Is there one that you feel is inherently best? Why or why not?
3. How would the consistency model in Chapter 6 fit into a theory of organization?
4. When a source is highly credible, would you advise him or her to organize the message anyway? Why or why not?

SUGGESTIONS FOR FURTHER READING

BETTINGHAUS, E.   *Persuasive communication*. New York: Holt, Rinehart, and Winston, 1980.
BEIGHLEY, K.   The effect of four speech variables on comprehension. *Speech Monographs*, 1952, *19*, 249–258.
SCOTT, W., OSGOOD, D. & PETERSON, C.   *Cognitive structure: theory and measurement of individual differences*. New York: John Wiley and Sons, 1979.

CHAPTER ELEVEN
THE RECEIVERS: INDIVIDUAL FACTORS AFFECTING PERSUASION

Almost every theory of persuasion since Aristotle's has recognized that the individual receiver is an important variable in the persuasive process. Some persons are persuadable—the pushovers—whereas others are not. Given identical persuasive messages and situations, one person will be affected and another will not. Past theories have attributed this difference to personality, to outlook, to situation, or to any one of a number of factors. In this chapter we will examine a few of these.

PERSONALITY AND PERSUASION

There are many ways to define personality. One of the most common ways utilizes the concept of *predisposition*. Our behavior is usually thought of as influenced by *precipitation* factors and *predisposing* factors. For example, in a family crisis, one member may storm and rage, and another may drink. The crisis was the precipitating factor and the personality of the member was the predisposing factor. We would believe, then, that one kind of person drinks when confronted with a crisis and another storms and rages (Shaffer and Shoben, 1956, p. 310). There are many naive theories of personality that all of us use in evaluating others. What is personality? How is it related to communication and attitude change? How does personality differ from other individual factors?

There are a number of characteristics that form our personalities. One of the original notions of personality was proposed by Jung, who classified persons as introverted and extroverted. Many different kinds of personality types have been proposed by a number of researchers, such as ascendant-submissive, rigid-flexible, and so on. What kinds of personality factors might be related to the process of persuasion?

General Personality Factors

R.C. Adams (1972), in a comprehensive study, examined a number of standardized personality tests, in order to find what kind of empirical relationships might exist between these tests and persuasibility. He found only one factor, attentional constancy, to relate significantly to persuasibility. This certainly is not a promising beginning to a study of personality and persuasability. However, suppose that these factors were not originally designed to measure the kinds of responses we see in a persuasive interaction? After all, most personality tests are used to diagnose mental illness. Is it possible that we could define persuasibility as a personality factor of its own?

Persuasibility as Personality

In one of the original efforts of the Yale studies in attitude and communication, the topic of personality came under careful scrutiny. These researchers made the assumption that an important aspect of anyone's personality was persuasibility, and set out to study some of the factors that determined this characteristic. The result was the volume *Personality and Persuasibility* (Hovland and Janis, 1959). In addition to devising measures of persuasibility, various other personality factors were studied as they related to communication. No clear evidence was produced that would indicate a separate personality factor called persuasibility.

Authoritarianism

Linton and Graham (1959), working in the Yale group, examined the effects of authoritarianism on persuasibility. This personality factor (Adorno and others, 1950), is defined as a number of characteristics: submission, aggression, anti-intraception, power, cynicism, and projection. Linton and Graham found significant differences in changers in power and anti-intraception. The changers, in other words, admired power and toughness in persons, and were suspicious of intellectualizing and thoughtfulness. Linton and Graham conclude that this personality trait did indeed distinguish between changers and nonchangers, but unfortunately, their results could easily have occurred by chance, because a number of statistical tests were performed.[1]

---

[1] If ten statistical tests are performed, the "significance" level of the statistical test needs to indicate that the probability has been raised to ten times the original value. Linton and Graham did nine different tests but did not adjust the test values.

Dogmatism

In his seminal book *The Open and Closed Mind*, Milton Rokeach (1960) hypothesized that the ability to examine incoming data and evaluate argument is an important personality characteristic. Rokeach began his study with the general concept of authoritarianism, much like Hovland and Janis. However, Rokeach felt the the F scale, as a measure of general authoritarianism, had a pronounced bias toward right-wing authoritarianism and ignored what he called the special case of left-wing authoritarianism (1960, p. 13). Rokeach attempted to study the *structure*, not the *content* of authoritarianism. He designed his approach around cognitive behavior as a personality structure. He measured this factor in a test commonly called the dogmatism test because it measures the degree to which individuals are dogmatic. You will remember that individuals typically exhibit central-peripheral categories in their attitude structures (Chapter 3, p. 60). Rokeach hypothesized that these structures would also be closed or open depending on the nature of each individual.

We would expect this characteristic to be significantly related to persuasion because an open-minded person logically would be more persuadable than a closed-minded one. However, not all investigations of the relationships between dogmatism and persuasion show clear outcomes.

Bostrom (1964) reported that dogmatic persons tended to agree with persuasive communications more than nondogmatic persons did. Mertz, Miller, and Ballance (1966) also reported that closed-minded persons showed greater post-communicative attitude change. Hunt and Miller (1967), in a different type of study, reported results that demonstrated the same trend but were not statistically significant. In other words, these studies seem to indicate that dogmatism does not inhibit the effect of a persuasive communication but rather enhances it.

However, Jones and Dieker (1966) reported data that had exactly the opposite indication, namely, low-dogmatic persons changed more than high-dogmatic persons did. Powell (1962) discovered that low-dogmatic persons were better able to distinguish between sources and messages in persuasion, which may explain some of the findings.

In an attempt to explain some of these contradictory findings, Bostrom and Tucker (1969) hypothesized that the amount of evidence in the persuasive communication would be a logical factor to account for some of the differences. Unfortunately, they found that the expected interaction between type of evidence and the dogmatism of the receivers did not appear. Only the evidence affected the outcome, and the dogmatism of the receivers did not affect any of the results. In addition, Adams and Beatty (1979) also failed to find any real difference in resistance to persuasion that was due to dogmatism. Neal Miller (1965) demonstrated that dogmatism had only a mild inhibitory effect on attitude change, but that involvement in the subject (defined in a situation where individuals had to take an active part in the task) was much more important.

Although open-mindedness might seem to be a promising concept for the study of the interaction of personality and attitude change, little of the research demonstrates a conclusive effect. We can only conclude that the dogmatism as defined by Rokeach operates only in situations that are not as closely related to persuasion.

Need for Social Approval

Another interesting personality factor is that of need for social approval developed by Crowne and Marlow (1964). This factor seems to have a logical connection to persuasive activities, that is, if one needs the approval of others, then persuasive appeals ought to be more strongly felt. Baseheart (1971) examined this factor in persuasion and showed that opinionated statements were more effective for receivers who had high need for approval. Adams and Beatty (1977), however, failed to find a significant effect for need for social approval on attitude change; in their study, the specific persuasive strategy accounted for much more of the effect. Because these two studies have contradictory findings, we must conclude that the relationship between need for approval and persuasion, although a logical one, has not been strongly demonstrated.

Self Esteem

Spillman (1979) demonstrated that self esteem is an important audience variable, especially when the message threatens one's self-esteem. In her study, a persuasive appeal based on threatened self-esteem, which made no reference to value inconsistency, provided stronger motivation for individuals to modify their values toward consistency than did a message that directly made individuals aware of the value of inconsistency. This certainly is a logical relationship.

OTHER INDIVIDUAL DIFFERENCES

Some of the other more interesting variations in receivers are not as stable as personality factors, in that we generally believe that a personality factor is relatively constant over time and issues. Some factors of this type might be termed social attitudes rather than personality. We will examine a few of these.

Involvement

What does it mean when we say that a receiver is *involved* in a topic? Most of us would conclude that it means that a given subject is of interest, of importance, or of significance to the person. We might be interested in the outcome of a specific resolution on the floor of the United Nations, but we are really *involved* when the university starts talking about raising tuition. We all know persons who are as involved in the outcome of the U.N. debates as they are in the mythical tuition raise.

How do we decide if someone is involved, and what effect does it have on the process of persuasion?

Measuring Involvement

The initial problem in measurement is the definition of involvement. Muzafer Sherif (Sherif, Sherif, and Nebergall, 1969) decided to approach the problem by examining the *latitudes of acceptance and rejection*. These latitudes were the distances from one's own position that would be considered acceptable. For example, suppose an individual is asked to respond to the following statement: Israel has a moral right to defend herself by attacking and destroying nuclear reactors in neighboring countries. The individual's response moderately agrees with the statement. If this person would accept that a neutral response moderately agrees with the statement. If this person would accept that a neutral response or a strong agreement would also be acceptable responses, then the latitude of acceptance is somewhat large. On the other hand, if the person could accept only moderate agreement, then the latitude of acceptance would be smaller. Sherif defined involvement as the size of this latitude. A person with a wide latitude of acceptance was deemed as not involved, while a person with a narrow latitude of acceptance was considered to be highly involved.

Sereno and Mortenson (1969) demonstrated that this involvement had a strong effect on the effect of a persuasive message, and Mortenson and Sereno (1970) showed that this effect interacts with message discrepancy. Generally, involvement inhibits acceptance. You will remember that involvement was an important factor in the construction of RSO theory (Chapter 5). Sereno and Bodaken (1972) demonstrated an even more interesting effect concerning involvement, namely, the nature of the involvement also changes as a result of persuasive communication. They demonstrated that highly involved subjects (who had previously been shown to resist persuasion) actually changed the nature of their attitudes, first by decreasing their latitudes of rejection, and second by increasing their latitudes of noncommitment. This interesting finding means that a great many socio-psychological studies that have shown negative results may well have produced changes but not in the unidimensional attitude measures that the experimenters have used.

Interest vs. Involvement

Chaiken (1980) has studied involvement as it relates to information processing in a persuasive situation. In this study, he defined involvement as a topic that had consequences for the receiver. This is a poor definition of an important variable in the persuasive interaction. Chaiken probably ought to have used *interest* instead. After the careful work of Sherif and the attention to latitudes of acceptance and rejection, it is disappointing to see Chaiken misuse *involvement* in this fashion. Further, the same error is made by Petty, Cacioppo, and Heesacker (1981). This confusion is unfortunate. However, these studies report that individuals who exhibit greater *interest* in a topic resist persuasion more than those not as interested.

Attitudinal Factors

You will remember in the RSO theory model of persuasion that the initial position that receivers hold is one of the principal determinants of the amount of change that will occur in the sources and in the attitudes. But there are many other characteristics of attitude that also affect the results of persuasion.

Discrepancy of attitude. One interesting factor in an audience is how far away from the advocated position they are. Mortenson and Sereno (1970) showed that discrepancy plays an important role in the persuasive process. It is wise, according to this study, not to advocate too much.

Intensity of initial attitude. Mehrley and McCroskey (1970) showed how the initial position on an issue determines a good deal of the outcome on that issue. They found that when receivers held an initially neutral attitude towards the topic, a message containing opinionated-rejection statements was more effective than a message containing nonopinionated statements. However, when receivers were intense about the attitude, a selected message containing nonopinionated messages was more effective in producing attitude change and postcommunicative credibility measurements.

Intelligence

This is probably one of the most critical factors in the interaction of receivers and a message, but, unfortunately, it has received less attention than it deserves. Whitehead (1971), for example, found that more intelligent persons were affected more by a persuasive speech, but that the evidence introduced in the speech seemed to make little difference. Less intelligent persons gave speakers using authority-based assertions higher ratings in credibility. However, Wheeless (1971) found no significant relationship between comprehension of a message and its persuasiveness. If intelligence is a factor, then it probably operates in some other way.

Sex

Few myths are more deeply ingrained that that of the persuadable female and the hardheaded male. If women are indeed weak and compliant, then we might conclude that they are a soft touch for a persuasive message. And indeed, some researchers think that this is true. Cronkhite has written, "The evidence seems to indicate overwhelmingly that women are generally more persuasible than men" (1969, p. 36). Although it is true that many studies (you will remember the Scheidel study in Chapter 2) show women to be more persuadable, many others, such as Bostrom and Kemp (1968), fail to show such a relationship. Rosenfeld and Christie (1974), in a comprehensive attempt to solve the interrelatedness of topic, situation, and other factors in the persuasibility problem, have concluded that sex is not as important as other variables. They examine 21 different studies in which the receiver's sex had been a variable in the assessment of attitude change. They found that in nine cases, no significant differences were found. In nine other cases, females were found to be significantly more persuaded than males. In several other cases, females were more persuaded than males but the change was mitigated by some other variable, such as logic in the message. *In none of the studies were males found to be more affected by the persuasive message than the females.* Rosenfeld and Christie designed a content-free task to test persuasibility, and found that males were more susceptible! They concluded that at one time, women were indeed more susceptible to persuasion because of social constraints, but that modern women (they wrote this in 1974) were becoming less so. Their conclusions are convincing ones.

The definition of *sex* in these studies has been biological. The question of persuasibility ought to be more strongly associated with the maleness or femaleness of the person's personality than with biological classification. Sandra Bem (1974) has constructed a test of *androgyny*, which she defined as the ability to take on the viewpoint of the opposite sex. Then we could classify males as either traditionally male in attitude or as androgynous. Using this classification system, Montgomery and Burgoon (1977) examined persuasibility scores for traditional males and females as well as androgynous males and females. They found that androgyny makes a difference in males but not in females. In other words, androgynous males are more persuadable than traditionally oriented males. This is not surprising, since many of the test items of the androgyny test are involved with factors such as social sensitivity and concern for others; factors that should logically predict more change as a result of persuasive communication.

Cognitive Complexity

This interesting variable should logically make a difference in the persuasive interaction. You will remember that consistency was theorized to be affected by the complexity of individuals (O'Keefe, 1980). Cognitive complexity has generated a good deal of theoretical writing concerning the relationships between this variable and possible persuasive effects (Clark and Delia, 1977; Reardon, 1980). Theoretically, more complex persons will be able to handle inconsistency better than noncomplex persons and, thus, be less persuadable. In this respect, complexity is posited to interact exactly the same as dogmatism. However, the real evidence for any such relationship is sketchy at best.

Superstition as a System of Belief

Little systematic research is available concerning the extent to which most persons employ superstitious or nonrational belief systems. From time to time, various polling organizations present evidence that substantial numbers of citizens utilize superstition in some form or another. However, little serious research has been conducted on the nature or extent of superstitious beliefs in people generally.

One group of researchers has touched on this problem peripherally. In their study of authoritarianism, Adorno and others (1950) assumed that one of the characteristics of authoritarian persons was a belief in "superstition and stereotypy." A subscale of their authoritarianism test (the F scale) represents a rather clear antiscientific approach to human information processing.

Unfortunately, this potentially interesting variable has been largely ignored by the communication researchers who have studied the relationship of authoritarianism and the impact of messages. When Linton and Graham (above, p. 000) studied the relationships between persuasibility and authoritarianism, they eliminated the superstition and stereotypy scales from their analyses. The authoritarianism scales have fallen into general disrepute among scholars. Kirscht and Dillehay (1960, p. 130) conclude that authoritarianism as defined is a significant phenomenon, but they do not feel that the original F test can stand up as a coherent and unified set of dispositions.

Jahoda (1969) has authored a careful study of the theoretical issues involved in superstition. He sees the phenomenon as a natural outcome of the desire for certainty. Superstition often provides an answer to a social or political problem that would otherwise be unanswered. Jahoda reports two sets of historical data about the frequency of superstitious beliefs. These figures indicate that as many as 40 percent of the populations sampled entertain superstitious beliefs of one kind or another.

Logically a message containing more evidence from authoritative sources should have greater impact than a message without authoritative sources and without evidence. Many studies have shown, however that the addition of evidence does not always produce greater effect.

THE PHYSIOLOGY OF
PERSUASION

An area in persuasion that we often overlook is the physiological condition of the receiver. We react very differently to persuasive communication when we are tired, hungry, or our physiology is altered for some reason. To illustrate how this might happen, let us look at a representative study.

Janis, Kaye, and Kirschner (1965) asked individuals to read a message designed to change attitudes concerning the future of three-dimensional movies. The readers were divided into two groups: one was served soft drinks and some peanuts while reading the message; the other group received no refreshment. The group that ate and read exhibited more attitude change than did the other group. Janis and his associates attributed this effect to a more positive attitude toward the experimenter when the food was present, which these authors assume would create a differential effect. Insko (1967) attributes the differences in the two groups to a reinforcing effect, but he does not specify what was supposedly reinforced. Learning theories usually state that reinforcement operates upon a response being performed. Once reinforced, the response is likely to appear more often. In this experiment, the subjects were reading and conceivably could have been responding either positively or negatively. No opportunities for responses (at least overt ones) were present in the experiment. Why, then, would eating a small snack create the additional attitude change?

Perhaps the answer can be found in some theoretical explanation other than reinforcement. In discussing contemporary attitude theories, Fishbein and Azjen (1975) list (in addition to learning or reinforcement theories) expectancy-value theories, consistency theories, and attribution theories. The expectancy-value theories are informational in nature and predict that attitudes change when information changes concerning the potential utility of the attitude to the receiver. It is difficult to see how a bottle of soda and a package of peanuts would add to these portions of the respondents' information systems. Consistency theories might explain the effect, if we can assume that Janis, Kaye, and Kirschner are correct and the receivers attributed more positive affect to the experimenters as the result of the food, and that the experimenters were perceived as the source of the persuasive messages. Neither of these assumptions can be made in this case, at least not with any confidence. The attribution theories hold that external cues cause us to attribute attitudes to ourselves and to others. Bem's example (1967) of the use of external cues as measures of internal states cites the case of an individual who, when asked, "Do you like brown bread?" responds, "I guess I do, I'm always eating it." Receivers in the Janis, Kaye, and Kirschner study might have asked themselves "Do you find this message convincing?" and then answered "I guess it is, I feel pleasant and relaxed here."

All in all, the theories of attribution, reinforcement, consistency, and expectancy-value do not provide a really satisfactory explanation of the phenomenon of eating while reading. There are, of course, many other theories of attitude change, and we could continue to look for explanations of the Janis, Kaye and Kirschner effect from other theories, none of which seem any more satisfactory than the four discussed above. How, then do we explain this experiment?

To begin with, at least two elements were involved, one cognitive and the other physiological. Any theory that is employed to explain the findings of Janis and his associates should involve an altered physiological state. The incorporation of physiological state, communicative attempt, and resulting attitude change could result in a more general theory of communication and persuasion.

Altered physiological states can produce altered states of awareness, arousal, and methods of information processing. These states would seem to be very important in the context of persuasive communication. For the most part, however, theories of communication and persuasion have ignored the possible presence of fatigue, psychosis, pain, and the many possible states arising from the use of drugs. These inherently interesting psychological states have clear correlations in altered behavior. Why then, have most researchers ignored these variables when they study persuasion? At least part of the answer to this question lies in the way in which we think persuasion ought to work in our society.

A primarily manipulative model of persuasive communication creates some ethical problems in many persons, but these problems are minor compared with those created by the coupling of persuasion and physiological control. A manipulative model involving only words is quite different from a manipulative model involving physiological states. When we hear that a standard technique utilized by Chinese interrogators in the Korean war was to deprive the subject of food and reward him with a potato when the desired response was obtained (Schein, 1956), we are horrified. This technique seems to us to be morally equivalent to persuading someone with a blackjack. Rewards for correct behavior seem acceptable for modern childrearing, for our economic system, and even in the annual merit-review procedures of a university. However, altering the reception of a message through the use of hunger or drugs is quite distasteful to most of us. Nonetheless, the exploration of altered physiological states as they relate to attitude change is an interesting problem and should not be ignored simply because of our aversion to its use. Certainly, some segments of our society have used physiological manipulation to enhance acceptance or rejection of ideas. A popular consciousness-raising course (*EST*) involves some physical deprivation as part of the systematic teaching of self-awareness (Gorden, 1979). Participants in this program apparently find it effective.

At the roots of the problem is our strong reaction to the study of phenomena that we find unpleasant. Most of us wish to believe that behavior is not determined by extraneous forces beyond our control. Unfortunately, many forces shape our beliefs and attitudes that are out of our control and of which we may not even be aware. B.F. Skinner, who has been interested in this kind of control for many years, has repeatedly stated that studying behavioral manipulation is certainly not the same as advocating it. Control, to Skinner, is a fact of life and should be studied. As long ago as 1955 he wrote

> We cannot make wise decisions if we continue to pretend that human behavior is not controlled, or if we refuse to engage in control when valuable results might be forthcoming. Such measures weaken only ourselves, leaving the strength of science to others . . . The first step in a defense against tyranny is the fullest possible exposure of the controlling techniques. (1955, p. 15)

Reactions to Skinner's interest in control are varied but usually negative. One typical response appeared in a popular magazine when the writer admitted he knew little about psychology, but did "know something about freedom and dignity!" (Pearce, 1972).

Altered physiological states occur in persons for reasons entirely separate from persuasive attempts, and could interact with persuasive communication in interesting ways. Tranquilizers, for example, are widely used by a variety of persons, and it is usually impossible to detect their use. Tranquilizers might well influence the audience of persuasive attempts. All in all, it seems shortsighted to ignore the relationships between physiological conditions and attitude change out of fear that such study will hasten the onset of the brave new world. On the contrary, we ought to seek better understanding so that we cope with the phenomenon of persuasion in a number of widely varied circumstances.

It is often a surprise to students of communication to discover that there is a well-developed literature on the manipulation of human behavior. For example, Gottschalk (1961) explored the possible use of some of the common drugs used in psychotherapy as facilitators of police interrogations. Kubzanksy (1961) similarly speculated about how stimulus deprivation affects behavior, especially in suggestibility.

Nonetheless, most research done on the process of attitude change has been done using individuals (subjects) whose thought processes are considered normal and in situations in which central nervous system (CNS) activity will not be altered. When we examine the ordinary world, however, we see that we cannot safely assume that these conditions will prevail. Alchohol, for example, is extremely widely used; over 100 million Americans use alcohol in some form or another (Straus, 1976). Tobacco is another drug that significantly alters the CNS; over 50 million Americans use tobacco in the form of cigarettes, and these users are exposed fairly constantly to its effects.

Tranquilizers also enjoy fairly wide use, and the exact proportion of our population using them is not known. Estimates run as high as 10 million daily users of tranquilizing substances. Then when we add the users of controlled substances, epinephrines, marijuana, and other drugs, we are forced to conclude that the possibility of encountering an individual whose CNS activity has been altered by chemical means is quite high.

Other conditions significantly alter the CNS level. Fatigue, psychosis, pain, and many other physiological variants are important. A substantial portion of our population is overweight and is involved in various dieting methods. Hunger significantly affects the CNS and might affect attitude change. In short, the assumption that potential audiences for persuasive communications will have normal CNS activity is probably a naive one. On the other hand, the probability that an ordinary audience will be affected in some way by altered CNS condition seems rather high.

In the rest of this chapter, we will examine some of the factors that create alterations of the CNS, together with the possible influences of some of these effects: CNS arousal, subject awareness of this arousal, and the relationship of these factors to attitude change. Then the effect of CNS depression will be explored. Following this discussion, we will examine some of the specific causes of alterations in CNS states, such as epinephrine, caffeine, ethanol, tobacco, and other drugs. Then we will examine some of the effects of the environment, such as the presence of others, hunger, and fatigue.

Effects on Arousal

You will recall that our model of the effects of persuasive communication stems from consistency theories in which the inconsistent elements in the message are held to create a psychological state similar to drive or motivation (Festinger, 1957). Dissonant elements do not always unequivocally create physiological effects (Cronkhite, 1965), but, by and large, there is ample evidence to indicate that dissonance and arousal may be said to be similar states (Pallak and Pittman, 1972).

This would lead us to believe that arousal should have a simple effect on the process of persuasion, that is, enhanced arousal ought to lead to an enhanced attitude change, and the lack of arousal should have the opposite effect. Unfortunately, the relationship is not that simple. Two crucial elements in the process are the degree to which the individual being aroused is aware of the arousal and the source to which the arousal is attributed.

An interesting demonstration of the role of awareness and arousal was done by Schacter and Singer (1962). In an experiment in which individuals were told that the principal purpose was a test of vision, the experimenter injected the subjects with a solution of epinephrine bitartrate, a symathomimetic drug whose effects bear a marked similarity to arousal of the central nervous system. These individuals were told that they received an injection of a vitamin supplement designed to affect their vision. Some were correctly informed of the effects of epinephrine, some were not told of any effects, and a third group was misinformed, that is, they were told to expect symptoms of an entirely different nature. Then all individuals were placed in an emotion-producing condition, in which a confederate of the experimenters attempted to produce either euphoria or anger. Following the inducement, each person was asked to report his or her emotional state. Both emotions were induced, but, interestingly enough, the group that was misinformed of the possible effects of the epinephrine reported that they felt much more euphoric than the informed group. In other words, persons were more susceptible to the confederate's moods when they had no explanation of their own bodily states than when they did. In the anger inducement, persons were measured as to amount of angry behaviors present following the inducement. Again, more behaviors were present when the persons were ignorant of the possible effect of the epinephrine on their own bodily states. The attribution of the source of arousal, then, seemed to be a crucial factor in the evaluation of the situation.

In a similar experiment, Schacter and Wheeler (1962) injected persons with both epinephrine and chlorpromazine. Following an appropriate period for the drugs to take effect, they showed an amusing film to these persons and measured the number of behavioral indications of positive affect, such as smiles, laughter, and so forth. The epinephrine had produced more responses than the placebo but the responses fell short of significance. Both groups were far more stimulated than those with the chlorpromazine. The degree of amusement was interpreted to be directly related to the degree of CNS activation. Schacter (1964) sums up the results of these studies:

> Given a state of sympathetic activation, for which no immediately appropriate explanation is available, human subjects can be manipulated into states of euphoria, anger, and amusement at a movie. Varying the intensity of sympathetic activation serves to vary the intensity of variety of emotional states in both rat and human subjects. (1964, p. 69)

Often however, we are aware of CNS arousal when we experience it, and are accustomed to interpret it. But what happens when we think that we are experiencing CNS arousal even if we are not? Kerber and Coles (1978) conducted an experiment to answer this question. Subjects were led to believe that they were aroused when actually they were not. In this study, individuals were monitored on two physiological measures, heart rate and skin conductivity, while they judged the attractiveness of nude females. The heart rates were fed back so that the subjects could monitor their own responses. In one group, a false feedback gave the impression of increased CNS activity, and this false feedback produced higher rates of perceived attractiveness than did the ordinary feedback. Actual physiological measures (both heart rate and skin conductivity) had little relation to judgments. This, of course, is direct support for Bem's self-perception theory.

In a similar study, Mintz and Mills (1971) gave individuals pills containing caffeine and either told them about the true effect of the drug or described an irrelevant side-effect. All then read a fear-arousing communication. Persons who were not told the effects of the drug were significantly more persuaded than those who were informed of the drug's effects.

These studies provide support for consistency interpretations of attitude change, but whether the individuals in these studies are aware of the effective inconsistencies is not entirely clear. It may be that CNS arousal is associated with attitude change, and that a simple association is enough to explain the effect. Results of this kind seem to be fairly consistent across many kinds of CNS arousal. For example, Pittman (1975) created CNS arousal by placing subjects in a situation that appeared threatening. The threat interacted with the other elements of the dissonance-producing situation in much the same manner as did the drug induced arousals in the Schacter studies and the Mintz and Mills experiment. In other words, CNS arousal seems to be quite general in its effects, whether it is induced by epinephrine, caffeine, fear, or false feedback. If individuals are aware of the source of the arousal, then no particular effects can be attributed to the CNS. If, however, individual attribute the CNS arousal to the stimuli they have experienced, then CNS arousal will significantly affect the result in attitude change.

This process of attribution provides the first really adequate explanation of the findings of Janis and his associates mentioned earlier. The individuals experienced heightened CNS arousal as a result of the snack and could possibly have attributed it to the message. We might consider this a special case of attribution theory, or we might label it a special kind of misattribution that has cognitive consequences, especially on attitudes.

The nature of this misattribution is not always clear. Worschel and Arnold (1974) showed that arousal from other sources is easily misattributed to dissonance. This misattribution seems to be reversible. Zanna and Cooper (1974) placed subjects in situations that would create dissonance-related attitude change. Then they gave each subject a pill (a placebo) and told them that the pills would make them tense. When the pill was given, attitude change resulted. The pill did not reduce the tension, but only explained it for the participants. In a more complete study of the misattributions, Cooper, Zanna, and Taves (1978) placed persons in a forced compliance situation and varied the decision freedom in order to vary the amounts of dissonance produced. Then they gave these persons either a tranquilizer, a placebo, or an amphetamine. The placebo results are similar to other dissonance experiments because the high decision freedom resulted in more change. The effect was enhanced in the amphetamine condition and was nonexistent in the tranquilizer condition.

The effects of CNS arousal and its attribution seem consistent. Small changes in CNS states lead to rather pronounced attitudinal consequences, and the strongest of these is when the CNS change is attributed falsely to the attitudinal stimuli. Most of the studies previously cited, however, are of situations in which communication has not played a prominent part in bringing about the attitude change. Can we see the same effects in a more usual communication experiment? Harris and Jellison (1971) provide evidence that these processes apply to communicative situations. They studied the interaction of a fear-arousing communication and false feedback of CNS condition. One group of their subjects was given false feedback indicating arousal during the portion of the message in which the fear appeals was contained; then they were given false feedback indicating that the arousal was diminished during the section of the message in which the recommendations were contained. This group experienced a substantial degree of attitude change compared with the other groups in the study.

CNS arousal, then, cannot by itself be said to be a significant factor in attitude change. Only when the arousal is either created by the message or attributed to the message does arousal have an effect. In those instances, its effects are quite strong; in most cases it nearly doubled the effect of the message alone. Persuasive messages addressed to persons already experiencing some sort of CNS arousal are likely to be effective, especially if the individuals are not aware of the source of the arousal.

Effects of Depression

Depressing the CNS logically should have the reverse effect of arousal on attitude change. Some evidence for this reversal is furnished by two of the studies cited above. Schacter and Wheeler (1962) administered chlorpromazine as a blocking agent and Cooper, Zanna, and Taves (1978) used tranquilizing substances. In both studies the drug produced less attitude change than in the normal subjects. We might interpret these effects as simply the absence of arousal, that is, if arousal creates attitude change, then any tranquilizing substance merely prevents that effect.

Probably the clearest indication of the effects of CNS depression on attitude change is found in a study by Bostrom and White (1979). Their respondents were informed that they were involved in a study concerned with gathering data on the relationship between information retention and alcohol consumption, and that they might be asked to drink an alcoholic beverage. All persons completed an inventory that measured their attitudes toward three cultural truisms adapted from those employed by McGuire (1961). All were then given a large glass of a soft drink (Fresca), but some received a high alcohol dose (0.770 ml per kg body weight),

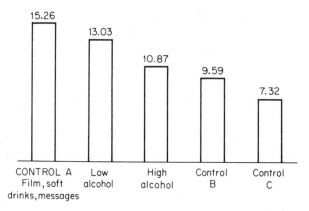

FIGURE 11-1

others a moderate dose (0.517 ml per kg), and others received none. Then all respondents viewed a film (a 20-minute animated feature concerning conformity) while they consumed their drinks.

Each person then read three messages attacking the validity of the cultural truisms. Each of these was a short, 500-word essay containing factually oriented material that attacked the truism in question. Following the essays were factual questions concerning their general sobriety and motivation level. Last, the individuals were asked to identify counterarguments, if any, that had occurred to them while reading the essays. Two additional control groups were used, one which had no drinks or movie but which read the messages, and one which only took the posttest.

The results for these groups are shown in Figure 11-1. Clearly, the presence of alcohol in the drinks had a deleterious effect on attitude change, but it is interesting to note that even the high-alcohol condition produced more attitude change (though not significantly so) than the control groups who heard the message alone. The soft drinks apparently served as the same sort of social facilitator that the drinks and the peanuts did in the Janis study, and the alcohol served to diminish the effect. No difference was observed in the number of counterarguments formed, but the same perception of their motivational levels were higher for the two alcohol groups than for the no-alcohol condition. In other words, subjects with high-alcohol dosages felt motivated but simply did not exhibit the attitude change that ought to accompany high motivation. Here we have an interesting contrast to the role of awareness in the CNS arousal states. CNS depression, at least when it is due to alcohol, produces an entirely opposite effect.

The state of the central nervous system would seem to be an extremely important factor in the determination of subsequent attitude effects arising from persuasive communications. However, the practical value of some of the conclusions might be less interesting to many of us; after all, it would be unusual to inject a receiver with epinephrine prior to hearing a persuasive speech and then tell that same receiver that the injection would be harmless so that misattribution could occur. But the use of drugs that affect the CNS is certainly not rare, as observed earlier in this chapter; it may be rarer to find individuals whose CNSs have not been affected in some way by some drug. In addition, our environment has clear effects on CNS states, and these certainly have a potential influence on the process of attitude change. If we are to include the less formal interpersonal interactions as an integral part of our study of persuasion, then the use of tobacco, alcohol, tranquilizers, and even marijuana becomes more important for the study of persuasion. In the next section, some specific substances commonly used by large segments of our population will be briefly discussed together with the possible effects that they might cause in the persuasive interaction. Following this substance inventory, specific environmental effects such as the presence of others, hunger, and sensory deprivation will also be examined.

Specific Drugs and Their Effects

Tobacco.   Although public use of tobacco is under attack by various groups, it is probably safe to say that it remains one of the most commonly used drugs in social situations and, by extension, in communicative interactions. The active agent in tobacco use is nicotine, and it is through the effects of nicotine that tobacco has its strongest effect on the CNS. Nicotine is readily absorbed through the mucous membranes, not only in the lungs, but in the oral and gastrointestinal tract as well as the skin (Goodman and Gilman, 1958). This means that cigar and pipe smokers, as well as cigarette smokers, are probably ingesting some amount of nicotine through tobacco usage. The principal method of deciding whether or not an individual is addicted seems to lie in the frequency of use and the effects of deprivation, not the method of ingestion.

What are the physiological effects of tobacco use? The U.S. Surgeon General's Report (1964) was quite specific about CNS effects. They report that smoking even one cigarette evinces strong effects: increasing heart rate, respiration, blood sugar level, and cardiac output. These symptoms are exactly the same as those experienced in emotional states (Woodworth and Schlosberg, 1958). Nesbitt (1972) found that chronic smokers are more emotional than nonsmokers, so it would seem that the relationship between smoking and CNS activity is fairly well established. However, specific effects of nicotine on the CNS depend to a degree on whether the smoker is in a state of withdrawal or satiation. Schacter (1978) gathered evidence to show that smokers who were not allowed to smoke, as well as smokers who were allowed to smoke only low-nicotine cigarettes, showed a much greater degree of irritability than did nonsmokers and smokers who were allowed as many high-nicotine cigarettes as they wished. Schacter finds that addiction is the only psychological concept that entirely explains the effect of smoking:

> Again and again, then, one finds the same pattern. Smoking does not improve the mood or calm the smoker or improve his performance when compared with the

nonsmoker. However, not smoking or insufficient nicotine makes him considerably worse on all dimensions. Given this persistent fact, how, then, to account for the fact that the smoker smokes more when he is stressed? One can, obviously, account for the generally debilitating effects of no or low nicotine by assuming the deprived smoker is in withdrawal, but this assumption alone cannot account for the effects of stress on smoking rate unless one assumes that stress in some way depletes the available supply of nicotine. (Schacter, 1978, p. 439)

Schacter goes on to demonstrate that when stress is present, the urine is acid, and when the urine is acid, more nicotine is excreted, leading to nicotine deficiency and more smoking.

In addition, tobacco affects the fashion in which information is acquired. Kleinman, Vaughan, and Christ (1973) found that smokers who had been deprived of cigarettes for 24 hours learned better on more highly meaningful tasks but did more poorly on low meaningful tasks. They explained their finding by assuming that withdrawal of nicotine created CNS arousal that facilitated performance on the easy task but retarded it on the difficult one. Anderson and Hockey (1977) found that serial learning was not affected by the presence of nicotine, but incidental memory was affected. In general, then, there seem to be at least two ways in which nicotine affects the CNS: as an immediate stimulus to CNS activity when the nicotine content of the body falls below acceptable levels, and as a depressant to the CNS in anxiety-related situations. The effects of the CNS arousal-depression should, therefore, have considerable influence on the evaluation of persuasive messages if individuals are aware of them and can attribute the CNS arousal to the effects of nicotine. If users are not aware of the effects, then they should attribute the effects to the persuasive message and, therefore, experience more attitude change.

Do smokers have a clear knowledge of the effects of smoking on different physiological measures? To determine, at least partially, the extent of such knowledge, a questionnaire was given to 97 undergraduate students at the University of Kentucky (Bostrom, 1980). Of these students, 65 classified themselves as nonsmokers or as smokers using less than five cigarettes per day. Thirty-two reported that they used more than five cigarettes per day. They were asked if the use of cigarettes raised or lowered heart rate, respiration rate, blood sugar, general emotionality, and irritability. The results are tabulated in Table 11-1. Smokers differ slightly from nonsmokers in proportion of their responses, but the discrepancies are not significant. Most smokers correctly respond that smoking raises heart rate, but only half correctly responded that smoking raises respiration rate. Only 31.2 percent of the smokers correctly identify a rise in emotionality with smoking; 37.5 percent felt that emotionality decreased; 31.2 percent did not know. A separate sample of faculty members and adults produced proportions very similar to those in Table 11-1.

Although the sample reported certainly would not meet the requirements of a national poll, it seems reasonable to assume that a substantial number of persons who use tobacco are at least unaware of a portion of the effects it produces and would fit well into the paradigm of aroused-ignorant receivers, with the subsequent enhancement of attitude change. Interestingly, a large proportion of smokers seem

TABLE 11-1 Proportions Responding to Questionnaire of Physiological Effects of Cigarettes

	PERCENT RESPONDING RAISES		PERCENT RESPONDING LOWERS		PERCENT RESPONDING DON'T KNOW	
	NON SMOKERS ($n=65$)	SMOKERS ($n=32$)	NON SMOKERS ($n=65$)	SMOKERS ($n=32$)	NON SMOKERS ($n=65$)	SMOKERS ($n=32$)
Heart rate	64.6	84.3	10.7	6.2	24.6	9.3
Respiration rate	60.0	50.0	21.5	25.0	18.4	25.0
Blood sugar	18.4	12.5	30.7	50.0	50.7	37.5
General emotionality	27.6	31.2	29.2	37.5	43.0	31.2
Irritability	35.3	31.2	29.2	50.0	35.3	18.7

Source: R. Bostrom, Altered physiological states: The central nervous system and persuasive communication. In M. Roloff and G. Miller (Eds.), *Persuasion: New directions in theory and research.* Beverly Hills: Sage, 1980. Reprinted by permission of Sage Publications.

to know that smoking increases heart rate but also feel that it reduces emotionality, which they may be identifying as stress. This is consistent with Schachter's analysis of the interaction of nicotine and stress (1978).

Caffeine. Caffeine appears in an amazing number of foods commonly consumed, and many consumers are ignorant of the specific caffeine content in most foods. An ubiquitous source of caffeine is coffee. Some individuals drink up to 20 cups daily, which is a heavy dose of caffeine in the bloodstream. Another source of caffeine is cola-type soft drinks; in some of these, the caffeine content often is the equivalent of several cups of coffee. Television ads promoting decaffeinated coffee should lead us to believe that heavy coffee drinkers might attribute their emotional state to the caffeine intake, but most soft drink consumers seem unaware of the caffeine content of the beverages.

Mintz and Mills (1971) provide the best direct evidence of the effects of caffeine. They showed that individuals who ingested caffeine but who misattributed the effects to a persuasive message exhibited much more attitude change than did individuals who ingested caffeine but attributed their arousal to the drug. Although caffeine is a CNS stimulant, Franks and his associates (1975) found that it could not counteract the depression introduced by ethanol. Thus, in terms of its cognitive effects caffeine must be described as a very mild stimulant but one whose presence will enhance attitude change, especially if the recipient of the message has no knowledge of its effect.

Cannabis. Cannabis, or marijuana, usually produces significant psychological effects. It apparently acts as a mild CNS stimulant; thus, its effects would be similar to caffeine. However, other effects usually accompany the marijuana high.

Salzman, VanderKolk, and Shader (1976) reported that marijuana increased hostility, both in verbal aggression and in reported inner feelings. Hill, Schwinn, Goodwin, and Powell (1974) found that marijuana increased sensitivity to painful and nonpainful stimuli, and reduced the general tolerance for pain.

There is some evidence of particular effects that marijuana has on cognitive functioning as well. Crockett, Klanoff, and Clark (1976) report that marijuana disrupts cognitive processes and emotional tone. Miller, McFarland, Cornett, and Brightwell (1977) found that marijuana dosages significantly decreased immediate and final free recall but only slightly influenced recognition memory. In a study to determine possible long-term effects of heavy cannabis use, Weckowitz, Collier, and Spreng (1977) studied 24 heavy users. They found evidence for more field dependence, and users had better control of attention processes than did 24 matched nonusers. The users also did slightly better on tasks designed to measure originality, cognitive flexibility, and general cognitive functioning. It is entirely possible that the 24 users differed from the nonusers in these characteristics prior to heavy cannabis use; no real causal attribution can be drawn from these data.

The effects of marijuana on the reception of a persuasive messages are problematical at best. The most salient characteristic of the use of the drug is the factor of subject awareness. In fact, Schachter (1964) suggests that whatever pleasurable sensations arise from its use are at least partially determined by the user's expectations and the socialization inherent in the situation. Therefore, it seems apparent that one principal effect on persuasion would be to diminish perceptions of arousal and to attribute these sensations to the use of the drug. Another would certainly be inattention and lack of acquisition memory (Abel, 1971). All in all, it would seem that marijuana would seriously diminish persuasibility.

Alcohol.   Most researchers agree that alcohol acts as a depressant on the CNS. Beyond this generalization, however, the effects of alcohol on cognitive tasks is less well known. A review of 41 studies involving alcohol dosage concluded that cognitive and perceptual activities are affected more than are psychomotor tasks (Levine, Kramer, and Levine, 1975). The CNS effects are not without ambiguity. Crow and Ball (1975), for example, found that alcohol dosage increased heart rates, although the effect depended on order of dosage. However, in general, alcohol dosage affects cognitive tasks rather markedly. Carpenter (1962) demonstrated that alcohol increases response latency on a variety of tasks, and Moskowitz and Burns (1973) produced this same effect on an information-processing task. Alcohol has a deleterious effect on immediate and short-term memory, but it does not seem to affect the forgeting rate as much as the learning rate (Wickelgren, 1975). Experience, or familiarity, seems to mitigate some of these effects (Jones, 1972).

McGonnel and Beach (1968) found that alcohol reduced subjects' anxiety about a 50-watt shock, and Smart (1965) found that alcohol reduced anxiety in conflict situations. Alcohol definitely seems to decrease general affect. The study by Bostrom and White (1979) clearly indicated that the act of ingesting any kind of drink enhanced persuasive effects, but the presence of alcohol in such drink decreased persuasive effects so that an alcoholic drink was approximately equal to no drink at all. Alcohol *per se*, then, inhibits persuasion, but drinking in general enhances it.

Tranquilizers.   Many kinds of tranquilizing substances are commonly available today to most segments of the population, even though most of them require a physician's prescription. Kleinkecht and Smith-Scott (1977) report, for example, that over 37 percent of college students in their sample used tranquilizer substances in one form or another. It may well be that college students are subject to particular forms of anxiety that makes their use of tranquilizers less representative than a true national sample, but even so, it seems reasonable to assume that the national proportion is high. Tranquilizers generally depress the CNS, but have a milder depressant effect than does alcohol. They produce state-dependent learning, which may influence the retention of the persuasive message. But their primary influence is to lessen the amount of CNS arousal and subsequently lessen the impact of a persuasive message.

In addition, there is some evidence that tranquilizers may inhibit memory processes as well. Tranquilizers as well as alcohol produce state-dependent learning (Carpenter and Ross, 1965; Goodwin, 1969). Material acquired in one state is poorly remembered if the same state is not present during the recall period. The total effect of tranquilizers on persuasibility should be that of a strong inhibitor.

Amphetamines.   Another very common drug, amphetamines are normally used to allay fatigue and relieve pain. Dieters use them to combat the debilitating effects of hunger. In large doses, however, they have the capacity to bring on the symptoms of paranoid schizophrenia. According to Marshall (1979), professional football players who received large doses of amphetamine could be induced into a state of rage, and were less reluctant to perform when tired or injured. Schacter's demonstration of the interaction of epinephrine and behavioral inductions probably best illustrates the effects of amphetamines. When individuals taking the drug fully understand its effects, then the result on persuasive communication is likely to be minimal. However, when they either expect no particular arousing effect or expect one that is less than is likely to occur, the probability is high that they will attribute the arousal state to the act of persuasion and as a consequence experience a heightened effect.

Effects of the Environment

There are many environmental effects that strongly affect the reception of persuasive communications, and these effects are especially interesting because most of them are not perceived by the individual experiencing them. As most of them heighten CNS activity, we can say usually that most of these environmental effects would increase the effectiveness of a persuasive message.

The presence of others.   Zajonc (1965) was one of the first to note that the presence of others could create CNS arousal. He cited instances of increased level of hydrocortisone in the bloodstream of individuals who were performing in groups rather than alone, and he also observed that this enhancement inhibited the acquisition of new responses but facilitated the performance of previously learned activities. A similar effect was recently reported by Markus (1978), who studied the performance of individuals who operated either alone or in a situation in which they were watched by others. When watched, people's performance on a well-learned task was facilitated, but more complex tasks were hindered.

The presence of others may inhibit CNS arousal when the arousal comes from another source. For example, pain typically creates CNS arousal, but the presence of others not only inhibits overt expressions of pain but also inhibits the CNS arousal that usually accompanies pain.

The nature of the effect of the presence of others is not universally agreed upon. Many researchers attribute it to a kind of anxiety, but we could make a strong case for calling it an embarrassment effect. In an interesting attempt to resolve some of this ambiguity, Rajecki, Ickes, Corcoran, and Lenerz (1977) tested individuals in the presence of others who were blindfolded and, therefore, could not observe the individual performing. They found that the presence of a nonblindfolded peer reduced the error rate on a cognitive task, but the presence of a blindfolded peer caused individuals to complete the trials faster and make fewer errors than they did in isolation. These authors conclude that observation is an important effect but that mere presence is also efficacious in bringing about increased performance. Because little is known about these effects by most individuals, we would expect a strong facilitation of persuasive effects in the presence of others. Although this may seem contradictory (persuasive interactions *per se* seems to imply the presence of at least one other person), the effects of others' presence can be detected in the situation where the persuasive message is read rather than delivered in person.

Hunger.   During the latter part of World War II, 36 young men volunteered for a study involving semistarvation at the University of Minnesota. After six months of a sharply attenuated diet, the volunteers were carefully studied, and marked changes were noted.

> They have become distractable, unable to study effectively . . . . They had become inefficient in other tasks as well. They were irritable, unable to control their actions for social acceptability, although somewhat recovered in this respect from a nadir during semistarvation. A number of them had become addicted to activities that had not figured in their earlier lives—to drinking tea and coffee, smoking tobacco, and chewing gum. Most of them had also become addicted to eating as much as possible and had ceased to display earlier discriminative tastes in doing so. Their table manners were neglected. (Easterbrook, 1978, pp. 51-52)

Where we would expect hunger to be simply an actuator or a creator of drive (Hull, 1943), it appears that prolonged hunger produces an entirely different set of reactions. While no specific evidence is available, we would expect a mild amount of hunger to facilitate persuasion and a prolonged amount to inhibit it.

The DDD syndrome.   DDD is the acronym given by Farber, Harlow, and West (1957) to the factors present in prison camps: debility, dependence, and dread. The three factors interact to produce a situation in which the individual experiences a generalized state of hyporesponsiveness, a loss of time concept, and self-disorganization. The similarity to the hunger symptoms presented above is responsible for its inclusion here. Although we might expect individuals in a normal environment to be free of these characteristics, it is entirely possible that many persons at particular times are experiencing the DDD syndrome. Medical students, for example, may neglect their nutrition because of the extreme anxiety caused by a scheduled examination and fear their professors in much the same way that prisoners fear their guards. Older persons often report the same kinds of reactions to the threats of decreasing resources, a hostile environment, and inactivity. Persons experiencing the DDD syndrome are extremely persuasible when the source of the message is one of the sources of DDD. According to news reports, American hostages held by Iranian students in 1979 showed signs of the DDD syndrome, and were consequently more persuadable.

Other factors.   There are a number of other factors that could possibly affect the CNS and the reception of persuasive communication. Boredom (Heron, 1972), biorhythms (Lane, 1971), fatigue, and even meditation strongly affect the CNS. However, the lack of strong evidence for consistent effects in each of these sources of CNS alterations should lead one to be cautious about possible effects. However, each of these is an important factor and should be considered.

We have seen that altered CNS states are common in ordinary audiences, and even that normal CNS states might be the exception to the rule. The use of cigarettes, alcohol, and tranquilizers are very common. In addition, environmental factors such as hunger, fatigue, and the presence of others have significant effects on the CNS. All of these effects are easily classifiable into two categories: stimulants and depressants. Depressants inhibit persuasive effects because they apparently inhibit cognitive processing and the subsequent discomfort caused by attitude-discrepant messages. Stimulants enhance persuasive effects if and only if the individual does not attribute the arousal to the drug or the environment; then the arousal is apparently attributed to the persuasive message and persuasion is enhanced. Most persons do not seem to understand the physiological effects of common drugs on their central nervous systems, and so we might expect the overall effect of CNS arousal to be facilitative.

The implications of this information are profound. A successful persuasive strategy might include the presence of a small amount of hunger, some sort of CNS stimulant administered in the form of a social ritual, and attribution of the subsequent arousal to the persuasive communication. It is a common practice in many organizations to invite candidates for new positions to cocktail parties, to lunches, dinners, coffees, and many other social functions. This practice usually is called hospitality, but its implications could easily be seen as somewhat more sinister. Fortunately, few, if any, interviewers involved in these practices have any Machiavellian purpose in mind. Many political figures have favorite theories about the proper time of day for political broadcasts. Dinnertime would seem to be an efffective choice because persons usually eat their meals in groups and can experience arousal while eating and smoking. Franklin Roosevelt made effective use of dinnertime speeches on Thanksgiving and Christmas. Who knows how much of Walter Cronkite's popularity might be due to the time of his broadcasts?

Probably the most important potential use of this kind of information lies in our understanding of the persuasive process. In an area where inoculation was once thought of as a topic of major importance, we ought to see clear implications of knowledge concerning CNS arousal as an inoculating device. When correct attributions about arousal are made, then subsequent persuasive effects will be minimized, and, when present, would be due solely to the messages-sources interaction. Such understanding ought to be an important part of any educational effort where the persuasive process is involved.

SUMMARY

Individuals vary widely in their reactions to persuasion, but no specific personality factors can be said to operate in all circumstances. Early theories in this area centered on authoritarianism and dogmatism, but these characteristics only affected specific persuasive situations. Involvement and attitude discrepancy are two factors that do influence receivers' processing of persuasive messages. Sex differences can probably be attributed more to personality factors and sex roles than to biological sex.

Physiological factors are extremely important in persuasion, because physiological arousal is fairly common in modern life. The effects of arousal on the CNS are facilitating if the individual is not aware of the source of the arousal and attributes it to the message. A number of commonly used substances have profound effects on CNS arousal and depression.

QUESTIONS FOR FURTHER STUDY

1. Why would dogmatism affect attitude change? Discuss the various studies concerning dogmatism.
2. Why would self-esteem play a significant role in persuasion? Has self-esteem ever caused you or your audience to accept a message?
3. Have you ever become involved in a message? How do you react to fiery opinionated statements? Are they effective? Explain.
4. Why are females generally thought to be more persuadable than males? Cite examples. Have you ever found this to be true? Explain.

5. Discuss the effects of cognitive and physiological states on attitude change (separately and as they relate to each other).

6. Why do people typically think that alcohol facilitates attitude change? Did you think so before reading this chapter? Explain. Be sure to discuss the amount of consumption and its effect.

7. Which of the drugs discussed in this chapter do you feel would produce a greater attitude change? Why?

8. Discuss the effects of applied mental stress on attitude change.

SUGGESTIONS FOR FURTHER READING

BOSTROM, R.   Altered physiological states: the central nervous system and persuasive communications. In M. Roloff & G. Miller (Eds.), *Persuasion: New directions in theory and research.* Beverly Hills: Sage, 1980.

HOVLAND, C. & JANIS, I.   *Personality and persuasibility.* New Haven: Yale, 1959.

JAHODA, G.   *The psychology of superstition.* Baltimore: Penguin, 1971.

JANIS, I., KAYE, D., & KIRSCHNER, P.   Facilitating effects of "eating while reading" on responsiveness to persuasive communications. *Journal of Personality and Social Psychology*, 1965, *1*, 181–186.

ROKEACH, M.   *The open and closed mind.* New York: Basic Books, 1960.

SCHACTER, S.   The interaction of cognitive and physiological determinants of emotional state. In L. Berkowitz (Ed.), *Advances in experimental social psychology.* New York: Academic Press, 1964.

CHAPTER TWELVE
PERSUASION IN
SMALL GROUPS

Small groups are one of the most important communicative settings in our daily lives. In our jobs, in our families, and in our social lives, we find ourselves making decisions in small groups, usually trying to act as a collective unit. Persuasion is an important part of the small-group process, but it usually operates differently there than in other settings.

How did group life get to be so important in human affairs? No one really knows, but we do know that almost everything we do involves groups in some way or another. Society, of course, is composed of groups. Large organizations are only groups of groups. Even in situations where we would think that order and structure would not be present, groups appear and are usually the principal focus of experience.

Let us look at one example. In September, 1971, one of the worst prison riots in American history took place in the state prison in Attica, New York. On September 9, Thursday morning, 1,280 prisoners had rebelled and taken over one quarter of the prison, holding a number of guards hostage. But they did not remain unorganized for long. Tom Wicker, an editor for *The New York Times*, was summoned to act as part of the negotiation team for the state. He later wrote in his book, *A Time To Die*:

> By midafternoon, the rebelling men had nominated numerous leaders, or members of a "negotiating team"—two from each cell block. They had organized a sort of police or security force to maintain order, and had appointed guards for the hostages, who had been located within a ring of wooden benches not far from the center of D-yard, and who were being guarded by the ever-alert Muslims. Cleanup details were sent out and homosexual couples were told to come out from under the blankets and make

love later on. Rationing of captured food was imposed. Leaders also demanded—and got—the voluntary surrender of some drug stocks taken from the hospital in C-block. (Wicker, 1975, p. 29)

Wicker also goes on to describe how the prisoners set up a sick bay, and many other organized functions during the riot period. It is clear that group activity was one of the central functions during this prison disturbance.

It is not often that we are taken out of the usual structures of our society. But when we do, our first instinct is to get organized, that is, form ourselves into functional groups. This activity is viewed by some as evidence that mankind—the social animal—has a deep-rooted need to operate as a member of a group.

GROUPS AND ATTITUDE CHANGE

Groups have a number of significant influences on attitude change. You will remember in Chapter 4, when the kind of sources that were homophilious were being discussed, that this kind of source influence was derived from the group as an extension of the individual's perception system. Sherif (1958), Asch (1962), and Deutsch and Gerard (1955) all demonstrated some of the ways in which this group influence is felt. Let us look at some of the specific factors in this influence.

Characteristics of Groups

What are some of the characteristics of a small group? This may seem like a meaningless question to many of us; a group is more than one or two individuals. It comes as a surprise to may of us to realize that not every aggregation of individuals can be thought of as a real group. In real groups there is a sense of belongingness or groupness that mere aggregations of individuals do not have.

In a popular modern novel, the hero is confronted by an older couple who come from the same state that he does. "You are a Hoosier!" they cry, feeling that his former residence automatically places him in the same group as them. He, on the other hand, does not feel that being a Hoosier is sufficiently distinctive to qualify them to spend their vacation with him.

Each of us belong to many nominal groups, that is groups that exist in name only. We are juniors, art majors, Sigma Nu's, Kennedy Democrats, Gophers, or humanists. It is true that sometimes each of these identifications can awake feelings of loyalty and dedication. Like the couple in the novel, being a Hoosier can be very important to us, and we are proud of the designation. But how do we distinguish these casual, or nominal groups from the real groups in which significant activity takes place?

We may not be sure when exactly an aggregation of individuals turn into a group, but we are usually sure that a group exists when we see one. John Brilhart (1978) likens this process to the assembling of 12 lines on a piece of paper to form a representation of a cube. The 12 lines each have the same potential when they are not arranged that way, but when they form the cube, there is no doubt in any one's mind that they are part of a single entity.

There are three important characteristics that define groups: *cohesiveness, structure,* and *identity.* Let us look at each of these in turn.

Cohesiveness.   This characteristic refers to the quality some aggregations have of clinging together. Cohesiveness can be created by a number of factors. Some typical ones are common goals, common background, liking for one another, and external forces or pressure. A group that is cohesive is one that has some force tending to hold it together. Casual aggregations lack cohesiveness.

Structure.   We may not recognize it, but almost every real group has some kind of structure. Structure does not necessarily manifest itself in a formal table of organization or a specific designation of a leader and followers. Structure is apparent every time a group member takes on a specific function. Almost always structure is related to an individual's personality, the task needs, and the situation. In family groups, structure is largely determined by traditional factors. Not all groups are so formally organized. But every real group has some structure which importantly influences its activity. For example, consider a parent-teacher organization that has sponsored parent visitations on a specific evening. A small group of parents may meet with one or more teachers concerning specific programs. The fact that some of the group members are parents and the others are teachers powerfully determine the structure of the resulting group. The roles that persons take are determined at least partially by this structure.

Identity.   One thing that is vital before we can consider an aggregation a group is a *sense* of the group, or identity. In other words, the members of the group must feel that the group is real and that they do indeed belong to it. Typically, identity comes about as the result of some naming procedure. Coaches and sports writers are fond of picking out subgroups of athletic teams and applying catchy names to them. For example, the defensive football team at Louisiana State University was once called the Chinese Bandits to give them a specific identity. The Miami Dolphins had a no-name defense and the Los Angeles Rams had a Fearsome Foursome.

In real groups, these terms are usually more prosaic. "The girls on the third floor" or "the guys in the machine tool room" are two examples. Sometimes we hear terms like "the neighborhood," or other less formal designations. Clubs and formal organizations, of course, almost always have specific identities. But formal organization is not essential to a sense of identity.

Groups and the Influence Process

We typically think of persuasion as something that happens when a single source influences others, but persuasion definitely takes place in small group settings. How do groups change responses of their members? There are a number of general ways. One important effect is the reaching of a group *consensus,* or a general conclusion that is acceptable to all in the group. Another outcome is to achieve solidarity or to intensify attitudes about the subject in question. A term that is currently used for this effect is consciousness raising. Chesebro, Cragan, and McCullough (1973) studied conscious-raising groups in detail and reported on some of the techniques using groups for this method.

Irving L. Janis (1977) has defined a particular type of group influence as groupthink. It is characterized by a situation in which loyalty to the group is more paramount than good decisions. Janis noticed some high-level policy decisions in the U.S. government which exhibited some of these characteristics, and also demonstrated some of them in the laboratory. Courtwright (1978) has been able to provide a clear illustration of the process of groupthink in an experimental situation.

FACTORS INVOLVED IN ANALYSIS OF GROUPS

What are some of the factors that lead to persuasion in the small group? One way of approaching this question would be to examine the group inputs. Hackman and Morris (1975) characterized these inputs as belonging to three main types: individual factors (skills, attitudes, personal characteristics), group-based factors (structure, size, cohesiveness), and environmental factors (task characteristics, reward structure, level of stress).

In this chapter we will examine only four main types of group factors: membership characteristics, leadership and structure, amount of participation, and type of communicative activity.

Membership Characteristics

Who the members of a group are and what they think is probably one of the most important factors in bringing about group change. Personality is one of a number of ways that membership has an effect.

Personality characteristics.   For example, Alderton (1980) showed that individuals whose personality could be described as generally internal in locus of control ascribed more personal responsibility as a result of a group discussion. Sex differences can play a role in the kinds of group influences present. Baird (1976) reviewed the relevant literature concerning sex differences in group research. He found that definite sex roles had been observed: women had been encouraged to be more reticent, less aggressive, noncompetitive, more sensitive to needs, more yielding to social pressure, and other typical stereotypical behavior. However, before you take Baird's conclusions too seriously, you might wish to reread the section on sex and persuasibility in the last chapter. If androgyny is the principal determinant there, it ought logically to be the principal determinant in the small-group experience as well.

TABLE 12-1 Verdicts and Initial Opinions about the Prosecution

	GUILTY VERDICT	HUNG JURY	NOT GUILTY VERDICT
Proprosecution	20	9	11
Moderate	16	9	12
Prodefense	11	10	18

Initial attitude. Jurma (1979) showed that individuals who were high in task orientation were effective, regardless of whether the leaders were structuring. This is an example of an initial attitude that affects group outcomes. However, we are usually more interested in the initial attitude toward the topic—that is, preconceptions—than on the way that a particular group's deliberations will come out. You will remember that the Asch effect depended on a unanimous majority for its force, but recently some researchers have been studying the initial attitudes of groups to see how they affect outcomes.

For example, Bray and Noble (1978) varied the composition of mock juries so that some were composed of high authoritarians and others were composed of low authoritarians (see Chapter 11, p. 181). The deliberations in these groups led to more severe punishment recommended by the high authoritarians and less by the low authoritarians. Deliberation, in other words, produced greater polarization.

How do minorities influence a group in reaching decisions? Many persons feel that prior attitude is the principal mechanism for bringing this about. Much of this research has been conducted in studying mock juries. Unfortunately, a good deal of this research suffers from serious methodological difficulties.

One good example occurs in a study conducted by Davis and his associates (1978). They studied the general effects of bias on the nature of decisions rendered in 6-person juries. They believed that initial bias would affect the outcome of a jury's deliberation as well as the kind of verdicts rendered. 708 persons were asked a series of questions to measure possible bias toward the prosecution or the defense in a rape trial. On the basis of these questions, the experimenters divided the jurors into three groups: proprosecution (34%), moderate (33%), and prodefense (33%). All of these persons watched a videotaped trial, and then indicated their preference for the guilt or innocence of the defendant. Of the total of 708 persons 447 (63%) indicated that they thought him guilty, while 261 (37%) thought him innocent. The initial predisposition had only a slight effect on the judgments of innocent or guilty. Then these persons were divided into 128 6-person juries, and were allowed to deliberate. In spite of the overwhelming number of guilty predispositions, only 49 of these groups (41.1%) were able to reach a verdict of guilty in the alloted time. Of all the juries 41 (35.9%) voted not guilty, and 28 of the groups were unable to reach a decision. Davis and his coauthors claim that initial bias had significantly affected the number of guilty verdicts. This bias is illustrated in Table 12-1. The frequencies reported do not produce a significant chi-square (4.32, $df=4$). Then the authors

TABLE 12-2 Majority Size, Initial Bias, and Results of Jury Deliberations

Majority Size	PROSECUTION			MODERATE			PRODEFENSE		
	G	H	NG	G	H	NG	G	H	NG
5-1	7	0	2	7	2	1	0	0	0
4-2	6	5	1	5	3	3	4	5	5
3-3	0	2	6	1	4	4	1	5	1
2-4	0	2	2	0	0	3	0	0	5

present an analysis of the results of the deliberations broken down in terms of the composition of the juries. Juries were constructed according to the posttrial, predeliberation judgements of the jurors. These groups were 6-0, 5-1, 4-2, 3-3, 2-4, 1-5, and 0-6 in favor of a guilty verdict. These outcomes are reported in Table 12-2. In this analysis, they reported the following:

> Moderate and pro-prosecution matrices are rather similar, but the pro-defense matrix is somewhat different from the first two. We lack a standard, straightforward means of assessing the intercondition agreement among the matrices, but inspection (of the table) offers no clear evidence that group decision processes vary with condition. (1978, p. 42)

These authors overlooked a very efficient means of assessing the "intercondition agreement among the matrices," namely, the partitioning of chi-square for multiple interactions.

This three-factor partition can be constructed by eliminating the 6–0 juries (they routinely returned a verdict of guilty, as we might suspect), the 1–5, and the 0–6 juries (they also produced no surprises, that is, they produced routine verdicts of not guilty). This three-element matrix can be analyzed into several components: the main effects; the interactions among majority, bias, and verdict; and the triple interaction among all three. Because the verdict rendered is the dependent variable in this interaction, the triple partition of chi-square is analogous to a two-way interaction in an analysis of variance. When this chi-square is calculated, it yields a value of 15.26, which, with $df = 12$, is not significant. Therefore, we cannot conclude, as these authors did, that the "pro-defense matrix was somewhat different from the first two." We may forgive the authors their use of the word "somewhat" in this context, perhaps. Because the triple interaction was not significant, we may collapse the frequencies into more simple comparisons. The bias by majority size interaction is of little theoretical interest, because these two factors were varied by the experimenters. Initial attitude and the verdict produced are of the greatest theoretical and practical interest. This interaction only produced a chi-square of 0.268, which is far from significant. The majority size by verdict interaction, on the other hand, produced a chi-square value of 43.231, significant at the 0.001 level ($df = 6$). It is worth examining this matrix separately: Table 12-3 presents this analysis and shows clear evidence for the strength of the jury composition effect as

TABLE 12-3 Majority Size, and Verdicts Reached

	VERDICTS		
	G	H	NG
Distribution			
5-1	20	2	3
4-2	15	13	9
3-3	2	11	11
2-4	0	2	10

opposed to the initial bias of the jurors. On the other hand, bias, as such had little effect, as Table 12-4 demonstrates. The interesting fact of the outcome of this experiment (and one that apparently escaped the authors of it) was that the trial (and by extension, the messages in the trial) did produce some slight differences in the initial judgments, but *the manner in which these judgments were arranged in the juries was of much greater importance in predicting the outcome of the deliberations.*

These judgments, and the nature of the group composition have not been studied as much as we would like. The effect of the not-guilty minority seems out of proportion to its size. These and other questions are beginning to be studied by communication researchers.

Participation and Group Influence

The amount that each member participates has a strong effect on whether or not that member has an influence on the outcome. Bavelas (1953), in his studies of centrality and structure, showed that central persons had more influence and were more satisfied than peripheral persons. Bostrom (1968) showed that this was also true of groups where the centrality was not formally constituted. Both of these studies show that participation is one of the principal indices of group influence. The member that participates more is the one that has the most influence on the outcome of the group decisions. However, not all persons participate equally. What are the factors that lead one person to be influential and another to hold back?

Judee Burgoon (1977) identified some of the characteristics that lead to reticence in a small group (reinforcement and approach-avoidance). The reticent person was one that received little reinforcement from this kind of activity and that had established a pattern for avoiding communication. Burgoon devised a test that was a good predictor of actual participation. Apprehension may also be a factor. Jablin, Siebold, and Sorenson (1977) showed that apprehensiveness about communication significantly limited the participation in brainstorming groups.

Participation is not only a good thing for individuals in the group; it seems to be a good thing for the group as a whole. Groups that have more varied inputs may do a better job in making decisions. Hirokawa (1980) showed that groups that had

TABLE 12-4   Juror Bias and Verdicts Reached

	VERDICTS REACHED		
Initial Bias	G	H	NG
Proprosecution	13	9	11
Moderate	13	9	11
Prodefense	11	10	11

a good deal of interaction were more effective decision-makers and that they tended to interact on substantive matters until a decision was reached.

Sorenson and McCroskey (1977) studied the types of personality that interact in small groups and discovered that this factor affected the amount of interaction present in a group. The kinds of personalities that went into the group also strongly affected the type of interaction that the group performed. Harper and Askling (1980) demonstrated that leadership, openness, and amount of participation predict success of groups. In addition, Bochner and Bochner (1972) suggest that Machiavellianism and task structure determine the amount of participation in a group. High Machiavellians participated more than low Machiavellians, apparently out of a desire to be of greater influence in the group.

Type of Communication Activity

Not only is participation important, but the type of interaction is important. However, the general classification of communicative activity in small groups is not always agreed upon. Bales (1958) proposed an elaborate classification scheme for small-group activity, but it is not easy to code and sometimes the group activity is simpler than that. For example, Mabry (1975) showed that interaction could be defined into three main stages: boundary-seeking, ambivalence, and actualization. Ellis and Fisher (1975) also showed that conflict in small groups went through three stages, which they called interpersonal conflict, confrontation, and substantive conflict. Decision-making only occurred during the last phase. These systems might be an easier way to look at the communication types in the group. Mabry (1975) developed a model of group activity that included latency, adaptation, integration, and goal-attainment. He showed that a group must progress from one stage to another if it is to accomplish its goal. Poole (1981) showed that no one model could be claimed as an archetypical description for all group phenomena; different groups followed different patterns in achieving a decision.

Some kinds of group interaction are more persuasive than others. Knutson (1972) showed that orientation behavior produced more consensus than groups where no one engaged in orientation. This was defined as an "aligning" phenomenon rather than a straightforward influence attempt. Knutson and Holdridge (1975) also showed that orientation was a factor in the determinations of leadership. Leaders were those who were more likely to be orienting than the others. Prentice (1975) showed that trust-destroying communications inhibited the verbal fluency of groups. It would be logical to expect that these kinds of communication would lead to less group productivity.

Knutson and Kowitz (1977) suggest that groups utilize three types of activity: informational, procedural, and interpersonal. The first refers to data input, empirical analysis, and logical analysis. The second includes leader and follower behavior. The third involves relational elements among the members independent of the first two. They also show that different kinds of conflict should call for different kinds of group activity. They do not suggest which ought to be better. Gouran and Baird (1972) demonstrated differences in communication structure between task-oriented groups and informal groups. Baird (1974) further reported that preparation and member motivation both had an effect on these structures.

Gouran, Brown, and Henry (1978) concluded that behaviors contributing to the substance of the decision-making, such as introducing relevant issues, amplifying ideas, and documenting assertions, as well as procedural behaviors, such as goal orientation and pursuing issues systematically, had greater effect on preceptions of quality than did member involvement and behaviors focusing on the socio-emotional quality of the group. This sounds like a straightforward persuasion approach to group activity, one that is message and source oriented. In a similar study, Bell (1979) showed that discussion groups were more open to changing their minds when the content of the communications were highly substantive rather than when they were not.

Another way of looking at communication quality is in its effect. Leathers (1972) hypothesized that communications of better quality would be indicated by the amount of feedback they generated. In his study, he showed that communication of this type produced a better group product than low-quality communications. However, we might simply reason that these groups had more and better interaction; hence, they made the better decision. It is important for the communication in the group to stick to the point. Kline and Hulinger (1973) showed that more group consensus was present when individual communication in the groups was not redundant.

Leadership and Structure

It is always difficult to distinguish between structure and leadership. Leaders often are those persons in positions of influence. They may not necessarily have inherent leadership qualities. In the network studies, the central position usually had the most influence, and could be equated with leadership. Another problem lies in the definition of leadership. A leader may simply be that person that handles group maintenance tasks, that is, a facilitator. The real influence may come from other members. Nonetheless, we all recognize that leadership is one of the most interesting factors in the study of small groups, simply because of the influence potential that the leaders have.

When a group is highly centralized, all of its communication needs to be cleared by the leader. When one person has power, it is typically utilized this way. For example, Bradley (1978) demonstrated that power had more influence on the characteristics of upwardly-directed communications than did status. In large groups, some of this is necessary. Not everyone can talk at once in a large group, so formal procedure has evolved. Most of us now call this parliamentary law: the chairperson assigns the floor and action is only taken in the form of motions. Gouran and Geonetta (1977) have shown that in small groups some formality helps them stay on the topic better, which indicates that perhaps a little formality is not a bad thing. In spite of common sense, many small groups rigidly adhere to procedures. A school board, for example, may consist of only five members, but it may deliberate as if it were the U.S. House of Representatives, with questions of order and other nonsense interfering with group interaction.

Some persons may like this sort of activity. For example, Rosenfeld and Plax (1975) studied the nature of the autocratic leader. They found that autocratic leaders (as defined by a leadership questionnaire) were those who scored low in achievement versus independence, intraception, nurturance, and social values; while scoring high on abasement, achievement, and aggression. To be classified as a democratic leader, the scoring would be reversed. These persons probably would not like the formal-group situation.

Leadership is often designated in some formal fashion like an election or an appointment. Often leaders emerge from the group because of some personal characteristic they have, or some ability the group happens to need at the time. These leaders are typically more influential than other group members. We might even say that they are more persuasive. How do they go about exerting this influence?

Hill (1976) showed that when leaders exhibited a great many opinionated statements, the groups did not come as close to consensus as when the groups had a leader that was unopinionated. In addition, members rated unopinionated leaders as more competent. Wood (1977) showed that leaders tend to adapt themselves to different discussion situations.

Downs and Picket (1977) showed that group compatibility of a particular type was important in reactions to leaders. The leadership type that emphasized equally tasks and concerns for people was the best in terms of productivity, and the compatible groups were also the most productive. However, the incompatible groups did not suffer as much as has been predicted.

A special problem in recent years has been the role of the female leader in mixed and male groups. Yerby (1975) studied the success in groups of female leaders. She found that the composition of the group was an important factor. When the group was balanced (two males and two females) there was more satisfaction. In addition, more positive attitudes about sex roles predicted greater satisfaction with group activity with a female leader. Wood (1979) also showed that the group purpose was an important factor in the evaluation of leaders, and that the sex of group members would interact with the group's purpose in influencing these evaluations. In other words, the acceptance of female leaders may depend on the type of group that it is.

Perhaps the real purpose of a creative group is to have no leaders. Jablin and Sussman (1978) have shown, in a study examining real brainstorming groups, that individuals who are productive in ideas perceive fewer status differences among group members, perceive themselves as high status group members and are less apprehensive.

THE "CHOICE-SHIFT" PHENOMENON

The choice-shift phenomenon is the name given to the tendency of groups to chose more risky alternatives than an individual would in the same situation. This has led many to call it the risky-shift effect (Meyers and Lamm, 1976). Though many studies of this effect have been conducted, no real explanation for it is commonly accepted by researchers (Cartwright, 1971). However, group activity does produce this effect, and two main explanations are usually offered for it. One is the social comparison of one's own opinion with that of others; and the other is the new information or arguments concerning the decision alternatives (Meyers and Lamm, 1976, 620-21). The first emphasizes normative influence processes, and the second emphasizes persuasion processes. Much research has also tended to focus on the role of one or the other of these two mechanisms in producing group influence.

The Social Comparison Explanation

It is entirely possible that a person may hold an extreme opinion but, for fear of being labeled extreme or unreasonable, may express a more moderate position than that which he or she prefers. Then others in the group reveal that they also espouse positions closer to his or her personal ideal or more extreme than was expressed originally. The release from fear of negative evaluation allows such a person to express more risky position than was done initially. Because this process presumably operates in varying degrees for several of the group members, it could account for the polarization effect. This is hardly a persuasive effect, because it is only a release of inhibitions. If this is the true explanation for the risky-shift phenomenon, perhaps it is not a true influence in the sense that we have been using the word. It is more likely that individuals simply are influenced by the presentation of others' opinions in the groups—in other words, less risky members perceive the individuals that argue for the risky alternative as attractive and, hence, emulate them.

The Persuasion Explanation.

The persuasion explanation states that mere knowledge of others' positions *per se* is not the critical ingredient for group polarization effects. Instead, it is the information that is exchanged during the course of the discussion that plays the major role. According to this interpretation, the group produces arguments that favor a more extreme position. Though individual group members may have been aware of some of these supporting elements, most were not aware of all of them. Thus, the net effect is a shift as a result of the new persuasive information to which group members are exposed. In fact, most groups move toward decisions involving greater risk. The persuasion explanation, then, must include some cultural value to account for the preponderance of persuasive arguments in favor of risk. Burnstein and Vinokur (1975), for example, favor cultural values as a complete explanation.

Those who have read this far in this book now know that a great deal of research has been done to give us a truly comprehensive picture of individuals influencing each other. It is, therefore, astonishing to observe that small-group researchers do not make use of the research in risky shift, and usually they do not even observe communicative behavior in their experiments. No systematic investigation of the choice shift phenomenon has attempted to measure group members' perceptions of each other in even rudimentary credibility terms, to observe the resulting group interactions and the influence attempts, and then measure the outcomes. Until this is done, the choice shift phenomenon will have to be treated as an interesting curiosity.

Researchers in communication have demonstrated the weaknesses of the usual interpretations of the risky shift. For example, Fontes and Bundens (1980) demonstrate that the foreperson in jury studies usually has much more influence than other jury members. The significant phenomenon might be communicative activity. Cline and Cline (1980) showed that choice shifts were directly influenced by the patterning of communicative activity in small groups. Their data demonstrate conclusively that risky choices are accomplished by kinds of communicative patterning that "spread the responsibility" in the group.

New Approaches to Small Group Research

One interesting development is the possibility of reducing the persuasive-arguments explanation to a mathematical model. Boster, Mayer, Hunter, and Hale (1980) have made a strong beginning in this kind of study, and it shows great promise for the future. The model is particularly strong because it incorporates features of the persuasive-arguments theory and group-composition theory. Boster and his associates have shown that actual groups correspond closely in their behavior to this model.

Another theory that offers much promise in small-group interaction is that proposed by Siebold, Poole, and McPhee (1980). Drawing on Giddens' theory of structuralization, they propose an interaction system based on message analysis. They ask that we study the *valence* of a message, its quality as *argument*, and the influence *strategy* it demonstrates. They hypothesize that groups organize "decision schemes" that stem from the character of the interaction system. This theoretical approach should be especially valuable in interpreting some of the theoretical issues already discussed. It should be especially valuable in clearing up some of the problems inherent in choice-shift theory and group-composition problems.

In another seminal approach to group interaction, Hewes, Planalp, and Streibel (1980) have proposed a comprehensive mathematical treatment characterizing the nature of dyadic interactions in a small group. This model, though complex, demonstrates a usable method of studying mutual influence in the small-group context. Their technique could be used to provide a more precise, flexible, and complete representation of group interaction. With this representational scheme, development of hypotheses concerning the principal issues in small-group processes should be facilitated.

SUMMARY

Groups are influential in and of themselves; typically they enhance the persuasive process. Not every aggregation is a group, and not every group is influential. Groups typically have identity, structure, and cohesiveness. Groupthink is one of the unfortunate byproducts of group activity.

Group influence can be analyzed in many ways. Personal characteristics of the members is one important input. Initial attitude or predisposition is another. Member participation is probably one of the most persuasive activities observed.

Leaders are typically more persuasive than other members in groups, either because of groups' structure or because of their personal ability.

One important group influence is called the risky shift, but very little research shows us exactly how this phenomenon may work.

QUESTIONS FOR FURTHER STUDY

1. How much influence does a sorority or fraternity have on its members? Explain. How much cohesiveness do these groups have?
2. How much influence does a group leader usually hold? Explain. What type of characteristics should a group leader possess?
3. Do you believe that orientation is a factor in group leadership and group consensus? Why?
4. What is the most effective group of which you have been a member? Why do you consider it effective? Do any of the studies described in this chapter support your reasoning? If so, which ones?

SUGGESTIONS FOR FURTHER READING

BRANDSTATTER, H., DAVIS, J., & SCHULER, H. (Eds.) *Dynamics of group decisions*. Beverly Hills: Sage, 1978.
BURGOON, J.   Unwillingness to communicate as a predictor of small group discussion behaviors and interactions. *Central States Speech Journal*, 1977, *28*, 122–133.
CARTWRIGHT, D. & ZANDER, A. (Eds.)   *Group dynamics*. New York: Harper and Row, 1953.

JANIS, I.   Groupthink. *Psychology Today*, 1971, *5*, 6, 43–46.
LEATHERS, D.   Quality of group communication as a determinant of group product. *Speech Monographs*, 1972, *39*, 166–93.
TUBBS, S.   *A systems approach to small group interaction.* Reading, Mass.: Addison-Wesley, 1978.

CHAPTER THIRTEEN
BARGAINING AND NEGOTIATION — COMPETITIVE PERSUASION

We are all used to thinking of communication as an essentially cooperative activity. Just a moment's reflection, however, should be enough to convince us that this certainly is not the case with a great many personal interactions. When we deal with the automobile repairman, the IRS representative, and the headwaiter in the restaurant, often we do not share mutually cooperative motives. In fact, in many of these situations, *a gain for one person in the interaction results in a loss for the other*. The technical term for these kinds of interactions is mixed-motive interactions. It would be strange if these kinds of interactions were the same as common motive interactions, and, indeed, they are not. How does persuasion work in mixed-motive groups?

These kinds of interactions are usually called bargaining or negotiation. In the usual persuasive situation, the source's credibility depends a great deal on safety-trustworthiness, which, you will recall, was defined as the lack of self-interest on the part of the source. However, in bargaining, the individuals are both heavily involved, and neither can be thought of as a source or a receiver primarily. This makes this kind of situation quite different from the typical persuasive interaction, and, as you might guess, the kinds of techniques that should be followed are quite different. Let us first look at some of the characteristics of bargaining and negotiation.

COMMUNICATION IN
MIXED-MOTIVE
INTERACTIONS

What is a mixed-motive interaction? This typically refers to situations in which individuals are in *conflict*, but conflict is not always that easy to demonstrate. Ruben (1978), for example, has noted that we use the word *conflict* to designate disaffection, lack of tolerance, or shortsightedness. Persons seem to believe that conflict exists whenever someone feels upset about an interaction. Ruben urges that conflict be based on the realities of the system, which depends on the input and desired outputs of the process. Putting this more simply, we may say that a mother and daughter are in real conflict if they cannot agree about their interdependent behavior with regard to who does the dishes and who is to carry out the garbage. If they are merely uncomfortable with each other's value systems or lifestyle, then we could not call this a real conflict.

You will remember that at the beginning of this chapter, we defined mixed-motive interactions as those in which a gain for one was also a loss for another. Games fit this definition because usually one person or side is the "winner." However, these are artificially contrived interactions primarily for entertainment. In real life, do we have "games" that result in winners and losers? Unfortunately, yes. When you finish your college work, you will undoubtedly seek a job, and you will often be pitted against another person, competing for one position. After you get the job, you will probably find that the method of promotion in the company is based on a competitive merit system. Your corporation itself may be competing against another corporation for a finite share of the market. Competition is a way of life in the business world.

Classes that are graded on a strict curve are those in which only a predetermined number of persons receive A and B grades, regardless of the quality of work or learning achievement of the students. Students often feel that this is unfair and that all who do A work ought to receive this kind of mark.

Morton Deutsch (1949) defined cooperative and competitive behavior in this framework. Competitive behavior was that which was created by situations in which only one individual could enter the goal area at one time. Cooperative behavior results when the presence of another in the area did not inhibit the achievement of another. Whether communication *should* be cooperative or competitive is truly irrelevant to the problem of coping with bargaining or negotiation behavior; the fact is that much of our society is competitive and we must learn to adapt. There may be situations where we can convert competitive behavior into cooperative, but we must also be able to cope with the competitive when we have to. The predominant position that sports occupies in our civilization illustrates how intensely most of us feel about competition. It is truly amazing how important a championship trophy or a winning game is viewed by otherwise rational citizens of a city or a university. Competition seems to fill some deep-seated need for many of us.

It is this approach to bargaining and negotiation that has placed it in a framework that is antagonistic and noncommunicative. To communicate about motives and goals was a sign of weakness, and a good bargainer was supposed to be the strong and silent type. However, more recently, we see some real values in the mutual influence process and the ways in which mutually acceptable solutions can be reached, even in a competitive framework. As a consequence, many researchers have become interested in the way that bargainers influence each other by varying the cooperativeness implicit in their moves. In other words, the bargaining researchers have discovered persuasion!

RESEARCH IN BARGAINING

Research in bargaining has followed the development of laboratory techniques for its study. One of the original devices was the Acme-Bolt trucking game, devised by Deutsch and Kraus (1960). As you might guess, this was not a real game but a contrived interaction to test certain kinds of competitive and cooperative behavior. In the Acme-Bolt game, each player is designated as the proprietor of a trucking company, either Acme or Bolt. The playing board had three roads on it along which players move their trucks. The center road is the shortest route for both Acme and Bolt to achieve their objective. The two exterior roads are long and tortuous, about twice the distance for each player. So each player may choose to take the exterior road, which is long and difficult, or the interior road, which is short and easy. The problem is that the interior road is shared by both players and both cannot use it at once. If Acme chooses the center road, Bolt cannot use it and must go around the exterior road or wait till Acme gets done. However, Bolt can enter the center road and block Acme's progress. In short, if both Bolt and Acme choose to use the center road, neither will succeed. If both Bolt and Acme choose the exterior routes, they will both succeed but at greater cost. Finally, if Bolt chooses the interior route while Acme chooses the exterior route, Bolt wins (and vice versa). This game affords clear examples of cooperative and competitive choices and has been used extensively in the study of conflict. In some versions one player or another can close a gate that blocks the other from using the center route.

This trucking game is typical of most of the experimental instances of competitive behavior. Cooperation could be established by taking turns or some other agreement. Competition can be exhibited by blocking behavior.

Another example of laboratory manipulation of bargaining is the prisoner's dilemma game, which takes its name from the following situation: .

> Two suspects are taken into custody and separated. The district attorney is certain that they are guilty of a specific crime, but she does not have adequate evidence to convict them at a trial. She points out to each prisoner that they have two alternatives:

TABLE 13-1 Possible Outcomes for the Prisoner's Dilemma

PRISONER 1

		CONFESS	NOT CONFESS
PRISONER 2	CONFESS	2 years (P1) 2 years (P2)	10 years (P1) 1 year (P2)
	NOT CONFESS	1 year (P1) 10 years (P2)	5 years (P1) 5 years (P2)

to confess to the crime the police are sure they committed, or remain silent. If they both do not confess, then the district attorney will book them on some trumped-up charge such as petty larceny or illegal possession of narcotics, and they will both receive minor punishment. If they both confess, they will be punished, but the district attorney will recommend lighter sentences. But if one confesses and the other does not, both will be implicated. The confessor, however, will receive an extremely light sentence for turning state's evidence, but the other who did not confess will get the maximum penalty. (Rubin and Brown, 1975, p. 20)

Table 13-1 illustrates the possible outcomes for the prisoner's dilemma. At the side of the table are the two choices for the first prisoner, and at the top of the table are the two choices for the second prisoner. This table can be thought of as a *matrix* and the manner in which the matrix is entered can be termed a *game*.

These are only two of the ways in which psychologists have studied bargaining and negotiation. We can all agree that persons involved in real conflict might well react differently, although some researchers have indeed made use of real rewards and found that experimental outcomes are essentially the same (Steinfatt, 1973). Morely (1978) has provided an illuminating analysis of the kinds of laboratory studies that bargaining researchers have typically used. Although all are not directly related to real interactions between real people, it is Morely's contention that most are highly relevant and that their conclusions are highly useful.

Usually there are two main variables that affect the outcome of the bargaining interactions: the content of the bargainer's position (often called the *moves*) and the manner of presentation (communicative variables). Let us first look at some of the results of the kinds of moves bargainers make.

Moves, or Strategic Choices

In this section we will examine only a representative sample of some of the hundreds of studies that have been conducted in bargaining and negotiation. Typically these studies provide each player a set of circumstances in which a given set of payoffs will be appropriate, and then let the players bargain among themselves to see what kinds of choices are made.

Making concessions.   There have been a number of studies that indicate that an individual who makes concessions is more likely to elicit cooperation than one who makes demands or no concessions. Pilisuk and Skolnick (1968) had students play an arms-race–disarmament game against a simulated opponent who employed one of two experimental strategies: matching (the number of missiles produced by the opponent was equal to the number produced by the student on the previous trial); or conciliatory (the number of missiles produced by the opponent was equal to one less than the student's number on the previous trial). The conciliatory strategy was more likely to induce cooperation than the matching one.

Some other researchers have found that conciliatory strategies are least effective in inducing cooperation. They often result in exploitation by subjects. Although Marwell, Schmitt, and Boyesen (1973) have obtained evidence to the contrary, and have indicated that a pacifist strategy may elicit cooperation (at least among Norwegian subjects), other studies support more cooperative behavior in the outcomes (Meeker and Shure, 1969). Why should a pacifist strategy be ineffective? Bixenstine and Gaebelein (1971) suggest one possible answer. They placed persons in a prisoner's-dilemma game and forced them to play against a strategy that was programmed to match their prior cooperative or competitive behavior in reciprocal fashion, either immediately or gradually. The investigators expected the greatest cooperation to be elicited when the individuals played against a strategy that was quick to reciprocate cooperation and slow to reciprocate competitive behavior (retaliate). Instead they found that persons exploited each other in this condition, taking advantage of the eagerness to cooperate by choosing competitively. The greatest cooperation was achieved when the bargainer was slow to compete and slow to respond to cooperation by others. Because a bargainer was slow to reciprocate with cooperation, the cooperative behavior may have appeared all the more valuable, and, therefore, subjects' temptation to defect was reduced. This is a somewhat depressing finding. Certainly one must be cautious about the process of making concessions in bargaining.

Sequence of moves.   Another way that bargainers attempt to exert influence over each other is by varying the sequence in which the moves or offers are arranged. By first making hard demands and then softening them by making concessions, a person may indicate a desire to settle for a division of resources.

Studies in which the prisoner's-dilemma game was utilized to study strategy shift are interesting. Schellenburg (1964), for example, found no systematic difference between shifts in cooperativeness and subject behavior. Other studies, however, demonstrate that a change in the other's behavior from low to high cooperativeness induces greater cooperation than either a shift from high to low or a pattern of high unchanging cooperativeness (Bixenstine and Wilson, 1963). This research seems to indicate that an individual who makes concessions is more likely to elicit cooperation from the other than one who makes demands but no concessions.

Concessions have also been observed in studies using the Acme-Bolt trucking game. Usually, persons start out by blocking in the center of the one-lane section of road. This usually results in some unproductive interactions, in which both players lose. The impasse is only broken when one individual elects to make a concession at some point to allow the other person through. Of course, in the next trial, the conceder usually expects the opponent to take a turn at backing up. If all is normal and communication is allowed, this is the pattern that is followed. However, when a bargainer refuses to carry out the pattern, the result is usually another impasse and the game comes to an unsatisfactory conclusion.

Concessions are also apparent in studies using the bilateral-monopoly game. Bilateral monopoly is a game in which players must set prices for property exchange, based on amounts of property traded. Here the size and rate of the concessions tend to influence the other player to match the same size and rate (Druckman, Zechmeister, and Solomon, 1972). In this game, the starting-tough strategy is usually more effective than a consistent-concession strategy.

The tendency of bargaining pairs to settle on a mutually favorable contract is described by Kelley and Schenitzki (1972) and is called the systematic-concessions model. In this model, each person starts by proposing contracts for which personal profits are high. As these offers and counteroffers are rejected, the next step is to propose deals that are less profitable. The net result of making a number of concessions is to enlarge the size of interactions that are acceptable to each person. If the process continues, the pair ought to reach a point where they can agree. This process has a degree of rationality about it that some of the others lack.

The research on concession making shows that often concessions present information about the preferences and intentions. A bargainer who makes frequent concessions will probably be viewed as willing to settle for less than one who makes concessions only occasionally. Also, a person who concedes up to a certain point and then refuses to move beyond this point will probably be seen as being close to some cutoff point below which he or she will leave the relationship rather than settle. However, threats toughen the position.

Second, concessions reveal our perception of the other person. If a person systematically refuses to concede, we might arrive at the conclusion that we are not as important in the value system as we would like to be.

Third, concessions and their pattern offer an opportunity for the expression of personal goals and values. The individual who finds making concessions highly upsetting is probably expressing a particular outlook on life. This pattern may be highly revealing to the other person in the interaction.

Most of these interpretations of bargaining, you may have noticed, are primarily communicative. The logical extension of this approach is to allow the bargainers free and full communicative opportunity. What happens when we do this? What are the effects of extensive communication in the bargaining process?

Communication Variables
and Bargaining

Beisecker (1970b) discovered that individuals who perceived a great deal of issue conflict generated more interaction in bargaining than those who saw little conflict. In addition, individuals that rigidly held to a position generated more interaction than did flexible individuals. The interesting question is what kind of interaction is the best, or most productive? What kinds are there?

One of the first kinds of communicative behavior in bargaining is the threat. Though Bowers (1974) has coined the word *thromise*, which is somewhere between threat and promise, most bargaining uses implied or explicit threat somewhere. Marr (1974) compared the results of threats and orientation communications in interactions. Orientation seemed to be much more effective in bringing about cooperative behavior.

Clearly, a cooperative bargainer ought to elicit more cooperation. Johnson, McCarty, and Allen (1976) studied four kinds of bargaining behaviors: cooperative and competitive, expressed by verbal and nonverbal means. Actors were trained to express cooperativeness and competitiveness by means of nonverbal cues such as sympathetic facial expressions, good eye contact, and the like. When individuals were presented with these persons as bargainers, the experimenter hypothesized that the nonverbal messages would convey as much cooperativeness as the verbal messages. However, this hypothesis was not confirmed. No differences could be ascribed to the nonverbal aspects of bargaining behavior. The general cooperativeness, however, did have a strong effect.

Many persons have hypothesized that the personal element is the important part of bargaining. A depersonalized interaction should result in less cooperative behavior. Face-to-face interactions, then, should produce more cooperation that mediated ones. This idea led Turnbull, Strickland, and Shaver (1976) to hypothesize that the medium of the communicative interaction might well interact with the power of the person who is bargaining. They placed persons into a simulated disarmament talk and gave one set of bargainers more power than others (represented by the hypothetical number of missiles each country had). Power had some effect on the attribution of motive in the bargainers, but there was little interaction with the type of medium in which bargaining was conducted. Face-to-face interactions, however, were consistently better. Donohue (1978), however, found that social power had a significant effect on bargaining outcomes. He also studied the interaction of personality and initial expectations in bargaining situations, and personality did not seem to have much effect.

In an interesting approach to bargaining and negotiation, Donohue (1981) devised a coding system to designate attack, defense, and regression interactions. Attacks were threats, charges, and offers, defenses were denying fault and answering, and regressions were disconfirmation, concessions, and miscellaneous communications. Donohue coded the utterances into cues and responses. The intensity of these cues and responses was scored. From these indices, a relative advantage index was constructed. This index should predict which individual in a negotiation engaged in the most advantageous verbal behavior. In most of Donohue's bargaining pairs, the relative advantage was a good predictor of bargaining success.

All in all, the literature in bargaining suggests that the principal method in arriving at a cooperative best solution is inextricably tied to the processes of information exchange and persuasion. When game situations were first studied, it was thought that they formed a model of competitive interactions only. In 1968, however, game theory was offered as a model of the cooperative process and was demonstrated to serve as well in this capacity (Bostrom, 1968). This view was not readily accepted at the time (Beisecker, 1970a), but since then it has come to be the dominant paradigm of bargaining and negotiation research.

TOWARD CONCILIATION—
GAME THEORY SOLUTIONS
OF CONFLICT

If persons are to arrive at mutually cooperative interactions, they need a method of formalizing their solutions. Most interactive situations are complex and do not have immediately obvious solutions that are fair to both parties. Game theory offers an approach to this problem. Hamburger (1979) has provided an illuminating analysis of the manner in which social interactions can be thought of as games and vice versa. His illustrations include the negotiation processes involved in nuclear disarmament as well as those of the marketplace. The method of analysis that leads to solutions of the games is called *theory of games*, and it is a useful tool in studying bargaining. To apply game theory to personal interactions, it is necessary to think of each person as a player and the outcomes of the interaction as payoffs. To see how this works, let us examine a social interaction from an early analysis of game theory and communication (Bostrom, 1968).

Professor Applegate has had a hard morning of grading papers, talking to students, and thinking. He wishes to have a quiet lunch at the local diner, and as he enters the establishment he has several clear-cut goals in mind. He wishes a quiet lunch away from the students who frequent the place. He also wishes to read the daily *Herald*, so that he can check his horoscope and do the puzzle. He also wishes to have the best lunch possible for the least money.

As the proprietor of the diner sees Applegate approach, he winces. Applegate usually stays two hours, uses valuable seating space, and is not a spectacular tipper. The proprietor also has some clear-cut goals in this interaction. He would like to see Applegate sit at the counter rather than at a booth so that less valuable seating will be occupied. He would also rather that Applegate not read the paper because it takes forever.

You will notice immediately that each person in this interaction has control over only part of the interaction. The choices can be divided into two main categories: those in control of the professor and those in control of the proprietor. In this situation, let us suppose that Applegate can sit wherever he wishes (which is true in most diners) and that he can order anything he wants (we will here simplify this to either steak or hamburger). The proprietor, on the other hand, can either hide the *Herald* or leave it out where Applegate can find it, and he can either prepare the meal nicely or make a mess of it. Each choice on either side has value for each person (or each player, if we think of them that way). These values may be

TABLE 13-2   Pattern of Utility for Each Outcome

PROFESSOR		PROPRIETOR	
OUTCOME	VALUE	OUTCOME	VALUE
Steak	2	Hamburger	1
Booth	1	Counter	4
Paper	2	No paper	2
Good meal preparation	3	Poor meal preparation	1

called each player's *subjective utility*, in that the value, or utility, is entirely subjective and determined by each person's values or attitudes. Part of the utility in this interaction is determined by money, but part is also determined by relatively abstract wants. Chapter 4 should have convinced all of us that we can measure attitudes, so we ought to be able to measure utilities in the same way. *Let us assume that we do this, and elicit a pattern of utility (or* value, *or attitude) for each outcome, as shown in Table 13-2.*

You will notice that these values are not exactly symmetrical. In other words, the proprietor would rather that Applegate order a hamburger, because they are easier to prepare and do not have to be thawed out, but it is not as important to him as the steak is to Applegate. To mess up the meal is a saving to the proprietor, but it is not as important as a good meal is to the professor. The proprietor has four options, and so does the professor. These options and their respective values are displayed in Table 13-3. Notice that each choice is lettered for each person and that in the table there are two values, one for the professor and one for the proprietor. Thus *A* for the proprietor stands for the option of preparing the meal well and hiding the paper. *C* for the professor stands for ordering a steak and sitting in a booth. Option *CD* stands for the interaction where the professor chooses *C* and the proprietor chooses *D* (we have, chauvinistically, put the professor first). Table 13-3 illustrates the possible outcomes for each of the sixteen interactions. You will note that the professor's subjective utility is in the upper left hand section of each cell and the proprietor's is in the lower right. Thus, in outcome *BB* the professor gets 0 and the proprietor gets 8. The professor ordered hamburger when he would rather have had steak, he sat at the counter when he would rather have sat at a booth, he got a poorly prepared meal, and the paper was hidden. The proprietor, on the other hand, got everything he wanted. Outcome *CC* illustrates the opposite interaction. Clearly neither of these is fair and if these are the only two choices, the interaction is going to be an unpleasant one for each of the players.

The utility of game theory is that it offers a method of solving this matrix so that each person gets a fair outcome. There are several ways of solving this kind of matrix (Bostrom, 1968). In this example, probably the best method is that pro-

TABLE 13-3 Options of the Proprietor and the Professor

		PROPRIETOR			
		A GOOD MEAL NO PAPER	B POOR MEAL NO PAPER	C GOOD MEAL PAPER	D POOR MEAL PAPER
PROFESSOR	A HAMBURGER BOOTH	4 / 3	1 / 4	6 / 1	3 / 2
	B HAMBURGER COUNTER	3 / 7	0 / 8	5 / 5	2 / 6
	C STEAK BOOTH	6 / 2	3 / 3	8 / 0	5 / 1
	D STEAK COUNTER	5 / 6	2 / 7	7 / 4	4 / 5

posed by Hamburger (1979). In these kinds of matrices, graphing the outcomes is an easy way to see how they compare to each other. In Figure 13-1, the various choices are plotted against each other on a graph. The bottom scale represents the value to the professor and the scale going up the left-hand side represents the value to the proprietor. Thus choice *AD* shows three units of value for the professor and only two units of value for the proprietor. Hamburger (1979, p. 62) has shown that any choice that is northeast of another is a better choice, and can be said to dominate it. Thus *AA* is obviously better than *AD* and *BC* is obviously better than either of them (because the interactions that are above and to the right of other interactions have greater value to both players).

But there are some interactions that are on the northeast border. How can we choose among them? First we extend a line from *BB* to *BA* to *DA* to *DC* and then to *CC*. This line defines what Hamburger calls the solution set, that is, the set of options from which we can draw our solution. Figure 13-2 illustrates how all other interactions are dominated by the solution set and by definition will not be chosen. But how to choose among *BB*, *BA*, *DA*, *DC*, or *CC*? Hamburger suggests that we use the principle of equivalency, that is, the assumption that each player is equal and that the best solution should be as nearly equal as possible. Figure 13-3 illustrates the line of equivalency, which is a line in the graph that expresses exactly equal outcomes. If you look at the dotted line in Figure 13-3, you will see that it is the expression of equal outcomes for each person. It travels through *CB* and *EC*, and if we refer back to Table 13-2, we see that these choices are indeed exactly equal

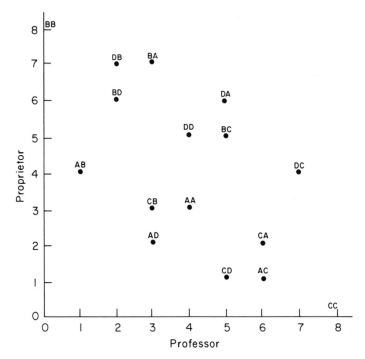

FIGURE 13-1 Interaction outcomes plotted by values of each participant

for each person. However, Figure 13-3 shows us that some judicious mix of *DA* and *DC* will result in a solution that will have greater utility for each. How can we mix these?

The position of the intersection between the equivalency line and the solution set provides the answer. The equivalency line (the dotted line in Figure 13-3) intersects $\overline{DADC}$ at a point that cuts $\overline{DADC}$ into two segments, one being exactly one-fourth of the other.[1] Therefore, the best solution to the interaction will be one in which *DA* is chosen three times as often as *DC*. In other words, in every four noon hours, *DA* should be chosen three times and *DC* chosen once. Putting this another way, the professor should always sit at the counter and order steak. The proprietor should always prepare the meal well and should hide the *Herald* three

---

[1]To prove this, drop a perpendicular line from *DA* toward the bottom of the graph, and a horizontal line toward the left border of the graph. These lines intersect at a point that we can call *x*. We have now created a triangle $\overline{DAxDC}$. Then let the point on the line $\overline{DADC}$ be called *y*. Extend a line from *x* to *y*, and we have now created two right triangles, $\overline{DAxy}$ and $\overline{DCxy}$. The line of equivalency passes through $\overline{DAx}$ at *BC*, a point that (only coincidentally) is exactly one-half of $\overline{DAx}$. Let the point where the line of equivalency intersects $\overline{DADC}$ be called *z*. Now we have created a new right triangle, $\overline{DABCz}$. This triangle and $\overline{DAxy}$ are similar triangles (remember your tenth-grade geometry?), because they have two angles that are equal. Similar triangles have proportions that are equal. Therefore, because $\overline{DABC} = \frac{1}{2} \overline{DAx}$, then $\overline{DAz} = \frac{1}{2} \overline{DAy}$. $\overline{DAy} = \frac{1}{2}$ of $\overline{DADC}$, so $\overline{DAz} = \frac{1}{4} \overline{DADC}$.

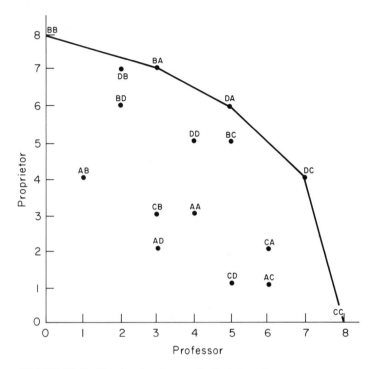

FIGURE 13-2 Dominant outcomes in the interaction

times out of four. If each person has correctly chosen the values that go into this system, then this solution will guarantee each the best subjective utility over the long run.

If this mathematical tool is available for the solution of bargaining interactions, why don't people use it? In the 1971 Attica prison riot, the prisoners and the officials were bargaining about conditions for ending the riot, and parts of the negotiation showed promise of arriving at a solution. However, Governor Rockefeller chose to storm the prison and put the riot down by force, resulting in the death of 10 hostages and 29 prisoners. All hostages were killed by gunfire from the assaulting forces and none were killed by the prisoners (Wicker, 1975, p. 400). We will never know why Rockefeller acted as he did, rather than extending the bargaining process further. Clearly, there were more desirable solutions than killing 39 persons and wounding 89 others.

In the summer of 1981, the baseball season was interrupted by a strike that suspended play for a good part of the summer. The most interesting part of the negotiation was that little of it went on at all before the strike. How can we bring about some give in these bargaining situations? Each person in the interaction must stand ready to make some concessions and, in addition, must be open to communicative interaction. Perhaps the total breakdown of the bargaining situation is in

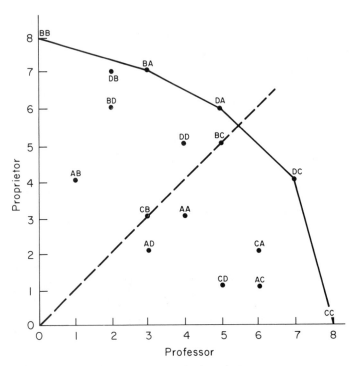

FIGURE 13-3 Line of equivalency in the solution

itself a message that one of the bargainers feels strongly about the situation, but it seems to be a real waste of time and money not to give bargaining a real chance in these kinds of problems.

Part of the limitations of bargaining behavior is that usually no real creative alternative arises from the situation. Steinfatt, Siebold, and Frye (1974) examined a prisoner's dilemma in a bargaining situation in which the prisoner might resort to an exchange of points, that is, bribe, for cooperative solution. In other words, they provided an opportunity to break out of the two-by-two matrix, as a creative alternative. Only one pair of their respondents arrived at this kind of solution. It seems clear that many of us are too heavily bound by the situation that a bargaining problem presents us. More creative constraints might well be the answer to this important psychological problem.

SUMMARY

The truly impressive part of real-life bargaining and negotiation seems to be the fact that little of us actually do it. We began this chapter with the hope of discovering how bargainers might influence each other, but we end it with the dismal notion that most mixed-motive interactions do not get to the bargaining stage. Perhaps the *really* important persuasive task is to get individuals to bargain at all.

Persuasion clearly plays an important part in mixed-motive interactions, but this role is far from clear. The sequence of moves is important. Most mixed-motive interactions can be solved with game theory, but few persons are aware enough of this kind of analysis to make it a popular technique.

QUESTIONS FOR FURTHER STUDY

1. Set up an experimental-monopoly game where none of the participants can bargain or trade. How did it work? Would you do it again?

2. Interview the customer service representative at any large store in your area (Wards, Sears). Do they make bargaining part of their job? How?

3. When was the last time you dickered about the price of any product? How did you feel about it?

4. Read Wicker's book about the Attica riots. If you had been one of the convicts, what changes in bargaining strategy would you have tried? Why did the governor react the way he did?

SUGGESTIONS FOR FURTHER READING

BOSTROM R.   Game theory in communication behavior. *Journal of Communication*, 1968, *18*, 369–380.

BEISECKER, T.   Game theory in communication research: a reaction and reorientation. *Journal of Communication*, 1970, *20*, 105–120.

DONOHUE, W.   Analyzing negotiation tactics: development of a negotiation interact system. *Human Communication Research*, 1981, *7*, 273–287.

HAMBURGER, H.   *Games as Models of Social Phenomena*. San Francisco: W.H. Freeman, 1979.

RUBIN, J. & BROWN, B.   *The social psychology of bargaining and negotiation*. New York: Academic Press, 1975.

WICKER, T.   *A time to die*. New York: Ballantine Books, 1975.

CHAPTER FOURTEEN
PERSUASION IN ORGANIZATIONS

Up to this point we have examined persuasion in the general sense, and in two interpersonal settings bargaining and small groups. Persuasive activity, of course, takes place in many other specific settings, and of these, one of the most important is the organization. Most of us spend a great deal of our lives in large organizations. These "groups of groups" do our banking for us, provide our groceries, organize our educational experiences and bring us entertainment. Individual enterprise, while romanticized by many, is definitely a thing of the past.

For example, this book that you are reading is nicely printed, interestingly bound, and distributed widely. This did not happen by accident. The author, though talented, could neither print a book nor design one, and he would be hard put to figure out how to ship them to the various colleges and universities that use it. The large organization that produced this book is called Prentice-Hall, and employs 100 college editors, 165 college sales representatives, 10 college executives, 6 college designers, as well as a multitude of advertising and marketing people, secretaries, and so forth. All in all, a large enterprise.

Levinson (1973) estimates that 90 percent of the persons who work do so in organizations. These organizations depend on communication, much of which is persuasive in nature, to coordinate their activities. The purpose of this chapter is to examine the organizational setting to see how persuasive activity functions there.

THE NATURE OF ORGANIZATIONS

One of the best definitions of an organization is that offered by Goldhaber: "a network of interdependent relationships" (1974, pp. 14–19). This may not have been the way that some of us would have defined organization, but because we assume Goldhaber knows what he is talking about, let us probe a little. First, let us explore the organizational idea behind networks.

Networks

A network is the general pattern in which the organization is put together. You will remember that small groups all have *structure*, and before an aggregation can be said to be a real group, some sort of structure is necessary. In large organizations, structure takes on a different kind of meaning. Part of organizational structure is usually determined by questions of ownership, authority relationships, and tradition.

In medieval times, merchants and artisans usually dealt directly with their clientele. As commerce developed, the artisans began to acquire structure in the master-journeyman-apprentice system. The master was responsible for the overall operation of the shop, the journeymen did the skilled labor, and the apprentices did the unskilled work. Any customer had access to the master because he was always in the shop. However, as soon as one person acquired a second shop, then a line of responsibility developed, and the two shops were connected by the fact of their common ownership. The concept of ownership of private property was a fundamental aspect of this development, because it made it possible for a shoemaker to buy or own a tailor shop and a hatter's shop, thereby, and to become a clothing company. The network concept described the ownership pattern of these shops.

Once a company developed, the individual clients were no longer able to have direct access to the owner because the owner might well be in another part of the city or country. Problems had to be relayed through the network leading to the owner and down again.

In modern organizations, these networks are extremely complex and sometimes very frustrating. For example, in a typical hospital, there are two different networks that operate to keep the hospital running. One of these is administrative, consisting of the people who work in food services, provide janitorial services, and the like. This well-defined network is usually headed by a hospital administrator. At the same time, there is another network dealing with medical matters. This network is headed by a chief of medicine and deals with questions of what doctors are allowed to practice in the hospital, whether an expensive piece of equipment is needed, and how the operating rooms should be scheduled. Part of the problems in modern hospitals (and part of the reason that they cost so much) is inherent in this dual network system.

You can see how important the specific network system is to any organization. We are interested in it because the network typically prescribes how communication will flow in the organization. There are formal networks in organizations and informal ones. Sometimes the formal ones are more effective in getting information through the organizational structure.

Networks of authority involve power relationships. It is often the case that superiors in a formal network try to persuade their subordinates to perform certain tasks. In the same organization, other superiors simply tell their employees what to do. In more progressive organizations, superiors attempt to sell employees on their work, not tell them. Networks will function, in a large part, according to the philosophy an organization has, and within each philosophy formal networks will vary.

Interdependent Relationships

The second element in Goldhaber's definition of an organization was interdependent relationships. Everyone in a large organization is related to every other person on some way or another. These relationships vary in type, in intensity, and in structure. An employee's position in the network partially accounts for the kind of relationship that they have with those above and below them in the network hierarchy.

Personal characteristics also account for part of the relational structure. Let us look at some of these relational elements.

Position.   The organization typically has a number of levels of responsibility and activity. Depending on where individuals are in the network, their relationships can be seen as upward, downward, or level. In addition, each organization has relational elements derived from factors other than the formal structures. These informal relationships are often more important and effective in communication than the formal ones.

Function.   Because the organization depends heavily on the division of labor for its efficiency, the kind of activity each individual engages in will importantly affect the relational elements involved. Most organizations distinguish between *staff* and *line* functions. Line functions are those that actually advance the work of the organization. In an auto manufacturing plant, the line is the actual manufacturing process. In a university, the professors are the line persons who actually do the work. In the armed forces, a line officer is an officer who operates in one of the combat arms.

Staff persons, on the other hand, are those whose work benefits and assists the line functions. In the auto manufacturing plant, the personnel department is usually considered a staff department, because auto manufacturing could conceivably take place without personnel records being kept. Universities, similarly, could do without student-affairs functions such as student unions and student loans. The military could carry out its mission without a finance department. Staff functions have occupied a larger and larger part of most organizations, and depend increasingly on communication as the basic tool for their operation.

Organizations and Communication

What kind of communication takes place in organizations? Let us turn once again to Goldhaber for a definition. He defines communication in organizations as: "verbal/nonverbal messages orally diffused to internal audiences for task, maintenance, and human purposes" (1974, p. 14). "Task" refers to the daily activity of the organization. "Maintenance" relates to matters that keep the organization in good health, such as personnel and supportive activity. And "human purposes" means that individuals in the organization will maintain friendship and human contact in ways sometimes irrelevant to organizational activity. As we might expect, the typical divisions of communicative purpose are also found in the organization. We will examine some of these first, and then look at upward, downward, and lateral messages later in this chapter.

Informative messages.   Information is absolutely vital in any large organization. As a consequence, a great deal of the messages sent internally have to do with procedures, operations, addresses, instructions, and the like. Typical methods used in corporations are bulletin boards, company publications, and meetings. In other words, oral and printed channels are typically used.

Persuasion.   Few writers in organizational communication use the word *persuasion*. Tompkins, for example, in describing the functions of an executive, tells us that an executive must ". . . induce cooperation by communication" (1977, p. 24). Many others use the word *influence* almost exclusively (Jablin, 1979). Regardless of the terminology, the motivation of others is an important organizational process. Few managers understand it and rely heavily instead on coercion to achieve organizational goals.

Approaches to Organizational Theory

Early in this chapter we observed that organizational life is quite different from the other kinds of human activity that we all engage in. How exactly do organizations function? The answer, as you might expect, is not known exactly, but there are a number of general views about it that are quite useful to the study of organizational communication. There is no one view of large organizations that is commonly accepted by all. Each approach has an important influence on how an organization works. Let us look at a few of these.

McGregor's theory X and theory Y.   One of the most interesting approaches to basic organizational thinking is the contrast between theory-X and theory-Y management. These two approaches were originally proposed by Douglas McGregor (1960), to account for the assumptions managers make about their subordinates. Theory X assumes that most persons naturally dislike work and avoid it. Therefore, most persons must be coerced into working and threatened with punishment. In addition, most persons prefer to be directed and wish security above other desires. Theory Y, on the other hand, assumes that people enjoy work naturally, and self-control and self-direction are the natural way to supervise activities. The average worker does not avoid responsibility but, instead, seeks it.
    Which of these views of human nature is correct? Probably neither, but the

assumptions make an enormous difference in the manner in which organizations are structured. You probably know many American organizations that are structured according to theory X. Robert Townsend's illuminating report of his experiences in reorganizing the Avis corporation (1970) makes us think that perhaps all businesses ought to be reorganized following theory-Y principles.

Content theories vs. process theories.   Luthans and Kreitner (1975) have described organizational theories as being divided into two main types: process theories and content theories. Both theory X and theory Y are content theories, because they attempt to provide the cognitive processes that lead to individual motivation in an organization. You will recall that in Chapter 3 we discussed the general differences between cognitive psychology and behavioral psychology. The content theories generally belong in the cognitive category.

On the other hand, the process theories ignore the inner aspects of human experience and focus on the stimuli and responses, that is, the inputs and outputs of the organization. Luthans and Kreitner advocate the process approach and apply techniques of behavioral modification to achieve organizational goals. In their view, a reinforcement schedule will be the most effective persuasive system in bringing about behavioral change in an organization. In this view, then, communication is the vehicle by which the reward schedules could be made explicit to employees. With this process, persuasion is linked to identifying specific behaviors that will and will not be rewarded.

ORGANIZATIONAL COMMUNICATION

As you might have expected, the problem of communication in organizations has had some systematic study by researchers in communication. As we mentioned earlier, specific attention to persuasion has not been part of this research. Nonetheless, some extremely interesting data has been gathered concerning the nature of organizational communication. If we look at some specific instances of this research, we can probably see how some of them relate to persuasion in the organization.

Communication and Influence

One whose principal job in an organization is communicative ought logically to have more influence than one whose principal function is a direct line operation. The organizational communicators ought logically to be more influential than the line persons, at least on the face of it. In an attempt to examine the influence of these persons, MacDonald (1976) studied those workers in an organization whose direct function was liaison. These persons' principal job was to act as a communicative relay between one part of the organization and the other. MacDonald found that

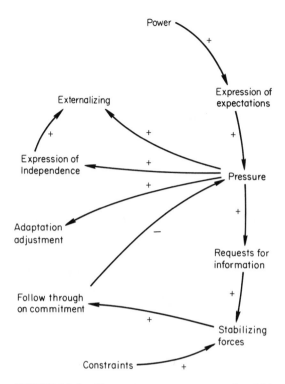

FIGURE 14-1. The power-pressure group of variables.

Source: L. Browning, A grounded organizational communication theory derived from qualitative data. Communication Monographs, 1978, 45, p. 95. Reprinted by permission of the Speech Communication Association.

most members of the organization felt that these liaison persons were much more influential than other persons. In actuality, the influence that they had was no more than any other person in the organization. In other words, persons *perceive* liaison persons as more influential than they actually are.

Browning (1978) has constructed an elaborate model of the pressure aspects of organizational communication. In his study he performed detailed analyses of communication incidents that occurred in a large organization. He organized and classified these into three main clusters: power-advancement; power-pressure; and central figure. The second cluster, the power-pressure cluster, most corresponds to the persuasive function in this organization. Figure 14-1 illustrates the relationships among these clusters. The person with power, through expression of expectations, exerts pressure that, in turn, creates externalization, expressions of independence, and adaptation adjustment. It also leads to requests for information that, in turn, lead to stabilizing forces. You may recognize in Figure 14-1 a system of communication. Browning did not attempt to explain this system in terms of any particular organization communication theory, but only describe what happens in an organization when pressure is attempted.

Superior-Subordinate Relationships

Fred Jablin, in an extremely detailed analysis of the problems involved in superior-subordinate communications, has examined several of the characteristics of this kind of organizational communication (1979).

Upward influence.   Interestingly enough, the upward influence of a superior has a strong effect on subordinates. Employees are satisfied with their superior much more when that superior exercises a great deal of influence with the superior's superiors. In addition, these subordinates will then interact more with the superior with upward influence. Jablin, however, urges that this conclusion be accepted only tentatively (p. 1207). No real reason has been proposed for this phenomenon, but it seems reasonable to conclude that those persons who excel in upward persuasive communication are also good at it in downward persuasive communication. This may also be a credibility effect because an individual judged to have influence within the organization may be viewed as being high in qualification-expertness.

Personal characteristics.   Another factor discussed by Jablin is the personal characteristic of both the superior and the subordinate. One interesting characteristic is the internal vs. external perception of locus of control. Internal persons feel that their behavior is inner-directed, and that they are in charge of their life. Externals, on the other hand, feel that other persons, circumstances, and the organization have more effect on outcomes than they do themselves. Internal supervisors tend to use persuasion more than do external supervisors. In other words, if an individual is confident in his or her ability and position in an organization, then that person will tend to use persuasive rather than coercive influence on others. On the other hand, internals will be more susceptible to persuasive messages aimed at higher-level needs and externals will be more susceptible to persuasive messages aimed at lower-level needs.

In addition, subordinates are more satisfied with a superior when the superior has high credibility, is not apprehensive, and is usually nonauthoritarian. Whether these satisfaction indices can be translated into successful persuasive ability has not been demonstrated, though it seems reasonable to conclude that one is more easily persuaded by a source who is considered a more satisfactory supervisor than another.

Semantic-information distance.   A third variable summarized by Jablin is the semantic-information distance that exists between superiors and subordinates. This distance is usually defined as disparity in the way in which superiors and subordinates use words to describe reality and structure. When this distance is high, subordinates' morale is low. Management, for example, tends to describe itself in terms not used by workers. Probably the most significant aspect of the semantic-information distance is that managers typically tend to misperceive the attitudes held by their subordinates. This means that often managers will be confronted with significant problems in persuasive communication without knowing that these problems exist.

INDUCING ORGANIZATIONAL CHANGE

One of the most common persuasive tasks in an organization is that of bringing about some change in the organization. There are many problems involved in changing the character of an organization. Organizations resist change, depending on (1) the size of the organization, (2) the number of levels that are involved in the network, (3) the length of time that members of the organization have been involved in it, and (4) the perceptions of the members about the present structure.

In addition, any group (as you will recall from Chapter 12) has its own norms and standards. This is especially pertinent in organizations in which a group has established its own work norms. Then those who produce more or work harder are viewed as extremely threatening to the work group as a whole.

In spite of organizational inertia, change in organizations can be accomplished. Let us look at some of the approaches to change that are typically advocated.

Motivational Patterns

Katz and Kahn (1966) assert that four principal motivational structures are present in any organization, and to bring about change, one or more of these patterns ought to be employed. These motives are (1) legal compliance, (2) seeking rewards, (3) self-determination, and (4) internalization of rewards. If, these seem familiar, they should! Those are an extremely close paraphrase of the general social-influence processes proposed by Herbert Kelman (1961). You might wish to review these and the four principal types of source credibility in Chapter 4. Katz and Kahn's first two methods, legal compliance and seeking rewards, were grouped together by Kelman and called compliance. Katz and Kahn's last two are also the same as Kelman's internalization. What Kelman offered was the identification factor that Katz and Kahn ignored. One would certainly feel that persons in an organization would be as susceptible to internalization as they would be anywhere.

Motivational approaches in organizations depend on what Lathans and Kreietner (1975) call process approaches to organizations. Other approaches of this type include Maslow's hierarchy of needs (1943) and other theories of internal motivation. The principal problem with those approaches is that, like some general models of persuasion (see Chapter 6), they depend on rational models of human behavior. Nonetheless, they have been proved successful in many different settings.

Organizational Goal Integration

Kathleen Kelly Reardon (1981) has proposed an extremely interesting approach to organizational persuasion that she calls "organizational goal integration." This process, says Reardon, is accomplished by the *integration of organization goals and personal goals*. Three separate techniques are used to bring this about. The first is the exchange process, in which money and other rewards are traded for work. The second is the socialization process, in which "people can be persuaded to value activities that help the organization" (1981, p. 178). Third is the accommodation process, in which the organization *accommodates* to the persons involved, rather than the other way around. Reardon's approach is extremely interesting and seems to be valid for most organizations.

Counterattitudinal Advocacy

You will remember from Chapter 3 that counterattitudinal advocacy is the process in which we advocate something that we really do not believe in. You will also remember that this process is an effective method of inducing attitude change and can be thought of as a separate kind of persuasion (Miller and Burgoon, 1975). Reardon (1981) feels that counterattitudinal advocacy is one of the most powerful methods by which large organizations bring about change in their members. Although this may disturb some of us, we need to recognize that this process is probably universal. Almost every organization occasionally induces its members to say things that they do not really believe.

An interesting example of this is reported by Altheide and Johnson (1980). They interviewed officers and men of the U.S.S. *Walden*, a warship assigned to the bombardment of the Vietnamese coast during the war in Vietnam. One of these officers reported that the aerial spotters would often exaggerate the amount of damage done by a particular salvo. When asked why, the officer reported:

> It was written in the regulations that damage assessment will be given at the completion of each mission. So even if there wasn't any damage, they'd give you some, because they had to justify—eventually the ship had to justify sending 300 shells onto a beach only to come back with no damage. I mean, no damage? The Type Commander is going to want to know why I am spending 18,000 dollars a shell, or whatever it is, and why are you firing 300 of these shells against no target? (1980, p. 211)

Altheide and Johnson further report on the procedure for enforcing this kind of fraudulent report. In another interview, a gunnery officer related:

> One time, I don't remember whether we had just arrived on the gun line in a particular area or whether we'd been firing there for a couple of days, but anyway, this time we

ran into a green spotter. This was his first time out, although we didn't find this out until a couple of months later. It was our first mission of the day, I think, and he came over the phone and said due to the dense foliage he couldn't give us any battle damage assessment. The Old Man asked to ask him again, to tell him that we *had* to have damage, but the spotter repeated the same thing again, that he couldn't give us any. Well, the Captain got on the circuit and gave a call to the spotter's Commanding Officer and said, very to the point, I thought, no damage assessment for our rounds, and we pick up our marbles and go home. He didn't say it exactly that way, of course, but that was the message. Following this, we could hear the spotter's Commanding Officer get on the same circuit and he told him to fly a little lower and see if he couldn't find a few bunkers. The spotter could hear all of this, of course, and by this time, he knew what it was all about. He found some, too. (1980, p. 212)

After a period of this activity, it is quite reasonable to see how those who are rewarded for this counterattitudinal reporting may easily come to believe that what they are saying is true.

Leadership in Organizations

Many persons are convinced that organizational change is a clear function of the characteristics of the leaders in the organizations. Often we are disappointed when a new leader (such as a president) finds that the federal government is the same old thing, regardless of who is at the top. When universities are disgusted with their football teams, it is the coach that gets fired, not the players. But you will remember from Chapter 12 that leadership is a complex process and depends as heavily on the members of a group as it does on the leader. This is especially true in large organizations.

One of the most interesting approaches to leadership in organizations is that of Fred Fiedler (1968). Fiedler measured the manner in which leaders perceived other members of the work group. He used two techniques, the ASO score and the LPC score. The first is based on the "assumed similarity of opposites" and is measured by having each member rate every other member on semantic differential scales, such as friendly-unfriendly and pleasant-unpleasant. Then each person designates one person in the work group that is the most preferred and the least preferred. The difference between those two persons in the scales measures is the ASO. The LPC measure is similar, in that it stands for "least-preferred coworker." A leader that has a high LPC score is one that views even the least preferred coworker in favorable terms. This would seem to indicate a homogeneous group, or at least a positive attitude on the part of the leader for all of the group members.

Fiedler's second aspect of leadership depends on task structure. Given tasks in the organization can be structured or unstructured, depending on the situation. Often the organizational constraints determine structure. The military, for example, is highly structured. Other organizations have much more flexibility. The latitude of choice offered to any leader is determined by the structure.

The third characteristic is that of position power. Fiedler defines this variable as the amount of reward and punishment available to the leader in the organization. In a university department, for example, the department chairperson may be the designated leader, but the amount of salary the faculty gets each year may be determined either by a salary schedule or by a dean. In this case, the chairperson has very little position power. Leaders with real power in organizations are those who can hire or fire employees, can determine their work schedules, and can determine raises in pay.

Putting these three characteristics together, Fiedler constructed what he called a contingency model of leadership. In short, this model states that in given situations, the LPC or ASO scores of the leader will have differing effects on the group's performance. For example, if the group has good leader-member relations, is unstructured, and the leader position power is weak, high LPC scores will contribute to positive group performance. When the leader-member relations are poor, the situation is structured and the leader's position power is strong, the LPC will also contribute positively to the group's performance. However, when leader-member relationships are good, the task is unstructured and position power is weak, LPC will not contribute to good group performance. (For a complete layout of the contingency model, see Fiedler, 1968, p. 371.)

There are a number of other leadership theories used in the organizational setting (see Chapter 12), but Fiedler's is probably the most useful. One important factor that characterizes Fiedler's research is that it has been carried out in real organizations and not in artificially constructed laboratory settings. Fiedler has probably one of the most comprehensive approaches to organizational leadership. In his view, persuasion or motivation in an organization will be seriously modified by the circumstances and position in which the leader operates.

Planned Change

Another worthwhile approach to organizational change is the planning approach advocated by Lippit, Watson, and Westley (1958). Here the focus is on relevant information coming in from outside the organization or created inside the organization. One organization member or a group of members is a change agent who oversees the planning and the implementation of the change. This process is a formal, participative effort at change and has often been implemented by those interested in modernization. The role of the change agent is extremely important in this process, and it is typical to see an outside consultant in this role. One important part of the process is the stabilization of change after the planning phase. Organizations tend to revert to older patterns, and one of the important processes of the change agent is to see that stabilization takes place. Participation at every level in each of the phases of planning is advocated as the principal method of stabilization.

SUMMARY

It should be clear that persuasion in a large organization is simply not a matter of selecting a highly credible source and constructing an impressive and intense message. The complexity of the organizational structure together with the interchange of relational elements indicate that those who attempt change in organizations use many different techniques at many different places in the organization. At the same time, persons in organizations are the same as persons anywhere else, so that general principles of persuasion can be expected to apply. The organizational setting provides an interesting challenge to persuaders to fit these techniques into the specific functions in the organization.

QUESTIONS FOR FURTHER STUDY

1. Examine the four main motivational patterns hypothesized by Katz and Kahn (1966) and compare them to Kelman's three influence processes and the four credibility factors in Chapter 4.
2. Try to trace the paperwork and the steps necessary to change a grade at your school. What does this tell you about authority?
3. Interview someone in a relatively low-status job in a large organization (use yourself, if you have such a job). What varying perceptions are there of the superiors? How would you go about persuading them of anything?
4. What was the last major change you observed in your school's organizational structure? Try to find out how it came about.
5. Attempt to find an organizational chart for an organization. Then interview individuals in those positions and find out if it works or not.

SUGGESTIONS FOR FURTHER READING

ALTHEIDE, D. & JOHNSON, J. *Bureaucratic propaganda*. Boston: Allyn and Bacon, 1980.

FIEDLER, F. Personality situational determinants of leadership effectiveness. In D. Cartwright & A. Zander, (Eds.) *Group dynamics*. New York: Harper and Row, 1968.

GOLDHABER, G. *Organizational communication*. Dubuque: Brown, 1974.

JABLIN, F. Superior-subordinate communication: the state of the art. *Psychological Bulletin*, 1979, *86*, 1201–1222.

CHAPTER FIFTEEN
PERSUASION AND YOU

By now you know a great deal more about persuasion than the average person, and you certainly must have formed some general ideas about the way the process affects you, your loved ones, and friends, not to mention your society as a whole. We may have all admitted at the beginning that persuasion is probably a better method of bringing about social change than coercion, but under some circumstance we may not be so sure. A coercive society is at least honest with its relationships with its people. High-conforming organizations, like the military, are frank in their expectations that individual freedom of action is severely circumscribed. Not all organizations are so direct with their members. The American university system, where individual freedom is loudly advocated, may in fact be rigid in its behavioral expectations. This kind of influence is more insidious because it wears the cloak of reasonableness and openness.

The basic decision every person must make is the ethical one. How ethical is it to persuade another person? In Chapter 1, we introduced a few basic statements about the ethicality of the persuasive act. Let us review these statements:

1. Persuasion can be viewed as an ethically neutral act, one that can be employed for ethical or nonethical ends.
2. Persuasion will be employed by many varieties of persons. Knowledge of the persuasive processes will often be useful as a defense against unscrupulous practitioners.
3. Ethical systems are often relative and can admit several acceptable answers to the same question.

These statements are true as far as they go, but there are a number of problems with them, especially with the first one. Let us look for a moment at some of the ethical problems inherent in the view that persuasion is ethically neutral.

THE ETHICS OF
PERSUASION

Persuasion as an Ethically
Neutral Act

Persuasion is certainly not *always* ethically neutral because there are a number of techniques used by persuaders that are certainly questionable. For example, consider these recommendations by Ewbank and Auer (1951) for the conduct of debate: It is considered ethically wrong to falsify evidence, to use emotional appeals when facts and logic are available, to divert attention from your own weakness by attacking the opponent, to conceal your true purpose, and to pose as an authority when you actually possess only a layperson's knowledge. Modern advertisers, evangelists, political candidates, governments, professors, and, indeed, each of us are probably guilty of one of Ewbank and Auer's five violations at some time or another. Often we simply invoke a relativistic ethic, state that "the times, they are a'changing," and simply classify Ewbank and Auer as a couple of old fuddy-duddies. However, if we think about it for a moment, *none* of us would like to be persuaded in the fashion that Ewbank and Auer describe.

So the point of view that persuasion is an ethically neutral act is probably not defensible, it depends on *what kind* of persuasion. You will recognize in this position the ends-means argument, that is, if the act produces an ethically good result, then an ethically questionable means is, therefore, justified. For example, President Roosevelt may have had to shade the truth slightly to involve the United States in World War II, and most historians seem to feel that the fight against Hitler was certainly justification for this act. However, when President Johnson did the same thing in the war in Vietnam, he was roundly condemned; the nature of the conflict did not have the same moral character as the war against Germany and Japan. If we accept the ends-means argument, then we might say that Hitler was morally correct in exterminating six million Jews, because this act resulted directly in the establishment of a Jewish homeland in Israel, which was a morally "good" outcome.

It is easy to see that this argument is fraught with difficulty. It may indeed be ethical to disfigure a woman with a mastectomy if you really believe that in so doing you are saving her life, but it may be entirely unethical to advocate the discontinuance of black-lung benefits for coal miners because you feel that energy is too expensive. So some other standard ought to be applied other than the ends-means standard.

Altruism

A simple standard against which to test the ethicality of persuasive acts is that of altruism. A persuader who sincerely has the best interests of the receivers in mind cannot be totally at fault. For example, suppose a policeman poses as a minister in order to talk a would-be suicide off a window ledge. The policeman has committed an unethical persuasive act, but there is no prospect of personal gain for the persuader here. Conversely, an evangelist who poses as a family counselor so that he can charge for marriage counseling is clearly in the wrong.

The phenomenon of helping others has received a good deal of attention recently from contemporary social psychologists. The result of most of this study shows that most of us are not as willing to help others as we probably ought to be. For example, Bostrom, Humphreys, and Roloff (1980) found that only half of the respondents in a large sample were willing to help by making a simple telephone call. This rate of response is disconcerting.

Altruism can be defined as that quality in an act in which no personal reward is expected. It is probably true, as Roloff (1981) has maintained, that a great deal of human interaction is motivated by *exchange* considerations (you do something for me, and I will do something for you). Many exchanges are ethical in that they are fair, but for an excellent test of the ethicality of a persuasive act, the altruistic standard is probably the best.

Ethics and Credibility

An encouraging sign for all of us involved in communication is that the general examination of credibility reveals a fairly strong ethic. You will remember that in Chapter 4, we examined four different factors of credibility. One, safety-trustworthiness, is intensively ethical. A source is judged to be high in this factor when he or she is considered to be a truth-teller. Many times polling organizations ask the general public about what occupations are credible. Almost all of these list used-car salespersons at the bottom of the list, preceded closely by politicians. Years ago, the medical profession was highly regarded in such polls, but has slipped seriously in recent years, perhaps reflecting the public's perception that physicians are becoming more and more interested in the financial aspects of their profession. Typically underpaid groups—for example, ministers and school teachers—remain at the top of these kinds of lists.

You will remember that Ewbank and Auer condemned the tendency to pose as an expert, and to use emotional appeal rather than factual ones. These recommendations are reflected in the qualification-expertness credibility factor. In other words, in the belief that all persuasive sources should be expert, we are taking an ethical position, whether we like it or not.

Two credibility factors are probably not related to ethical positions, namely, compliance-dynamism and normative-identificatory. We have little choice over the latter, since it is rooted in our social and residential group memberships. Compliance-dynamism, on the other hand, seems to be an unethical form of persuasion. The source who persuades through position power has little to offer to mitigate the unpleasantness of this act. We might take heart, however, in that Bostrom (1981) found that compliance-dynamism evaluations did not conform to other credibility evaluations in the RSO theoretical predictions, and McCroskey and Young (1981) view compliance-dynamism with great suspicion.

As we review the credibility literature, we see, inherent in the general perception of sources, a strong dimension of ethicality. However much sources might feel that they can manipulate audiences by use of unethical tactics, it should be clear that in order to be credible, some attention must be paid to the ethical dimension. Perhaps Ewbank and Auer were not so out of date after all! It is, after all, perfectly possible to be ethical *and* persuasive. B.J. Diggs (1964) summed this up rather well:

> At its best, persuasion is not a matter of means and ends or of cause and effect. It is a sharing of reason, a union of rational beings in which foggy vision in one is made up for by the keen sight of another. Or more aptly, it is a union in which men mutually contribute, through a variety of persuasive roles, to the clear vision and well-being of all. Its goal is mutual understanding of the best thing to do. (1964, p. 373)

RESISTANCE TO PERSUASION

Though we feel that all persons *should* be ethical, it is our sad experience that many of them are not. In many cases, it is our duty to *resist* persuasion when it is attempted. Fortunately, there is a great deal that we now know about this interesting topic.

Why Resist?

One difficulty that we all must face is the fact that we live in a pluralistic society where persuasion is not always used for good ends. Almost every large organization is interested in a certain amount of conformity and would wish most of its employees to have a more positive attitude than they do.

Day in and day out we are all bombarded with persuasive messages from a variety of sources such as advertisers, political candidates, utility companies, government agencies, and others. Without ever really noticing it, these messages subtly become part of our culture, and we are persuaded without being aware of it.

Our government was formed with a strong desire for civil liberties together with a desire for individual freedom that is not seen in much of the world. The very size of the modern corporation, together with the power inherent in contemporary government presents, *in and of itself*, serious assaults on the real liberty of individuals. We do possess a great deal of political freedom, but our economic freedom is another thing.

Throughout this book we have seen a great deal of attention given to research in finding new ways to persuade persons. The technology available to carry out these techniques is awesome. In order to preserve even some semblance of individual dignity, the citizen's duty is resistance to persuasion.

How do we show people that they are being manipulated? Ellul's injunction has great meaning for all of us:

> The only truly serious attitude is to show people the extreme effectiveness of the weapons used against them, to rouse them to defend themselves by making them aware of their frailty and their vulnerability, instead of soothing them with the worst

illusion, that of a security that neither man's nature nor the techniques of propaganda permit him to possess. (1965, p. 257)

Edelman (1977) has examined some of the persuasive techniques used by the establishment, and the assumption that when someone is out of step with the established norm they are deviant and must be corrected. Edelman cites examples occurring among psychiatric patients and welfare recipients that indicate that both of these groups have been taught to think of themselves as inadequate. The use of the health metaphor is common among groups of this type. Individuals are taught to think of themselves as sick and to think of the institutions, such as mental hospitals and welfare agencies, that are trying to treat them as well. Group meetings, in which pseudodemocracy is encouraged, are in fact insiduous methods for stamping out resistance, and keeping clients in a powerless state, ambivalent about their roles and their identity. Edelman believes that when a leadership springs up that encourages alliances among these client groups, such as a welfare rights organization, the result is more self-respect and confidence, and even more power in the process of extracting concessions from the authorities.

Early Work in Inoculation

It is not enough to feel that we must resist; it is crucial to know *how* to do it. Fortunately, some research is available to provide some guidelines to this important process.

A great deal of the earliest research in resistance to persuasion was done by William McGuire (1964) who used the term inoculation to describe the attribution of greater resistance to individuals. McGuire studied various means of inoculation, but he was principally interested in the process of supplying information to receivers *before* the communication takes place in the hope that the information would make the receiver more resistant. This information may be thought of as an inoculation in the biological sense, in that a less harmful disease often confers immunity to a more harmful one. McGuire thought that some counterpersuasion in advance of the persuasive message would serve in the same fashion. Whether we can consider persuasion a disease is an interesting question. However, McGuire's basic technique involves supplying information prior to the reception of the message so that the receiver will be more resistant.

McGuire's basic method was to construct a persuasive message attacking a cultural truism, such as "Everyone should brush their teeth after each meal if at all possible." The message would contain statements like "too much brushing wears down the teeth prematurely." Then prior to the message, material would be introduced that should strengthen the belief in the truism. McGuire wondered if this information should be supportive—that is, if it should support the truism—or refutational—that is, if it should refute any possible attacks on the truism.

Another one of McGuire's first questions involved the nature of the presentation of the message. One method was passive reading, in which receivers merely read the defensive material. Another method was to read the refutational material

TABLE 15-1   Mean Belief Levels after Attacks Preceded by Refutational—Same vs Supportive Defenses[a,b]

TYPE OF PARTICIPATION	REFUTATIONAL DEFENSE THEN ATTACK	SUPPORTIVE DEFENSE THEN ATTACK	REFUTE MINUS SUPPORT
Passive reading	11.51	7.47	+4.04
	(35)	(32)	
Reading and underlining	11.13	7.63	+3.50
	(31)	(32)	
Writing from outline	9.19	7.94	+1.25
	(31)	(32)	
Writing without guidance	9.46	6.53	+2.93
	(35)	(32)	
Weighted mean	10.33	7.39	+2.94
	(132)	(128)	

[a]Control levels: neither attack nor defense — 12.62 (N — 130); attack only (with no prior defense) — 6.64 (N — 130).

[b]15.00 indicates complete adherence to the truism; 1.00 indicates complete disagreement.

Source: Adapted from *The Study of Attitude Change* by R.V. Wagner and J.J. Sherwood. Copyright © 1969 by Wadsworth Publishing Company, Inc. Reprinted by permission of the Publisher, Brooks/Cole Publishing Company, Monterey, California.

and underline significant passages relative to the arguments presented in the defense. A third method was to write out the defensive material, based on an outline supplied by the experimenters. A fourth method was writing out the arguments without any guidance.

Table 15-1 presents McGuire's initial findings. The refutational material was better in all cases. In addition, the reading of the material was also better than the writing of the defensive material. It also seems likely that the receivers got more information from the reading conditions than from any of the writing conditions.

McGuire studied a number of other methods of inducing resistance to persuasion: foreknowledge of a persuasive attempt, active and passive participation in refutational activities, and persistence of the effects. None of these produced as many interesting findings as the initial study of types of participation and types of defense.

Sometimes the inoculation can take place immediately before the message in an active situation. Infante (1973a) studied the kind of inoculation present in the following situation: information was presented in the form of a transcript of a symposium, in which the following exchange took place:

> MODERATOR: I would like for us to turn to another area, the safety of the community's habits regarding the consumption of carbonated cola soft drinks. Yes, Dr. Eugene Abelson, you have something to say on this?

TABLE 15-2 Character and Authoritativeness of Warner and Speaker

	OPINIONATED WARNING[a]			
	A WARNS ABOUT A	A WARNS ABOUT LA	LA WARNS ABOUT A	LA WARNS ABOUT LA
Char. of Warner	10.41	9.65	10.82	11.59
Auth. of Warner	12.65	13.06	9.06	9.41
Char. of Speaker	15.71	14.41	15.88	14.06
Auth. of Speaker	17.82	15.94	17.12	17.35

	NONOPINIONATED WARNING			
	A WARNS ABOUT A	A WARNS ABOUT LA	LA WARNS ABOUT A	LA WARNS ABOUT LA
Char. of Warner	10.21	10.47	11.82	10.53
Auth. of Warner	12.82	13.18	10.12	11.53
Char. of Speaker	14.88	15.00	15.06	15.00
Auth. of Speaker	17.94	16.71	18.18	17.35

	CONTROL	
	A SPEAKER ONLY	LA SPEAKER ONLY
Char. of Speaker	13.35	14.53
Auth. of Speaker	16.29	16.47

[a]Scale: 3, least favorable, 21, most favorable. A = initially authoritative source. LA = initially less authoritative source.

DR. DENNIS ALTERMAN: (Professor of Pharmacology at the University of Iowa) Just a moment; I am very familiar with what Dr. Abelson is going to say on this issue. So before he begins, I would just like to say a few things. I do not think that carbonated cola soft drinks are harmful for the individual. Also, I do not accept the arguments that he is going to present on cola soft drinks being associated with malnutrition, insomnia, heart disease, dental disease, and sclerosis of the liver (1973a, p. 190).

The persuasive speech by Dr. Alterman then followed. These warnings were couched in both ordinary language (above) and opinionated language. Infante compared the results of such warnings when preceding an authoritative speaker as well as an unauthoritative speaker. Table 15–2 presents Infante's findings. In this table, the lower the mean, the more persuasive was the speech. You can see that the warning was effective with the authoritative speaker only if couched in opinionated language, but it was ineffective for nonauthoritative speakers. Apparently the opinionated language applied to the nonauthoritative source backfired on the warner. Infante also tested the effects of opinionated language as it interacts with the warner's position, before or after the speaker (1975b). He found that the language still had the same effect, but that the position of the warner had little effect. In other words, the forewarning could have been an afterwarning just as easily. This finding does serious harm to the inoculation notion, and forces us to look for some other explanation of the resistance phenomenon. What is present here is the effects of two messages presented to the same persons, not an induction of resistance.

This means that the so-called inoculation is only the presentation of another message, following the same rules of any other message. For example, McCroskey, Young, and Scott (1972) found that two-sided inoculation attempts were more effective than one-sided ones, and that evidence in the inoculation was not a significant factor. You will remember some of the ambivalent findings concerning evidence in Chapter 8.

Counterarguments and Persuasion

One technique that many persons probably use in resisting persuasive messages is the invention of counterarguments. For example, you may hear someone argue that television causes violent behavior in young persons, and while you listen, you might say to yourself, "But would they have been as violent without television?" This is a counterargument, which may succeed in defusing the effect of the message. No one knows, of course, what goes on inside someone's mind while a message is being presented. Festinger and Maccoby (1964) got around this difficulty by distracting a group of receivers. They reasoned that if they were distracted, they would not be able to come up with the effective counterarguments and, thus, the receivers would be more persuaded. Festinger and Maccoby did indeed show that persons who were distracted while a persuasive communication was being presented were persuaded more as a result. You will remember that in Chapter 11 we examined the Janis, Kaye, and Kirschner study (1965) in which individuals were given food and a soft drink while receiving the persuasive communication. Janis, Kaye, and Kirschner explain their findings by asserting that the receivers who ate were probably distracted. You will remember that Chapter 11 disagreed with this interpretation and attributed the results to elevated affect. However, a small amount of distraction might also have been involved.

David Brandt (1979) examined two items: the distraction that was involved in heckling a persuasive speech. In addition, he gave the listeners a paper-and-pencil test that measured the propensity to counterargue. He found that the heckling was effective only among those persons who were not likely to counterargue. Those who were high counterarguers were not affected by the heckling at all. Brandt's data adds credibility to Festinger and Maccoby's contentions about distractions. Heckling, you will remember, decreased the credibility of a source. We would conclude that any kind of heckling would reduce persuasive impact. But among those who were low in propensity to counterargue, heckling actually *increased* persuasive impact, making the communication more effective.

Individual Differences
and Resistance

Adams and Beatty (1977) tested the interaction between dogmatism, the need for social approval, and the resistance to persuasion. You will remember from Chapter 11 that certain kinds of listener personalities often affect persuasion. Adams and Beatty studied dogmatism (Rokeach, 1960), and need for social approval (Crowne and Marlow, 1964). However, neither of these personality variables had any affect on the subsequent resistance. On the other hand, the supportive strategy was much more effective in inducing resistance than was the refutational, but this difference did not reach statistical significance.

Infante (1976) found that receivers that were told that they were successful in an earlier communicative situation were more resistant to a persuasive attack than those that were told that they were failures.

There have been many studies that have examined threat, motivation, and warning as variables affecting individuals' ability to resist. Hollander (1974) has examined a number of them, but could not find any consistent finding that he would label generalizable.

Montgomery and Burgoon (1980) examined the possible interactions of sex and resistance to persuasion. You will remember that, although sex differences in persuasibility were not clear, Montgomery and Burgoon (1977) did demonstrate that androgynous men were more persuadable. However, the results were not the same in this study, which was also designed to test source-expectancies in resistance. Montgomery and Burgoon's findings are worth examining in some detail.

They hypothesized that traditional receivers (nonandrogynous) who receive messages advocating traditional behaviors will change more; that nontraditional receivers (androgynous) who receive nontraditional messages will change more. When androgynous persons received an unexpected message from a traditional source, there was much more change than when these same receivers received an expected message from that same traditional source. This difference was a large one, and could account for all of the interactions in Montgomery and Burgoon's data. This difference was so large, that it may well have obscured any sex differences in the traditional (nonandrogynous) groups.

Supportive or
Refutational Inoculation?

One interesting problem in the study of resistance to persuasion is what kind of inoculation to use. Burgoon and King (1974) studied inoculations of three types: supportive, refutational, or both in combination. They also varied the manner of encoding these messages, whether active or passive (passive encoders merely read the messages, active encoders had to supply parts of the messages themselves), and they varied the (language) intensity of the messages.

The type of inoculation did not make any difference in this study. However, the intensity of language was a factor when the individuals actively participated. In other words, highly intense language led to more resistance to a subsequent persuasive message when individuals were active encoders, and low intensity in language was more effective when individuals were passive.

Pryor and Steinfatt (1978) examined the interaction of supportive-refutational inoculation and the initial-belief level of the receivers. They found that McGuire's original contentions about belief level need to be carefully considered. In their study, supportive messages provided significant resistance, even in the high range of beliefs. This finding was at odds with McGuire's. Pryor and Steinfatt conclude that more substantial study is necessary before complete picture of supportive and refutational messages emerges.

Kinds of Attitudes under Attack

Whether or not an attitude is easily defended will depend on the nature of the attitude. Ullman and Bodaken (1975) examined attitudes that were formed by passively reading a persuasive communication as opposed to attitudes that were formed through the process of counterattitudinal advocacy. They found that the latter attitudes are much more strongly held and resist attack better than the former.

Resistance in Active Interpersonal Settings

McLaughlin, Cody, and Robey (1980) studied the interaction of intimacy, consequences, and rights to resist on the strategies chosen in resisting persuasive attempts. Their conclusions are worth reporting in detail:

> Identity managing strategies, such as comparing the other (unfavorably) to oneself, acting hurt, and pretending astonishment so that the other will feel guilty, can be expected to occur most frequently in intimate situations. Identity managing should be less effective with non-intimates simply because there is no feeling of relational commitment to exploit. The influence of intimacy will be mediated somewhat by the user's feelings of righteousness. Further, identity managing may be used only with great discretion in intimate situations with long term consequences, on the chance that it might backfire and force an angry other into a position threatening the relationship. (1980, pp. 33–34)

Clearly, resistance in intimate situations may not be worth the trouble. And a different set of standards obviously applies to the general problem of resistance.

SUMMARY

Our initial conclusions that persuasion is ethically neutral may have been too simple, but clear standards about what is ethical may be difficult to establish. This chapter takes the point of view that altruism is the single best standard for judging the ethicality of persuasive acts. Reviewing credibility findings reveals an inherent ethical system that significantly affects persuasion.

The lack of ethicality (altruism) in powerful persuaders points up the need for resistance to persuasion. Resistance was originally thought of as inoculation. A variety of techniques have been shown to be effective against persuasion.

QUESTIONS FOR FURTHER STUDY

1. How do you feel about persons who try to persuade you? Why?
2. If you could persuade someone who has a drinking problem to stop drinking by exaggerating a little, would you do it? How about using fictitious medical evidence? How far would you go? Defend your answer.
3. Advertisers claim that our economy must grow or we will have a depression. How do you feel about this?
4. Get the EPA's mileage for new cars for this year. Then examine a few commercials in which mileage is mentioned. What effect did your prior knowledge have on your reactions to the commercials.

REFERENCES

ABEL, E.   Marijuana and memory: Acquisition or retrieval? *Science*, 1971, *173*, 1038-1040.

ABELSON, R.   The structure of belief systems. In R. Schank and K. Colby (Eds.) *Computer models of thought and language*. San Francisco: Freeman, 1973, 287-340.

ABELSON, R. & ROSENBERG, M.   Symbolic psychologic: A model of attitudinal cognition. *Behavioral Science*, 1958, *3*, 1-13.

ADAMS, R.   Persuasibility as a correlate of certain personality factors. *Western Speech*, 1972, *36*, 187-197.

ADAMS, C. & BEATTY, M.   Dogmatism, need for social approval, and the resistance to persuasion. *Communication Monographs*, 1977, *44*, 321-325.

ADDINGTON, D.   The effect of vocal variations on ratings of source credibility. *Speech Monographs*, 1971, *38*, 242-247.

ADORNO, T., FRENKEL-BRUNSWIK, E., LEVENSON, D. & SANFORD, R.   *The authoritarian personality*. New York: Harper and Row, 1950.

AJZEN, I. & FISHBEIN, M.   Attitude-behavior relations: A theoretical analysis and review of empirical research. *Psychological Bulletin*, 1978, *84*, 888-912.

ALDERTON, S.   Attributions of responsibility for socially deviant behavior in decision-making discussions as a function of situational locus of control of attributor. *Central States Speech Journal*, 1980, *31*, 117-127.

ALLPORT, G.   Attitude. In M. Fishbein (Ed.), *Readings in attitude theory and measurement*. New York: John Wiley, 1967.

ALLYN, J. & FESTINGER, L.   The effectiveness of unanticipated persuasive communications. *Journal of Abnormal and Social Psychology*, 1961, *62*, 35-40.

ALTHEIDE, D. & JOHNSON, J.   *Bureaucratic propaganda*. Boston: Allyn and Bacon, 1980.

ANDERSON, D. C.   The effect of various uses of authoritative testimony in persuasive speaking (Doctoral Dissertation, Ohio State, 1958).

ANDERSEN, K. & CLEVENGER, T., JR.   A summary of experimental research in ethos. *Speech Monographs*, 1963, *30*, 59-78.

ANDERSON, K. & HOCKEY, G.   Effects of cigarette smoking on incidental memory. *Psychopharmacology*, 1977, *52*, 223-226.

ANDERSON, L. J. & ANDERSEN, K. E.   *Research on the relationship of reasoning and evidence to message acceptance.* Paper presented to the annual meeting of the Speech Communication Association, November, 1980.

ANDERSON, L. & FISHBEIN, M.   Prediction of attitudes from the number and evaluative aspects of beliefs about the attitude object. *Journal of Personality and Social Psychology*, 1965, *3*, 437-443.

ANDERSON, N.   Cognitive algebra: Integration theory applied to social attribution. In L. Berkowitz (Ed.) *Advances in experimental social psychology.* New York: Academic Press, 1974, *7*, 2-101.

ANDERSON, N. & GRAESER, C.   An information integration analysis of attitude change in group discussion. *Journal of Personality and Social Psychology*, 1976, *34*, 210-222.

APPLBAUM, R. & ANATOL, K.   Dimensions of source credibility: A test for reproducibility. *Speech Monographs*, 1973, *40*, 231-237.

APPLEGATE, J.   *A constructivist outline for cultural communication studies.* Paper presented at the annual meeting of the Speech Communication Association, New York, 1980(a).

APPLEGATE, J.   Person- and position-centered teacher communication in a day-care center: A case study triangulating interview and naturalistic methods. In Denzin, N. (Ed.), *Studies in symbolic interaction* (Vol. 3). Greenwich, Connecticut: JAI Press, 1980(b).

APPLEGATE, J.   *The impact of construct system and persuasive strategy development on face to face persuasive interaction.* Unpublished manuscript, University of Kentucky, 1981.

ARMSTRONG, B., FINK, E., BAUER, C. & KAPLOWITZ, S.   The persistence of attitude change induced by varying levels of message discrepancy. Paper presented at the annual meeting of the International Communication Association, Minneapolis, 1981.

ARNOLD, W. E. & McCROSKEY, J. C.   The credibility of reluctant testimony. *Central States Speech Journal*, 1967, *18*, 97-103.

ARONSON, E. & GOLDEN, B.   The effect of relevant and irrelevant aspects of communicator credibility on opinion change. *Journal of Personality*, 1962, *30*, 135-146.

ARONSON, E. & MILLS, J.   Effect of severity of initiation on liking for a group. In D. Cartwright & A. Zander (Eds.) *Group dynamics* (2nd ed.). Evanston: Row, Peterson, 1962.

ARONSON, E., TURNER, J. & CARLSMITH, M.   Communicator credibility and communication discrepancy as determinants of opinion change. *Journal of Abnormal and Social Psychology*, 1963, *67*, 31-36.

ASCH, S.   Studies of independence and conformity: A minority of one against a unanimous majority. *Psychological Monographs*, 1956, *70*, (9, Whole No. 416).

ASCH, S.   Effects of group pressure on the modification and distortion of judgement. In D. Cartwright and A. Zander (Eds.) *Group dynamics* (2nd ed.). Evanston: Row, Peterson, 1962.

BAIRD, J.   A comparison of distributional and sequential structure in cooperative and competitive group discussion. *Speech Monographs*, 1974, *41*, 226-232.

BAIRD, J.   Sex differences in group communication: a review of relevant research. *Quarterly Journal of Speech*, 1976, *62*, 179-192.

BAKER, E. & REDDING, W.   The effects of perceived tallness in persuasive speaking. *Journal of Communication*, 1962, *12*, 51-58.

BALES, R.   Task roles and social roles in group problem-solving. In E. Maccoby, T. Newcomb, & E. Hartley (Eds.) *Readings in social psychology* (3rd ed.). New York: Henry Holt and Company, 1958.

BANTZ, C. & SMITH, D.   A critique and experimental test of Weick's model of organizing. *Communication Monographs*, 1977, *44*, 171–184.

BARKER, L.   *Communication*. Englewood Cliffs, N.J.: Prentice-Hall, 1978.

BARNLUND, D.   A transactional model of communication. In K. Sereno & D. Mortenson (Eds.) *Foundations of communication theory*. New York: Harper and Row, 1970, 83–102.

BASEHEART, J.   Message opinionation and approval-dependence as determinants of receiver attitude change and recall. *Speech Monographs*, 1971, *38*, 302–310.

BASEHEART, J. & BOSTROM, R.   Credibility of source and self in attitude change. *Journalism Quarterly*, 1972, *49*, 742–745.

BASKERVILLE, B.   The illusion of proof. *Western Speech*, 1961, *25*, 236–242.

BASSETT, R., STATON-SPICER, A. & WHITEHEAD, J.   Effects of source attire on judgements of credibility. *Central States Speech Journal*, 1979, *30*, 282–285.

BAUDHUIN, S. & DAVIS, M.   Scales for the measurement of *ethos*: Another attempt. *Speech Monographs*, 1972, *39*, 296–301.

BAVELAS, A.   Communication patterns in task-oriented groups. In D. Cartwright & A. Zander, (Eds.) *Group dynamics*. Evanston: Row, Peterson, 1953.

BEIGHLEY, K.   The effect of four speech variables on comprehension. *Speech Monographs*, 1952, *19*, 249–258.

BEISECKER, T.   Game theory in communication research: A reaction and a reorientation. *Journal of Communication*, 1970, *20*, 105–120(a).

BEISECKER, T.   Verbal persuasive strategies in mixed-motive interactions. *Quarterly Journal of Speech*, 1970, *54*, 149–160(b).

BELL, M.   The effects of substantive and affective conflict in problem-solving groups. *Speech Monographs*, 1974, *41*, 19–23.

BELL, M.   The effects of substantive and affective verbal conflict on the quality of group discussion. *Central States Speech Journal*, 1979, *30*, 75–82.

BEM, D.   An experimental analysis of self-persuasion. *Journal of Experimental Social Psychology*, 1965, *1*, 199–218.

BEM, D.   Self-perception: An alternative interpretation of cognitive dissonance phenomena. *Psychological Review*, 1967, *74*, 183–200.

BEM, S.   The measurement of psychological androgyny. *Journal of Consulting and Clinical Psychology*, 1974, *42*, 155–162.

BERELSON, B.   *The behavioral sciences today*. New York: Harper and Row, 1963.

BERGER, C.   Toward a role-enactment theory of persuasion. *Speech Monographs*, 1972, *39*, 260–276.

BERGER, C., GARDNER, R., PARKS, M., SCHULMAN, L. & MILLER, G.   Interpersonal epistemology and interpersonal communication. In G. Miller (Ed.) *Explorations in interpersonal communication*. Beverly Hills: Sage, 1980.

BERGMANN, G. & SPENCE, K.   Operationism and theory in psychology. *Psychological Review*, 1941, *48*, 1–14.

BERKOWITZ, L.   *Cognitive theories in social psychology*. New York: Academic Press, 1978.

BERKOWITZ, L. & COTTINGHAM, D.   The interest value and relevance of fear arousing communications. *Journal of Abnormal and Social Psychology*, 1960, *60*, 37–43.

BERLO, D.   *The process of communication*. New York: Holt, Rinehart, & Winston, 1960.

BERLO, D., LEMMERT, J. & MERTZ, R.   Dimensions for evaluating the acceptability of message sources. *Public Opinion Quarterly*, 1969, *33*, 563–576.

BERLO, D. K. & GULLEY, H. E.   Some determinants of the effect of oral communication in producing attitude change and learning. *Speech Monographs*, 1957, *24*, 10–20.

BETTINGHAUS, E.   The relative effect of the use of testimony in a persuasive speech upon the attitudes of listeners. Master's thesis, Bradley University, 1953.

BETTINGHAUS, E.   The operation of congruity in an oral communication situation. *Speech Monographs*, 1961, *28*, 131-143.

BETTINGHAUS, E.   *Persuasive communication*. New York: Holt, Rinehart, & Winston, 1980.

BETTINGHAUS, E., MILLER, G. & STEINFATT, T.   Source evaluation, syllogistic content, and judgment of logical validity by high- and low-dogmatic persons. *Journal of Personality and Social Psychology*, 1970, *16*, 238-244.

BIXENSTINE, V. & GAEBELINE, J.   Strategies of "real" opponents in eliciting cooperative choice in a prisoner's dilemma game. *Journal of Conflict Resolution*, 1971, *15*, 157-166.

BIXENSTINE, V. & WILSON, K.   Effects of level of cooperative choice by the other player in a prisoner's dilemma game. *Journal of Abnormal and Social Psychology*, 1963, *67*, 139-147.

BLANKENSHIP, J. & SWEENEY, B.   The "energy" of form. *The Central States Speech Journal*, 1980, *31*, 172-183.

BOCHNER, A. & BOCHNER, B.   A multivariate investigation of machiavellianism in four-man groups. *Speech Monographs*, 1972, *39*, 277-285.

BODAKEN, E., LASHBROOK, W. & CHAMPAGNE, M.   PROANA5: A computerized technique for analysis of small group interactions. *Western Journal of Speech Communication*, 1971, *35*, 112-115.

BORING, E.   *A history of experimental psychology*. New York: Appleton-Century-Crofts, 1950.

BORMANN, E.   *Communication theory*. New York: Holt, Rinehart, & Winston, 1980.

BOSTER, F., MAYER, M., HUNTER, J. & HALE, J.   Expanding the persuasive arguments explanation of the polarity shift: a linear discrepancy model. In D. Nimmo (Ed.) *Communication yearbook IV*. Brunswick, New Jersey: Transaction Press, 1980.

BOSTROM, R.   Dogmatism, rigidity, and rating behavior. *Speech Teacher*, 1964, *13*, 283-287.

BOSTROM, R.   Motivation and argument. In G. Miller and T. Nilsen (Eds.) *Perspectives in argumentation*. Chicago: Scott, Foresman, 1966, 110-128.

BOSTROM, R.   Theory of games and communication theory. *Journal of Communication*, 1968, *18*, 369-380.

BOSTROM, R.   Patterns of communicative interaction in small groups. *Speech Monographs*, 1970, *37*, 257-263.

BOSTROM, R.   Altered physiological states: the central nervous system and persuasive communications. In M. Roloff and G. Miller (Eds.), *Persuasion: new directions in theory and research*. Beverly Hills: Sage, 1980.

BOSTROM, R.   The interaction of sources, receivers and objects: RSO theory. In M. Burgoon (Ed.), *Communication yearbook V*. Brunswick, New Jersey: Transaction Books, 1981.

BOSTROM, R., BASEHEART, J. & ROSSITER, C.   The Effects of three types of profane language in persuasive messages. *Journal of Communication*, 1973, *23*, 461-475.

BOSTROM, R., HUMPHREYS, R. & ROLOFF, M.   Comunicacion y comportamiento serviciales: los efectos de informacion, refuerzo, y sexo en reacciones serviciales. Paper presented at the International Communication Association, Acapulco, 1980.

BOSTROM, R. & HURT, T.   *The credibility of policemen as message sources*. Law Enforcement Assistance Administration (unpublished), 1973.

BOSTROM, R. & KEMP, A.   Type of speech, sex of speaker and sex of subject as factors influencing persuasion. *Central States Speech Journal*, 1968, *30*, 245-252.

BOSTROM, R. & TUCKER, R.   Evidence, personality, and attitude change. *Speech Monographs*, 1969, *36*, 22-27.

BOSTROM, R., VLANDIS, J. & ROSENBAUM, M.   Grades as reinforcing contingencies and attitude change. *Journal of Educational Psychology*, 1961, *52*, 112-115.

BOSTROM, R. & WHITE, N.   Does drinking weaken resistance? *Journal of Communication*, 1979, *29*, 73-80.

BOWERS, J.   Congruity principle in oral communication. *Central States Speech Journal*, 1963, *14*, 88-91.

BOWERS, J.   The influence of delivery on attitudes toward concepts and speakers. *Speech Monographs*, 1965, *32*, 154-158.

BOWERS, J.   Beyond threats and promises. *Speech Monographs*, 1974, *41*, ix-xi.

BOWERS, J. & OCHS, D.   *The rhetoric of agitation and control.* Reading, Mass.: Addison-Wesley, 1971.

BOWERS, J. & OSBORN, M.   Attitudinal effects of selected types of concluding metaphors in persuasive speeches. *Speech monographs*, 1966, *34*, 147-155.

BOWERS, J. & PHILLIPS, W.   A note on the generality of source-credibility scales, *Speech Monographs*, 1965, *32*, 85-86.

BRADAC, J., BOWERS, J. & COURTWRIGHT, J.   Three language variables in communication research: Intensity, immediacy, and diversity. *Human Communication Research*, 1979, 7, 257-269.

BRADAC, J., KONSKY, C. & DAVIES, R.   Two studies of linguistic diversity upon judgments of communicator attributes and message effectiveness. *Communication Monographs*, 1976, *43*, 70-79.

BRADLEY, P.   Power, status, and upward communication in small decision making groups. *Communication Monographs*, 1978, *45*, 33-43.

BRANDES, P.   Evidence in Aristotle's Rhetoric. *Speech Monographs*, 1961, *28*, 21-28.

BRANDSTATTER, H., DAVIS, J. & SCHULER, H.   *Dynamics of group decisions.* Beverly Hills: Sage Publications, 1978.

BRANDT, D.   Listener propensity to counterargue, distraction, and resistance to persuasion. *Central States Speech Journal*, 1979, *30*, 321-331.

BRAY, R. & NOBLE, A.   Authoritarianism and decisions of mock juries: Evidence of jury bias and group polarization. *Journal of Personality and Social Psychology*. 1978, *36*, 1424-1430.

BRAYBROOKE, D.   *Philosophical problems of the social sciences.* New York: Macmillan, 1965.

BREHM, J.   Post-decision change in the desirability of alternatives. *Journal of Abnormal and Social Psychology*, 1956, *52*, 384-389.

BREHM, J. & LIPSHER, D.   Communicator-communicatee discrepancy and perceived communicator trustworthiness. *Journal of Personality*, 1959, *27*, 352-361.

BREWER, W.   There is no convincing evidence for operant or classical conditioning in adult humans. In W. Weimer & D. Palermo (Eds.) *Cognition and symbolic processes.* Hillsdale, N.J.: Erlbaum, 1975.

BRILHART, J.   *Effective group discussion.* Dubuque, Iowa: William C. Brown, Publishers, 1978.

BRINGHAM, J. & GREISBRECHT, L.   "All in the Family": Racial attitudes. *Journal of Communication*, 1976, *26*, 69-74.

BROOKS, R.   The generality of early reversals on attitudes toward communication sources. *Speech Monographs*, 1970, *37*, 152-155.

BROOKS, R. & SCHEIDEL, T.   Speech as process: A case study. *Speech Monographs*, 1968, *35*, 1-7.

BROWN, J.   Problems presented by the concept of acquired drives. *Current theory and research in motivation* (Lincoln, Nebraska: University of Nebraska, 1953).

BROWN, J.   *The motivation of behavior.* New York: McGraw-Hill, 1960.

BROWN, W.   Will Rogers: Ironist as persuader. *Speech Monographs*, 1972, *39*, 183-192.

BROWNING, L.   A grounded organizational communication theory derived from qualitative data. *Communication Monographs*, 1978, *45*, 93-109.

BRUNER, J. & C. GOODMAN.   Value and need as organizing factors in perception. *Journal of Abnormal and Social Psychology*, 1947, *42*, 33-44.

BURGESS, P.   Old time *gsr* and a new approach to the analysis of public communication. *The Quarterly Journal of Speech*, 1973, *59*, 61–74.

BURGOON, J.   Conflicting information, attitude and message variables as predictors of learning and persuasion. *Human Communication Research*, 1975, *1*, 133–144.

BURGOON, J.   Unwillingness to communicate as a predictor of small group discussion behaviors and evaluations. *Central States Speech Journal*. 1977, *28*, 122–133.

BURGOON, J., BURGOON, M., MILLER, G. & SUNNAFRANK, M.   Learning theory approaches to persuasion. *Human Communication Research*, 1981, *7*, 160–179.

BURGOON, M.   A factor-analytic examination of messages advocating social change. *Speech Monographs*, 1972, *39*, 290–295.

BURGOON, M. & CHASE, L.   The effects of differential linguistic patterns in messages attempting to induce resistance to persuasion. *Speech Monographs*, 1973, *40*, 1–7.

BURGOON, M., COHEN, M., MILLER, M. & MONTGOMERY, C.   An empirical test of a model of resistance to persuasion. *Human Communication Research*, 1978, *5*, 27–39.

BURGOON, M., JONES, S. & STEWART, D.   Toward a message-centered theory of persuasion: Three empirical investigations of language intensity. *Human Communication Research*, 1975, *1*, 240–256.

BURGOON, M. & KING, L.   The mediation of resistance to persuasion strategies by language variables and active-passive participation. *Human Communication Research*, 1974, *1*, 30–41.

BURGOON, M. & STEWART, D.   Empirical investigations of language intensity: I. The effects of source, receiver, and language intensity on attitude change. *Human Communication Research*, 1974, *1*, 244–248.

BURGOON, M. & MILLER, G.   Prior attitude and language intensity as predictors of message style and attitude change following counterattitudinal advocacy. *Journal of Personality and Social Psychology*, 1971, *20*, 246–253.

BURNSTEIN, E. & VINOKUR, A.   What a person thinks upon learning that he has chosen differently from the others: Nice evidence for the persuasive arguments explanation of choice shifts. *Journal of Experimental Social Psychology*, 1975, *11*, 412–496.

BURNSTEIN, E., VINOKUR, A. & TROPE, Y.   Interpersonal comparisons versus persuasive argumentation. *Journal of Experimental Social Psychology*, 1973, *9*, 236–245.

BYRNE, D.   Interpersonal attraction and attitude similarity. *Journal of Abnormal and Social Psychology*, 1961, *62*, 713–715.

CANTOR, J.   Grammatical variations in persuasion: Effectiveness of four forms of request in door-to-door solicitations for funds. *Communication Monographs*, 1979, *46*, 296–305.

CANTOR, J., ALFONSO, H. & ZILLMAN, D.   The persuasive effectiveness of the peer appeal and a communicator's first-hand experience. *Communication Research*, 1976, *3*, 293–310.

CAPPELLA, J.   Modeling interpersonal communication systems as a pair of machines coupled through feedback. In G. Miller (Ed.), *Explorations in interpersonal communication*. Beverly Hills: Sage, 1980, 59–86.

CAPPELLA, J. & FOLGER, J.   An information-processing explanation of attitude-behavior inconsistency. In D. Cushman & R. McPhee (Eds.) *Message-attitude-behavior relationship*. New York: Academic Press, 1980.

CARBONE, T.   Stylistic variables as related to source credibility. *Speech Monographs*, 1975, *42*, 99–106.

CARPENTER, J.   Effects of alcohol on some psychological processes. *Quarterly Journal of Studies on Alcohol*, 1962, *23*, 274–314.

CARPENTER, J. & ROSS, B.   Effects of alcohol on short-term memory. *Quarterly Journal of Studies on Alcohol*, 1965, *26*, 561–579.

CARTWRIGHT, D. & HARARY, F.   Structural balance: A generalization of Heider's theory. *Psychological Review*, 1956, *63*, 1–22.

CARTWRIGHT, D.   Risk-taking by individuals and by groups: An assessment of research employing choice dilemmas. *Journal of Personality and Social Psychology*, 1971, *20*, 361–368.

CATHCART, R.   An experimental study of the relative effectiveness of four methods of presenting evidence. *Speech Monographs*, 1955, *22*, 227–233.

CEGALA, D.   *An explication and partial test of a model of interpersonal persuasion.* Paper presented at the annual meeting of the Speech Communication Association, New York, 1980.

CHAIKEN, S.   Heuristic versus systematic information processing and the use of source versus message cues in persuasion. *Journal of Personality and Social Psychology*, 1980, *39*, 752–756.

CHANG, M. & GRUNER, C.   Audience reaction to self-disparaging humor. *Southern Speech Communication Journal*, 1981, *46*, 419–426.

CHAPANIS, N. & CHAPANIS, A.   Cognitive dissonance: Five years later. *Psychological Bulletin*, 1964, *61*, 1–22.

CHASE, L. & KELLEY, C.   Language intensity and resistance to persuasion: a research note. *Human Communication Research*, 1976, *3*, 82–85.

CHESEBRO, J., CRAGAN, J. & McCULLOUGH, P.   The small group technique of the radical revolutionary: A synthetic study of consciousness-raising. *Speech Monographs*, 1973, *40*, 136–146.

CHOMSKY, N.   *Language and mind.* New York: Harcourt, Brace, and World, Inc., 1968.

CLARK, D.   *Rhetoric in greco-roman education.* Morningside Heights, New York: Columbia University Press, 1957.

CLARK, R. A. & DELIA, J.   Cognitive complexity, social perspective-taking, and functional persuasive skills. *Human Communication Research*, 1977, *3*, 128–134.

CLARK, R.   Group-induced shift toward risk: A critical appraisal. *Psychological Bulletin*, 1971, *76*, 251–270.

CLINE, R. & CLINE, T.   A structural analysis of risky-shift and cautious-shift discussions: A diffusion-of-responsibility theory. *Communication Quarterly*, 1980, *28*, 26–36.

COCH, L. & FRENCH, J.   Overcoming resistance to change. In D. Cartwright, & A. Zander (Eds). *Group dynamics.* Evanston: Row, Peterson, 1953.

CODY, M. & McLAUGHLIN, M.   Perceptions of compliance-gaining situations: A dimensional analysis. *Communication Monographs*, 1980, *47*, 132–148.

CODY, M., McLAUGHLIN, M. & JORDAN, W.   *A multidimensional scaling of three sets of compliance-gaining strategies.* Paper presented at the annual meeting of the Speech Communication Association, New York, 1980.

COHEN, A.   *Attitude change and social influence.* New York: Academic Press, 1964.

COHEN, J. & COHEN, P.   *Applied multiple regression/correlation analyses for the behavioral sciences.* Hillsdale, N.J.: Erlbaum, 1975.

COLBY, K.   Simulation of belief systems. In R. Schank and K. Colby (Eds.) *Computer models of thought and language.* San Francisco: Freeman, 1973, 251–286.

COLLINS, B.   *Social psychology.* Menlo Park, California: Addison-Wesley, 1970.

COOK, S. & SELLTIZ, L.   A multiple-indicator approach to attitude measurement, *Psychological Bulletin*, 1964, *62*, 36–55.

COOPER, J. & POLLOCK, D.   The identification of prejudicial attitudes by the galvanic skin response. *Journal of Social Psychology*, 1959, *50*, 241–245.

COOPER, J., ZANNA, M. & TAVES, P.   Arousal as a necessary condition for attitude following induced compliance. *Journal of Personality and Social Psychology*, 1978, *36*, 1101–1106.

COPE, F. & RICHARDSON, D.   The effects of reassuring recommendations in a fear-arousing speech. *Speech Monographs*, 1972, *39*, 148–150.

COSTLEY, D.   An experimental study of the effectiveness of quantitative evidence in speeches of advocacy. Master's thesis, University of Oklahoma, 1958.

COTTON, J. & KLATZKY, R.   *Semantic factors in cognition.* Hillsdale, N.J.: Erlbaum, 1978.

COURTWRIGHT, J.   A laboratory investigation of groupthink. *Communication Monographs,* 1978, *45,* 229–246.

CRABLE, R.   *Argumentation as communication: Reasoning with receivers.* Columbus, Ohio: Charles E. Merrill, 1976.

CROCKER, L.   *Argumentation and debate.* New York: American Institute of Banking, 1962.

CROCKETT, D., KLANOFF, H. & CLARK, C.   The effects of marijuana on verbalization and thought procedures. *Journal of Personality and Assessment,* 1976, *40,* 582–587.

CRONEN, V. & CONVILLE, R.   Belief salience, summation theory, and the attitude construct. *Speech Monographs,* 1973, *40,* 17–26.

CRONEN, V. & CONVILLE, R.   Fishbein's conception of belief strength: A theoretical, methodological, and experimental critique. *Speech Monographs,* 1975, *42,* 143–150.

CRONEN, V. & MIHEVIC, N.   The evaluation of deductive argument: A process analysis. *Speech Monographs,* 1972, *39,* 124–131.

CRONEN, V. & PRICE, W.   Affective relationships between the speaker and listener: An alternative to the approach-avoidance model. *Communication Monographs,* 1976, *43,* 51–59.

CRONKHITE, G.   Autonomic correlates of dissonance and attitude change. *Speech Monographs,* 1966, *33,* 392–399.

CRONKHITE, G.   *Persuasion: Speech and behavioral change.* Indianapolis: Bobbs-Merrill, 1969.

CRONKHITE, G. & J. LISKA.   A critique of factor analytic approaches to the study of credibility. *Communication Monographs,* 1976, *43,* 91–107.

CRONKHITE, G. & LISKA, J.   Judgment of communicant acceptability. In M. Roloff and G. Miller (Eds.) *Persuasion: New directions in theory and research.* Beverly Hills: Sage, 1980.

CROW, L. & BALL, C.   Alcohol state-dependency and autonomic reactivity. *Psychophysiology,* 1975, *12,* 702–706.

CROWNE, D. & MARLOWE, D.   *The approval motive: Studies in evaluative dependence.* New York: Houghton-Mifflin, 1964.

CUNNINGHAM, F.   *Objectivity in social science.* Toronto: University of Toronto Press, 1973.

CUSHMAN, D. & CRAIG, R.   Communication systems: Interpersonal implications. In G. Miller (Ed.) *Explorations in interpersonal communication.* Beverly Hills: Sage, 1976.

CUSHMAN, D. & McPHEE, R.   *Message-attitude-behavior relationship.* New York: Academic Press, 1980.

CUSHMAN, D. & WHITING, G.   An approach to communication theory: Toward consensus on rules. *Journal of Communication,* 1972, *22,* 217–238.

DABBS, J. & LEVENTHAL, H.   Effects of varying the recommendations in a fear-arousing communication. *Journal of Personality and Social Psychology,* 1966, *4,* 525–531.

DANIELS, T. & WHITMAN, R.   The effects of message introduction, message structure, and verbal organizing ability upon learning of message information. *Human Communication Research,* 1981, *7,* 147–160.

DARNELL, D.   The relation between sentence order and comprehension. *Speech Monographs,* 1963, *30,* 186–192.

DAVIS, J., SPITZER, C., NAGAO, D. & STASSER, G.   Bias in social decisions by individuals and groups. In H. Brandstatler, J. Davis, and H. Schulz *Dynamics of group decisions.* Beverly Hills: Sage, 1978.

DEETZ, S.   Words without things: toward a social phenomenology of language. *Quarterly Journal of Speech*, 1973, *59*, 40-51.

DeFLEUR, M. & F. WESTIE.   Verbal attitudes and overt acts: An experiment on the salience of attitudes. *American Sociological Review*, 1958, *23*, 667-671.

DELIA, J.   Regional dialects, message acceptance, and perceptions of the speaker. *Central States Speech Journal*, 1975, *26*, 188-194.

DELIA, J.   A constructivist analysis of the concept of credibility. *Quarterly Journal of Speech*, 1976, *62*, 361-375.

DELIA, J.   Constructivism and the study of human communication. *Quarterly Journal of Speech*, 1977, *53*, 66-83.

DELIA, J., CROCKETT, W., PRESS, A. & O'KEEFE, D.   The dependency of interpersonal evaluations on context-relevant beliefs about the other. *Speech Monographs*, 1975, *42*, 11-19.

DELIA, J., KLINE, S. & BURLESON, B.   The development of persuasive communication strategies in kindergartners through twelfth-graders. *Communication Monographs*, 1979, *46*, 241-256.

DEUTSCH, M.   A theory of cooperative and competitive behavior. *Human Relations*, 1949, *2*, 129-152.

DEUTSCH, M. & GERARD, H.   A study of normative and informative influences upon individual judgement, *Journal of Abnormal and Social Psychology*, 1955, *54*, 629-636.

DEUTSCH, M. & KRAUSS, M.   The effect of threat on interpersonal bargaining. *Journal of Abnormal and Social Psychology,* 1960, *61*, 181-189.

DEUSTCHER, I.   *Why do they say one thing, do another?* Morristown, N.J.: General Learning Press, 1973.

DEWEY, J.   *How we think.* Boston: D.C. Heath, 1933.

DIGGS, B.   Persuasion and ethics. *Quarterly Journal of Speech*, 1964, *50*, 360-369.

DILLEHAY, R.   On the irrelevance of the classical negative evidence concerning the effects of attitudes and behavior. *American Psychologist*, 1973, *28*, 887-891.

DILLEHAY, R. & CLAYTON, M.   Forced-compliance studies, cognitive dissonance, and self-perception theory. *Journal of Experimental Social Psychology*, 1970, *6*, 458-465.

DONOHEW, L. & PALMGREEN, P.   A reappraisal of dissonance and the selective exposure hypothesis. *Journalism Quarterly*, 1971, *22*, 54-63.

DONOHEW, L., PALMGREEN, P. & DUNCAN, J.   An activation model of exposure. *Communication Monographs*, 1980, *47*, 295-303.

DONOHEW, L., PARKER, J. & McDERMOTT, V.   Psychophysical measurement of information selection: Two studies. *Journal of Communication*, 1972, *22*, 54-63.

DONOHEW, L. & TIPTON, L.   A conceptual model of information seeking, avoiding, and processing. In P. Clarke (Ed.) *Conceptual models of mass communication research.* Beverly Hills: Sage, 1973, 243-265.

DONOHUE, W.   An empirical framework for examining negotiation processes. *Communication Monographs*, 1978, *48*, 247-257.

DONOHUE, W.   Analyzing negotiation tactics: Development of a negotiation interact system. *Human Communication Research*, 1981, *7*, 273-287.

DOOB, L.   The behavior of attitudes. *Psychological Review*, 1947, *54*, 135-156.

DOWNS, C. & PICKETT, T.   An analysis of the effects of nine leadership-group compatibility contingencies upon productivity and member satisfaction. *Communication Monographs*, 1977, *44*, 220-230.

DRESSER, W. R.   Effects of "satisfactory" and "unsatisfactory" evidence in a speech of advocacy. *Speech Monographs*, 1963, *30*, 302-306.

DRUCKMAN, D., ZECHMEISTER, K. & SOLOMON, D.   Determinants of bargaining behavior in a bilateral monopoly game: Opponents concessions rate and relative defensibility. *Behavioral Science*, 1972, *17*, 514-531.

DULANY, D.   On the support of cognitive theory in opposition to behavioral theory: A methodological problem. In W. Weimer, & D. Palermo (Eds.) *Cognition and the symbolic process*. Hillsdale, N.J.: Erlbaum, 1974.

EAGLY, A. & CHAIKEN, S.   An attribution analysis of the effects of communicator characteristics on opinion change: The case of communicator attractiveness. *Journal of Personality and Social Psychology*, 1975, *32*, 136–144.

EASTERBROOK, J.   *The determinants of free will*. New York: Academic Press, 1978.

EBBSEN, E. & BOWERS, R.   Proportion of risk to conservative arguments in a group discussion and choice shift. *Journal of Personality and Social Psychology*, 1974, *29*, 316–327.

EDELMAN, M.   The language of participation and the language of resistance. *Human Communication Research*, 1977, *3*, 159–170.

EHNINGER, D.   *Influence and argument*. Chicago: Scott, Foresman, 1974.

EHNINGER, D., MONROE, A. & GRONBECK, B.   *Principles and types of speech communication*. Glenview, Ill.: Scott, Foresman, 1978.

EISENBERG, A. & ILARDO, J.   *Argument: Alternative to violence*. Englewood Cliffs, N.J.: Prentice-Hall, 1972.

ELLIS, D. & FISHER, B.   Phase of conflict in small group development. *Human Communication Research*, 1975, *1*, 195–212.

ELLUL, J.   *Propaganda: The formation of men's attitudes*. New York: Alfred Knopf, 1965.

EWBANK, H. & AUER, J.   *Discussion and debate*. New York: Appleton-Century-Crofts, 1951.

FARBER, I., HARLOW, H. & WEST, L.   Brainwashing, conditioning, and DDD. *Sociometry*, 1957, *20*, 271–283.

FEATHER, N.   A structural balance model of evaluative behavior. *Human Relations*, 1965, *18*, 171–185.

FEEZEL, J.   A qualified certainty: Verbal probability in arguments. *Speech Monographs*, 1974, *41*, 348–356.

FESTINGER, L.   A theory of social comparison processes. *Human Relations*, 1954, *7*, 117–140.

FESTINGER, L.   *A theory of cognitive dissonance*. New York: Harper and Row, 1957.

FESTINGER, L.   Informal social communication. In D. Cartwright & A. Zander (Eds.), *Group dynamics* (3rd ed.). New York: Harper and Row, 1968.

FESTINGER, L. & CARLSMITH, J.   Cognitive consequences of forced compliance. *Journal of Abnormal and Social Psychology*, 1959, *58*, 203–210.

FESTINGER, L. & MACCOBY, N.   On resistance to persuasive communications. *Journal of Personality and Social Psychology*, 1964, *68*, 359–366.

FESTINGER, L., RIECKEN, H. & SCHACTER, S.   *When prophecy fails*. New York: Harper and Row, 1956.

FIEDLER, F.   Personality and situational determinants of leadership effectiveness. In D. Cartwright & A. Zander (Eds.), *Group dynamics* (3rd ed.). New York: Harper and Row, 1968.

FISHBEIN, M.   A consideration of beliefs and their role in attitude measurement. In M. Fishbein (Ed.), *Readings in attitude theory and measurement*. New York: John Wiley, 1967.

FISHBEIN, M. & AJZEN, I.   *Belief, attitude, intention, and behavior*. Reading, Mass.: Addison Wesley, 1975.

FISHBEIN, M. & HUNTER, R.   Summation versus balance in attitude organization and change. *Journal of Abnormal and Social Psychology*, 1964, *69*, 505–510.

FISHER, W.   Toward a logic of good reasons. *Quarterly Journal of Speech*, 1978, *64*, 376–384.

FLORENCE, T.   An empirical test of the relationship of evidence to belief systems and attitude change. *Human Communication Research*, 1975, *1*, 145–158.

FONER, E.   The televised past. *Nation*, June 16, 1979, 724–726.

FONTES, N. & BUNDENS, R.   Persuasion during the trial process. In M. Roloff & G. Miller (Eds.) *Persuasion*. Beverly Hills: Sage, 1980.

FRANDSEN, K.   Effects of threat and media of transmission. *Speech Monographs*, 1963, *30*, 101–104.

FRANKS, H. AND OTHERS.   The effects of caffeine on human performance alone and in combination with ethanol. *Psychopharmacologica*, 1975, *45*, 51–63.

FRENCH, J. & RAVEN, B.   The bases of social power. In D Cartwright and A. Zander, *Group dynamics* (2nd ed.). Evanston, Row, Peterson, 1962, 607–623.

GARDNER, J. C.   An experimental study of the use of selected forms of evidence in effecting attitude change. Master's thesis, University of Nebraska, 1966.

GIBB, J.   Defensive communication. *Journal of Communication*, 1961, *11*, 141–148.

GIBSON, J., GRUNER, C., KIBLER, R. & KELLY, F.   A quantitative examination of differences and similiarities in written and spoken messages. *Speech Monographs*, 1966, *4*, 444–451.

GILKINSON, H., PAULSON, S. & SIKKINK, D.   Effects of order and authority in an argumentative speech. *Quarterly Journal of Speech*, 1954, *40*, 183–192.

GOLDHABER, G.   *Organizational communication*. Dubuque, Iowa: William C. Brown, 1974.

GOODMAN, L. & GILLMAN, A.   *The pharmacological basis of therapeutics*. New York: Macmillan, 1958.

GOODWIN, D.   Alcohol and recall: State-dependent effects in man. *Science*, 1969, *163*, 1358–1360.

GORDEN, W.   Experimental training: A comparison of t-groups, tavistock, and est. *Communication Education*, 1979, *28*, 39–48.

GOSS, B. & WILLIAMS, L.   The effects of equivocation on perceived source credibility. *Central States Speech Journal*, 1973, *24*, 162–167.

GOTTSCHALK, L.   The use of drugs in interrogation. In A. Biderman, and H. Zimmer, H. (Eds.), *The manipulation of behavior*. New York: John Wiley, 1961.

GOURAN, D. & BAIRD, J.   An analysis of distributional and sequential structure in problem-solving and informal group discussions. *Speech Monographs*, 1972, *39*, 16–22.

GOURAN, D., BROWN, C. & HENRY, D.   Behavioral correlates of perception of quality in decision-making discussions. *Communication Monographs*, 1978, *45*, 51–63.

GOURAN, D. & GEONETTA, S.   Patterns of interaction as a function of the degree of leadership centralization in decision-making groups. *Central States Speech Journal*, 1977, *28*, 47–53.

GREENBERG, B. & MILLER, G.   The effects of low-credible sources on message acceptance. *Speech Monographs*, 1966, *33*, 127–136.

GROSSBERG, L. & O'KEEFE, D.   Presuppositions, conceptual foundations, and communication theory: On Hawes' approach to communication. *Quarterly Journal of Speech*, 1975, *61*, 195–212.

GRUNER, C.   An experimental study of satire as persuasion. *Speech Monographs*, 1965, *32*, 149–154.

GRUNER, C.   Editorial satire as persuasion: an experiment. *Journalism Quarterly*, 1967, *44*, 727–730.

GRUNER, C.   The effect of humor in dull and interesting informative speeches. *Central States Speech Journal*, 1970, *21*, 160–166.

GUEST, R.   *Organizational change: The effect of successful leadership*. Homewood, Illinois: Richard C. Irwin, 1962.

GULLEY, H. & BERLO, D.   Effects of intercellular and intracellular speech structure on attitude change and learning. *Speech Monographs*, 1956, *23*, 288–297.

HACKMAN, J. & MORRIS, C.   Group tasks, group interaction process, and group performance effectiveness. In L. Berkowitz (Ed.), *Advances in experimental social psychology* (Vol. 8). New York: Academic Press, 1975.

HAIMAN, F.   An experimental study of the effects of ethos in public speaking. *Speech Monographs*, 1949, *16*, 190–192.

HAMBURGER, H.   *Games as models of social phenomena*. San Francisco: Freeman, 1979.

HAMPLE, D.   Testing a model of value argument and evidence. *Communication Monographs*, 1977, *44*, 106–120.

HAMPLE, D.   Predicting immediate change and adherence to argument claims. *Communication Monographs*, 1978, *45*, 219–228.

HAMPLE, D.   Predicting belief and belief change using a cognitive theory of argument and evidence. *Communication Monographs*, 1979, *46*, 142–146.

HAMPLE, D.   *Models of arguments using multiple bits of evidence*. Paper presented at the annual meeting of the International Communication Association, Minneapolis, 1981.

HARMS, L.   Listener judgements of status cues in speech. *Quarterly Journal of Speech*, 1961, *47*, 164–168.

HARPER, N. & ASKLING, L.   Group communication and quality of task solution in a media-producing system. *Communication Monographs*, 1980, *47*, 77–100.

HARRE', R. & SECORD, P.   *The explanation of social behavior*. Totowa, New Jersey: Littlefield, Adams, 1973.

HARRIS, V. & JELLISON, J.   Fear-arousing communications, false physiological feedback and the acceptance of recommendations. *Journal of Experimental Social Psychology*, 1971, *7*, 269–279.

HARRISON, A.   *Individuals and groups*. Monterey, California: Brooks/Cole, 1976.

HART, R. & BURKS, D.   Rhetorical sensitivity and social interaction. *Speech Monographs*, 1973, *39*, 75–91.

HART, R., CARLSON, R. & EADIE, W.   Attitudes toward communication and the assessment of rhetorical sensitivity. *Communication Monographs*, 1980, *47*, 1–22.

HARTE, T.   The effects of evidence in persuasive communication. *Central States Speech Journal*, 1976, *27*, 42–46.

HAWES, L.   A response to Grossberg and O'Keefe: Building a human science of communication. *The Quarterly Journal of Speech*, 1975, *61*, 209–219.

HAWES, L.   The reflexivity of communication research. *Western Journal of Speech Communication*, 1978, *42*, 12–20.

HAWES, L.   *Pragmatics of analoguing: Theory and model construction in human communication*. Reading, Mass.: Addison-Wesley, 1975.

HAWES, L. & FOLEY, J.   Group decisioning: testing in a finite stochastic model. In G. Miller (Ed.), *Explorations in interpersonal communication*. Beverly Hills: Sage, 1980, 237–254.

HAZEN, M. & KIESLER, K.   Communication strategies affected by audience opposition, feedback, and persuability, *Speech Monographs*, 1975, *42*, 56–68.

HEATH, R.   Variability in value system priorities as decision-making adaptation to situational differences, *Communication monographs*, 1976, *43*, 325–333.

HEIDER, F.   Attitudes and cognitive organization. *Journal of Psychology*, 1946, *21*, 107–112.

HEISENBERG, W.   *Physics and Philosophy*. New York: Harper and Row, 1958.

HENSLEY, W.   A criticism of "dimensions of source credibility: a test for reproducibility." *Speech Monographs*, 1974, *41*, 293–294.

HERON, W.   The pathology of boredom. In T. Tyler (Ed.), *Altered states of awareness*. San Francisco: Freeman, 1972.

HEWES, D., PLANALP, S. & STREIBEL, M.   Analyzing social interaction: Some excruciating models and exhilirating results. In D. Nimmo (Ed.) *Communication Yearbook IV*. Brunswick, New Jersey: Transaction, 1980.

HEWGILL, M. & MILLER, G.   Source credibility and response to fear-arousing communications. *Speech Monographs*, 1965, *32*, 95–101.

HIGBEE, K.   Fifteen years of fear arousal: Research on threat appeals. *Psychological Bulletin*, 1969, *72*, 426–444.

HIGGINS, T.   The "communication game": Its implications for social cognition and persuasion. In T. Higgins, P. Herman, & M. Zanna (Eds.) *Social cognition*. Hillsdale, New Jersey: Erlbaum, 1981.

HILL, S., SCHWIN, R., GOODWIN, D. & POWELL, B.   Marijuana and pain. *Journal of Pharmacology and Experimental Therapeutics*, 1974, *188*, 415–418.

HILL, T.   An experimental study of the relationship between opinionated leadership and small group consensus, *Communication Monographs*. 1976, *43*, 246–257.

HIROKAWA, R.   A comparative analysis of communication patterns within effective and ineffective decision-making groups. *Communication Monographs*, 1980, *47*, 312–321.

HOLLANDER, S.   Effects of forewarning factors on pre- and post-communication attitude change. *Journal of Personality and Social Psychology*, 1974, *30*, 272–278.

HOLTZMAN, P.   Conformation of ethos as a confounding element in communication research. *Speech Monographs*, 1966, *33*, 464–466.

HOVLAND, C., JANIS, I. & KELLEY, H.   *Communication and persuasion*. New Haven: Yale University Press, 1953.

HOVLAND, C. & JANIS, I.   *Personality and persuasibility*. New Haven: Yale University Press, 1959.

HOVLAND, C. & MANDELL, W.   An experimental comparison of conclusion drawing by the communicator and the audience. *Journal of Abnormal and Social Psychology*, 1952, *48*, 581–588.

HOVLAND, C. & WEISS, W.   The influence of source credibility on communication effectiveness. *Public Opinion Quarterly*, 1951, *15*, 635–650.

HOVLAND, C. AND OTHERS.   *Order of presentation in persuasion*. New Haven: Yale University Press, 1957.

HULL, C.   *Principles of behavior*. New York: Appleton-Century-Crofts, 1943.

HUNT, M. & MILLER, G.   Open and closed mindedness and assimilation and contrast effects. *Central States Speech Journal*. 1967, *18*, 292.

HURT, T. & SCOTT, M.   A multiple regression approach to attitude change. Paper delivered at the annual meeting of the International Communication Association, Chicago, 1975.

HURT, T. & BOSTROM, R.   The predictive value of the congruity theory. Paper presented at the Speech Communication Association meeting, San Francisco, 1971.

INFANTE, D.   Cognitive speech as a predictor of post speech attitude and attitude change. *Speech Monographs*, 1972, *39*, 55–61.

INFANTE, D.   Forewarnings in persuasion: effects of opinionated language and forewarner and speaker authoritativeness. *Western Speech*, 1973a, *37*, 185–195.

INFANTE, D.   The perceived importance of cognitive structure components: an adaptation of Fishbein's theory. *Speech Monographs*, 1973b, *40*, 8–16.

INFANTE, D.   Differential function of desirable and undesirable consequences in predicting attitude and attitude change toward proposals. *Speech Monographs*, 1975a, *42*, 115–134.

INFANTE, D.   Effects of opinionated language on communicator image and in conferring resistance to persuasion. *Western Speech Communication*, 1975b, *39*, 112–119.

INFANTE, D.   Persuasion as a function of the receiver's prior success or failure as a message source. *Communication Quarterly*, 1976, *24*, 21–26.

INFANTE, D.   The construct validity of the semantic differential scales for the measurement of source credibility. *Communication Quarterly*, 1980, *28*, 19–26.

INSKO, C.   *Theories of attitude change*. New York: Appleton-Century-Crofts, 1967.

INSKO, C., ARKOFF, A. & INSKO, V.   Effects of high and low fear-arousing communications upon opinions toward smoking. *Journal of Experimental Social Psychology*, 1965, *1*, 256-266.

ISAACSON, W.   Propaganda sweepstakes. *Time*, 1981, *61* (9), 15-16.

JABLIN, F.   Superior-subordinate communication: the state of the art. *Psychological Bulletin*, 1979, *86*, 1201-1222.

JABLIN, F., SIEBOLD, D. & SORENSON, R.   Potential inhibitory effects of group participation on brainstorming performance. *Central States Speech Journal*, 1977, *28*, 113-121.

JABLIN, F. & SUSSMAN, L.   An exploration of communication productivity in real brainstorming groups. *Human Communication Research*, 1978, *4*, 329-337.

JACCARD, J. & KING, W.   The relation between behavioral intentions and beliefs: a probabalistic model. *Human Communication Research*, 1977, *3*, 326-334.

JAHODA, G.   *The psychology of superstition*. Baltimore, Md: Penguin Books, 1971.

JANIS, I.   Groupthink. *Psychology Today*, 1971, *5* (6), 43-46.

JANIS, I.   Group identification under conditions of external danger. In D. Cartwright & A. Zander (Eds.) *Group dynamics*. New York: Harper and Row, 1953.

JANIS, I. & FESHBACH, S.   Effects of fear-arousing communications. *Journal of Abnormal and Social Psychology*, 1953, *48*, 78-92.

JANIS, I., KAYE, D. & KIRSCHNER, P.   Facilitating effects of "eating while reading" on responsiveness to persuasive communication. *Journal of Personality and Social Psychology*, 1965, *1*, 181-186.

JANIS, I. & KING, B.   The influence of role playing on opinion change. *Journal of Abnormal and Social Psychology*, 1954, *49*, 211-218.

JANIS, I. & TERWILLIGER, R.   An experimental study of psychological resistances to fear-arousing communications. *Journal of Abnormal and Social Psychology*, 1962, *65*, 403-410.

JELLISON, J. & RISKIND, J.   A social comparison of abilities interpretation of risk-taking behavior. *Journal of Personality and Social Psychology*, 1970, *15*, 375-390.

JOHANNESEN, R. (Ed.)   *The ethics of persuasion*. New York: Random House, 1967.

JOHNSON, D., McCARTY, K. & ALLEN, T.   Congruent and contradictory verbal and nonverbal communications of cooperativeness and competitiveness in negotiations. *Communication Research*, 1976, *3*, 275-292.

JONES, B.   Cognitive performance during acute alcohol intoxication: The effects of prior task on performance. *Psychonomic Science*, 1972, *26*, 327-329.

JONES, S. & DIEKER, R.   *A study of the effects of choice, justification, and dogmatism on responses to a belief-discrepant communication*. Paper presented to the Speech Association of America, Chicago, Illinois, December, 1966.

JORDAN, W.   A reinforcement model of metaphor. *Speech Monographs*, 1972, *39*, 223-226.

JURMA, W.   Effects of leader structuring style and task orientation characteristics of group members. *Communication Monographs*, 1979, *49*, 282-295.

KANOUSE, D. & ABELSON, R.   Language variables affecting the persuasiveness of simple communications. *Journal of Personality and Social Psychology*, 1967, *7*, 153-163.

KAPLAN, A.   *The conduct of inquiry*. Scranton, Pa.: Chandler, 1964.

KAPLAN, S.   Attribution processes in the evaluation of message sources. *Western Speech Communication*, 1976, *40*, 185-195.

KAPLAN, S. & SHARP, H.   The effect of responsibility attributions on message source evaluations. *Speech Monographs*, 1974, *41*, 364-370.

KATZ, D.   The functional approach to the study of attitudes. *Public Opinion Quarterly*, 1960, *24*, 163-204.

KATZ, D. & KAHN, R.   *The social psychology of organizations*. New York: John Wiley and Sons, 1966.

KELLEY, H.   Attribution theory in social psychology. In D. Levine (Ed.), *Nebraska symposium on motivation*, Lincoln: University of Nebraska Press, 1967, 192–238.

KELLEY, H. & SCHENETZKI, D.   Bargaining. In G. McClintock, (Ed.), *Experimental social psychology*. New York: Holt, Rinehart, & Winston, 1972.

KELMAN, H.   Compliance, identification, and internalization: three processes of attitude change. *Journal of Conflict Resolution*, 1958, *2*, 51–60.

KELMAN, H.   Processes of opinion change. *Public Opinion Quarterly*, 1961, *25*, 57–58.

KELMAN, H. & HOVLAND, C.   "Reinstatement" of the communicator in delayed measurement of opinion changes. *Journal of Abnormal and Social Psychology*, 1953, *48*, 327–335.

KENNEDY, A.   *The effect of humor upon source credibility.* Paper presented to the Speech Communication Association annual meeting, Chicago, Illinois, December, 1972.

KERBER, K. & COLES, M.   The role of perceived physiological activity in affective judgments. *Journal of Experimental Social Psychology*, 1978, *14*, 419–433.

KERRICK, J.   The effect of relevant and nonrelevant sources on attitude change. *Journal of Social Psychology*, 1958, *47*, 15–20.

KIESLER, C., COLLINS, B. & MILLER, N.   *Attitude change: A critical analysis of theoretical approaches.* New York: John Wiley, 1969.

KING, G.   An analysis of attitudinal and normative variables as predictors of intentions and behavior. *Speech Monographs*, 1975, *42*, 237–244.

KING, R.   *Forms of public address.* Indianapolis, Indiana: Bobbs-Merrill, 1969.

KING, S.   Reconstructing the concept of source perceptions: toward a paradigm of source appropriateness. *Western Speech Communication*, 1976, *40*, 216–225.

KING, S. & SERENO, K.   Attitude change as a function of degree and type of interpersonal similarity and message type. *Western Speech*, 1973, *37*, 218–232.

KIRSCHT, J. & DILLEHAY, R.   *Dimensions of authoritarianism.* Lexington: University of Kentucky Press, 1967.

KISSLER, G. & LLOYD, K.   Effect of sentence interrelation and scrambling on the recall of factual information. *Journal of Educational psychology*, 1973, *64*, 187–190.

KLAPPER, J.   *The effects of mass communication.* New York: Free Press, 1960.

KLAPPER, J.   Mass communication, attitude stability, and change. In C. Sherif and M. Sherif (Eds.), *Attitude, ego-involvement, and change.* New York: John Wiley, 1967, 297–311.

KLEINKNECHT, R. & SMITH-SCOTT, J.   Prevalence, sources, and uses of tranquilizers among college students. *Journal of Drug Education*, 1977, *7*, 249–257.

KLEINMAN, K., VAUGHAN, R. & CHRIST, S.   Effects of cigarette smoking and smoking deprivation on paired-associate learning of high- and low-nonsense syllables. *Psychological Reports*, 1973, *23*, 963–966.

KLINE, J.   Interaction of evidence and reader's intelligence on the effects of short messages. *Quarterly Journal of Speech*, 1969, *55*, 407–413.

KLINE, J. & HULINGER, J.   Redundancy, self-orientation, and group consensus. *Speech Monographs*, 1973, *40*, 72–74.

KLINE, J.   Dogmatism of the speaker and selection of evidence. *Speech Monographs*, 1971, *38*, 354–355.

KNAPP, M.   *Nonverbal communication in human interaction.* New York: Holt, Rinehart, & Winston, 1972.

KNOWER, F.   Experimental studies of changes in attitude: A study of the effect of printed argument on changes in attitude. *Journal of Abnormal and Social Psychology*, 1936, *30*, 522–532.

KNUTSON, T.   An experimental study of the effects of orientation behavior on small group consensus. *Speech Monographs*, 1972, *39*, 159–165.

KNUTSON, T. & HOLDRIDGE, R.   Orientation behavior, leadership, and consensus: a possible functional relationship. *Speech Monographs*, 1975, *42*, 107–114.

KNUTSON, T. & KOWITZ, A.   Effects of information type and level of consensus: achievement in substantive and effective small group conflict. *Central States Speech Journal*, 1977, *28*, 54–63.

KOEHLER, J.   Effects on audience opinion of one-sided and two-sided speeches supporting and opposing a proposition, examining opinions on speaker ethos, the topic, and open mindedness of listeners. Doctoral dissertation, Pennsylvania State University, 1968.

KUBZANSKY, P.   The effects of reduced environmental stimulation on human behavior: a review. In A. Biderman & H. Zimmer (Eds.), *The manipulation of behavior*. New York: John Wiley, 1961.

KURTZ, P.   Some people believe anything they see on TV. *U.S. News and World Report*, May 21, 1979, 52–54.

LANE, L.   Communicative behavior and biological rhythms. *Speech Teacher*, 1971, *20*, 16–20.

LaPIERE, R.   Attitudes *versus* actions. *Social Forces*, 1934, *13*, 230–237.

LARSON, C. & SANDERS, R.   Faith, mystery and data: an analysis of "scientific" studies of persuasion. *Quarterly Journal of Speech*, 1975, *61*, 178–194.

LARSON, M.   Some problems in dissonance theory research. *Central States Speech Journal*, 1973, *24*, 183–188.

LASHBROOK, W., SNAVELY, W. & SULLIVAN, D.   The effects of source credibility and message information quantity on the attitude change of apathetics. *Communication Monographs*, 1977, *44*, 252–262.

LEATHERS, D.   Quality of group communication as a determinant of group product. *Speech Monographs*, 1972, *39*, 166–173.

LEFKOWITZ, M., BLAKE, R. & MOUTON, J.   Status factors in pedestrian violation of traffic signals. *Journal of Abnormal and Social Psychology*. 1955, *51*, 704–706.

LEVINSON, H.   Asinine attitudes toward motivation. *Harvard Business Review*, 1973, *51*, 70–76.

LEVENTHAL, H.   Findings and theory in the study of fear communications. In L. Berkowitz (Ed.), *Advances in experimental social psychology* (Vol. 5). New York: Academic Press, 1970.

LEVENTHAL, H. & NILES, P.   A field experiment on fear arousal with data on the validity of questionnaire measures. *Journal of Personality*, 1964, *32*, 459–479.

LEVENTHAL, H. & NILES, P.   Persistence of influence for varying durations of exposure to threat stimuli. *Psychological Reports*, 1965, *16*, 223–233.

LEVENTHAL, H. & PERLOE, S.   A relationship between self-esteem and persuasibility. *Journal of Abnormal and Social Psychology*, 1962, *64*, 385–388.

LEVENTHAL, H., WATTS, J. & PAGANO, F.   Effects of fear and instructions on how to cope with danger. *Journal of Personality and Social Psychology*, 1967, *6*, 313–321.

LEVINE, J., KRAMER, G. & LEVINE, E.   Effects of alcohol on human performance: An integration of research findings based on an abilities classification. *Journal of Applied Psychology*, 1975, *60*, 285–293.

LEWIS, J.   A criticism of the factor structure of source credibility as a function of the speaking situation. *Speech Monographs*, 1974, *41*, 287–290.

LINTON, H. & GRAHAM, E.   Personality correlates of persuasibility. In I. Janis and others (Eds.) *Personality and persuasibility*. New Haven: Yale University Press, 1959.

LIPPITT, R., POLANSKY, N., REDL, F. & ROSEN, S.   The dynamics of power. In D. Cartwright & A. Zander (Eds.) *Group dynamics*. Evanston: Row, Peterson, 1953.

LIPPIT, R., WATSON, J. & WESTLEY, B.   *The dynamics of planned change*. New York: Harcourt, Brace, 1958.

LISKA, A.   *The consistency controversy*. New York: John Wiley, 1975.

LISKA, J.   Situational and topical variations in credibility criteria. *Communication Monographs*, 1978, *44*, 85–92.

LITTLEJOHN, S.   *Theories of human communication.* Columbus, Ohio: Charles E. Merrill, 1978.

LOTT, A. & LOTT, B.   A learning theory approach to interpersonal attitudes. In A. Greenwald, T. Brock, & T. Ostrom (Eds.) *Psychological foundations of attitudes.* New York: Academic Press, 1968, 67–88.

LOTT, B.   Attitude formation: The development of a color-preference response through mediated generalization. *Journal of Abnormal and Social Psychology.* 1955, *50*, 321–326.

LUCE, D. & RAIFFA, H.   *Games and decisions.* New York: John Wiley, 1957.

LUCHOK, J. & McCROSKEY, J.   The effect of quality of evidence on attitude change and source credibility. *Southern Speech Communication Journal.* 1978, *43*, 371–383.

LUMSDAINE, A. & JANIS, I.   Resistance to 'counterpropaganda' produced by one-sided and two-sided propaganda presentation. *Public Opinion Quarterly*, 1953, *17*, 311–318.

LUMSDEN, D.   An experimental study of source-message interaction in a personality impression task. *Communication Monographs*, 1977, *44*, 121–129.

LUTHANS, F. & KREITNER, R.   *Organizational behavior modification.* Glenview, Illinois: Scott, Foresman, 1975.

MABRY, E.   An instrument for assessing content themes in group interactions. *Speech Monographs*, 1975, *42*, 291–297.

MacDONALD, D.   Communication roles and communication networks in a formal organization. *Human Communication Research*, 1976, *2*, 365–375.

MANIS, M., GLEASON, T. & DAWES, R.   The evaluations of complex social stimuli. *Journal of Personality and Social Psychology*, 1977, *3*, 404–419.

MARKUS, H.   The effect of mere presence on social facilitation. *Journal of Experimental Social Psychology*, 1978, *14*, 389–397.

MARR, T.   Conciliation and verbal responses as functions of orientation and threat in group interaction. *Speech Monographs*, 1974, *41*, 6–18.

MARSHALL, E.   Drugging of football players curbed by central monitoring system. *Science*, 1979, *203*, 626–628.

MARWELL, G. & SCHMITT, D.   Dimensions of compliance-gaining behavior: an empirical analysis. *Sociometry*, 1967, *30*, 350–364.

MARWELL, G., SCHMITT, D. & BOYESEN, B.   Pacifist strategy and cooperation under interpersonal risk. *Journal of Personality and Social Psychology*, 1973, *28*, 12–20.

MASLOW, A.   A theory of human motivation. *Psychological Review*, 1943, *50*, 370–396.

McCOMBS, M.   Agenda-setting research: A bibliographic essay. *Political Communication Review.* 1976, *1*, 1–7.

McCLURE, R. & PATTERSON, T.   Television news and political advertising. *Communication Research*, 1973, *1*, 3–31.

McCROSKEY, J.   Scales for the measurement of *ethos*. *Speech Monographs*, 1966, *33*, 65–72.

McCROSKEY, J.   A summary of experimental research on the effects of evidence in persuasive communication. *Quarterly Journal of Speech*, 1969, *55*, 169–176.

McCROSKEY, J.   The effects of evidence as an inhibitor of counterpersuasion. *Speech Monographs*, 1970, *37*, 188–194.

McCROSKEY, J. & MEHRLEY, S.   The effects of disorganization and nonfluency on attitude change and source credibility. *Speech Monographs*, 1969, *36*, 13–21.

McCROSKEY, J., RICHMOND, V. & DALY, J.   The development of a measure of perceived homophily in interpersonal communication. *Human Communication Research*, 1975, *1*, 323–332.

McCROSKEY, J. & YOUNG, T.   Ethos and credibility: The construct and its measurement after three decades. *Central States Speech Journal*, 1981, *32*, 24–34.

McCROSKEY, J., YOUNG, T. & SCOTT, M.   The effects of message sidedness and evidence on inoculation against counterpersuasion in small group settings. *Speech Monographs*, 1972, *39*, 205–212.

McDERMOTT, V.   Interpersonal communication networks: An approach through the understanding of self-concept, significant others, and social influence process. *Communication quarterly*, 1980, *28*, 3–12.

McGONNEL, P. & BEACH, H.   The effects of ethanol on the acquisition of conditioned GSR. *Quarterly Journal of Studies on Alcohol*, 1968, *29*, 845–855.

McGREGOR, D.   *The human side of enterprise*. New York: McGraw-Hill, 1960.

McGUIRE, W.   Resistance to persuasion conferred by active and passive prior refutation of the same and alternative counterarguments. *Journal of Abnormal and Social Psychology*, 1961, *63*, 326–332.

McGUIRE, W.   Inducing resistance to persuasion: Some contemporary approaches. In R. Wagner & J. Sherwood (Eds.), *The study of attitude change*. Belmont, California: Brooks/Cole, 1969, 173–183.

McGUIRE, W.   Resistance to persuasion conferred by active and passive refutation of the same and alternative arguments. *Journal of Abnormal and Social Psychology*, 1961, *63*, 326–332.

McGUIRE, W.   Inducing resistance to persuasion. In L. Berkowitz (Ed.), *Advances in experimental social psychology I*. New York: Academic Press, 1964.

McGUIRE, W. & PAPAGEORGIS, D.   Effectiveness of fore-warning in developing resistance to persuasion. *Public Opinion Quarterly*, 1962, *26*, 24–34.

McLAUGHLIN, M.   Recovering the structure of credibility judgements: an alternative to factor analysis. *Speech Monographs*, 1975, *42*, 221–228.

McLAUGHLIN, M., CODY, M. & ROBEY, C.   Situational influences on the selection of strategies to resist compliance-gaining attempts. *Human Communication Research*, 1980, *7*, 14–36.

McLUHAN, M.   *Understanding media*. New York: McGraw-Hill, 1964.

McPHEE, R. & CUSHMAN, D.   Attitudes, behaviors, and messages: An introductory overview. In D. Cushman and R. McPhee (Eds.), *Message-attitude-behavior relationship*. New York: Academic Press, 1980.

MEEKER, R. & SHURE, G.   Pacifist bargaining tactics: Some "outsider" influences. *Journal of Conflict Resolution*, 1969, *13*, 487–493.

MEAD, G.   *On social psychology*. Chicago: University of Chicago Press, 1956.

MEHRLEY, S. & McCROSKEY, J.   Opinionated statements and attitude intensity as predictors of attitude change and source credibility. *Speech Monographs*, 1970, *37*, 47–52.

MERTZ, R., MILLER, G. & BALLANCE, L.   Open and closed mindedness and cognitive conflict. *Journalism Quarterly*, 1966, *43*, 429–433, 485.

MEYERS, D. & LAMM, H.   The group polarization phenomenon. *Psychological Bulletin*, 1976, *83*, 602–627.

MILLAR, F. & ROGERS, L.   A relational approach to interpersonal communication. In G. Miller (Ed.), *Explorations in interpersonal communication*. Beverly Hills: Sage, 1980, 87–104.

MILLER, G. A. & JOHNSON-LAIRD, P.   *Language and perception*. Cambridge, Mass.: The Belknap Press of Harvard University Press, 1976.

MILLER, G. R.   *Perspectives in argumentation*. Chicago: Scott, Foresman, 1966.

MILLER, G. R.   Some factors influencing judgements of logical validity of arguments: a research review. *Quarterly Journal of Speech*, 1969, *55*, 276–286.

MILLER, G. R.   Counterattitudinal advocacy: a current appraisal. In D. Mortenson and

K. Sereno (Eds.), *Advances in Communication Research*. New York: Harper and Row, 1973, 105–151.

MILLER, G. R.   Humanistic and scientific approaches to speech communication inquiry: Rivalry, redundancy, and rapproachment. *Western Journal of Speech Communication*, 1975, *39*, 230–239.

MILLER, G. R.   On being persuaded: Some basic distinctions. In M. Roloff and G. Miller (Eds.), *Persuasion: New directions in theory and research*. Beverly Hills: Sage, 1980, 11–28.

MILLER, G. R. & BASEHEART, J.   Source trustworthiness, opinionated statements, and responses to persuasive communications. *Speech Monographs*, 1969, *36*, 1–7.

MILLER, G. R. & BERGER, C.   On keeping the faith in matters scientific. *Western Journal of Speech Communication*, 1978, *42*, 44–56.

MILLER, G. R., BOSTER, F., ROLOFF, M. & SIEBOLD, D.   Compliance-gaining message strategies: A typology and some findings concerning effects of situational differences. *Communication Monographs*, 1977, *44*, 37–51.

MILLER, G. R. & BURGOON, M.   *New techniques of persuasion*. New York: Harper and Row, 1973.

MILLER, G. R. & BURGOON, M.   Persuasion research: Review and commentary. In B. T. Ruben (Ed.), *Communication yearbook II*. New Brunswick, N.J.: Transaction Books, 1978.

MILLER, G. R. & BURGOON, M.   The relationship between violations of expectations and the induction of resistance to persuasion. *Human Communication Research*, 1979, *5*, 301–313.

MILLER, G. R. & FONTES, N.   *Videotape on trial*. Beverly Hills: Sage, 1979.

MILLER, G. R. & HEWGILL, M.   Some recent research on fear-arousing message appeals. *Speech Monographs*, 1966, *33*, 377–391.

MILLER, G. R. & HEWGILL, M.   The effects of variations in non-fluency on ratings of source credibility. *Quarterly Journal of Speech*, 1964, *50*, 36–44.

MILLER, G. R. & LOBE, J.   Opinionated language, open and closed mindedness and response to persuasive communications. *Journal of Communication*, 1967, *17*, 33–341.

MILLER, G. R. & McREYNOLDS, M.   Male chauvinism and source competence. *Speech Monographs*, 1973, *40*, 154–155.

MILLER, G. R. & NICHOLSON, H.   *Communication inquiry: A perspective on a process*. Reading, Mass.: Addison-Wesley, 1976.

MILLER, L., McFARLAND, D., CORNETT, T. & BRIGHTWELL, D.   Marijuana and memory impairment: Effect on free recall and recognition memory. *Pharmacology, Biochemistry, and Behavior*, 1977, *7*, 99–103.

MILLER, N.   Involvement and dogmatism as inhibitors of attitude change. *Journal of Experimental Social Psychology*, 1965, *1*, 121–132.

MILLS, C.   Relationships among three sources of credibility in the communication configuration: speaker, message, and experimenter. *Southern Speech Communication Journal*, 1977, *42*, 334–351.

MILLS, G.   *Reason in controversy*. Boston: Allyn and Bacon, 1964.

MILLS, J.   Opinion change as a function of the communicator's desire to influence and liking for the audience. *Journal of Experimental Social Psychology*, 1966, *2*, 152–159.

MINICK, W.   *The art of persuasion*. New York: Houghton-Mifflin, 1968.

MINTZ, P. & MILLS, J.   Effects of arousal and information about its source upon attitude change. *Journal of Experimental Social Psychology*, 1971, *7*, 561–570.

MONTGOMERY, C. & BURGOON, M.   An experimental study of the interaction of sex and androgyny on attitude change. *Communication Monographs*, 1977, *44*, 130–135.

MONTGOMERY, C. & BURGOON, M.   The effects of androgyny and message expectations on resistance to persuasive communication. *Communication Monographs*, 1980, *47*, 56-67.

MORLEY, I.   Bargaining and negotiation: The character of experimental studies. In H. Bandstatter, J. Davis, & H. Shuler (Eds.), *Dynamics of group decisions*. Beverly Hills: Sage, 1978.

MORRIS, C.   *Signs, language, and behavior*. New York: George Braziller, 1946.

MORTENSON, C. & SERENO, K.   The influence of ego-involvement and discrepancy on perceptions of communication. *Speech Monographs*, 1970, *37*, 127-134.

MORTON, T., ALEXANDER, J. & ALTMAN, I.   Communication and relationship definition. In G. Miller (Ed.), *Explorations in interpersonal communication*. Beverly Hills: Sage, 1976, 105-126.

MOSKOWITZ, H. & BURNS, M.   Alcohol effects on information processing time with an overlearning task. *Perceptual and Motor Skills*, 1973, *37*, 835-839.

MUELLER, C.   *The politics of communication*. New York: Oxford University Press, 1973.

MULAC, A.   Effects of obscene language upon three dimensions of listener attitude. *Communication Monographs*, 1976, *43*, 300-307.

MUNN, W. & GRUNER, C.   "Sick" jokes, speaker sex and informative speech. *Southern Speech Communication Journal*, 1981, *46*, 411-418.

MURPHY, R.   *Mass communication and human interaction*. New York: Houghton Mifflin, 1977.

MYRDAHL, G.   *Objectivity in social science*. New York: Random House, 1967.

NESBITT, P.   Chronic smoking and emotionality. *Journal of Applied Social Psychology*, 1972, *2*, 187-196.

NEWCOMB, T.   Attitude development as a function of reference groups: The Bennington study. In E. Maccoby, T. Newcomb, and E. Hartley (Eds.) *Readings in social psychology* (3rd ed.). New York: Henry Holt and Company, 1958.

NORRIS, E.   Attitude change as a function of open- or closed-mindedness. *Journalism Quarterly*, 1965, *42*, 571-575.

NOWAK, S.   Values and attitudes of the Polish people. *Scientific American*, 1981, *245*, 45-53.

O'KEEFE, D.   The relationship of attitudes and behavior: a constructivist analysis. In D. Cushman & R. McPhee (Eds.), *The message-attitude-behavior relationship: Theory, methodology, and application*. New York: Academic Press, 1980.

O'KEEFE, D.   Logical empiricism and the study of human communication. *Speech Monographs*, 1975, *42*, 169-183.

O'KEEFE, D. & BRADY, R.   Cognitive complexity and the effects of thought on attitude change. *Social Behavior and Personality*, 1980, *8*, 49-56.

O'KEEFE, D. & DELIA, J.   Construct comprehensiveness and cognitive complexity as predictors of the number and strategic adaptation of arguments and appeals in a persuasive message. *Communication Monographs*, 1979, *46*, 231-240.

O'KEEFE, D. & SYPHER, H.   Cognitive complexity measures and the relationship of cognitive complexity to communication: a critical review. *Human Communication Research*. 1980 (in press).

OSGOOD, C.   Cross-cultural comparability in attitude measurement via multi-lingual semantic differentials. In I. Steiner & M. Fishbein (Eds.), *Recent studies in social psychology*. New York: Holt, Rinehart, and Winston, 1965.

OSGOOD, C., SUCI, G. & TANNENBAUM, P.   *The measurement of meaning*. Urbana: University of Illinois Press, 1957.

OSGOOD, C. & TANNENBAUM, P.   The principle of congruity in the prediction of attitude change. *Psychological Review*, 1955, *62*, 42-55.

OSTERMEIER, T.   An experimental study on the type and frequency of reference as used by an unfamiliar source in a message and its effect upon perceived credibility and attitude change. Unpublished doctoral dissertation, Michigan State University, 1966.

OSTERMEIER, T.   Effects of type and frequency of reference upon perceived source of credibility and attitude change. *Speech Monographs*, 1967, *34*, 137–144.

PALLAK, M. A. & PITTMAN, T.   General motivational effects of dissonance arousal. *Journal of Personality and Social Psychology*, 1972, *21*, 349–358.

PALMGREEN, P. & CLARKE, P.   Agenda-setting with local and national issues. *Communication Research*, 1977, *4*, 435–451.

PASTORE, N. & HOROWITZ, M.   The influence of attributed motive on the acceptance of statement. *Journal of Abnormal and Social Psychology*, 1955, *51*, 351–362.

PEARCE, B.   The effect of vocalic cues on credibility and attitude change. *Western Speech*, 1971, *35*, 176–184.

PEARCE, B.   The coordinated management of meaning: a rules-based theory of interpersonal communication. In G. Miller (Ed.), *Explorations in interpersonal communication*. Beverly Hills: Sage, 1976.

PEARCE, D.   God is a variable interval. *Playboy*, 1972, *19*, 81–86, 171–176.

PETERSON, R. & FRANDSEN, K.   Cognitive balance, structural models, and communicative influence: an explication and a proposed extension. *Western Journal of Speech Communication*, 1979, *43*, 246–259.

PETRIE, C. & CARREL, S.   The relationship of motivation, listening capability, initial information, and verbal organizational ability to lecture comprehension and retention. *Communication Monographs*, 1976, *43*, 187–194.

PETTY, R., CACIOPPO, J. & HEESACKER, M.   Effects of rhetorical questions on persuasion: a cognitive response analysis. *Journal of Personality and Social Psychology*, 1981, *40*, 432–440.

PHILLIPS, G.   Rhetoric and its alternatives as bases for examination of intimate communication. *Communication Quarterly*, 1976, *24*, 11–23.

PILISUK, M. & SKOLNICK, P.   Inducing trust: a test of the Osgood proposal. *Journal of Personality and Social Psychology*, 1968, *8*, 121–133.

PITTMAN, T.   Attribution of arousal as a mediator in dissonance reduction. *Journal of Experimental Social Psychology*, 1975, *11*, 53–63.

POHL, GAYLE.   Attitude change in college students: "Death of a princess." Master's thesis, University of Kentucky, 1981.

POOLE, M.   Decision development in small groups 1: A comparison of two models. *Communication Monographs*, 1981, *48*, 1–24.

POWELL, F.   Open and closed mindedness and the ability to differentiate source and message. *Journal of Abnormal and Social Psychology*, 1962, *65*, 61–64.

PRENTICE, D.   The effect of trust-destroying communication on verbal fluency in the small group. *Speech Monographs*, 1975, *42*, 262–270.

PRUITT, D.   Choice shifts and group discussions: An introductory review. *Journal of Personality and Social Psychology*, 1971, *20*, 339–360.

PRYOR, B. & STEINFATT, T.   The effects of initial belief level on inoculation theory and its proposed mechanisms. *Human Communication Research*, 1978, *4*, 216–230.

RAGSDALE, D.   Effects of selected aspects of brevity on persuasiveness. *Speech Monographs*, 1968, *35*, 8–13.

RAGSDALE, D. & MIKELS, A.   Effects of question periods on a speaker's credibility with a television audience. *Southern Speech Communication Journal*, 1975, *60*, 302–312.

RAJECKI, D., ICKES, W. CORCORAN, C. & LENEZ, K.   Social facilitation on human performance: Mere presence effects. *Journal of Social Psychology*, 1977, *102*, 297–310.

REARDON, K.   *Persuasion: Theory and context*. Beverly Hills: Sage, 1981.

REID, L.   *American public address*. Columbia: University of Missouri Press, 1961.

REINSCH, N.   An investigation of the effects of the metaphor and simile in persuasive discourse. *Speech Monographs*, 1971, *38*, 142–145.

REINSCH, N.   Figurative language and source credibility: A preliminary investigation and reconceptualization. *Human Communication Research*, 1974, *1*, 75-80.

RICHARDS, I.   *Philosophy of rhetoric*. New York: Oxford, 1950.

RING, K. & KELLEY, H.   A comparison of augmentation and reduction as modes of influence. In D. Cartwright & A. Zaner. *Group dynamics*. Evanston: Row, Peterson, 1953, 270-277.

ROBERTS, D. & MACCOBY, N.   Information processing and persuasion: counterarguing behavior. In P. Clarke (Ed.), *New models for mass communications research*. Beverly Hills: Sage, 1973, 269-280.

ROGERS, C.   Toward a science of the person. In T. Wann (Ed.), *Behaviorism and phenomenology*, Chicago: University of Chicago Press, 1964, 109-132.

ROGERS, E.   *The diffusion of information*. New York: Free Press, 1962.

ROGERS-MILLAR, E. & MILLAR, F.   Domineeringness and dominance: A transactional view. *Human Communication Research*, 1979, *5*, 238-246.

ROKEACH, M.   *The open and closed mind*. New York: Basic Books, 1960.

ROLOFF, M.   Communication strategies, relationships, and relational changes. In G. Miller (Ed.), *Explorations in interpersonal communication*. Beverly Hills: Sage, 1980, 173-196.

ROLOFF, M.   *Interpersonal communication: the social exchange approach*. Beverly Hills: Sage, 1981.

ROLOFF, M. & BARNICOTT, E.   The situational use of pro- and anti-social compliance-gaining strategies by high and low machivellians. In B. Ruben (Ed.), *Communication Yearbook 2*. New Brunswick, N.J.: Transaction Books, 1978, 193-206.

ROLOFF, M. & MILLER, G.   *Persuasion: New directions in theory and research*. Beverly Hills: Sage, 1980.

ROSENBERG, M. & ABELSON, R.   An analysis of cognitive balancing. In M. Rosenberg (Ed.), *Attitude organization and change*. New Haven: Yale University Press, 1960.

ROSENBERG, M. & HOVLAND, C.   Cognitive, affective, and behavioral components of attitudes. In M. Rosenberg (Ed.), *Attitude organization and change*. New Haven: Yale University Press, 1960.

ROSENFELD, L. & CHRISTIE, V.   Sex and persuasibility revisited. *Western Speech*, 1974, *38*, 224-253.

ROSENFELD, L. & FOWLER, G.   Personality, sex, and leadership style. *Communication Monographs*, 1976, *43*, 320-324.

ROSENFELD, L. & PLAX, T.   The relationship of listener personality to perceptions of three dimensions of credibility. *Central States Speech Journal*, 1975, *24*, 274-276.

ROSENTHAL, P.   The concept of the paramessage in persuasive communication. *Quarterly Journal of Speech*, 1972, *58*, 15-30.

ROSNOW, R. & ROBINSON, E.   *Experiments in persuasion*. New York: Academic Press, 1967.

ROSSITER, C.   The validity of communication experiments using human subjects: A review. *Human Communication Research*, 1976, *2*, 197-206.

RUBEN, B.   *Communication Yearbook 2*. New Brunswick, N.J.: International Communication Association, 1978.

RUBIN, J. & BROWN, B.   *The social psychology of bargaining and negotiation*. New York: Academic Press, 1975.

SALTIEL, J. & WOELFEL, J.   Inertia in cognitive processes: the role of accumulated information in attitude change. *Human Communication Research*, 1975, *1*, 333-344.

SALZMAN, C., VANDERKOLK, B. & SHADER, R.   Marijuana and hostility in a small group setting. *American Journal of psychiatry*, 1976, *133*, 1029-1033.

SANDERS, G. & BARON, R.   Is social comparison irrelevant for producing choice shifts? *Journal of Experimental Social Psychology*, 1977, *83*, 602-627.

SARNOFF, I.   Psychoanalytic theory and social attitudes. *Public Opinion Quarterly*, 1960, *24*, 251-279.

SCANLAN, R.   Adolf Hitler and the technique of mass brainwashing. In Bryant, D. (Ed.), *The rhetorical idiom*. Ithaca, N.Y.: Cornell University Press, 1958.

SCHACTER, S.   Deviation, rejection, and communication. *Journal of Abnormal and Social Psychology*, 1956, *46*, 190-207.

SCHACTER, S.   The interaction of cognitive and physiological determinants of emotional state. In L. Berkowitz (Ed.), *Advances in experimental social psychology* (Vol. 1). New York: Academic Press, 1964.

SCHACTER, S.   Second thoughts on biological and psychological explanation of behavior. In L. Berkowitz (Ed.), *Cognitive theories in social psychology*. New York: Academic Press, 1978.

SCHACTER, S., ELLERTSON, S., McBRIDE, D. & GREGORY, D.   An experimental study of cohesiveness and productivity. In D. Cartwright & A. Zander, *Group dynamics*. Evanston: Row, Peterson, 1953.

SCHACTER, S. & SINGER, J.   Cognitive, social and physiological determinants of emotional state. *Psychological Review*, 1962, *69*, 379-399.

SCHACTER, S. & WHEELER, L.   Epinephrine, chlorpromazine and amusement. *Journal of Abnormal and Social Psychology*, 1962, *65*, 121-128.

SCHEIDEL, T.   Sex and persuasibility. *Speech Monographs*, 1963, *30*, 353-358.

SCHEIN, E.   The Chinese indoctrination program for prisoners of war: A study of attempted brainwashing. *Psychiatry*, 1956, *19*, 149-172.

SCHELLENBURG, J.   Distributive justice and collaboration in zero-sum games. *Journal of Conflict Resolution*, 1964, *8*, 147-150.

SCHWEITZER, D.   The effect of presentation on source evaluation. *Quarterly Journal of Speech*, 1970, *56*, 33-39.

SCOTT, M. & HURT, T.   Social influence as a function of communicator and message type. *Southern Speech Communication Journal*, 1978, *43*, 146-161.

SCOTT, W.   Attitude change through reward of verbal behavior. *Journal of Abnormal and Social Psychology*, 1957, *55*, 72-75.

SCOTT, W., OSGOOD, D. & PETERSON, C.   *Cognitive structure: Theory and measurement of individual differences*. New York: John Wiley, 1979.

SEILER, W.   The effects of visual materials on attitudes, credibility, and retention. *Speech Monographs*, 1971, *38*, 331-334.

SERENO, K.   Ego involvement, high source credibility, and responses to a belief-discrepant communication. *Speech Monographs*, 1968, *35*, 476-481.

SERENO, K. & BODAKEN, E.   Ego-involvement and attitude change: Toward a reconceptualization of persuasive effect. *Speech Monographs*, 1972, *39*, 151-158.

SERENO, K. & HAWKINS, G.   The effects of variations in speaker's nonfluency upon audience ratings of attitude toward the speech topic and speaker's credibility. *Speech Monographs*, 1967, *34*, 58-64.

SERENO, K. & MORTENSON, D.   The effects of ego-involved attitudes on conflict negotiation in dyads. *Speech Monographs*, 1969, *36*, 8-12.

SHAFFER, L. & SHOBEN, F.   *The psychology of adjustment*. Boston: Houghton Mifflin, 1956.

SHANNON, C. & WEAVER, W.   *The mathematical theory of communication*. Urbana: University of Illinois Press, 1949.

SHERIF, M.   Group influences on the formation of norms and attitudes. In E. Maccoby, T. Newcomb, & E. Hatley, *Readings in social psychology*. New York: Henry Holt, 1958.

SHERIF, M., SHERIF, C. & NEBERGALL, R.   *Attitude and attitude change: The social-judgment-involvement approach*. Philadelphia: W.B. Saunders, 1965.

SIEBOLD, D.   Communication research and the attitude-verbal report-overt behavior relationship: a critique and theoretic reformulation. *Human Communication Research*, 1975, *2*, 3–33.

SIEBOLD, D., POOLE, M., & McPHEE, R.   New prospects for research in small group communication. Paper presented to the Central States Speech Association meeting, Chicago, 1980.

SIMONS, H.   Persuasion in social conflicts: a critique of prevailing conceptions and a framework for future research. *Speech Monographs*, 1972, *39*, 227–247.

SIMONS, H.   The rhetoric of science and the science of rhetoric. *Western Journal of Speech Communication*, 1978, *42*, 37–43.

SKINNER, B.   Superstition and the pigeon. *Journal of Experimental Psychology*, 1948, *38*, 168–172.

SKINNER, B.   Freedom and the control of men. *American Scholar*, 1955, *25*, 47–65.

SKINNER, B.   *Verbal behavior*. New York: Appleton-Century-Crofts, 1957.

SKINNER, B.   Behaviorism at fifty. In T. Wann, (Ed.) *Behaviorism and Phenomenology*. Chicago: University of Chicago Press, 1964.

SMART, R.   Effects of alcohol in conflict and avoidance problems. *Quarterly Journal of Studies in Alcohol*, 1965, *26*, 187–205.

SMITH, D.   Communication research and the idea of process. *Speech Monographs*, 1972, *39*, 174–182.

SMITH, D. & KEARNEY, L.   Organismic concepts in the unification of rhetoric and communication. *Quarterly Journal of Speech*, 1973, *59*, 30–38.

SMITH, M.   Effects of threats to attitudinal freedom as a function of message quality and initial receiver attitude. *Communication Monographs*, 1977, *44*, 196–206.

SMITH, R.   Source credibility context effects. *Speech Monographs*, 1973, *40*, 303–309.

SNYDER, M.   When believing means doing: Creating links between attitudes and behavior. In M. Zanna, C. Herman, & E. Higgins (Eds.) *Variability and consistency in social behavior: The Ontario Symposium*. Hillsdale, N.J.: Erlbaum, 1981.

SORENSEN, G. & McCROSKEY, J.   The prediction of interaction behavior in small groups. *Communication Monographs*, 1977, *44*, 73–80.

SPENCE, K.   *Behavior theory and conditioning*. New Haven: Yale University Press, 1956.

SPICER, C. & BASSETT, R.   The effect of organization on learning from a message. *Southern Speech Communication Journal*, 1976, *41*, 290–299.

SPILLMAN, B.   The impact of value and self-esteem messages in persuasion. *Central States Speech Journal*, 1979, *30*, 67–74.

STAATS, A.   Social behavior and human motives: Principles of the attitude-reinforcer-discriminative system. In A. Greenwald, T. Brock, & T. Ostrom (Eds.) *Psychological foundations of attitudes*. New York: Academic Press, 1968.

STAATS, A.   *Social Behaviorism*. Homewood, Illinois: Dorsey Press, 1975.

STEINFATT, T.   The prisoners dilemma and a creative alternative game: The effects of communication under conditions of real reward. *Simulation and Games*, 1973, *4*, 389–409.

STEINFATT, T.   A criticism of "Dimensions of source credibility: A test for reproducibility." *Speech Monographs*, 1974, *41*, 291–292.

STEINFATT, T.   *Human communication: An interpersonal introduction*. Indianapolis, Indiana: Bobbs-Merrill, 1977.

STEINFATT, T. & INFANTE, D.   Attitude-behavior relationships in communication research. *Quarterly Journal of Speech*, 1976, *62*, 267–278.

STEINFATT, T. & MILLER, G.   Communication in game theoretic models of conflict. In G. Miller & H. Simons (Eds.), *Perspectives on communication in social conflict*. Englewood Cliffs, N.J.: Prentice-Hall, 1975.

STEINFATT, T., MILLER, G. & BETTINGHAUS, E.   The concept of logical ambiguity and judgments of syllogistic validity. *Speech Monographs*, 1974, *41*, 317–328.

STEINFATT, T., SIEBOLD, D. & FRYE, J.   Communication in game simulated conflicts: Two experiments. *Speech Monographs*, 1974, *41*, 24–35.

STEPHENSON, W.   Michael Polyani, science, and belief. *Ethics in Science and Medicine*, 1980, *7*, 97–110.

STEWART, D.   Communication and logic: evidence for the existence of validity patterns. *Journal of General Psychology*, 1961, *64*, 304–312.

STEWART, J.   Foundations of dialogic communication. *Quarterly Journal of Speech*, 1978, *64*, 183–201.

STINNET, W.   An investigation into four factors of source credibility. Unpublished master's thesis, Ohio University, 1971.

STONER, J.   Risky and cautious shifts in group decisions: the influence of widely held values. *Journal of Experimental and Social Psychology*, 1968, *4*, 442–459.

STRAUS, R.   Alcoholism and problem drinking. In R. Merton & R. Nisbet (Eds.), *Contemporary and social problems*. New York: Harcourt, Brace Jovanovich, 1976.

STRODTBECK, R., JAMES, R. & HAWKINS, C.   Social status in jury deliberations. In E. Maccoby, T. Newcomb, & E. Hartley (Eds.) *Readings in social psychology*. New York: Henry Holt, 1958, 379–387.

TANNENBAUM, P.   Attitudes toward source and concept as factors in attitude change through communication. Unpublished doctoral dissertation. University of Illinois, 1953.

TANNENBAUM, P. & GENGEL, R.   Generalization of attitude change through congruity principle relationships. *Journal of Personality and Social Psychology*, 1966, *3*, 493–500.

TANNENBAUM, P., MACAUALY, J. & NORRISS, E.   The principle of congruity and reduction of persuasion. *Journal of Personality and Social Psychology*, 1963, *3*, 233–238.

THIBAUT, J. & STRICKLAND, L.   Psychological set and social conformity. *Journal of Personality*, 1961, *25*, 115–121.

THISTLETWAITE, D., DeHANN, H. & KAMENETZKY, J.   The effects of "directive" and "nondirective" communication procedures on attitudes. *Journal of Abnormal and Social Psychology*, 1955, *51*, 107–113.

THOMPSON, E.   An experimental investigation of the relative effects of organizational structure in oral communication. *Southern Speech Journal*, 1960, *26*, 59–69.

THOMPSON, E.   Effects of message structure on listener's comprehension. *Speech Monographs*, 1967, *34*, 51–57.

THONSSEN, L. & BAIRD, A.   *Speech Criticism*. New York: Ronald Press, 1948.

THURSTONE, L.   *The measurement of values*. Chicago: University of Chicago Press, 1959.

TOLMAN, E.   *Behavior and psychological man*. Berkeley: University of California Press, 1961.

TOMPKINS, P. & SAMOVAR, L.   An experimental study of the effects of credibility and the comprehension of content. *Speech Monographs*, 1964, *31*, 120–123.

TOMPKINS, P.   Management qua communication in rocket research and development. *Communication Monographs*, 1977, *44*, 1–26.

TOMPKINS, P.   Organizational metamorphosis in space research and development. *Communication Monographs*, 1978, *45*, 110–118.

TOWNSEND, R.   *Up the organization*. Greenwich, Conn.: Fawcett, 1970.

TRIANDIS, H. & FISHBEIN, M.   Cognitive interaction in person and perception. *Journal of Abnormal and Social Psychology*, 1963, *67*, 446–453.

TUBBS, S.   *A systems approach to small group interaction*. Reading, Mass.: Addison-Wesley, 1978.

TUBBS, S.   Explicit versus implicit audience conclusions and audience commitment. *Speech Monographs*, 1968, *35*, 14–19.

TUCKER, R.   General systems theory: A logical and ethical model for persuasion. *The Journal of the American Forensic Association*, 1971, *8*, 29–35.

TUCKER, R.   On the McCroskey scales for the measurement of *ethos*. *Central States Speech Journal*, 1971, *22*, 127–129.

TUCKER, R. & WARE, P.   Persuasion via mere exposure. *Quarterly Journal of Speech*, 1971, *57*, 437–443.

TURNBULL, A., STRICKLAND, L. & SHAVER, K.   Medium of communication, differential power, and phasing of concessions. *Human Communication Research*, 1976, *2*, 262–270.

ULLMAN, R. & BODAKEN, E.   Inducing resistance to persuasive attack: a test of two strategies of communication. *Western speech communication*, 1975, *39*, 240–248.

WAGNER, G.   An experimental study of the relative effectiveness of varying amounts of evidence in a persuasive communication. Unpublished thesis, Mississippi Southern University, 1958.

WAGNER, R. & SHERWOOD, J.   *The study of attitude change*, Belmont, California: Brooks/Cole, 1969.

WALL, V.   Evidential attitudes and attitude change. *Western Speech*, 1972, *36*, 115–123.

WALLACE, K.   The fundamentals of rhetoric. In L. Bitzer, & E. Black (Eds.), *The prospect of rhetoric*. Englewood Cliffs, N.J.: Prentice-Hall, 1971, 3–20.

WALSTER, E., ARONSON, E. & ABRAHAMS, D.   On increasing the persuasiveness of a low prestige communicator. *Journal of Experimental Social Psychology*, 1966, *2*, 325–342.

WALSTER, E., BERSCHEID, E. & WALSTER, G.   New directions in equity research. *Journal of Personality and Social Psychology*, 1973, *25*, 151–176.

WALSTER, E. & FESTINGER, L.   The effectiveness of "overheard" persuasive communications. *Journal of Abnormal and Social Psychology*, 1962, *65*, 395–402.

WARE, D. & TUCKER, R.   Heckling as distraction: an experimental study of its effect on source credibility. *Speech Monographs*, 1974, *41*, 185–188.

WECKOWITZ, T., COLLIER, G. & SPRENG, L.   Field dependence, cognitive functions, personality traits, and social values in heavy cannabis users and non-user controls. *Psychological Reports*, 1977, *41*, 291–302.

WEIMER, W. & PALERMO, D.   *Cognition and the symbolic processes*. Hillsdale, N.J.: Erlbaum, 1974.

WEISS, W.   A sleeper effect in opinion change. *Journal of Abnormal and Social Psychology*. 1953, *68*, 173–180.

WEISS, W.   Opinion congruence with a negative source on one issue as a factor influencing argument on another issue. *Journal of Abnormal and Social Psychology*, 1957, *54*, 180–186.

WESTLEY, B. & McCLEAN, M.   A conceptual model for communications research. *Journalism Quarterly*, 1957, *34*, 31–38.

WHEELESS, L.   The effects of comprehension loss on persuasion. *Speech Monographs*, 1971, *38*, 327–330.

WHEELESS, L.   Effects of explicit credibility statements by a more credible and a less credible source. *Southern Speech Communication Journal*, 1973, *39*, 33–39.

WHEELESS, L.   Attitude and credibility in the prediction of attitude change: A regression approach. *Speech Monographs*, 1974, *41*, 277–281.

WHEELESS, I. & McCROSKEY, J.   The effects of selected syntactical choices on source credibility, attitude, behavior, and perception of message. *Southern Speech Communication Journal*, 1973, *38*, 213–222.

WHETMORE, E.   *Mediamerica*. Belmont, California: Wadsworth, 1979.

WHITEHEAD, J.   Effects of authority-based assertion on attitude and credibility. *Speech Monographs*, 1971, *38*, 311–315.

WHITMAN, R. & TIMMIS, J.   The influence of verbal organizational structure and verbal organizing skills on select measures of learning. *Human Communication Research*, 1975, *1*, 293–301.

WHORF, B.   The relation of habitual thought and behavior to language. In S. Hayakawa (Ed.), *Language, meaning, and maturity*. New York: Harper Brothers, 1954.

WICKELGREN, W.   Alcoholic intoxication and memory storage dynamics. *Memory and Cognition*, 1975, *3*, 385–389.

WICKER, T.   *A time to die*. New York: Ballantine Books, 1975.

WIDGERY, R.   Sex of receiver and physical attractiveness of source as determinants of initial credibility perception. *Western Speech*, 1974, *38*, 13–17.

WILLIAMS, K.   Reflections on a human science of communication. *Journal of Communication*, 1973, *23*, 239–250.

WILLIAMS, L.   The effect of deliberate vagueness on receiver recall and agreement. *Central States Speech Journal*, 1980, *31*, 30–41.

WILLIAMS, L. & GOSS, B.   Equivocation: character insurance. *Human Communication Research*, 1975, *1*, 265–270.

WINTHROP, H.   The effect of personal qualities on one-way communication. *Psychological reports*, 1965, *2*, 323–324.

WHITEHEAD, J.   Factors of source credibility. *Quarterly Journal of Speech*, 1968, *54*, 59–63.

WOELFEL, J., CODY, M., GILLIAM, J. & HOLMES, R.   Basic premises of a multidimensional attitude change theory: An experimental analysis. *Human Communication Research*, 1980, *6*, 153–167.

WOODWORTH, R. & SCHLOSBERG, H.   *Experimental psychology*. New York: Holt, Rinehart & Winston, 1958.

WOOD, J.   Leading in purposive discussions: a study of adaptive behavior. *Communication Monographs*, 1977, *44*, 152–166.

WOOD, J.   Alternate portraits of leaders: A contingency approach to perceptions of leadership. *Western Journal of Speech Communication*, 1979, *43*, 260–270.

WOOD, M.   Williams Jennings Bryan: Crusader for the common man. In L. Reid (Ed.), *American public address: Studies in honor of Albert Craig Baird*. Columbia: University of Missouri, 1961.

WORSCHEL, S. & ARNOLD, S.   The effects of combined arousal states on attitude change. *Journal of Experimental Social Psychology*, 1974, *10*, 549–560.

WYER, R.   *Cognitive organization and change: An information processing approach*. New York: John Wiley, 1974.

YERBY, J.   Attitude, task, and sex composition as variables affecting female leadership in small problem-solving groups. *Speech Monographs*, 1975, *42*, 160–168.

ZAJONC, R.   Social facilitation. In D. Cartwright & A. Zander (Eds.) *Group dynamics*. Evanston: Row, Peterson, 1953, 63–73.

ZAJONC, R.   The concepts of balance, congruity and dissonance. *Public Opinion Quarterly*, 1960, *24*, 280–296.

ZAJONC, R.   Social facilitation. *Science*, 1965, *149*, 269–274.

ZAJONC, R.   Cognitive theories in social psychology. In G. Lindsey & E. Aronson (Eds.). *Handbook of Social Psychology* (Vol. I). Reading, Mass.: Addison, Wesley, 1968, 320–411.

ZANNA, M. & COOPER, J.   Dissonance and the pill: An attribution approach to the arousal properties of dissonance. *Journal of Personality and Social Psychology*, 1974, *29*, 703–724.

ZAREFSKY, D.   The Great Society as a rhetorical proposition. *Quarterly Journal of Speech*, 1979, *65*, 364–378.

ZELKO, H.   Do we persuade, argue, or convince? *Quarterly Journal of Speech*, 1939, *25*, 385–392.

ZIEGELMULLER, G. & DAUSE, C. *Argumentation: Inquiry and advocacy*. Englewood Cliffs, N.J.: Prentice-Hall, 1975.

ZILLMAN, D.   Rhetorical elicitation of agreement in persuasion. *Journal of Personality and Social Psychology*, 1972, *21*, 159–165.

AUTHOR INDEX

SUBJECT INDEX